Study Guide to Accompany

Smith and Roberson's

BUSINESS LAW

Ninth Edition

Richard A. Mann
Professor of Business Law
The University of North Carolina at Chapel Hill
Member of the North Carolina Bar

Barry S. Roberts
Professor of Business Law
The University of North Carolina at Chapel Hill
Member of the North Carolina and Pennsylvania Bars

Prepared by
Peter T. Kahn
University of Minnesota

Dennis R. Hower
University of Minnesota

West Publishing Company
Minneapolis/St. Paul   New York   Los Angeles   San Francisco

WEST'S COMMITMENT TO THE ENVIRONMENT

In 1906, West Publishing Company began recycling materials left over from the production of books. This began a tradition of efficient and responsible use of resources. Today, up to 95% of our legal books and 70% of our college texts and school texts are printed on recycled, acid-free stock. West also recycles nearly 22 million pounds of scrap paper annually—the equivalent of 181,717 trees. Since the 1960s, West has devised ways to capture and recycle waste inks, solvents, oils, and vapors created in the printing process. We also recycle plastics of all kinds, wood, glass, corrugated cardboard, and batteries, and have eliminated the use of Styrofoam book packaging. We at West are proud of the longevity and the scope of our commitment to the environment.

Production, Prepress, Printing and Binding by West Publishing Company.

 TEXT IS PRINTED ON 10% POST CONSUMER RECYCLED PAPER    PRINTED WITH SOY INK™

COPYRIGHT © 1994 by   WEST PUBLISHING CO.
610 Opperman Drive
P.O. Box 64526
St. Paul, MN 55164–0526

ISBN 0–314–03663–6

CONTENTS

PURPOSE OF THE STUDY GUIDE

PURPOSE OF THE STUDY GUIDE

Students in college business law courses are often studying law for the first time. As with other demanding and challenging areas of study, law uses a specialized vocabulary to convey complicated theories, concepts and principles. Such semantic and doctrinal complexities can pose difficulties. Acquiring a working understanding of the American legal system and its related fields of specific study is not an easy task.

For legal knowledge presented in text materials and classroom lectures to have value, students must apply their learning to everyday life. Clearly, the purpose of introductory law courses is not to train or prepare students to become legal experts qualified to handle legal matters with the same degree of precision and expertise as an attorney. The realistic goals of "first-exposure" courses in law include presenting the law, its terminology and basic principles, in a manner that enables students to: understand the legal system of which they are a part; apply the terms and concepts they have learned to their own lives; allow them to consider law as a future career; and effectively seek professional legal assistance when the need arises.

This *Study Guide* was written with these goals in mind. Used properly, the *Study Guide* will prove to be an invaluable learning tool in conjunction with textual readings and classroom instruction.

HOW TO USE THE STUDY GUIDE

By keeping pace with in-class lectures and text reading assignments with the related *Study Guide* chapters, students will incur the most beneficial use of the *Study Guide*. By completing *Study Guide* assignments topically concurrent with classroom instruction and textual material, students will be aided in comprehending the text and will be provided a useful frame of reference for organizing class notes. The *Study Guide* assignments have also been written to facilitate exam review and preparation.

The *Study Guide* format has been designed with study assignments related to each chatperss text. Answer keys for *Study Guide* chapters are included at the end of the *Study Guide*.

Each *Study Guide* chapter opens with a brief review of the textbook materials upon which it is based. These introductory SCOPE NOTES explain the major theme of a chapter, how it relates to the preceding material, and how it introduces subsequent chapters. Following the introductory comments, EDUCATIONAL OBJECTIVES focus student attention on important concepts and doctrines to remember from the chapter, which can prove useful in exam preparation.

The next section of the *Guide* is a CHAPTER OUTLINE. Its purpose is not to supplant careful reading of the text, but to assist in reading and studying the text by summarizing and highlighting major concepts of each chapter. The CHAPTER OUTLINE is followed by a series of objective questions intended to enhance student mastery of textual and classroom material. TRUE-FALSE questions have been written to facilitate an understanding of important legal doctrines and principles. To gain the most benefit from the TRUE-FALSE items, students should refrain from over-analyzing or reading too much into them. Thoughts, interpretations or assumptions that are not in the question itself should not be addressed. To challenge understanding of the legal principles from which the TRUE-FALSE questions are drawn, students should rephrase false statements to become true and vice-versa.

MATCHING EXERCISES are the next category. These items introduce terms and phrases that are vital to understanding various legal doctrines. The third set of objective exercises is comprised of MULTIPLE CHOICE items. They are designed to enhance comprehension of the important components and interconnections among the various doctrines, principles and concepts being studied.

The *Study Guide* assignments close with CASE ANALYSIS problems. These are written to help students apply academic principles to factual situations. After conceptualizing the problem developed in the facts, students should identify the pertinent legal issues. Recalling relevant text and classroom material, students reach a solution to the problem supported by coherent reasoning. It is important to read the facts slowly and carefully while working through the short answer essay problems. This is the only way to precisely define the nature of the dispute, its relevant legal issues, and reach a proper decision. In this manner, students will achieve a real understanding of the legal topics discussed in the text.

After completing the *Study Guide* chapter assignments, answers may be checked with the ANSWER KEY at the end of the *Guide*. Failure to understand why some answers are incorrect will make our study of law frustrating and fruitless.

The fifty-three text chapters are divided into ten separate study units. The *Study Guide* chapters that comprise a single study unit close with RESEARCH QUESTIONS drawn from the material for that unit. These QUESTIONS follow: Part One—Legal Environment of Business, Chapters 1-8; Part Two—Contracts, Chapters 9-18; Part Three—Agency, Chapters 19-20; Part Four—Sales, Chapters 21-25; Part Five Commercial Paper, Chapters 26-30; Part Six—Partnership, Chapters 31-34, Part Seven—Corporations Chapters 35-38; Part Eight—Debtor/Creditor Relations, Chapters 39-41, Part Nine—Regulation of Business, Chapters 42-48; and Part Ten—Property, Chapters 49-53. The RESEARCH QUESTIONS are designed to challenge student understanding of the basic principles, doctrines and concepts examined in the related text readings by asking students to apply such knowledge to broader, contemporary social issues and problems.

HOW TO STUDY LAW: TEXT, CLASS AND EXAMS

HOW TO STUDY LAW: TEXT, CLASS AND EXAMS

In response to the often asked question, "How should I study for a course of this nature?" the authors would like to offer some suggestions. First, be at ease with confusion. Since law is a difficult field of study, it is rare that a single reading of the text or attending class without taking notes will lead to an understanding of the material sufficient to handle exams adequately. Usually, the first reading of the text and noteless class attendance results in total confusion. What do these strange, seemingly foreign terms mean? How do these entangled, complicated legal principles and doctrines fit together? DON'T BECOME DISCOURAGED! Practicing attorneys and legal educators rarely grasp all the ramifications of a particular court decision, legislative enactment or administrative ruling after just one reading. It is only after many readings of the rule in question, prolonged study, review and discussion with colleagues that the fog of analytic confusion begins to lift. Be cautioned, however, that this short-term apparent understanding will, in many cases, give way to long-term mystification as the future implications, meanings and interpretations of the principle in question become clouded with speculation and uncertainty associated with change.

WRESTLING WITH THE TEXT

Review the Preface, Table of Contents and Introduction. This provides an overall perspective on the course and the approach to the material taken by the authors. Noting the organization of the text and determining how the chapters relate to one another enables students to see how the textual material integrates with classroom lecture. The text chapters contain both narrative (definitional) and case (illustrative) material. The cases, since they are applications of the legal principles discussed in the preceding textual material, should be read after the narrative portion to reduce confusion and to enhance understanding of the terms and doctrines developed in the chapter.

WRESTLING WITH EXAMS

Proper preparation for tests is crucial. Do not fall behind in text reading or class attendance. Keep up with text and lecture material. This allows concentration on exam preparation over an extended period of time rather than attempting to cover the material for the first time shortly before the exam. Since we are dealing with complicated terms and concepts, last minute cramming often triggers a sense of panic which can lower concentration levels and generally detract from effective studying. Outlining, underlining and note-taking have all proved effective. Taking complete class notes and participating in class discussion are also effective learning tools. They help to maintain attention and concentration, as well as indicate the material that the instructor considers most important — a clue to the content of an upcoming exam. Remember that most of the students in the class may be just as confused about certain topics as you are. Participating in class discussion contributes to overcoming this confusion.

Once an exam has begun, budget time carefully. Avoid spending too much time on a single question. Before answering an objective question (true-false, multiple choice, matching, etc.), make sure that its content is fully understood. Do not misread or overread a question. Read it slowly and carefully. Do not read into the question unstated interpretative information. Focus exclusively on the doctrine, principle or term addressed in the question.

For essay questions, several readings may be required. It might prove useful to diagram the facts. Make sure an answer addresses the significant legal issues and quotes relevant legal doctrines for its solutions. Be sure to develop the reasons for an answer. Don't make the exam grader read the exam writer's mind. Explain answers with full, pertinent information.

These suggestions are offered to assist understanding the material studied in your law course. Hopefully, they will make learning about the American legal system and its workings easier and more enjoyable. Happy reading in your journey through law.

Assistant Professor Peter T. Kahn, J.D.
Professor Dennis R. Hower, J.D.

PART ONE: *The Legal Environment of Business*

Chapter 1

INTRODUCTION TO LAW

SCOPE NOTE

As modern life has become increasingly crowded, complicated, and subject to fast-paced change, our everyday affairs have become more subject to legal scrutiny and regulation. Our daily activities carry profound legal implications. It is therefore important to gain a working understanding of this all-pervasive influencing force in our lives: the American legal system. Chapter One introduces basic terminology, concepts and principles relevant to the nature, origin, and growth of our system of laws. Through understanding the foundations of our legal identities (rights/duties), we will have a useful frame of reference when studying the specific areas of legal inquiry contained in the subsequent chapters. What is law? What is the legal reasoning process? What are the sources of law? These and other fundamental topics are the focus of discussion in Chapter One.

EDUCATIONAL OBJECTIVES

1. Define law and discuss the importance of the phrase, "a society governed by a system of laws."

2. Enumerate the functions of and purposes served by law.

3. Discuss the "legal analysis" process.

4. Explain the interrelationships among law, morality, and justice.

5. Differentiate among the various classifications of law.

6. Identify the law-making bodies within the American legal system.

7. Develop the importance of stare decisis in the formation of common law.

8. Trace the historical origins of America's system of laws.

9. Evaluate the significance of the movement towards uniform, codified laws in various arenas of legal regulation.

10. Define and explain the significance of equity.

1

CHAPTER OUTLINE

I. **Nature of Law**
   A. **Definition of Law** — "a rule of civil conduct prescribed by the supreme power in a state, commanding what is right, and prohibiting what is wrong"
   B. **Functions of Law** — the primary function is to maintain stability in the social, political and economic system while at the same time permitting change
   C. **Legal Sanctions** — the means by which the law enforces the decisions of the courts
   D. **Law and Morals** — are NOT the same. Law and ethics are similar but they differ because rules of law have sanctions; rules of ethics do not
   E. **Law and Justice** — without law there can be no justice, but law is no guarantee of justice

II. **Classification of Law**
   A. **Substantive and Procedural Law** — substantive laws create, define, and regulate legal rights and obligations; procedural law sets the rules for enforcing the rights that exist by substantive law
   B. **Public and Private Law** — public law consists of constitutional, administrative, and criminal law; private law includes civil and business law
   C. **Civil and Criminal Law** — civil law defines duties that, if violated, constitute a wrong against the party injured by the violation; criminal law establishes duties that, if violated, constitute a wrong against the whole community

III. **Sources of Law**
   A. **Constitutional Law** — is established by the U.S. Constitution and the individual state constitutions
   B. **Judicial Law** — is established by Federal and State courts
      1. Common law — also called case law (judge-made decisions)
      2. Equity — a supplementary court system to courts of law (common law) with its own remedies when no adequate remedy is available at common law
      3. Restatements of law — the authoritative statement of the common law of the United States
   C. **Legislative Law** — is established by Federal and State enactments (statutes)
      1. Treaties — agreements between or among independent nations
      2. Executive orders — laws issued by the President or by governors of the states
   D. **Administrative Law** — rules and regulations created by Federal, State and local administrative agencies

IV. **Legal Analysis** — the method of analyzing and briefing Federal and State judicial decisions

TRUE-FALSE: Circle true or false.

T F 1. In order to survive, a civilized society must have an efficient legal system.

T F 2. Civil law is concerned with a wrong against an injured party while criminal law is concerned with a wrong against the whole community.

T F 3. Stare decisis is a doctrine based on present court decisions following previous ones, and it should never be overturned.

T F 4. A "maxim" is a general legal principle formulated over the years by courts of equity.

T	F	5. The source of American law superior to all other sources within a state is the state statutes.
T	F	6. The government has the burden of proving a defendant guilty of a crime beyond a reasonable doubt.
T	F	7. The source of American law to which all other sources are subordinate is a President's executive order.
T	F	8. The person who sues in a lawsuit is called the plaintiff, the person being sued is the defendant.
T	F	9. The Uniform Commercial Code was prepared and developed to make the law governing commercial transactions uniform within the various jurisdictions of Minnesota.
T	F	10. Legal sanctions are the means by which the law enforces the decisions of the courts.
T	F	11. Statutory law results from the independent decisions of the state and federal courts.
T	F	12. An authoritative statement of the common law of the United States can be found in the Restatements of Law.

KEY TERMS—MATCHING EXERCISE: Select the term that best completes each statement below.

1. Federal Trade Commission	8. Maxims	15. Stare decisis
2. Federal statutes	9. Money damages	16. Uniform Probate Code
3. Uniform Commercial Code	10. U.S. Constitution	17. Administrative law
4. Crime	11. Tort law	18. Executive order
5. Substantive law	12. Restatements of Law	19. Rescission
6. Procedural law	13. Legal sanctions	20. Treaty
7. Injunction	14. Equity	

_____1. A public wrong committed against society or the state.

_____2. The law that establishes rules for enforcing rights.

_____3. The remedy obtainable from a court of law.

_____4. A guiding principle whereby a court follows previous decisions in deciding the present case before it.

_____5. A new system of judicial relief that developed because of a lack of a proper remedy from the common law system.

_____6. One type of remedy available only in a court of equity requiring a party to refrain from doing a specific act.

_____7. The means by which the law enforces judgments.

_____8. The supreme law of the land.

_____9. The law that governs commercial transactions in most states.

_____10. The law that defines, creates, and regulates legal rights and duties.

_____11. An agreement between or among independent nations.

_____12. General legal principles formulated by equity courts.

_____13. Legislative laws passed by the Federal government.

_____14. A governor of a state may issue this source of law.

_____15. A remedy in equity in which a party is allowed to invalidate a contract.

MULTIPLE CHOICE: Select the alternative that best completes each statement below.

_____1. Equitable remedies include (a) specific performance (b) rescission (c) reformation (d) all of the above.

_____2. Federal Court decisions are not found in which of the following? (a) Federal Reporter (b) Lawyers Edition (c) Federal Supplement (d) North Western Reporter.

_____3. Of the following, the one with present authority over commercial transactions is the (a) Uniform Commercial Code (b) Uniform Sales Act (c) Uniform Bills of Lading Act (d) Bulk Sales Act.

_____4. Which of the following is most accurate? (a) all states have adopted the Uniform Commercial Code (b) the majority of states have adopted the Uniform Commercial Code (c) only one state has not adopted the entire Uniform Commercial Code (d) all the statements are false.

_____5. An example of a legal sanction for a criminal conviction is (a) a fine (b) capital punishment (c) imprisonment (d) all of the above.

_____6. The branch of public law that deals with regulatory functions of the government as performed and supervised by public officials or commissions is (a) judicial law (b) legislative law (c) administrative law (d) none of the above.

_____7. Which of the following is not a "maxim" of equity? (a) Equity will not suffer a wrong to be without a remedy (b) He who comes into equity must come with clean hands (c) He who seeks equity must do equity (d) Equity favors a forfeiture.

_____8. Law can best be classified into categories as (a) procedural or substantive (b) public or private (c) civil or criminal (d) all of the above.

_____9. That law that deals with the rights and powers of the government is (a) private law (b) public law (c) administrative law (d) tort law.

_____10. A source of law in our American legal system includes (a) the Federal Constitution (b) court decisions (c) municipal ordinances (d) all of the above.

_____11. Torts and contracts are examples of (a) private law (b) public law (c) criminal law (d) all of the above.

_____12. A remedy in equity in which a party to a contract is required to perform her obligations according to the contract is (a) an injunction (b) specific performance (c) reformation (d) rescission.

_____13. Public law consists of (a) administrative law (b) constitutional law (c) criminal law (d) all of the above.

CASE PROBLEMS — SHORT ESSAY ANSWERS: Read each case problem carefully. When appropriate, answer by stating a Decision for the case and by explaining the rationale—Rule of Law—relied upon to support your decision.

1. Sarah is in her first year of law school. The teaching method used at the school is the "case method" in which the students read and analyze the reports of court decisions or "cases." One such case is Brown v. Board of Education of Topeka, 347 U.S. 686, 74 S. Ct. 686 (1954). Explain to Sarah how to find this case in a law library.

   Decision: _____

   _____

   Rule of Law: _____

2. Harold signs a contract to buy Maude's home. Although he has the funds, Harold breaches the contract. Maude sues, asking for the remedy of specific performance. Harold demands a jury trial. Is he entitled to one? Explain.

   Decision: _____

   _____

   Rule of Law: _____

3. Nathanial Horn was walking along the street when he was arrested and booked for arson. At his trial, the state brought evidence showing that Horn was indeed in the immediate area when the fire purportedly began. Has the state proven its case against Horn?

   Decision: _____

   _____

   Rule of Law: _____

4. Anita wins a civil suit against Baker for damages of $10,000. Anita is unable to satisfy the judgment (receive payment) by collecting money from Baker. In order to be paid, what other possible remedy is available to Anita?

Decision: _____

_____

Rule of Law: _____

5. John Powers, one of the best-known swimmers in America, was walking near a river one day when he saw Mollie drowning. John, who was wearing a brand new shirt, didn't feel like getting wet. Would the State have a criminal action against John for not attempting to rescue Mollie? Explain.

Decision: _____

_____

Rule of Law: _____

Chapter 2

BUSINESS ETHICS AND THE SOCIAL RESPONSIBILITY OF BUSINESS

SCOPE NOTE

This chapter focuses on the important areas of business ethics and its responsibilities to society. Ethical problems in business concerning the relationship of employers to employees, of business to its customers and its owners, of competing business to each other, and between business and society are identified. Various ethical theories are described and discussed. The chapter also examines ethical standards in business and concludes by explaining the ethical responsibilities of business.

EDUCATIONAL OBJECTIVES

1. Define and explain ethics and its subset — business ethics.

2. Explain the differences between law and ethics.

3. Identify, compare and contrast the various ethical theories.

4. Understand and explain the application of ethical theories to the world of business.

5. Explain and discuss Lawrence Kohlberg's stages of moral development.

6. Identify and explain the ethical responsibilities of business.

CHAPTER OUTLINE

I. **Law versus Ethics** — law and morality are not the same

II. Ethical Theories

A. **Ethical Fundamentalism** — is a theory in which individuals look to a central authority or set of rules to guide them in ethical decision making

B. **Ethical Relativism** — is a doctrine asserting that actions must be judged by what individuals feel is right or wrong for themselves

C. **Utilitarianism** — is a doctrine that assesses good and evil in terms of the consequences of actions

D. **Deontology** — the followers of this theory believe that actions cannot be measured simply by their results but must be judged by the means and motives as well

E. **Social Ethics Theories** — assert that special obligations arise from the social nature of human beings

F. **Other Theories** — several other ethical theories, including intuitionism, are mentioned

III. Ethical Standards in Business

A. **Choosing an Ethical System** — these ethical theories provide insight into ethical decision making and help us formulate issues and resolve moral dilemmas

B. **Corporations as Moral Agents** — the issue of whether or not corporations can or should be held morally accountable for their actions is debated

IV. Ethical Responsibilities of Business

A. **Regulation of Business** — the American economic system of capitalism has failed to accomplish its objective of efficient resource allocation, and it cannot be relied on to achieve all of the social and public policy objectives required by a pluralistic democracy. Increased governmental intervention has been necessary to preserve the competitive process in our economic system and to achieve social goals extrinsic to the efficient allocation of resources

B. **Corporate Governance** — the 5,000 largest U.S. corporations currently produce over half of the nation's gross national product. The economic power of these corporations is controlled by a handful of individuals. Therefore, many observers insist that corporations should have a responsibility to undertake projects that benefit society

C. **Arguments Against Social Responsibility**
   1. Profitability — businesses are established to permit people to engage in profit making, not social activities
   2. Unfairness — whenever corporations stray from their designated role of profit maker, they take unfair advantage of company employees and shareholders
   3. Accountability — corporations are private institutions that are subject to a lower standard of accountability than are public ones
   4. Expertise — corporations may not possess a talent for recognizing or managing socially useful activities

D. **Arguments in Favor of Social Responsibility**
   1. The social contract — corporations, just like other members of society, owe a moral debt to contribute to the overall well-being of society
   2. Less government regulation — the more responsibly corporations act, the less the government must regulate them. For example, if companies use more reasonable and voluntary methods of pollution control, then government will be less likely to legislate more regulations
   3. Long-run profits — when corporations are involved in social causes and problems, it improves the corporation's image and makes good business sense; consumers support corporations with good images and avoid those with bad images

TRUE—FALSE: Circle true or false.

T   F   1. Ethics can be distinguished from a religious approach to morality because it uses reason and not revelation.

T   F   2. Like the law, ethics has a central authority, like courts, that establishes universally agreed upon standards.

T   F   3. Law, ethics and morality are one and the same.

T   F   4. If a course of action is legal, it can be relied upon as an infallible guide to moral behavior.

T   F   5. The two ethical theories, ethical relativism and situational ethics, are substantially the same.

T   F   6. Today, a corporation may be held criminally liable for the improper conduct of the board of directors acting for the corporation.

T   F   7. The primary responsibility of business is to make a reasonable profit on its investment by producing a quality product at a reasonable price.

T   F   8. An indispensable component for repeat customers is the services and policies of a company that creates good will.

T   F   9. A major criticism of the theory of utilitarianism is that it ignores justice.

T   F   10. Under ethical fundamentalism, it would be ethical to compel a few people (e.g., convicts) to undergo fatal medical tests in order to develop cures for the rest of the nation.

T   F   11. Strict utilitarianism and absolutism are identical ethical codes.

T   F   12. The social ethics theory proposed by John Rawls is called social egalitarianism.

KEY TERMS — MATCHING EXERCISE: Select the term that best completes each statement below.

1. Ethical relativism	8. Experience	15. Corporation
2. Act utilitarianism	9. Adam Smith	16. Economic motivation
3. Ethics	10. Absolutism	17. Imprisonment
4. John Rawls	11. Robert Nozick	18. Intuitionism
5. Ethical fundamentalism	12. Fines	19. Education
6. A priori	13. Distributive justice	20. Immanuel Kant
7. Deontology	14. Rule utilitarianism	

_____1. The study of what is right or good for human beings.

_____2. Reasoning that is based on theory rather than experimentation and that draws conclusions from cause to effect.

_____3. Another name for ethical fundamentalism.

_____4. An ethical doctrine that holds that actions must be judged by what individuals feel is right or wrong for themselves.

_____5. A form of business organization that is an artificial entity created by the State.

_____6. The remedy imposed upon a corporation for illegal conduct.

_____7. The ethical theory that seeks to analyze the type of society that people would establish if they could not determine in advance which members would be talented, rich, healthy or ambitious.

_____8. The philosopher who stresses that the most important duty society owes its members is liberty.

_____9. The philosopher who professes the theory that one should not do anything that he or she would not have everyone do in a similar situation.

_____10. This ethical theory holds that actions cannot be measured simply by their results but must be judged by the means and motives as well.

_____11. This ethical theory holds that rational people possess inherent powers to assess the correctness of actions.

_____12. Lawrence Kohlberg noted that people progress through stages of moral development according to two major variables: one is age, name the other.

_____13. The author of *The Wealth of Nations* who explains and justifies the economic system of capitalism.

_____14. A form of utilitarianism that assesses each separate act according to whether it maximizes pleasure over pain.

_____15. One of Adam Smith's six "institutions" that combined to establish our capitalistic system.

MULTIPLE CHOICE: Select the alternative that best completes each statement below:

_____1. Ethics (a) is a rational systematic attempt to determine the rules that should govern human conduct (b) is an attempt to discover the values worth pursuing in life (c) concerns itself with human conduct that is done knowingly and willingly (d) all of the above.

_____2. Regulation of business may occur by (a) self-regulation (b) the "invisible hand" of competition (c) the government (d) all of the above.

_____3. The principal arguments opposing business involvement in socially responsible activities include (a) accountability (b) profitability (c) expertise (d) all of the above.

_____4. Immanuel Kant's philosophy (a) is premised on man's rationality (b) stems from a direct pronouncement from God (c) is the essential belief that universal revealed truths are derived from a central moral authority (d) is none of the above.

_____5. Our criminal laws apply the reasoning of the following ethical theory (a) ethical fundamentalism (b) deontology (c) ethical relativism (d) utilitarianism.

_____6. Libertarians (a) stress justice as the most important obligation owed by society to its members (b) require that the wealth of a nation be distributed to all its citizens (c) stress market outcomes as the basis for distributing society's rewards (d) all of the above.

_____7. The one ethical system subscribed to by all present-day philosophers is (a) egalitarianism (b) libertarianism (c) intuitionism (d) none of the above.

_____8. Immanuel Kant's "categorical imperative" theory (a) is one of the deontological theories (b) rejects notions of the end justifying the means (c) is a variation of the Golden Rule (d) all of the above.

_____9. According to Lawrence Kohlberg's conventional level stage of moral development, the motivation for people to conform their behavior to meet group expectations is (a) affection (b) loyalty (c) trust (d) all of the above.

_____10. To preserve the competitive process of our nation's economic system and to achieve desired social goals, the government has (a) regulated monopolies (b) protected specific groups (labor and agriculture) from failures in the marketplace (c) corrected imperfections in the market system (d) all of the above.

_____11. The ethical theory that holds that before evaluating a person's decision or act it must be viewed from the perspective of a person in the actor's shoes, is (a) ethical relativism (b) deontology (c) situational ethics (d) utilitarianism.

_____12. The following is not one of Adam Smith's six "institutions" that established industrial capitalism (a) private property (b) increased government intervention (c) free enterprise (d) competition.

_____13. Ethical fundamentalists who look to a central authority or set of rules to guide their ethical decisions may be followers of the (a) writings of Karl Marx (b) Bible (c) Koran (d) all of the above.

CASE PROBLEMS — SHORT ESSAY ANSWERS: Read each case problem carefully. When appropriate, answer by stating a Decision for the case and by explaining the rationale — Rule of Law — relied upon to support your decision.

1. Whenever they are together, Andy and Barney argue about what constitutes ethical conduct. Andy's position is that whatever is legal is also ethical. If you are Barney, how would you respond to Andy by differentiating between law and ethics?

Decision: _____

_____

Rule of Law: _____

2. America's Jerry Falwell and Iran's former Ayatullah Khomeini have been identified as ethical fundamentalists. Explain this ethical theory. From what source would each man derive his position as a proponent of absolutism? List two criticisms of this ethical doctrine.

Decision: _____

_____

Rule of Law: _____

3. The Boston Strangler was a widely publicized serial killer. Identify and explain the ethical theory our criminal laws would apply in determining the innocence or guilt of this man.

Decision: _____

_____

Rule of Law: _____

4. Psychologist Lawrence Kohlberg proposed that all people progress through stages of moral development according to two major variables: age and education. Explain Kohlberg's three stages of moral development and his conclusions drawn from this research.

Decision: _____

_____

Rule of Law: _____

5. You have been hired as a consultant by a major business corporation to improve the socially responsible activities of the corporation within its local community. List some of the activities you might recommend to make this improvement.

Decision: _____

_____

Rule of Law: _____

Chapter 3

LEGAL PROCESS

SCOPE NOTE

Over the past decades, increased demands have been placed on our legal system to solve a multitude of previously nonexistent societal and individual problems. Courts, informal dispute settling processes, and administrative bodies have been called upon not only to resolve such conflicts, but to carve out new directions in social, political and economic policy. As individuals and groups continue to make greater use of the legal process, knowledge of its operational dynamics becomes vital. Chapter Three introduces students to the principles and practices of the part of the American legal system responsible for dispute settling—courts. How does a particular dispute move through the American civil law trial process? What are the rights/duties of parties to litigation? These and other concerns are focused upon in the context of our two basic court systems, State and Federal, as well as from the perspective of the overriding concern for fairness (due process) in these dispute-settling arenas. Of major concern is understanding how courts apply legal principles to the facts of a controversy in performing a conflict-resolving function.

EDUCATIONAL OBJECTIVES

1. Outline the organization and the types of cases heard by State and Federal courts.

2. Chart the passage of a case through the judicial process, from the pleadings stage through an appeal of an adverse judgment.

3. Define and identify the basic elements of jurisdiction.

4. Develop the importance of venue.

5. Explain conflict of law problems from both a State and Federal court perspective.

6. Discuss the importance of arbitration as a court substitute for resolving conflict.

CHAPTER OUTLINE

I. The Court System
A. **The Federal Courts**
1. District courts — the trial courts in the Federal system
2. Courts of Appeals — the Federal courts that primarily hear appeals from Federal district courts and administrative agencies
3. The Supreme Court — the nation's highest court consisting of nine justices whose principal function is to review decisions of the Federal Courts of Appeals and the highest State courts
4. Special courts — include the U.S. Claims Court, the Tax Court, the U.S. Bankruptcy Courts, and the U.S. Court of Appeals for the Federal Circuit
B. **State Courts**
1. Inferior trial courts — decide the least serious criminal and civil cases; small claims courts — decide only civil cases involving a limited amount of money
2. Trial courts — State trial courts of general jurisdiction over civil and criminal cases
3. Special courts — include probate and family courts
4. Appellate courts — include the highest court of each state whose decisions are usually final

II. Jurisdiction
A. **Subject Matter Jurisdiction** — the authority of a particular court to adjudicate a controversy of a particular kind
1. Federal jurisdiction
   a. Exclusive Federal jurisdiction — Federal courts have exclusive jurisdiction over federal criminal cases, admiralty, bankruptcy, anti-trust, patent, trademark, and copyright cases
   b. Concurrent Federal jurisdiction — cases that may be heard by either State or Federal courts; it is either federal question jurisdiction or diversity jurisdiction
2. State jurisdiction
   a. Exclusive state jurisdiction — jurisdiction over all other cases
   b. Choice of law in State courts — a court in one state may be the proper forum for a case even though the relevant events occurred in another state
3. Stare decisis in the dual court system — only decisions of the U.S. Supreme Court are binding on all other courts, Federal or State
B. **Jurisdiction Over the Parties** — jurisdiction over the parties involved in the dispute
1. In personam jurisdiction — jurisdiction of the court over the parties to a lawsuit
2. In rem jurisdiction — jurisdiction over property
3. Attachment jurisdiction — quasi in rem jurisdiction over property
4. Venue — the location where a lawsuit should be brought

III. Civil Dispute Resolution
A. **Civil Procedure**
1. The pleadings — the purpose of pleadings is to establish the issues of fact and law presented and disputed
2. Pretrial procedure — each party has the right to obtain evidence from the other party by discovery
3. Trial — the proceeding to determine the outcome of a case with or without a jury
4. Appeal — the purpose is to determine whether the trial court committed prejudicial error
B. **Alternative Dispute Resolution**
1. Arbitration — the disputing parties select a third person who renders a binding decision
2. Conciliation — methods of resolving disputes by use of a conciliator
3. Mediation — a third party (the mediator) selected by the disputants helps them reach a resolution
4. Mini-trial — occurs when both disputants are corporations

TRUE-FALSE: Circle true or false.

T   F   1. Venue is the power and authority of a court to hear and decide a case.

T   F   2. A court may not render a binding decision unless it has jurisdiction over the dispute and over the parties to that dispute.

T   F   3. The only court expressly created by the Federal Constitution is the U.S. Supreme Court.

T   F   4. The decisions of a State Supreme Court are always final.

T   F   5. The purpose of discovery is to enable each party to be informed of the evidence so there will be no surprises at the trial.

T   F   6. A decision of the U.S. Supreme Court on Federal questions is binding on all other courts, Federal or State.

T   F   7. In arbitration, the decision of the arbitrator is generally binding on the parties involved in the dispute.

T   F   8. Generally speaking, appellate courts hear the same witnesses' testimony as the trial court.

T   F   9. The United States has a dual court system: separate State and Federal courts.

T   F   10. The examination or questioning of potential jurors in the jury selection process is called voir dire.

T   F   11. The membership of the U.S. Supreme Court consists of nine justices.

T   F   12. Disputes involving public employees, such as police officers or fire fighters, may require compulsory arbitration as stated in the U.S. Constitution.

KEY TERMS — MATCHING EXERCISE: Select the term that best completes each statement below.

1. Pleadings	8. Complaint	15. Verdict
2. Writ of certiorari	9. Summons	16. Conciliator
3. Mediator	10. Arbitration	17. Award
4. Discovery	11. Depositions	18. Mediation
5. Venue	12. Counterclaim	19. Judgment
6. Appellate jurisdiction	13. Jurisdiction	20. Interrogatories
7. Original jurisdiction	14. Instructions	

_____1.   The type of jurisdiction the U.S. Supreme Court has in cases coming from Federal Courts of Appeals.

_____2.   The place (county) where the lawsuit should be filed or has to be tried.

_____3.   The "charges" given by the judge for the purpose of aiding the jury in reaching its decision.

_____4.   The jury's decision.

_____5.   The use of a neutral person selected by the disputing parties to decide the dispute.

_____6.   Pretrial testimony under oath taken out of court that may be used at the trial.

_____7.   The document that contains the claims of the plaintiff which, when filed, commences a civil lawsuit.

_____8.   The pretrial procedure by which each party has the right to obtain evidence, or information that might lead to evidence, from the other party.

_____9.   A method of appealing a case to the U.S. Supreme Court.

_____10.   The power or authority a court must have to hear and decide a case.

_____11.   A claim by the defendant in a civil lawsuit that she has been damaged and claims compensation (money).

_____12.   Written questions submitted to the opposing party in a civil lawsuit requiring written answers made under oath but before the trial.

_____13.   A person who proposes possible solutions to disputing parties that are not binding.

_____14.   The decision of an arbitrator.

_____15.   Notice to a defendant that a civil lawsuit has been brought against the defendant.

MULTIPLE CHOICE: Select the alternative that best completes each statement below.

_____1.   Diversity of citizenship exists when (a) the plaintiff and defendant are citizens of different states (b) a foreign country brings an action against U.S. citizens (c) a dispute is between U.S. citizens and citizens of a foreign country (d) all of the above.

_____2.   The trial court in the Federal court system is the (a) Federal district court (b) Court of Appeals (c) U.S. Supreme Court (d) Court of Claims.

_____3.   A motion made by the losing party in a civil action to the judge after the jury's verdict is a (a) directed verdict (b) judgment (c) judgment n.o.v. (d) writ of execution.

_____4.   The majority of appellate cases that reach the U.S. Supreme Court come from (a) a State court declaring a Federal statute invalid (b) a State court declaring a treaty invalid (c) all appeals reach the U.S. Supreme Court (d) a writ of certiorari.

_____5.   The Federal Courts of Appeals (a) exist within judicial circuits in the United States (b) have nine justices who decide the cases (c) hear only cases from administrative agencies (d) all of the above.

_____6. The inferior State court that generally hears civil cases involving a limited amount of money is the (a) district court (b) circuit court (c) small claims court (d) none of the above.

_____7. Under its appellate jurisdiction, the U.S. Supreme Court (a) must hear and decide every case appealed to the court (b) hears all cases appealed to the court by writ of certiorari (c) hears only those cases in which a State court declares a Federal statute invalid (d) none of the above.

_____8. The special Federal court that hears claims against the Federal government is the (a) Tax Court (b) U.S. Claims Court (c) Customs Court (d) none of the above.

_____9. In order for a court to proceed with a lawsuit, it must have jurisdiction over the (a) plaintiff (b) defendant (c) subject matter of the case (d) all of the above.

_____10. In a civil lawsuit, the defendant's answer to the plaintiff's complaint may contain (a) admissions or denials (b) affirmative defenses (c) counterclaims (d) all of the above.

_____11. The Federal courts have exclusive jurisdiction over cases involving (a) patents (b) bankruptcy (c) copyrights (d) all of the above.

_____12. The purpose of this type of jurisdiction is to resolve conflicting claims to property (a) attachment jurisdiction (b) in personam jurisdiction (c) in rem jurisdiction (d) none of the above.

_____13. Alternative dispute resolutions include (a) arbitration (b) conciliation (c) mediation (d) all of the above.

CASE PROBLEMS — SHORT ESSAY ANSWERS: Read each case problem carefully. When appropriate, answer by stating a Decision for the case and by explaining the rationale—Rule of Law—relied upon to support your decision.

1. In a civil action, Mary Swift sues James Swanson in a State district court for negligently damaging her property. Mary wins, and James appeals to the State Supreme Court. The Supreme Court reverses and remands the decision of the district court. What does remand mean and, according to the rules of civil procedure, what happens to this case? Explain.

Decision: _____

_____

Rule of Law: _____

2. A labor management dispute occurs in the Ajax Corporation. Neither side wants to go through an expensive and lengthy civil lawsuit, and both sides want a binding resolution of their problem. What type of alternative dispute resolution would you recommend to the parties? Explain.

Decision: _____

_____

Rule of Law: _____

3. A Georgia Supreme Court decision in a civil law paternity suit favors the defendant — the man alleged to be the father. If a case involving the same facts was brought before a Texas court, would the Texas court be obligated to follow the Georgia decision under the "stare decisis" doctrine? Explain.

Decision: _____

_____

Rule of Law: _____

4. While on vacation in Colorado, Amy Burns negligently struck Malcolm Morris with her ski, causing Malcolm to lose his sight in one eye. Amy is a resident of (or domiciled in) the State of Minnesota, and Malcolm lives in Colorado. Can this case be heard in Federal district court? Explain.

Decision: _____

_____

Rule of Law: _____

5. Karla Johnson, a resident of Iowa, appeals a case to the Eighth Circuit Court of Appeals and wins. If a case involving the same facts was brought on appeal to the Fourth Circuit Court of Appeals, must that circuit court follow the decision of the Eighth Circuit? Explain.

Decision: _____

_____

Rule of Law: _____

Chapter 4

CONSTITUTIONAL LAW

SCOPE NOTES

The founding fathers of the American government feared powerful, centralized, and unitary government. They were committed to a political philosophy that stressed "limited government." The Federal Constitution, as the blueprint for governing authority, embodies the principles of limited government in its separation of powers, checks and balances, federalism, and other structural restrictions. Chapter Four examines the purpose and functions of the fundamental law of American society: the Federal Constitution.

EDUCATIONAL OBJECTIVES

1. Discuss policy underlying concepts of constitutional law.

2. Identify fundamental doctrines characterizing the U.S. Constitution.

3. Outline major powers held by the Federal and State governments.

4. Explain the limits the U.S Constitution places on the Federal government and the states.

CHAPTER OUTLINE

I. **Basic Principles of Constitutional Law**
   A. **Federalism** — means that governing power is divided between the Federal government and the states
   B. **Federal Supremacy and Preemption** — all law in the United States is subject to the U.S. Constitution, which is the supreme law of the land
   C. **Judicial Review** — the process by which the courts examine governmental actions to determine whether they conform to the U.S. Constitution
   D. **Separation of Powers** — our Constitution establishes three distinct and independent branches of government: executive, legislative, and judicial

E.   **State Action** — includes any actions of the Federal and state governments that are protected by the U.S. Constitution and its amendments

II. Powers of Government

A.   **Federal Commerce Power** — the Constitution gives Congress the power to regulate commerce with other nations and among the states

B.   **State Regulation of Commerce**— the commerce clause of the Constitution also restricts the States' power to regulate activities if the result obstructs interstate commerce
1.   Regulations — the U.S. Supreme Court decides the extent of permissible state regulation affecting interstate commerce
2.   Taxation — the commerce clause, in conjunction with the import-export clause, also limits the power of the states to tax

C.   **Federal Fiscal Powers** — including the power to tax, to spend, to borrow and coin money, and the power of eminent domain
1.   Taxation — the Constitution grants Congress broad powers to tax with three major limitations
2.   Spending power — an important way the Federal government regulates the economy
3.   Borrowing and coining money — enables the Federal government to establish a national banking system: the Federal Reserve System
4.   Eminent domain — the government's power to take private property for public use

III. Limitations Upon Government

A.   **Contract Clause** — this clause of the Constitution restricts states from retroactively modifying public charters and private contracts

B.   **First Amendment** — the protection of free speech with some limits
1.   Corporate political speech — is indispensable to the discovery and spread of political truth
2.   Commercial speech — is the expression related to the economic interests of the speaker and its audience, e.g., advertisements of a product or service
3.   Defamation — a tort consisting of a false communication that injures a person's reputation

C.   **Due Process** — the Fifth and Fourteenth Amendments prohibit the Federal and State governments from depriving any person of life, liberty, or property without due process of law
1.   Substantive due process — involves a court's determination of whether a particular governmental action is compatible with individual liberties
2.   Procedural due process — pertains to the governmental decision-making process that results in depriving a person of life, liberty, or property

C.   **Equal Protection** — the guarantee of equal protection requires that similarly situated persons be treated similarly by governmental actions
1.   Rational relationship test — a standard of review used by the Supreme Court to determine whether governmental action satisfies the equal protection guarantee
2.   Strict scrutiny test — another standard of review
3.   Intermediate test — a third standard of review

TRUE-FALSE: Circle true or false.

T   F   1. Public law is concerned with the rights and powers of government and its relation to individuals or groups.

T   F   2. The Constitution of the United States was adopted in Washington, D.C. on August 1, 1776.

T   F   3. The Federal commerce clause grants virtually complete power to the individual states to regulate the economy and business.

T   F   4. The Federal government regulates the nation's economy by its power to spend money.

T   F   5. The U.S. Supreme Court ruled that the contract clause of the Federal Constitution precludes the states from exercising eminent domain or their police powers.

T   F   6. The judicial branch of the U.S. government has the power to enforce the law.

T   F   7. Defamation is a crime that injures a person's reputation.

T   F   8. The first ten amendments to the U.S. Constitution are known as the Federalist Papers.

T   F   9. An example of a concurrent governmental power is police power.

T   F   10. An example of the Federal government's fiscal powers is the prosecution of crimes that violate Federal law.

T   F   11. The legislative branch of the U.S. government has the power to make law.

T   F   12. Judicial review is a function of the President of the United States.

KEY TERMS—MATCHING EXERCISES: Select the term that best completes each statement below.

1. Administrative law	8. Chief Justice	15. First Amendment
2. Marbury v. Madison	9. Procedural due process	16. Tenth Amendment
3. McCulloch v. Maryland	10. Equal Protection clause	17. President
4. Bill of Rights	11. Veto power	18. Fifth Amendment
5. Import-export clause	12. Federal Commerce clause	19. Constitutional law
6. Eminent domain	13. Federal fiscal powers	20. Thirteenth Amendment
7. Defamation	14. Judicial review	

_____1. The landmark Supreme Court decision that verified the supremacy of the Constitution over every other source of law.

_____2. The power of the government to take private property for public use.

_____3. The clause of the U.S. Constitution that grants complete power to Congress to regulate the economy.

_____4. The Federal power that allows the Federal government to tax, spend, borrow, and coin money.

_____5. A tort that consists of a communication that injures a person's reputation.

_____6. The right to a fair hearing (trial) before the government can deprive a person of life, liberty or property.

_____7. The procedure by which a President can reject legislation passed by Congress.

_____8. The Amendment to the Constitution that protects the right of free speech.

_____9. A type of public law other than constitutional or criminal law.

_____10. The guarantee that requires that similarly situated persons be treated the same by governmental actions.

_____11. The first ten Amendments to the U.S. Constitution.

_____12. The Amendment that abolished slavery.

_____13. The person who has the power to appoint federal judges.

_____14. The fundamental law that created the levels of government in the United States.

_____15. The process by which courts determine whether governmental actions conform to the U.S. Constitution.

MULTIPLE CHOICE: Select the alternative that best completes each statement below.

_____1. The source of law that is the "supreme law of the land" is (a) U.S. Supreme Court decisions (b) Federal statutes (c) the U.S. Constitution (d) none of the above.

_____2. The final arbiter of the constitutionality of any law in the U.S. is (a) the U.S. Constitution (b) Congress (c) the President (d) the U.S. Supreme Court.

_____3. The doctrine that divides the U.S. government into three branches — executive, legislative, and judicial—is the (a) separation of powers principle (b) Bill of Rights (c) Judicial Review (d) Federalist doctrine.

_____4. Public law consists of all of the following except (a) criminal law (b) tort law (c) constitutional law (d) administrative law.

_____5. Basic principles of the U.S. Constitution include (a) separation of powers (b) federalism (c) federal supremacy (d) all of the above.

_____6. Federalism means that (a) the U.S. Constitution is the supreme law (b) the federal government and the states divide the governing power (c) judicial review is constitutional (d) all of the above.

_____7. The standard the U.S. Supreme Court uses in determining whether legislation satisfies the equal protection guarantee is the (a) strict scrutiny test (b) rational relationship test (c) both a and b above (d) none of the above.

_____8. The equal protection guarantee (a) applies when governmental action involves classification of people (b) requires that persons similarly situated be treated similarly by the government (c) is included in the Fourteenth Amendment to the Constitution (d) all of the above.

_____9. Federal fiscal powers do not include the power (a) to pay debts of the federal government (b) of eminent domain (c) to allow the states to levy duties on exports (d) all of the above.

_____10. Procedural due process considers "property" to include (a) real property (b) personal property (c) social security payments and food stamps (d) all of the above.

_____11. The branch of the U.S. government that has the power to veto bills enacted by Congress is the (a) executive branch (b) legislative branch (c) judicial branch (d) none of the above.

_____12. The branch of the U.S. government that has the power to reject executive appointments is the (a) executive branch (b) legislative branch (c) judicial branch (d) none of the above.

_____13. The "one person, one vote" rule decided by the U.S. Supreme Court is an example of the Court's use of the (a) rational relationship test (b) due process test (c) intermediate test (d) strict scrutiny test.

CASE PROBLEMS — SHORT ESSAY ANSWERS: Read each case problem carefully. When appropriate, answer by stating a Decision for the case and by explaining the rationale—Rule of Law—relied upon to support your decision.

1. (Optional) Explain the reason President Richard Nixon's claim of executive privilege was denied by the U.S. Supreme Court, resulting in the requirement that certain presidential tapes be produced and ultimately in President Nixon's resignation. [See United States v. Nixon, 418 U.S. 683 (1974).] (NOTE: Outside research is necessary to answer this question.)

Decision: _____

_____

Rule of Law: _____

2. The State of Minnesota places an import tax on all foreign cars arriving at its international port, the city of Duluth. The Datsun Company of Japan refuses to pay the state tax. If a lawsuit between these parties commences, who would prevail? Explain.

Decision: _____

_____

Rule of Law: _____

3. Mai Thai Fong has immigrated to the United States. She asks you to explain the separation of powers doctrine, one of the fundamental principles upon which our government is based. What would be your response?

Decision: _____

_____

Rule of Law: _____

4. The powers of the Federal government are superior to any and all of our fifty states. Yet each state has its own constitution and sovereignty over its own courts and citizens. Which Amendment to the U.S. Constitution expressly grants this right of sovereignty to the states?

   Decision: _____

   _____

   Rule of Law: _____

5. Explain the strict scrutiny test used by the U.S. Supreme Court in its decision in the <u>Brown v. Board of Education of Topeka</u> case concerning the equal protection guarantee of the Fourteenth Amendment.

   Decision: _____

   _____

   Rule of Law: _____

Chapter 5

ADMINISTRATIVE LAW

SCOPE NOTE

This chapter discusses administrative agencies, sometimes referred to as the "fourth branch of government." In the complex, crowded urban society that constitutes present-day America, many complicated socioeconomic problems arise that demand attention and expertise beyond the capacity of traditional lawmakers, courts and legislatures. Chapter Five includes a discussion of the growth of administrative law as the primary responder to such complex problems. How administrative agencies function is examined. Students should remember that the federal agencies focused upon reflect the types of activities engaged in by similar lawmakers in their own states and towns.

EDUCATIONAL OBJECTIVES

1. Discuss policy underlying concepts of administrative law.

2. Explain the operation of administrative agencies.

3. List activities pursued by administrative lawmakers.

4. Distinguish among significant federal administrative lawmakers.

5. Identify the limits imposed on administrative agencies.

CHAPTER OUTLINE

I. **Operation of Administrative Agencies** — most of these agencies perform three basic functions
    A. **Rulemaking** — is the process by which an administrative agency enacts or promulgates rules of law
        1. Legislative rules — are called regulations and are issued by the agency
        2. Interpretative rules — are statements by the agency that explain how the agency construes its governing statute

   3. Procedural rules — establish rules of conduct for practice before the agency and describe its
      method of operation
B. **Enforcement** — agencies determine whether their rules have been violated
C. **Adjudication** — an agency may use informal or formal methods to resolve disputes; the formal
   method is called adjudication

II. Limits on Administrative Agencies
A. **Judicial Review** — acts as a control or check by a court on a particular rule or order of an
   administrative agency
B. **Legislative Control** — is exercised over administrative agencies through budget control or even
   by completely eliminating the agency
C. **Control by Executive Branch** — is exercised by the President's power to appoint and remove
   the chief administrator of the agency
D. **Disclosure of Information** — requires agencies to disclose information about their actions

TRUE-FALSE: Circle true or false.

T   F   1. An enabling statute is passed by Congress to create a federal agency.

T   F   2. The scope of administrative law has diminished dramatically in the past 50 years.

T   F   3. The rules created by administrative agencies are called statutes.

T   F   4. The President can abolish federal administrative agencies of the executive branch with
              the approval of Congress.

T   F   5. A jury will decide a controversy brought to an administrative hearing.

T   F   6. All administrative agencies receive their authority from the judicial branch of the federal
              government.

T   F   7. When a decision of a controversy is made by an administrative agency, that decision
              usually may be appealed to the appropriate state or federal court.

T   F   8. The adjudication of a controversy between an individual and one of the federal
              administrative agencies is presided over by an administrative law judge.

T   F   9. In the adjudication of a controversy between an individual and a federal administrative
              agency, the agency serves as both prosecutor and decision maker.

T   F   10. State administrative agencies play a very limited role in our society today.

T   F   11. Federal administrative agencies are classified as either independent or executive
              agencies.

T   F   12. Once Congress has created a federal administrative agency, it cannot terminate the
              agency.

KEY TERMS — MATCHING EXERCISE: Select the term that best completes each statement below.

1. Administrative law	8. Chief Justice	15. Enabling statute
2. Judgment	9. "Fourth branch of government"	16. First Amendment
3. Administrative process	10. Legislative control	17. President
4. Order	11. Procedural rules	18. Constitutional law
5. Executive control	12. Legislative rules	19. Administrative law judge
6. Rulemaking	13. Interpretive rules	20. Adjudication
7. Administrative agency	14. Judicial review	

_____1. The entire set of activities in which administrative agencies engage while carrying out their functions.

_____2. The process by which an administrative agency enacts rules of law.

_____3. These rules are also called regulations.

_____4. Rules that explain how an administrative agency construes its governing statute.

_____5. The party who acts as prosecutor of an administrative hearing.

_____6. Another name for administrative agencies.

_____7. Rules that establish proper conduct for practice before an administrative agency.

_____8. The law that creates an administrative agency.

_____9. Public law that governs the powers and procedures of administrative agencies.

_____10. When Congress amends an enabling statute it exercises this control.

_____11. The name for the final disposition of an adjudication.

_____12. The formal procedure by which an administrative agency resolves a case.

_____13. The person who has the power to appoint and remove the chief administrator of an agency.

_____14. The person who presides over an administrative agency hearing.

_____15. The process by which courts determine whether governmental actions conform to the U.S. Constitution.

MULTIPLE CHOICE: Select the alternative that best completes each statement below.

_____1. Federal administrative agencies are not responsible for (a) taxation (b) elections (c) workers' compensation (d) all of the above.

_____2. Federal administrative agencies are responsible for (a) national security (b) commerce (c) labor relations (d) all of the above.

_____3. Basic functions performed by administrative agencies include (a) making rules (b) making statutes (c) presiding over administrative hearings (d) all of the above.

_____4. Public law consists of all of the following except (a) criminal law (b) tort law (c) constitutional law (d) administrative law.

_____5. Administrative agencies (a) create more legal rules than Congress (b) adjudicate more controversies than our state and federal courts (c) have increased in number tremendously in the past 50 years (d) all of the above.

_____6. Administrative agencies do not (a) make rules and regulations (b) create statutes (c) enforce the agency's rules (d) adjudicate controversies.

_____7. In essence, an adjudication is (a) a civil trial (b) a criminal trial (c) an administrative trial (d) none of the above.

_____8. Administrative agencies are (a) governmental entities (b) controlled by the legislative branch of government (c) called boards or commissions (d) all of the above.

_____9. Activities of the numerous administrative agencies are referred to as the (a) legislative process (b) judicial process (c) administrative process (d) none of the above.

_____10. If Congress amends the enabling statute, the administrative agency's authority may be (a) increased (b) modified (c) decreased (d) all of the above.

_____11. The branch of the U.S. government that has the power to impound money appropriated to an agency by Congress is the (a) executive branch (b) legislative branch (c) judicial branch (d) none of the above.

_____12. The branch of the U.S. government that has the power to reject executive appointments to administrative agencies is the (a) executive branch (b) legislative branch (c) judicial branch (d) none of the above.

_____13. In a judicial review of an order of an administrative agency, the court (a) decides questions of law (b) interprets statutory provisions (c) determines the meaning of terms (d) all of the above.

CASE PROBLEMS — SHORT ESSAY ANSWERS: Read each case problem carefully. When appropriate, answer by stating a Decision for the case and by explaining the rationale — Rule of Law — relied upon to support your decision.

1. Mary has been denied benefits under her state's Medical Assistance program. She has appealed the denial to the state's Department of Health. A hearing before an administrative law judge is being scheduled. Mary requests a jury trial for this administrative hearing. Is she entitled to a jury trial? Explain.

Decision: _____

_____

Rule of Law: _____

2. The increase in the number of federal, state and local administrative agencies in our country has been astounding. William and Howard are arguing the merits of this proliferation and specifically, the need for uniformity and consistency in running these agencies since, in the past, rules of evidence varied from agency to agency. Name and explain the law enacted by Congress that helped to resolve this concern.

Decision: _____

_____

Rule of Law: _____

3. As in question #2, William and Howard are continuing their discussion of administrative agencies. Howard tells William there are three sources of law that control the formation of an agency and the issuance of valid legislative regulations by the agency. Name the three and explain each one.

Decision: _____

_____

Rule of Law: _____

4. Formal rulemaking procedures for administrative agencies require that the agency must hold a hearing resembling a trial in civil court. The agency must base the rule it creates on the record of the trial-like hearing. If the rule is challenged in court as part of the judicial review process, the factual determination by the court must abide by the standard called the "substantial evidence test." Explain this test.

Decision: _____

_____

Rule of Law: _____

5. The Clean Air Act authorizes the Environmental Protection Agency (EPA) to issue regulations banning fuel additives that pollute the air and endanger the public health. When the EPA, using informal rulemaking procedures, banned lead additives to gasoline, the manufacturers of the additives challenged the regulations. Although the EPA could only establish the relationship between lead, in general, and health hazards, the federal court held the EPA did not need rigorous proof of cause and effect. Where regulations deal with health hazards, courts defer to the agency's judgment so long as it is based on more than wild guesses. What standard of review of factual determinations was used in this case? Explain.

Decision: _____

_____

Rule of Law: _____

Chapter 6

CRIMINAL LAW

SCOPE NOTE

The preceding materials have examined the American legal system from the perspective of civil law, usually involving disputes between private individuals. This chapter undertakes a different approach. That aspect of the American legal process that addresses disruptions of the public interest and society at large — criminal law — is discussed. The significant concepts and doctrines of both substantive and procedural criminal law are developed.

EDUCATIONAL OBJECTIVES

1. Evaluate various policy assumptions underlying American criminal law.

2. Distinguish tort law from criminal law.

3. Differentiate civil from criminal procedures.

4. Identify sources of criminal law.

5. Explain major classifications of criminal law.

6. Discuss the essential elements of a crime.

7. Outline prosecutorial burden of proof requisites for various specific crimes.

8. Discuss white-collar crimes and crimes against business.

9. Explain common defenses to criminal charges.

10. Discuss criminal procedure.

CHAPTER OUTLINE

I.   **Nature of Crimes**
   A.   **Essential Elements** — of a crime consists of two elements
      1. The wrongful or overt act
      2. Criminal intent
   B.   **Classification** — of crimes range from the most serious — a felony — to a misdemeanor
   C.   **Vicarious Liability** — is liability imposed upon one person for the acts of another person
   D.   **Liability of the Corporation** — historically, corporations were not held criminally liable; today, corporations can be liable and punished by a fine

II. **White-collar Crime**
   A.   **Computer Crime** — includes the use of a computer to steal money or services, or to tamper with information
   B.   **Racketeering Influenced and Corrupt Organizations Act** — its purpose is to stop the infiltration of organized crime into legitimate business

III. **Crimes Against Business**
   A.   **Larceny** — is the trespassory taking and carrying away of personal property of another with the intent to deprive the victim permanently of the goods
   B.   **Embezzlement** — is the fraudulent conversion of another's property by one who was in lawful possession of it
   C.   **False Pretenses** — is a crime enacted to close a loophole in the requirements of larceny
   D.   **Robbery** — is a larceny in which the property is forcibly taken from the victim
   E.   **Extortion and Bribery** — extortion is blackmail, while bribery is the offer of money or property to a public official to influence a decision by the official
   F.   **Burglary** — according to modern law, is an entry into a building with the intent to commit a felony
   G.   **Forgery** — is the falsification of a document with the intent to defraud another person
   H.   **Bad Checks** — is knowingly writing a check with insufficient funds in the account to cover the check

IV. **Defenses to Crimes**
   A.   **Defense of Person or Property** — individuals may use reasonable force to protect their property
   B.   **Insanity** — the traditional and most common test for insanity is the M'Naghten test
   C.   **Infancy** — minors under eighteen are brought before a juvenile court, not an adult criminal court
   D.   **Intoxication** — the majority position is that voluntary intoxication is not a defense
   E.   **Duress** — is a valid defense to criminal conduct other than murder
   F.   **Mistake of Fact** — an honest and reasonable mistake of fact will justify the defendant's conduct
   G.   **Entrapment** — arises when a law officer induces a person to commit a crime when that person would not have done so otherwise

V.   **Criminal Procedure**
   A.   **Steps in Criminal Prosecution** — a basic overview of the procedures in a criminal prosecution is presented
   B.   **Fourth Amendment** — protects individuals against unreasonable searches and seizures
   C.   **Fifth Amendment** — protects persons against self-incrimination, double jeopardy, and being charged with a capital crime except by grand jury indictment
   D.   **Sixth Amendment** — provides the accused with a speedy and public jury trial and the right to counsel for her defense

TRUE—FALSE: Circle true or false.

T   F   1. The standard by which the government has to prove the defendant guilty of a crime is "guilt by a preponderance of the evidence."

T   F   2. The same act (conduct) may constitute both a tort and a crime.

T   F   3. The distinction between the crimes of larceny and false pretenses is that in the latter, possession of the personal property is voluntarily transferred to the thief.

T   F   4. All jurisdictions (states), except Nevada, have passed legislation making it a crime to issue bad checks.

T   F   5. A criminal defense that arises when an official induces a person to commit a crime is duress.

T   F   6. A "bench trial" is a case tried by a judge without a jury.

T   F   7. In order to obtain a search warrant, the judge or magistrate issuing the warrant must believe that probable cause exists that the search will reveal evidence of a crime.

T   F   8. Civil law is private law; criminal law is public law.

T   F   9. Computer crime is an example of one type of white-collar crime.

T   F   10. Extortion and bribery are identical crimes.

T   F   11. Federal crimes are exclusively covered by statutory law.

T   F   12. Today, a corporation cannot be found guilty of a crime because it cannot be imprisoned.

KEY TERMS — MATCHING EXERCISE: Select the term that best completes each statement below.

1. White-collar crime	8. Deadly force	15. Misdemeanor
2. Search warrant	9. Due process	16. Durham test
3. Nondeadly force	10. Equal protection	17. Arraignment
4. True bill	11. Actus reus	18. Entrapment
5. Murder	12. Mens rea	19. Duress
6. Racketeering	13. Felony	20. Information
7. Defamation	14. Ordinance	

_____1. A pattern of criminal conduct that is defined as the commission of two or more predicate acts within a period of ten years.

_____2. The crime for which duress is not a valid defense.

_____3. The criminal intent required for a crime to exist.

_____4. The type or classification of crime punishable by death or imprisonment.

_____5. The type of nonviolent crime involving deceit or breach of trust.

_____6. The right to a fair hearing (trial) before the government can deprive a person of life, liberty or property.

_____7. The wrongful act that is a necessary element of a crime.

_____8. A crime punishable by fine or imprisonment in a local jail.

_____9. The kind of force that is generally never reasonable to use to protect property.

_____10. A grand jury's decision to indict the defendant in a criminal case.

_____11. The formal accusation of a crime brought by a county prosecutor.

_____12. The hearing at which the accused is informed of the charge against him and a plea is entered.

_____13. A document that allows a legal search of a person's home.

_____14. A criminal defense when a law officer induces a person to commit a crime that the person would not have committed otherwise.

_____15. A criminal defense in which a person is threatened with serious bodily harm unless the person participates in committing a crime.

MULTIPLE CHOICE: Select the alternative that best completes each statement below:

_____1. The amendment to the U.S. Constitution that prohibits double jeopardy in criminal cases is the (a) Eighth Amendment (b) Sixth Amendment (c) Fourth Amendment (d) Fifth Amendment.

_____2. Robbery differs from larceny in that the stolen property may be taken (a) directly from the victim (b) by force (c) by the threat of deadly force (d) all of the above.

_____3. The purpose of the exclusionary rule is to (a) deter all police activity (b) hinder the search for the truth in the case (c) protect individual liberty (d) none of the above.

_____4. The privilege against self-incrimination as guaranteed by the Fifth Amendment protects the accused from being forced to (a) testify against himself (b) stand in a "line up" for identification purposes (c) provide a handwriting sample (d) take a blood test.

_____5. A search warrant is not necessary (a) to search a person's luggage (b) when voluntary consent to search is given (c) to search a person's home (d) all of the above.

_____6. The accused in a serious criminal case (a) is not always entitled to a jury trial (b) if found guilty, may request a new trial (c) if acquitted must allow the State the right to appeal the acquittal to a higher court (d) must be proven guilty by a preponderance of the evidence.

_____7. Punishment for criminal conduct does not include (a) fines (b) imprisonment (c) a lawsuit for money damages (d) the death penalty.

_____8. Under our legal system, (a) a defendant's guilt is presumed (b) the defendant must testify in her own defense (c) the burden of proof of innocence or guilt is on the defendant (d) none of the above.

_____9. The amendment of the U.S. Constitution that protects individuals from unreasonable searches and seizures is the (a) First Amendment (b) Second Amendment (c) Fourth Amendment (d) Fifth Amendment.

_____10. The U.S. Supreme Court has ruled that juries deciding criminal cases (a) may consist of twelve jurors (b) may consist of six jurors (c) need not reach unanimous verdicts in all State court cases (d) all of the above.

_____11. The membership of a grand jury consists of not more than (a) six persons (b) twelve persons (c) twenty-three persons (d) none of the above.

_____12. Criminal liability imposed upon one person for the criminal acts of another person is (a) computer crime (b) racketeering (c) voluntary manslaughter (d) vicarious liability.

_____13. The amendment of the U.S. Constitution that provides for the assistance of counsel (an attorney) for the person accused of a crime is the (a) Fourth Amendment (b) Fifth Amendment (c) Sixth Amendment (d) Eighth Amendment.

CASE PROBLEMS — SHORT ESSAY ANSWERS: Read each case problem carefully. When appropriate, answer by stating a Decision for the case and be explaining the rationale — Rule of Law — relied upon to support your decision.

1. Allen Johnson, an undercover FBI agent, convinces Melvin Howard, an industrialist whose company is in financial trouble, to participate in the purchase and resale of narcotics. If Melvin is arrested, what defense would you recommend for him? Explain.

   Decision: _____

   _____

   Rule of Law: _____

2. Carol Olson is convicted by a six-member jury of the crime of embezzlement from the bank where she is employed. Carol appeals her conviction on the grounds she was wrongfully deprived of a jury of twelve persons in violation of her Constitutional rights. What result? Explain.

   Decision: _____

   _____

   Rule of Law: _____

3. Karla Johnson is arrested for first degree murder in her home through the use of an arrest warrant, together with an "information" of the charge at the time of arrest. What other method could be used to initiate prosecution of Karla for this crime? Explain.

Decision: _____

_____

Rule of Law: _____

4. Thelma and Louise decide to rob a bank. They spend two days planning every detail they believe will be necessary to execute their plan successfully. Then they change their minds. Have Thelma and Louise committed a crime? Explain.

Decision: _____

_____

Rule of Law: _____

5. In a famous Supreme Court case, Gideon v. Wainwright, 372 U.S. 335, 9 L. Ed. 799 (1963), the defendant, Gideon, charged with the commission of a felony, was unable to afford a lawyer for his defense, and the trial court denied his request to appoint a lawyer for him. Gideon was found guilty, and he was imprisoned. On appeal, the U.S. Supreme Court reversed the conviction and ordered his release. On what grounds did the Court make its decision?

Decision: _____

_____

Rule of Law: _____

Chapter 7

INTENTIONAL TORTS

SCOPE NOTE

Causing harm to people and property, apart from possible criminal implications, can often result in the injured party (victim) having a right of civil recovery against the wrongdoer. Torts is that area of the law that concerns injury-causing conduct and compensation to a victim. The vocabulary and principles of private, civil wrongs stemming from breaches of legal duties to act without danger to others, is focused on in Chapters Seven and Eight. Because tort law is essentially an exercise in loss-shifting (the recovering victim transfers to the injury-causer the financial liability for the loss suffered through the injury), our attention will be directed towards those types of acts that trigger the loss-shifting mechanism: deliberate, intentional harm to others, discussed in Chapter Seven; careless conduct resulting in accidental harm and the concept of "strict liability," both focused on in Chapter Eight.

Chapter Seven introduces the terminology and basic concepts of intentional torts. What acts constitute the deliberate injuring of another person or their property? What excuses or justifications for such conduct are recognized that absolve the actor from liability? These and other concerns are addressed in relation to the overriding purpose of tort law — compensation to the injured party.

EDUCATIONAL OBJECTIVES

1. Be familiar with the range of conflicts brought to tort law for resolution.

2. Differentiate among the various legal/equitable remedies available to a tort victim.

3. Identify and distinguish among the various acts recognized as intentional harm to business, property or persons.

4. Discuss the plaintiff's burden of proof in the context of intentional torts.

5. Enumerate the various valid defenses and their respective required elements associated with an intentional tort theory of recovery.

CHAPTER OUTLINE

I. Harm to the Person
   A. **Battery** — an intentional infliction of harmful or offensive bodily contact
   B. **Assault** — intentional conduct toward another person that puts him in fear of immediate bodily harm
   C. **False Imprisonment** — or false arrest, is the intentional confining of a person against her will
   D. **Infliction of Emotional Distress** — atrocious, intolerable conduct beyond all bounds of decency

II. Harm to Right of Dignity
   A. **Defamation** — false communication that injures a person's reputation
     1. Elements of defamation — include libel and slander (written and spoken defamation)
     2. Defenses to defamation — truth and privilege are defenses to defamation
   B. **Invasion of Privacy** — consists of four distinct torts; defenses include absolute, conditional and constitutional privilege
     1. Appropriation — of a person's name or likeness
     2. Intrusion — unreasonable and offensive interference with the solitude or seclusion of another
     3. Public disclosure of private facts — offensive publicity of private information
     4. False light — unreasonable and untruthful publicity that places another in a false light that is highly offensive
   C. **Misuse of Legal Procedure** — consists of three torts
     1. Malicious prosecution — wrongfully bring about a criminal proceeding without probable cause
     2. Wrongful civil proceedings — are similar to malicious prosecution except the legal proceeding is a civil lawsuit
     3. Abuse of process — is the use of a civil or criminal proceeding to accomplish a purpose for which it is not designed

III. Harm to Property
   A. **Real Property** — land and anything attached to it such as buildings, trees, and minerals
     1. Trespass — entering on, remaining on, and failing to leave land in possession of another
     2. Nuisance — a non-trespassory invasion of another's interest in the private use and enjoyment of land
   B. **Personal Property, or Chattel** — is any property other than an interest in land
     1. Trespass — an intentional taking or unauthorized use of another's personal property
     2. Conversion — an intentional exercise of dominion or control over another's property that justly requires the payment of full value for the property

IV. Harm to Economic Interests
   A. **Interference with Contractual Relations** — subjects a person to liability for the monetary loss that results
   B. **Disparagement** — publication of false statements about the title or quality of another's property or products
   C. **Fraudulent Misrepresentation** — a false representation of fact, opinion, or law to induce another to act or to refrain from action

V. Defenses to Intentional Torts
   A. **Consent** —willingness that an act shall occur that negates the wrongfulness of the act
     1. Exceeding consent — the defendant is limited to conduct to which the plaintiff consents
     2. Consent to a criminal act — may or may not be a valid defense

B.   Privilege
   1. Self-defense — action taken to prevent harm to oneself
   2. Defense of others — action taken to prevent harm to another
   3. Defense of property — a possessor may use reasonable force, not intended or likely to cause death or serious bodily harm, to protect real or personal property

TRUE-FALSE: Circle true or false.

T   F   1. A tort is a private wrong generally resulting in personal injury or in property damage or destruction.

T   F   2. Battery is the threat of bodily harm by the tortfeasor.

T   F   3. An example of the tort of emotional distress is rude and abusive language.

T   F   4. An obvious defense to the tort of trespass is that the trespasser mistakenly was unaware of the trespassing.

T   F   5. Any force by an owner, including deadly force, can be used to prevent a trespass across the owner's property.

T   F   6. One defense to the commission of an intentional tort is the plaintiff's consent to the defendant's conduct.

T   F   7. If the accused in a criminal case is found not guilty, that person can sue the public prosecutor for malicious prosecution.

T   F   8. Like other subject matter areas of the law such as contracts, tort law is static, i.e., it never changes.

T   F   9. Truth is the only complete defense to a lawsuit for defamation.

T   F   10. The privilege of self-defense to prevent harm to oneself may exist whether or not danger actually exists.

T   F   11. Tort law is primarily based upon common law.

T   F   12. The law protects the rights of the possessor of real property to its exclusive use and quiet enjoyment.

KEY TERMS — MATCHING EXERCISE: Select the term that best completes each statement below.

1.	Tort	8.	False imprisonment	15.	Defamation
2.	Slander	9.	Malicious prosecution	16.	Intrusion
3.	Battery	10.	Conditional privilege	17.	Appropriation
4.	Assault	11.	Absolute privilege	18.	False light
5.	Disparagement	12.	Nuisance	19.	Libel
6.	Chattel	13.	Conversion	20.	Exemplary
7.	Privilege	14.	Duress		

_____1. The kind of conduct that furthers an important social interest and creates immunity from tort liability.

_____2. A wrongful act causing personal injury or property damage or destruction.

_____3. A threat to do immediate bodily harm.

_____4. Intentionally confining a person against her will within fixed boundaries and without an available alternative exit.

_____5. An unjust commencement of a criminal proceeding without probable cause and for an improper purpose.

_____6. Like the defense of truth, this type of privilege protects the defendant from liability for defamation regardless of motive or intent.

_____7. Another name for personal property.

_____8. A non-trespassory invasion of another's interest in the use and enjoyment of land.

_____9. Interference with another's right of control of personal property as to require full payment for the property.

_____10. False statements intended to cast doubt upon the quality of another's products.

_____11. Another name for punitive damages.

_____12. The type of defamatory communication that is written.

_____13. The use of a plaintiff's name or photograph for the benefit of a defendant.

_____14. The type of invasion of privacy that is an unreasonable and highly offensive interference with the solitude of another.

_____15. The type of defamatory communication that is oral.

MULTIPLE CHOICE: Select the alternative that best completes each statement below.

_____1. Which of the following are responsible for their intentional torts? (a) adults (b) minors (c) incompetent persons (d) all of the above.

_____2. The tort of defamation includes (a) libel and slander (b) assault and battery (c) trespass and public nuisance (d) all of the above.

_____3. A person may commit the tort of trespass (a) on land (b) beneath the ground (c) above the surface of the land (d) all of the above.

_____4. Concerning chattels, the measure of damages (a) for the tort of trespass is the amount of damage for the actual harm to the chattel (b) for the tort of conversion is the full value of the chattel (c) for both trespass and conversion is the amount of damages for the loss of possession of the chattel (d) only a and b above.

_____5. An example of a tort that is not intentional is (a) defamation (b) negligence (c) invasion of privacy (d) emotional distress.

_____6. The tort of invasion of privacy does not include (a) the appropriation of a person's name (b) the unreasonable publication of private facts (c) trespassing on another's property (d) entering of another's home uninvited.

_____7. Interference with the performance of a contract by another may be (a) by the use of physical force (b) by threats (c) by an offer of higher pay for the performer (d) all of the above.

_____8. Consent to conduct, resulting in damage to the consenter's property but no liability, is valid if made by (a) an adult (b) a minor (c) an incompetent (d) an intoxicated person.

_____9. The privilege of self-defense exists (a) but not as an act of revenge (b) provided the defendant reasonably believed that it was necessary (c) even if the defendant could avoid the threatened contact by retreating (d) all of the above.

_____10. A fraudulent misrepresentation that induces another to enter a written agreement could involve a lawsuit within the law of (a) torts (b) contracts (c) both torts and contracts (d) none of the above.

_____11. The type of invasion of privacy that imposes liability for false publicity that places another in a position that is highly offensive is (a) intrusion (b) appropriation (c) false light (d) all of the above.

_____12. Privilege is a defense to intentional torts and it includes (a) defense of property (b) defense of other persons (c) self-defense (d) all of the above.

_____13. Intentional interference with property rights includes the torts of (a) trespass to real or personal property (b) conversion (c) nuisance (d) all of the above.

CASE PROBLEMS—SHORT ESSAY ANSWERS: Read each case problem carefully. When appropriate, answer by stating a Decision for the case and by explaining the rationale—Rule of Law—relied upon to support your decision.

1. While playing ice hockey, A knocks B down and continues to slam B's head against the ice. B's right eye is injured, and B sues. A argues that everyone knows hockey is a "violent" sport and that B's consent to play the game discharges any liability of A to B. Who wins? Explain.

   Decision: _____

   _____

   Rule of Law: _____

2. A says to B, "I'm going to beat you up." There is no way B can avoid the fight. A starts the fight. B grabs a rock and smashes A's head with it. A is seriously injured. What kind of tort liability, if any, would B have in this case? Explain.

   Decision: _____

   _____

   Rule of Law: _____

3. A newspaper prints a photograph of A with a caption stating that A has been accused of rape. In fact, the newspaper printed a photograph of the wrong person. Have the torts of defamation and invasion of privacy both been committed? Explain.

Decision: _____

_____

Rule of Law: _____

4. A says to B that C has a venereal disease. A's statement is not true. C learns of A's comment and sues. What tort has been committed? Explain.

Decision: _____

_____

Rule of Law: _____

5. As a practical joke, A calls B on the phone and tells B that B's child has been hit by a car and is in the hospital. B sues A. Who wins? Explain.

Decision: _____

_____

Rule of Law: _____

Chapter 8

NEGLIGENCE AND STRICT LIABILITY

SCOPE NOTE

The basic elements associated with recovery to the victim of careless conduct (negligence) or ultra-hazardous behavior (strict liability) are the focus of attention in Chapter Eight. What is negligence? How does the law determine whether an accident was unavoidable (no victim recovery) or avoidable (negligence)? What types of behavior fall within the strict liability category? These and other issues developed in Chapter Eight close out our discussion of tort law.

EDUCATIONAL OBJECTIVES

1. Define and discuss the basic elements of negligence.

2. Distinguish among the various sources of duty of care.

3. Develop the meaning and significance of the res ipsa loquitur doctrine vis-a-vis the burden of proof of the victim/plaintiff.

4. Define and explain the importance of proximate causation.

5. Differentiate among the various defenses to a complaint of negligence.

6. Enumerate the types of harm falling under strict liability.

7. Develop the defenses that can be successfully asserted in response to a strict liability complaint.

CHAPTER OUTLINE

I. **Negligence**
   A. **Breach of Duty of Care**
      1. Reasonable person standard — the degree of care that a reasonable person would exercise in a given situation
         a. Children — a child's conduct must conform to that of a child of like age, intelligence and experience
         b. Physical disability — a disabled person's conduct must conform to that of a reasonable person under like disability

   c. Mental deficiency — a mentally deficient person is held to the reasonable person standard

   d. Superior skill or knowledge — professionals must exercise the care and skill of members in good standing within their profession

   e. Emergencies — the standard is still the reasonable person but under emergency circumstances

   f. Violation of statute — the reasonable person standard of conduct may be established by statute

  2. Duty to act — generally, no one is required to aid another in peril

  3. Duties of possessors of land

   a. Duty to trespassers — generally, none

   b. Duty to licensees — the possessor of land owes a higher duty of care to licensees than to trespassers

   c. Duty to invitees — duty to exercise reasonable care to protect invitees against dangerous conditions

  4. Res ipsa loquitur — a rule that permits the jury to infer both negligent conduct and causation from the mere occurrence of certain types of events

 B. **Proximate Cause**

  1. Causation in fact — the defendant's conduct was the actual cause of the injury

  2. Limitations upon causation in fact

   a. Unforeseeable consequences — may negate the defendant's liability for negligence

   b. Superseding cause — an intervening act that relieves the defendant's liability to the plaintiff

 C. **Injury** — the defendant's negligence must have caused harm or injury

 D. **Defenses to Negligence**

  1. Contributory negligence — both parties contribute to the negligence that causes the harm; damages cannot be recovered

  2. Comparative negligence — damages are apportioned between the parties in proportion to their degree of negligence

  3. Assumption of risk — a plaintiff who voluntarily and knowingly assumes the risk of harm arising from the negligence of the defendant cannot recover for such harm

II. Strict Liability

 A. **Activities Giving Rise to Strict Liability**

  1. Abnormally dangerous activities — for harm resulting from such activities, strict liability is imposed

  2. Keeping of animals

   a. Trespassing animals — owners are generally strictly liable for harm caused by trespass of their animals

   b. Nontrespassing animals — keepers of wild animals are strictly liable for damage they cause, whether or not they are trespassing

  3. Products liability — a form of strict liability upon manufacturers and merchants who sell goods in a defective condition

 B. **Defenses to Strict Liability**

  1. Contributory negligence — is not a defense to strict liability

  2. Comparative negligence — some states apply this doctrine to products liability cases

  3. Assumption of risk — is a defense to an action based upon strict liability

TRUE—FALSE: Circle true or false.

T   F   1. The basis of liability for negligence is the failure to exercise reasonable care for the safety of other persons or their property.

T   F   2. Generally, the burden of proof in a civil action for negligence is on the plaintiff.

T   F   3. A physically disabled person and a mentally deficient person are held to the standard of conduct of a reasonable person with like disabilities or deficiencies.

T   F   4. Manufacturers and merchants who sell defective goods that are unreasonably dangerous to a consumer are strictly liable regardless of due care.

T   F   5. Keepers (owners) of dangerous and domestic animals are strictly liable for the injuries the animals cause only if the keeper is aware that the animals are dangerous.

T   F   6. Keepers of domestic animals are only liable for the injuries caused by their animal to other people.

T   F   7. Strict liability refers to a defendant's absolute liability without regard to negligence or intent on the part of the tortfeasor (defendant).

T   F   8. No one is under an affirmative duty to aid another who is in danger under any circumstances.

T   F   9. It is possible for a person to be injured by another without the latter having any liability.

T   F   10. The courts have traditionally allowed recovery for negligently inflicted emotional distress.

T   F   11. Parents are liable for all of the torts committed by their minor children.

T   F   12. The reasonable person standard means that a reasonable person is always careful, prudent and never negligent.

KEY TERMS—MATCHING EXERCISE: Select the term that best completes each statement below.

1. Res ipsa loquitur	8. Contributory negligence	15. Proximate cause
2. Reasonable person	9. Products liability	16. Last clear chance
3. Strict liability	10. Assumption of risk	17. Conversion
4. Licensee	11. Comparative negligence	18. Substantial factor test
5. Trespasser	12. Act of God	19. Superseding cause
6. Negligence	13. Propensity	20. Business visitor
7. Public invitee	14. But for rule	

_____1. Conduct that falls below the standard established by law for protection of others against unreasonable risk of harm.

_____2. The term that identifies the dangerous inclination of a domestic animal to cause injury.

_____3. The doctrine that apportions damages between parties in proportion to the degree (percentage) of fault.

_____4. A person privileged to enter upon land only with the consent of the lawful possessor.

_____5. The rule that means "the thing speaks for itself."

_____6. A widely applied test for causation in fact.

_____7. A standard of conduct involving the duty of care and imposed by law.

_____8. A business invitee such as a plumber who enters a home for the purpose of making repairs.

_____9. A common law defense available in negligence cases in which the plaintiff and defendant are both at fault and neither can recover damages.

_____10. A person who enters on the land of another without permission.

_____11. A person who enters a municipal pool to swim.

_____12. An intervening event that may relieve the defendant of liability.

_____13. Another name for absolute liability or liability without fault.

_____14. A valid defense to a charge of negligence that prohibits the plaintiff's recovery because of the plaintiff's consent to encounter a known danger.

_____15. A form of strict liability imposed on manufacturers who sell defective goods.

MULTIPLE CHOICE: Select the alternative that best completes each statement below.

_____1. Which of the following is not a defense to strict liability? (a) contributory negligence (b) comparative negligence (c) assumption of risk (d) all of the above.

_____2. The possessor of land owes no duty of care to (a) a child trespasser (b) licensees (c) business visitors (d) an adult trespasser.

_____3. Domestic animals that are generally considered safe to mankind include (a) cats and dogs (b) horses and sheep (c) cattle (d) all of the above.

_____4. Dangerous animals, whose keepers are held strictly liable for the harm they cause, include all of the following except (a) lions (b) cows (c) monkeys (d) raccoons.

_____5. Which of the following is not a defense to a charge of negligence? (a) assumption of risk (b) contributory negligence (c) proximate cause (d) comparative negligence.

_____6. The reasonable person standard (a) is what a judge or jury determines that a reasonable person would have done in specific circumstances (b) requires a child who drives a boat or car to be held to the standard of care of a child of like age, intelligence and experience under the same circumstances (c) does not hold insane persons responsible for their negligent acts (d) all of the above.

_____7. Which of the following professional or skilled persons would not be required to exercise special care and skill normally possessed by those practicing their professions or trade? (a) doctors and attorneys (b) teachers and professors (c) carpenters and electricians (d) architects and engineers.

_____8. The duty of affirmative action is not imposed on a defendant to aid or protect the plaintiff if the parties are (a) parent and child (b) employer and employee (c) best friends and neighbors (d) innkeeper and guest.

_____9. Strict liability will be imposed regardless of intent or negligence for (a) crop dusting that kills other life (b) faulty merchandise that results in injury (c) the use of dynamite in populated areas (d) all of the above.

_____10. If the plaintiff is aware of the dangerous or negligent conduct of the defendant and ignores it and is subsequently injured, the plaintiff cannot recover damages due to the doctrine of (a) contributory negligence (b) comparative negligence (c) assumption of risk (d) last clear chance.

_____11. A parent is responsible for the torts of her minor children if the parent (a) authorizes the tort (b) ratifies the tort (c) does not properly control her child's behavior (d) all of the above.

_____12. The possessor of land owes a duty of care to (a) licensees (b) child trespassers (c) business visitors (d) all of the above.

_____13. Which of the following is not a factor that imposes limitations on the causal connection between the defendant's negligence and the plaintiff's injury? (a) foreseeable events (b) superseding causes (c) unforeseeable consequences (d) none of the above.

CASE PROBLEMS — SHORT ESSAY ANSWERS: Read each case problem carefully. When appropriate, answer by stating a Decision for the case and by explaining the rationale — Rule of Law—relied upon to support your decision.

1. While flying her airplane and performing various stunts, Joelene Brady loses control of the plane and crashes into Sarah Johnson's home. Sarah sues. Joelene claims it was an unintentional accident. Who wins? Explain.

   Decision: _____

   _____

   Rule of Law: _____

2. Mark Benson is taking care of five-year-old Kathy Walsh while Kathy's mother is in the hospital. Kathy wanders from the house onto a nearby railroad track. Mark sees her on the track and a train is approaching. To avoid liability, must Mark make an attempt to rescue Kathy at the risk of his own life? Explain.

   Decision: _____

   _____

   Rule of Law: _____

3. While crossing a street, Abner and Baker meet in the middle of the street, have an argument, and begin fighting. Abner knocks Baker down, causing him to strike his head on the pavement and rendering him unconscious. Abner walks away. Carol unavoidably runs over the unconscious Baker with her car, seriously injuring him. Was the intervening force (Carol's car striking Baker) a superseding cause that relieves Abner of liability? Explain.

Decision: _____

_____

Rule of Law: _____

4. In a state that has a comparative negligence statute, a jury determines that the plaintiff, Susan, has sustained damages of $50,000 and that the percentages of fault of the parties to the case, Susan and the defendant, Michael, are: plaintiff — 10% negligent; defendant — 90% negligent. What would be Susan's judgment award in damages in this case?

Decision: _____

_____

Rule of Law: _____

5. The Swanberg Soup Company has shipped cases of its soup that are contaminated with botulism food poisoning to its retailers. Matthew purchases a can of the soup, eats some of it, and becomes very sick. Explain the type of liability the company has to Matthew in this case.

Decision: _____

_____

Rule of Law: _____

LEGAL ENVIRONMENT OF BUSINESS RESEARCH QUESTIONS: Drawing upon information contained in the text, as well as outside sources, discuss the following questions:

1. Common law does not impose a legal duty on persons to assist endangered strangers. Some states have enacted "Good Samaritan" Statutes eliminating this common law rule and creating a legal duty, under certain circumstances, to assist strangers facing danger. Has your state enacted such a statute? What are the advantages/disadvantages associated with laws creating such a legal duty of assistance?

2. Some jurists and social commentators have pointed out the necessity for calling a Constitutional Convention to address various amendments to the Constitution, including equal rights, right to life, balanced budget, anti-flag desecration, and right to die. Should such a Convention be called? What would be gained by such action and at what cost?

Chapter 9

INTRODUCTION TO CONTRACTS

SCOPE NOTE

Contracts is an area of law that touches nearly all other branches of business law. Understanding contract law provides a useful foundation for learning and applying principles associated with other specific fields of business law. Chapter Nine focuses on basic concepts of contract law, the various types of binding agreements recognized by courts and important introductory terminology. This knowledge provides a crucial frame of reference for the successful study of the principles and vocabulary that comprise the specific areas of contract law that will occupy our further inquiry into the arena of binding agreements.

EDUCATIONAL OBJECTIVES

1. Discuss the importance of contracts in business.

2. Identify present day controlling sources of contract law.

3. Define what is meant by "contract."

4. Differentiate the various classifications of contracts based on such factors as extent of performance, validity, method of creation and type of use.

5. Enumerate the particular elements that make up a contract.

6. List examples of contracts that you have entered into during recent weeks.

CHAPTER OUTLINE

I. **Contracts**
   A. **Development of the Law of Contracts**
      1. Common law — contracts are primarily governed by state common law
      2. The Uniform Commercial Code — governs all sales contracts concerning personal property
      3. Types of contracts outside the Code — general contract law governs these contracts

B. **Definition of a Contract** — a contract is a set of promises that the courts will enforce
C. **Essentials of a Contract** — the four basic requirements of a contract are mutual assent, consideration, legality of object, and capacity
D. **Classification of Contracts**
   1. Express and implied contracts — contracts created either by express language or by conduct of the parties
   2. Unilateral and bilateral contracts — contracts created by a promise for an act or by an exchange of promises
   3. Valid, void, voidable, and unenforceable contracts — contracts classified according to their enforceability
   4. Executed and executory contracts — contracts that are completed or unperformed
   5. Formal and informal contracts — contracts based upon a particular form or those that are not dependent upon formality for their validity
E. **Promissory Estoppel** — under this doctrine, some noncontractual promises are enforceable in order to avoid injustice
F. **Quasi Contracts** — are implied-in-law contracts

TRUE—FALSE: Circle true or false.

T	F	1. Contract law could be referred to as the law of enforceable promises.
T	F	2. A source of law upon which much of contract law is based is state common law.
T	F	3. The Uniform Commercial Code (U.C.C.) is the sole source of contract law in the United States today.
T	F	4. According to the U.C.C., all contracts are promises and all promises are contracts.
T	F	5. A bilateral contract results from the exchange of one promise for another.
T	F	6. When it is not clear whether a unilateral or bilateral contract has been formed, a unilateral contract will be presumed by the courts.
T	F	7. Both the defrauded and fraudulent parties to a contract may declare the contract void.
T	F	8. A void contract may be enforceable.
T	F	9. To be executed, a contract must be fully performed by all parties.
T	F	10. A quasi contract may be considered an obligation imposed by law and based upon equitable principles.
T	F	11. In a bilateral contract there are two promisors and two promisees.
T	F	12. Only written contracts, not oral ones, are binding and enforceable.

KEY TERMS—MATCHING EXERCISE: Select the term that best completes each statement below.

1. Common law	8. Forbearance	15. Goods
2. Uniform Commercial Code	9. Quasi	16. Promisor
3. Voidable	10. Promissory estoppel	17. Formal
4. Bilateral	11. Void	18. Breach
5. Implied	12. Unilateral	19. Informal
6. Executory	13. Executed	20. Promisee
7. Recognizances	14. Fraudulent	

_____1. The U.C.C. term for movable, tangible personal property.

_____2. An enforceable contract formed by conduct.

_____3. A contract created by a promise for a performance.

_____4. The primary source of contract law.

_____5. A contract that either may be avoided or enforced.

_____6. Formal acknowledgments of indebtedness made in court.

_____7. A promise not to do an act.

_____8. A contract in which there are one or more unperformed promises.

_____9. A contract imposed by law where there has been no expressed assent.

_____10. The source of contract law governing the sale of personal property.

_____11. The failure to properly perform a contract.

_____12. The person who makes a promise.

_____13. The person to whom the promise is made.

_____14. A contract created by an exchange of promises.

_____15. Simple contracts that do not depend upon formality for their legal validity.

MULTIPLE CHOICE: Select the alternative that best completes each statement below.

_____1. The U.C.C. modifies contract law and applies to a type of contract involving (a) the transfer of title to goods from seller to buyer for a price (b) employment contracts (c) contracts for the sale of patents and copyrights (d) all of the above.

_____2. Contracts may be (a) oral (b) written (c) implied from the parties' conduct (d) all of the above.

_____3. An example of a formal contract is (a) a promise under seal (b) a negotiable instrument (c) a recognizance (d) all of the above.

_____4. A says to B, "If you paint my garage, I will pay you one hundred dollars." B paints the garage. This creates a (a) bilateral contract (b) unilateral contract (c) void contract (d) all of the above.

_____5. A contract induced by fraud is (a) void (b) express (c) voidable (d) unenforceable.

_____6. An essential element of all contracts is (a) manifestation of mutual assent (b) consideration (c) legality of the object (d) all of the above.

_____7. The party entitled to elect to avoid a contract induced by fraud is called (a) a minor (b) the defrauded party (c) the fraudulent party (d) none of the above.

_____8. The law of contracts is also basic to which of the following fields of law (a) agency (b) commercial paper (c) sales (d) all of the above.

_____9. An authoritative reference book that gives an orderly presentation of the law of contracts is the (a) Reporter (b) American Law Institute (c) Restatement (d) none of the above.

_____10. The only state that has not adopted all sections of the U.C.C. is (a) Minnesota (b) Georgia (c) Louisiana (d) Arizona.

_____11. General contract law governs all of the following except (a) sales of personal property (b) sales of real property (c) insurance contracts (d) service contracts.

_____12. A contract that fails to satisfy the requirements of the Statute of Frauds is classified as (a) valid (b) unenforceable (c) void (d) voidable.

_____13. An oral or written contract in which all the terms have been definitely stated and agreed upon by the parties is an (a) informal contract (b) implied contract (c) express contract (d) none of the above.

CASE PROBLEMS—SHORT ESSAY ANSWERS:
Read each case problem carefully. When appropriate, answer by stating a Decision for the case and by explaining the rationale — Rule of Law — relied upon to support your decision.

1. When Sara became ill, Mary performed housekeeping services for Sara without any agreement that Mary be paid. Sara requested the services, and Mary expected to be paid. Sara died. In a lawsuit seeking compensation for Mary, the court ruled a contract existed. What kind of contract is it? Explain.

Decision: _____

_____

Rule of Law: _____

2. Julie plans a summer trip to Europe. Her best friend, Karen, has been accepted to medical school in the fall. Karen says, "Julie, while on your trip, if you buy a microscope for me, I will give you $100.00." Julie buys the microscope in Europe and returns home. Does a contract exist? Explain.

Decision: _____

_____

Rule of Law: _____

3. Barry says to Arnold, "I will sell you my motorcycle for $400." Arnold replies, "O.K." Neither party used the word promise in their negotiation. Was a bilateral contract created? Explain.

Decision: _____

_____

Rule of Law: _____

4. Michael lied to Joyce about important terms of their contract. On the basis of Michael's statement, Joyce agreed to the terms and signed the contract. How would such a contract be classified? Explain.

Decision: _____

_____

Rule of Law: _____

5. An employee of Harold's Hardware and Appliances Store delivers a TV set to Mary Martin mistakenly believing she had ordered it. Would the hardware store be entitled to the return of the set? Explain the legal concept of contract law involved in this case.

Decision: _____

_____

Rule of Law: _____

Chapter 10

MUTUAL ASSENT

SCOPE NOTE

An agreement (meeting of the minds) is the basis for a contract. All contracts must be agreements, but all agreements are not contracts. The first and most important area of contract study is how the parties to a contract reached an agreement. Meeting of the minds, as a primary factor in creating a legally valid and enforceable agreement, concerns the process by which the parties come to an understanding of the crucial terms that embody an agreement.

EDUCATIONAL OBJECTIVES

1. Identify the acts that together form an agreement.

2. Discuss the various requirements for a valid offer and acceptance.

3. Discuss the types of conduct of the parties and events that bring the life of an offer to an end.

4. Enumerate the significance of silence at the agreement formation stage.

CHAPTER OUTLINE

I. **Offer**
   A. **Essentials of an Offer**
      1. Communication—mutual assent to form a contract requires that the offeree must have knowledge of the offer that was made by the offeror to the offeree
      2. Intent—to have legal effect, an offeror must manifest an intent to enter into a contract
         a. Preliminary negotiations—are not valid offers that can create a contract
         b. Advertisements—a merchant invites customers to make offers to buy goods
         c. Auction sales—the auctioneer does not make offers to sell but invites offers to buy
      3. Definiteness—the terms of a contract must be reasonably certain
         a. Open terms—the Code provides standards by which omitted terms may be determined
         b. Output and requirements contracts—are enforceable agreements under the Code when based upon the good faith of the parties

53

B. **Duration of Offers**
  1. Lapse of time—if no time is stated in the offer, an offer will terminate after a reasonable time
  2. Revocation—an offer may be revoked any time before it is accepted
      a. Option contracts—the offeror is bound to hold open an offer for a specified time
      b. Firm offers under the Code—are those made by a merchant in writing and signed
      c. Statutory irrevocability—certain offers are irrevocable by statute
      d. Irrevocable offers of unilateral contracts—the Restatement holds that once performance begins, the offeror is obligated not to revoke the offer for a reasonable time
      e. Promissory estoppel—a noncontractual promise may be enforced to avoid an injustice
  3. Rejection—a refusal of the offer terminates it
  4. Counter-offer—is a counter-proposal that also terminates the original offer
  5. Death or incompetency—of either party terminates the offer
  6. Destruction of subject matter—of an offer terminates the offer
  7. Subsequent illegality—discharges the obligations of both parties under the contract

II. **Acceptance**
  A. **Communication of Acceptance**
    1. General rule—in all bilateral contracts, acceptance must be communicated to the offeror; in unilateral contracts, notice of acceptance to the offeror may not be required
    2. Silence as acceptance—generally, silence or inaction is not an acceptance of the offer
    3. Effect moment—a contract is formed when the last act necessary to its formation is done
        a. Stipulated provisions in the offer—of the means of acceptance must be followed
        b. Authorized means—the means of communication expressly authorized by the offeror
        c. Unauthorized means—if the medium of communication used by the offeree is unauthorized, it still may be effective if it is received in a timely manner
        d. Acceptance following a prior rejection—must be received by the offeror prior to the receipt of the rejection
  B. **Variant Acceptances**
    1. Common law—an acceptance must be positive and unequivocal; it must be the mirror image of the offer
    2. Code—because of the realities of modern business practices, the Code modifies the common law

TRUE-FALSE: Circle true or false.

T   F   1. One of the essentials of a contract is the agreement between two or more parties.

T   F   2. Parties usually manifest their mutual assent by means of an offer and an acceptance.

T   F   3. An auction sale is a binding offer to sell the property being auctioned.

T   F   4. It is essential to the contractual relationship that the offeree have knowledge of the offer.

T   F   5. After rejecting an offer, the offeree no longer has the power to bind the parties by accepting.

T   F   6. Illegality subsequent to the formation of a contract will discharge the contractual obligations of the parties.

T   F   7. The acceptance of an offer can create a contract only if the offer was communicated to a specifically named offeree.

T   F   8. As a general rule, silence on the part of a person to whom an offer is made is considered an acceptance of the offer.

T   F   9. After an offer has expired, there can be no acceptance of it.

T   F   10. An authorized means of communicating an acceptance is the method stated by the offeror in the offer or, if none is stated, it is the method used by the offeror.

T   F   11. Retail prices listed by merchants on items in a clothing or appliance store are not considered offers made by the merchants that a customer may accept.

T   F   12. The incompetency of either the offeror or the offeree ordinarily terminates an offer.

KEY TERMS — MATCHING EXERCISE: Select the term that best completes each statement below.

1. Offeree	8. Firm offer	15. Acceptance
2. Offeror	9. Inverted unilateral contract	16. Output contract
3. Option	10. Jest	17. Invitation
4. Mirror image rule	11. Counter-offer	18. Unilateral contract
5. Definiteness	12. Good faith	19. Merchant
6. Revocation	13. Auctioneer	20. Forbearance
7. Alternative	14. Silence	

_____1. An overt act by the offeree that manifests assent to the terms of the offer.

_____2. An act by the offeree that will terminate the offer yet indicates a willingness to contract.

_____3. Inaction by the offeree that may result in an acceptance under special circumstances.

_____4. The person who makes the offer in a contractual dealing.

_____5. A circumstance where one may lack the required intent to form a contract.

_____6. The person to whom an offer is made.

_____7. This term is defined as "honesty in fact in the conduct or the transaction concerned."

_____8. A contract in which the offeror is bound to keep open an offer for a specified time.

_____9. A contract created by an act for a promise.

_____10. No contract exists under common law because similar terms of agreement, contained in printed forms used by both buyers and sellers, are not present.

_____11. An agreement of a buyer to purchase the entire production of a seller's factory.

_____12. The person who is bound to keep a written offer to buy or sell goods open for up to three months.

_____13. The promise to refrain from doing an act.

_____14. The withdrawal of an offer that occurs before the offer is accepted.

_____15. A contract created by a promise exchanged for an act.

MULTIPLE CHOICE: Select the alternative that best completes each statement below.

_____1. The terms of an offer may be accepted by (a) spoken words (b) a letter (c) a telegram (d) all of the above.

_____2. An offer may terminate by (a) revocation (b) rejection (c) death of either party (d) all of the above.

_____3. A definite contractual proposal requesting a forbearance and made by one person to another is (a) an offer (b) an invitation (c) an acceptance (d) a quasi contract.

_____4. To create a contract, an offer must (a) be definite and certain (b) be communicated (c) have contractual intent (d) all of the above.

_____5. When the auctioneer brings the hammer down on the bidding, the result is (a) a withdrawal (b) an offer (c) a manifestation (d) a contract.

_____6. If the offeror has the power to terminate the offer before acceptance, the offeror has (a) rejection power (b) the power to lapse (c) irrevocable options (d) the power of revocation.

_____7. The manifestation of an unwillingness to accept an offer is called a (a) revocation (b) rejection (c) withdrawal (d) counter-offer.

_____8. An offer (a) may be a promise for a promise (b) must manifest intent to create a contract (c) that consists of a statement indicating a willingness to offer is not itself a binding offer (d) all of the above.

_____9. The following is generally effective upon being sent (dispatched): (a) an offer (b) an acceptance (c) a rejection (d) a revocation.

_____10. The standard the law applies to determine if a manifestation of mutual assent has occurred by the words or acts of the parties is (a) an objective standard (b) a subjective standard (c) a relative standard (d) none of the above.

_____11. An offer (a) may be a promise for an act (b) may be in the form of an act for a promise (c) requires an offeror and an offeree (d) all of the above.

_____12. Lapse of time of an offer (a) may terminate the offer (b) will terminate the offer after a reasonable period of time if no time for termination is stated (c) may be for one day if perishable goods are involved (d) all of the above.

_____13. A counter-offer (a) has no effect on the original offer (b) indicates a total rejection of the original offer (c) operates like a rejection (d) none of the above.

CASE PROBLEMS — SHORT ESSAY ANSWERS: Read each case problem carefully. When appropriate, answer by stating a Decision for the case and by explaining the rationale — Rule of Law — relied upon to support your decision.

1. Sam sent a telegram to Jerome offering Jerome the exclusive rights to a certain line of goods. Sam requested a reply by telegram. Jerome sent a registered letter to Sam saying he accepts. Sam refused to comply, and Jerome brings suit. Who prevails? Explain.

    Decision: _____

    _____

    Rule of Law: _____

2. A mailed a box of candy to B, stating that if B wanted to keep the candy, it would cost $5. B never requested the candy. B keeps the candy but refuses to pay. What result?

    Decision: _____

    _____

    Rule of Law: _____

3. A pays B $1,000 for a one-year option to buy five acres of land. Ten months later the value of the land has doubled, and B suddenly dies. B's executor refuses to honor the option, alleging B's death as a termination of the offer. Who prevails? Explain.

    Decision: _____

    _____

    Rule of Law: _____

4. William, whose child is trapped in his burning house, screams hysterically that he will pay $100,000 to anyone who will save the child. Sharon, a bystander, hears William and, at the risk of her life, rescues the child. Was William's statement an offer? Explain.

    Decision: _____

    _____

    Rule of Law: _____

5. Suppose that A mailed B a letter stating, "I wish I could find someone to buy my cattle for $10,000." B knows that $10,000 is a reasonable price. Therefore, B mails a letter to A stating, "I will buy your cattle for $10,000." Does a contract exist? Explain.

    Decision: _____

    _____

    Rule of Law: _____

Chapter 11

CONDUCT INVALIDATING ASSENT

SCOPE NOTE

This chapter focuses upon factors that distinguish an enforceable contract from a voidable or unenforceable contract due to unfairness/inequality in the manner in which the parties reached their agreement. Contracts that seem, on the face, to be valid because essential formation elements are apparently present may, however, be voidable as a result of "contaminations" (misconduct of the parties) in the negotiation (agreement formation) process. What are the "wrongful acts" or misdeeds that remove "reality of consent" from the meeting of the minds process? What remedies are available to contracting parties when "reality of consent" is absent?

EDUCATIONAL OBJECTIVES

1. Define and identify the essential elements of fraud and discuss the consequences of fraud.

2. Differentiate fraud from innocent misrepresentation and discuss the significance of the latter.

3. Define and identify examples of and discuss the differences between duress and undue influence.

4. Distinguish between and discuss the significance of unilateral and bilateral mistakes.

5. Identify situations where a contracting party faces a duty of disclosure and the consequences of failing to meet that duty.

CHAPTER OUTLINE

I. **Duress** — the law will not enforce any contract induced by improper physical force or improper threats
   A.   Physical compulsion — a type of duress using actual physical force
   B.   Improper threats — include economic and social coercion to compel a person to enter a contract
II. **Undue Influence** — is taking unfair advantage of a person by reason of a dominant position based upon a confidential relationship
III. **Fraud**—the following are the two types of fraud:
   A.   **Fraud in the Execution** — a misrepresentation that deceives the defrauded person as to the nature of the contract

B. **Fraud in the Inducement** — an intentional misrepresentation of a material fact on which the defrauded person enters the contract in reliance upon the misrepresentation; five requisite elements of fraud in the inducement are:
1. False representation
2. Fact
3. Materiality
4. Knowledge of falsity and intention to deceive
5. Justifiable reliance

IV. **Nonfraudulent Misrepresentation** — a majority of courts permit a rescission of a contract for negligent or innocent misrepresentation if all of the remaining elements of fraud are present

V. **Mistake** — an understanding or belief that is not in accord with facts
A. **Mutual Mistake** — occurs when both parties are mistaken as to the same facts
B. **Unilateral Mistake** — occurs when only one party is mistaken
C. **Assumption of Risk of Mistake** — will not allow a party to avoid the contract
D. **Effect of Fault upon Mistake** — generally does not allow a party who fails to read a contract to avoid it; a party is held to what she signs
E. **Mistake in Meaning of Terms** — generally, there is no mutual assent if both parties in good faith attach different meanings to the terms of their agreement

True-False: Circle true or false.

T   F   1. When undue influence is the issue in a legally challenged contract, the law presumes that advantage was taken by the dominant party.

T   F   2. Sellers are allowed some leeway to puff their goods to the public.

T   F   3. Forcing a person to create a contract against the person's will is called fraud.

T   F   4. All fraudulent contracts are void.

T   F   5. Generally, when a person signs a contract without reading it, the person is bound by its terms.

T   F   6. Duress is always either a tort or a crime.

T   F   7. An example of duress is a threat to sue another for civil damages.

T   F   8. Most courts today allow a rescission of a contract even if the false misrepresentation of a material fact that induces the plaintiff to enter the contract is innocently done.

T   F   9. If there is a mutual mistake between the parties concerning a material fact, the contract may be avoided.

T   F   10. If a contracting party makes a mistake as to the value of the subject matter, the court will rescind the contract.

T   F   11. To establish fraud, the misrepresentation must be known by the fraudulent party to be false and must be made with an intent to deceive.

T   F   12. As a general rule, silence alone does not constitute fraud.

KEY TERMS—MATCHING EXERCISE: Select the term that best completes each statement below.

1. Materiality	8. Mistakes of law	15. Ward
2. Rescission	9. Fiduciary	16. Damages
3. Mistake	10. Duress	17. Unilateral mistake
4. Concealment	11. Scienter	18. Valid
5. Undue influence	12. Mutual	19. Fraudulent person
6. Defrauded person	13. Voidable	20. Silence
7. Opinion	14. Void	

_____1. Conduct in which a parent, through unfair persuasion, induces a child to enter a contract.

_____2. A statement by a seller that a car is the best "deal" in town.

_____3. An element of fraud of sufficient substance to induce reliance in another to enter a contract.

_____4. A belief that is not in accord with the facts.

_____5. The kind of mistake in which both parties are mistaken.

_____6. The Restatement treats some of these beliefs the same as mistakes of fact.

_____7. The remedy that returns the parties to the status quo by canceling the contract.

_____8. The person who is often unduly influenced by a guardian.

_____9. One who is in a relationship of trust and confidence with another.

_____10. The classification of a contract induced by improper threats or undue influence.

_____11. The classification of a contract induced by actual physical force.

_____12. The element of fraud that consists of knowledge of the falsity of the intentional misrepresentation.

_____13. The innocent person upon whom fraud is committed.

_____14. The use of improper physical coercion to create a contract.

_____15. The person who commits fraud.

MULTIPLE CHOICE: Select the alternative that best completes each statement below.

_____1. When the courts decide that one should not be held to a contract that was not entered into voluntarily, they are speaking of (a) a mistake of the facts (b) a mistake of the law (c) duress (d) none of the above.

_____2. A creditor could threaten to (a) sue a debtor in civil court (b) criminally prosecute the debtor (c) do both of the above (d) do both but be guilty of duress in each instance.

_____3. A contract obtained by fraud in the inducement is generally (a) void (b) voidable (c) enforceable (d) none of the above.

_____4. A contract obtained by fraud in the execution is generally (a) void (b) voidable (c) mutually enforceable (d) none of the above.

_____5. A necessary element for fraud is a false representation concerning (a) a material fact (b) an opinion (c) a prediction (d) none of the above.

_____6. Generally, when a person gives an opinion that later proves to be erroneous, the person is liable for (a) fraud (b) duress (c) undue influence (d) none of the above.

_____7. A seller is obligated to disclose to a buyer (a) all defects concerning the subject matter (b) latent defects concerning the subject matter (c) defects that would be discovered by an ordinary examination (d) none of the above.

_____8. The denial of knowledge of a fact that one knows to exist can form the basis for (a) mistake (b) fraud (c) conversion (d) all of the above.

_____9. The required elements for fraud in the inducement are (a) a false representation of a material fact (b) a false representation made with knowledge of its falsity and intent to deceive (c) a false misrepresentation that is justifiably relied upon (d) all of the above.

_____10. An erroneous understanding or an inaccurate belief that, if acted upon, may produce an unfortunate result for the acting party is (a) fraud (b) duress (c) undue influence (d) a mistake.

_____11. Courts will grant relief from (a) duress (b) fraud (c) undue influence (d) all of the above.

_____12. An example of a confidential relationship in which one party could unfairly persuade another to create a contract is (a) an attorney and client (b) a physician and patient (c) a trustee and beneficiary (d) all of the above.

_____13. A voidable contract is created when (a) one person unduly influences another (b) an agent breaches her fiduciary duty to her principal (c) there has been a mutual mistake of a material fact (d) all of the above.

CASE PROBLEMS — SHORT ESSAY ANSWERS: Read each case problem carefully. When appropriate, answer by stating a Decision for the case and by explaining the rationale — Rule of Law — relied upon to support your decision.

1. Abner, who is negotiating the sale of his business to Betty, informs Betty that his business made a $10,000 profit during the last year. Betty tells Abner she will let him know of her decision to buy in one week. During this week, but before Betty gives her decision, Abner finds a mistake in the books that shows that he made only a $5,000 profit last year. Betty accepts Abner's offer. Betty now wants to rescind for misrepresentation concerning last year's profit. Can Betty rescind? Explain.

Decision: _____

_____

Rule of Law: _____

2. X points a gun at Y and orders Y to sign a written contract or be shot. X knows the gun is not loaded; Y does not. Later, Y repudiates the contract, and X claims the contract exists because the gun was empty. Does a contract exist? Explain.

Decision: _____

_____

Rule of Law: _____

3. Barney signs a document without reading it. Later he discovers the document is a written contract. Since no fraud was involved, Barney claims he had no knowledge that he was signing a contract and therefore lacked contractual intent. Does a contract exist? Explain.

Decision: _____

_____

Rule of Law: _____

4. Seller, in good faith, informs buyer that the stock of a certain corporation will probably be listed on the New York Stock Exchange within two weeks. Buyer, relying on this statement, buys the stock. Can buyer rescind when it is discovered the statement was incorrect? Can buyer sue for damages?

Decision: _____

_____

Rule of Law: _____

5. Seller offers to sell buyer 1,000 bushels of potatoes growing on seller's farm. Buyer accepts the offer. The potatoes were destroyed by a flood three hours before the contract was signed. Neither buyer nor seller knew of the flood. Can the buyer recover from the seller, if the seller fails to deliver the potatoes? Explain.

Decision: _____

_____

Rule of Law: _____

Chapter 12

CONSIDERATION

SCOPE NOTE

Parties bargaining for an exchange of items of value is a central factor in the creation of a contract. Understanding the function and purpose of consideration in the formation of valid, enforceable agreements is crucial. What is legally sufficient consideration? How do courts address the issue of adequacy of consideration? How do "moral consideration" and legal consideration differ? These and other issues associated with consideration are developed in this chapter.

EDUCATIONAL OBJECTIVES

1. Define and explain the central position occupied by consideration in the formation of a contract.

2. Enumerate the types of acts/promises that constitute legally sufficient consideration.

3. Distinguish between the various tests used to determine legally sufficient consideration.

4. Discuss the meaning and importance of forbearance in the context of consideration.

5. Clarify the doctrine of consideration in debtor-creditor agreements.

6. Point out situations and related rationale where binding agreements exist even without consideration.

CHAPTER OUTLINE

I. **Legal Sufficiency**
    A. **Adequacy** — legal sufficiency has nothing to do with adequacy of consideration
    B. **Unilateral Contracts** — a promise for an act or a forbearance to act
    C. **Bilateral Contracts** — a promise for a promise
    D. **Illusory Promises** — are statements that are in the form of a promise but impose no obligation on the maker of the statements
        1. Output and requirement contracts — an agreement to sell the entire production of a seller or to purchase all the materials of a particular kind that the purchaser needs

2. Exclusive dealing contracts — a manufacturer grants an exclusive right to a distributor to sell her goods in a designated area
3. Conditional promises — a contract does not exist until a specific happening or nonhappening of an uncertain event occurs

E. **Pre-existing Public Obligation** — such a duty is not consideration
1. Modification of a pre-existing contract — must be supported by mutual consideration according to common law, but the Code modifies that law
2. Substituted contracts — such contracts are valid and discharge the original contract
3. Settlement of an undisputed debt — is not legally sufficient and thus is not consideration
4. Settlement of a disputed debt — acceptance of the lesser amount discharges the debt but see the position of the Restatement

II. **Bargained for Exchange**
A. **Past Consideration** — is no consideration and unenforceable
C. **Third Parties** — may be consideration if the promisor requests the benefit be given to a third person

III. **Contracts Without Consideration**
A. **Promises to Perform Prior Unenforceable Obligations**
1. Promise to pay debt barred by the Statute of Limitations — an action to enforce a debt must be initiated within a set time period after the debt was due
2. Promise to pay debt discharged in bankruptcy — another exception to the requirement of consideration if allowed by the Bankruptcy Act
3. Voidable promises — another promise that is enforceable without new consideration is a new promise to perform a voidable obligation that has not previously been avoided
4. Moral obligation — under the common law, a promise made to satisfy a pre-existing moral obligation lacks consideration and is unenforceable

B. **Promissory Estoppel** — if detrimental reliance on a noncontractual promise occurs, the promisor is prohibited from denying the promise
C. **Contracts Under Seal** — a formal or solemn promise executed under seal
D. **Promises Made Enforceable by Statute**
1. Contract modifications — the Code has abandoned the common law rule requiring that a modification of an existing contract be supported by consideration in order to be valid
2. Renunciation — a written and signed waiver that can discharge a contract without consideration
3. Irrevocable offers — a written offer signed by a merchant to keep open the offer to buy or sell goods is not revocable for lack of consideration during the time stated that it is open, not to exceed three months, or if no time is stated, for a reasonable time

True and False: Circle true or false

T   F   1. Consideration is basically whatever is given in exchange for a promise.

T   F   2. The central idea behind consideration is that the contracting parties have entered into a bargained exchange with one another.

T   F   3. Valid consideration may exist even though the promises of both parties to a contract are not legally sufficient.

T   F   4. Legal sufficiency is equivalent to adequacy of consideration.

T	F	5. A legal detriment to you may be nothing more than attending a college, at the request of another, that you might not have attended otherwise.
T	F	6. Past consideration is not valid consideration, therefore, no contract exists.
T	F	7. An exchange of the offeror's promise for the offeree's forbearance is consideration.
T	F	8. A new promise of an obligor to perform a pre-existing contractual duty is a legal detriment.
T	F	9. Promises to purchase as much of an item as one may want or desire are generally upheld.
T	F	10. If, before maturity of a debt, the creditor accepts from the debtor a lesser sum offered in full satisfaction, the entire debt will be canceled.
T	F	11. Under the Uniform Commercial Code, a contract for the sale of goods can be effectively modified by the parties without new consideration so long as the modification was intended and in good faith.
T	F	12. Under common law, a promise made to satisfy a pre-existing moral obligation does constitute valid consideration.

KEY TERMS — MATCHING EXERCISE: Select the term that best completes each statement below.

1. Disputed debt	8. Legal benefit	15. Consideration
2. New promise	9. Firm offer	16. Statute of Limitations
3. Charitable subscriptions	10. A promise to satisfy a moral obligation	17. Bankruptcy
4. Legal sufficiency	11. Output contract	18. Renunciation
5. Illusory promise	12. Promissory estoppel	19. Statute of Frauds
6. Requirements contract	13. Undisputed debt	20. Past consideration
7. Legal detriment	14. Contracts under seal	

_____1. A debt that is certain as to the monetary amount.

_____2. One way in which the Statute of Limitations time period may be extended.

_____3. Although technically a gift, courts generally rule such promises are binding.

_____4. The result when a promisee takes definite and substantial action in reliance on the promisor's promise.

_____5. Doing something you are under no prior legal obligation to do.

_____6. The test for consideration that is not dependent on the adequacy of the consideration.

_____7. A promise that is so indefinite that no obligation is imposed on the promisor.

_____8. An agreement that affords sellers an assured market for all their goods.

_____9. An agreement to purchase all the materials of a particular kind that the purchaser needs.

_____10. A promise to pay the previous debts of an elderly parent is an example of this unenforceable promise.

_____11. A contested obligation to pay a sum certain in money.

_____12. The reason that a promise made on account of something that the promisee has already done is unenforceable.

_____13. Laws that provide a prescribed period of time in which actions to enforce payment of debts must be initiated after the debts become due.

_____14. The Uniform Commercial Code has specifically eliminated the use of these contracts for the sale of goods.

_____15. A procedure whereby a claim in a breach of contract case can be discharged without consideration by a written waiver signed and delivered by the aggrieved party.

MULTIPLE CHOICE: Select the alternative that best completes each statement below.

_____1. Consideration for a promise may be defined as (a) an act other than a promise (b) a forbearance (c) the creation, modification or destruction of a legal relation (d) all of the above.

_____2. The receipt by the promisor of that which the promisor had no prior legal right to receive is a (a) legal benefit (b) legal detriment (c) contract (d) gift.

_____3. An event, the happening of which qualifies the duty of performance of a promise, is called a (a) consideration (b) condition (c) gratuitous promise (d) none of the above.

_____4. The contract created when a promise is exchanged for an act or a forbearance to act is a (a) bilateral contract (b) void contract (c) gratuitous contract (d) unilateral contract.

_____5. The person to whom a promise is made is called the (a) offeree (b) promisor (c) promisee (d) donee.

_____6. Where the amount of the debt to be paid has not been agreed upon by the parties, there is (a) an exclusive dealing (b) an undisputed debt (c) a disputed debt (d) none of the above.

_____7. A promise made to perform a pre-existing public or contractual obligation is generally (a) binding (b) a contract (c) unenforceable (d) none of the above.

_____8. According to the U.C.C., a binding promise that requires no consideration is (a) an agreement made in good faith modifying a contract for the sale of goods (b) a written offer to buy or sell goods by a merchant during the time the offer is open (c) a written waiver, signed and delivered by the aggrieved party, of a claim due to an alleged breach of contract (d) all of the above.

_____9. A promise that the promisor should reasonably expect to induce action or forbearance by the promisee may be binding under the doctrine of (a) gratuitous contracts (b) waiver (c) promissory estoppel (d) none of the above.

_____10. An exception to the requirement of consideration is (a) a new promise by a debtor to pay a debt dismissed by the Statute of Limitations (b) a promise to pay a debt discharged in bankruptcy (c) a promise under seal in some states (d) all of the above.

_____11. Which of the following facts operates as a sufficient promise to renew the running of the Statute of Limitations? (a) a voluntary, unqualified admission that the debt is owed (b) a partial payment of the debt (c) a statement that the Statute will not be used as a defense (d) all of the above.

_____12. Contracts under seal (a) require consideration to be binding in all states (b) require an impression on wax to be binding today (c) are required by the Uniform Commercial Code to contain seals in all contracts for the sale of goods (d) none of the above.

_____13. A promise to give a person a present on the person's birthday (a) is a contract (b) is a condition (c) lacks consideration (d) none of the above.

CASE PROBLEMS — SHORT ESSAY ANSWERS: Read each case problem carefully. When appropriate, answer by stating a Decision for the case and by explaining the rationale — Rule of Law — relied upon to support your decision.

1. In early 1993, Mrs. Good signed a pledge to the All Heart Fund for the sum of $25,000. Later, she was hardpressed for money and wished to rescind. As attorney for the fund, what could you argue?

Decision: _____

_____

Rule of Law: _____

2. Samantha fixed Ray's car and tendered a bill of $75.00. Ray, in good faith, disputed the debt and returned $60.00 by check to Samantha stating on the check, "payment in full." Samantha cashed the check and months later sued for the $15.00. What results?

Decision: _____

_____

Rule of Law: _____

3. Amy sells a piano to Betty for $1,000. The next day, Betty asks Amy to guarantee (warrant) the condition of the piano, and Amy agrees. How would this case be decided by the U.C.C.? Explain.

Decision: _____

_____

Rule of Law: _____

4. If Mary saves the life of Bill's son, and one week later Bill, in a moment of gratitude, tells Mary he will pay her $5,000 for her heroism, can Mary demand the $5,000 in a court of law? Explain.

Decision: _____

_____

Rule of Law: _____

5. William's uncle, Ben, promises William that if he does not drink or smoke until he is 30, Ben will pay William $10,000. William fulfills his part of the agreement. Ben refuses to pay. What right does William have?

Decision: _____

_____

Rule of Law: _____

Chapter 13

ILLEGAL BARGAINS

SCOPE NOTE

A valid, binding agreement must contain acts and promises that are legal. Illegal acts and promises generally make an agreement void. Validity of subject matter, as an essential element of a contract, is discussed in this chapter in terms of the types of restricted/unlawful acts and promises that invalidate an agreement, as well as the remedial consequences of such illegality.

EDUCATIONAL OBJECTIVES

1. Define and give examples of "invalid subject matter."

2. Enumerate different classes of illegal agreements.

3. Discuss the relationship between illegality and divisible contracts.

4. Describe how types of illegality influence the availability of remedies.

5. Give examples of how illegality of bargain varies among states.

CHAPTER OUTLINE

I. **Violations of Statutes**
   A. **Licensing Statutes**—may be regulatory to protect the public from unqualified persons or merely for the purpose of raising revenue
   B. **Gambling Statutes**—are generally not enforceable with some exceptions such as state regulated and operated lotteries
   C. **Sunday Statutes**—some states have blue laws that prohibit certain types of commercial activity on Sundays
   D. **Usury Statutes**—laws that establish a maximum rate of permissible interest on contract loans

II. **Violations of Public Policy**
   A. **Tortious Conduct**—a promise to commit a tort is unenforceable on public policy grounds

B. **Common Law Restraint of Trade**—made such contracts illegal
1. Sale of a business—today if restraints covering territory and time are reasonable, they are allowed
2. Employment contracts—contracts not to compete may be allowed if reasonable and necessary
C. **Obstructing the Administration of Justice**—such agreements are illegal and unenforceable
D. **Corrupting Public Officials**—also illegal and unenforceable
E. **Exculpatory Clauses**—a clause that excuses one party from liability for his or her tortious conduct is usually unenforceable
F. **Unconscionable Contracts**—the Code and Restatement may deny enforcement to such contracts

III. **Effect of Illegality**
A. **General Rule: Unenforceability**—if an agreement is illegal neither party can successfully sue and recover
B. **Exceptions**
1. Party withdrawing before performance—can recover
2. Party protected by statute—can recover
3. Party not equally at fault—can recover
4. Excusable ignorance — can recover
5. Partial illegality—provides two possibilities: either the contract is wholly unenforceable or only the illegal part of the contract will be unenforceable

TRUE-FALSE: Circle true or false.

T   F   1. The term "illegal bargain" is directly equivalent to "illegal contract."

T   F   2. A bargain is "illegal" when its formation or performance is criminal or tortious or opposed to public policy.

T   F   3. One who has practiced a trade in violation of a regulatory statute will normally be able to collect a fee for services.

T   F   4. A revenue measure seeks to protect the public against the incompetent or unqualified practitioner.

T   F   5. Normally, the courts have refused to recognize the enforcement of a gambling contract.

T   F   6. At common law, a valid contract could be made on Sunday.

T   F   7. A "usury law" will protect the borrower by providing for a minimum interest rate.

T   F   8. At common law, any restraint upon an individual's right to engage in a trade was illegal.

T   F   9. Managers must sign employment contracts prohibiting them from competing with their current employers for the rest of their lives.

T   F   10. In all cases, the entire contract is void if any part of it is illegal.

T   F   11. The Code and the Restatement define the word unconscionable as "exceeding that which is reasonable or customary."

T   F   12. Statutes that prohibit commercial activity on Sunday are Blue Laws.

KEY TERMS—MATCHING EXERCISE: Select the term that best completes each statement below.

1. Revenue license	8. "Blue sky law"	15. Unconscionable
2. Lotteries	9. Exculpatory clause	16. Reasonable
3. Injunction	10. An agreement (covenant) not to compete	17. Forbearance
4. Time-price differential	11. Regulatory license	18. Criminal conduct
5. "Public policy"	12. Licensing statute	19. Employment contracts
6. Usury law	13. Unenforceable	20. Garnishment
7. Adhesion contract	14. Blue Laws	

_____1. A contract term that excuses one party from liability for that person's own negligence.

_____2. A typical restraint that usually accompanies the sale of a business.

_____3. A standard form contract in which one party offers the other party a contract on a "take-it-or-leave-it" basis.

_____4. A statute that historically protected a borrower of money from excessive interest charges on the loan.

_____5. A statute that prohibits the sale of unregistered securities.

_____6. A law commonly applied to the professions of law, medicine and dentistry.

_____7. A form of gambling that, if permitted at all, is usually state regulated and operated.

_____8. Statutes that prohibit certain types of commercial activity on Sunday.

_____9. The rationale used by a court that may allow a statute to reach beyond its stated bounds.

_____10. A contract of sale, the terms of which are unscrupulous, unprincipled or unjust.

_____11. A license designed for the protection of the public against unqualified persons.

_____12. The type of restraint of trade that is enforceable.

_____13. A court order prohibiting an employee from competing with her former employer in a described area for a given time.

_____14. The agreement managers are often required to sign restraining them from competing with their employers during the time of their employment.

_____15. A license regarded as a taxing measure.

MULTIPLE CHOICE: Select the alternative that best completes each statement below.

_____1. "Blue Laws" are state statutes that (a) follow the common law rule that a valid contract can be made on Sunday (b) prohibit certain types of commercial activity on Sunday (c) prohibit acts of "necessity" or "charity" from being performed on Sunday (d) none of the above.

_____2. A common example of a licensing statute would be one (a) prohibiting larceny (b) prohibiting forgery (c) requiring professional people to register d) all of the above.

_____3. A statute that requires the licensing of plumbers but does not establish standards of competence would be a (a) revenue statute (b) criminal statute (c) regulatory statute (d) usury statute.

_____4. A scheme for the distribution of property by chance among persons who have paid or agreed to pay a valuable consideration for the chance is a (a) usury loan (b) gambling statute (c) lottery (d) all of the above.

_____5. A statute establishing a maximum rate of permissible interest is a (a) Sunday statute (b) gambling statute (c) usury law (d) revenue statute.

_____6. To find a transaction usurious, the courts have traditionally required the following factor(s) (a) a loan or forbearance (b) money that is repayable absolutely (c) an interest charge exacted in excess of the interest rate allowed by law (d) all of the above.

_____7. Common examples of professions to which licensing statutes apply would be (a) brokers (b) accountants (c) dentists (d) all of the above.

_____8. The usual method by which an employer seeks to enforce a covenant not to compete by a former employee is (a) specific performance (b) rescission of the employment contract (c) an injunction (d) none of the above.

_____9. If a seller takes unfair advantage of a buyer in an unequal bargaining position and extorts an exorbitant price for the purchased goods, the contract is (a) a gambling contract (b) a usury contract (c) an exculpatory contract (d) an unconscionable contract.

_____10. The typical restraint of trade could occur in a situation such as a (a) sale of a business, including the good will (b) sale of merchandise (c) sale of a covenant (d) none of the above.

_____11. The classification of an agreement to commit a tort is (a) valid (b) voidable (c) unenforceable (d) none of the above.

_____12. Generally, when an agreement is illegal (a) neither party can win a lawsuit against the other for breach (b) neither party can recover damages for any services rendered (c) the court will leave the parties where it finds them (d) all of the above.

_____13. The type of reasonable restraint on the seller of a business that a court will enforce is a restraint that covers (a) time (b) territory (c) both time and territory (d) none of the above.

CASE PROBLEMS—SHORT ESSAY ANSWERS: Read each case problem carefully. When appropriate, answer by stating a Decision for the case and by explaining the rationale—Rule of Law — relied upon to support your decision.

1. The maximum rate of annual interest in state Z is 8%. The legal rate is 6%. If A loans B $1,000 and the parties agree that B is to pay $72.00 as interest each year ($6.00 per month), is the contract usurious? Explain.

   Decision: _____

   _____

   Rule of Law: _____

2. Adam had Barbara, a plumber, install a shower in Adam's home. When Adam learned Barbara wasn't licensed, he declined to pay. The pertinent statute has the payment of $10.00 as its only requirement for a plumber's license. Barbara sues. Decide and discuss.

   Decision: _____

   _____

   Rule of Law: _____

3. After searching three weeks for an apartment to rent, Abby finds one suitable for her family. Daniel, the landlord, adds to the lease agreement Abby must sign if she wants the apartment, a clause stating that he will not be liable for any negligence he might cause while the apartment is rented. Is this clause enforceable? Explain.

   Decision: _____

   _____

   Rule of Law: _____

4. A sold a barber shop to C. The contract called for A not to enter the barber business in the county for a period of five years. Two years later, A opened a barber shop across town from C and C sued. Decide and discuss.

   Decision: _____

   _____

   Rule of Law: _____

5. A contracts with B whereby B is to kill C for $50,000. Although B could be criminally prosecuted for this act, B wanted the contract with A enforced. What result?

Decision: _____

_____

Rule of Law: _____

Chapter 14

CONTRACTUAL CAPACITY

SCOPE NOTE

Another basic requirement of a valid, enforceable contract is capacity — the ability of a party to make a binding agreement. Various groups of people are deemed to lack such ability, either completely or partially. Who are these persons and what tests are applied to determine when someone possesses or lacks contractual capacity? This is the focus of Chapter 14.

EDUCATIONAL OBJECTIVES

1. Distinguish between classes of persons considered totally incompetent and those who are only partially limited relevant to contractual capacity.

2. Discuss the rationale for excusing certain persons from contractual obligations that they have entered.

3. Identify minimal obligations ("necessaries") to which incapacitated parties are held.

4. Understand the significance of and restrictions on affirmance/disaffirmance.

5. Clarify the consequences of false representations of capacity as they relate to disaffirmance.

CHAPTER OUTLINE

I. **Minors**—A person who is not of legal age
   A. **Liability on Contracts**—general rule: minor's contracts are voidable at the minor's option
      1. Disaffirmance—the right of a minor to avoid a contract through words or conduct
      2. Ratification—is binding on the minor but only if it occurs after the minor reaches legal age
   B. **Liability for Necessaries**—a minor is liable for the reasonable value of necessaries actually delivered to the minor
   C. **Liability for Misrepresentation of Age**—the majority of states still allow the minor to disaffirm the contract
   D. **Liability for Tort Connected With Contract**—generally minors are liable for their torts but if the tort is so connected to a contract that a court must enforce both the tort action and the contract, the minor in such cases is not liable for the tort

II. Incompetent Persons—persons who lack mental capacity
   A.   **Person Under Guardianship**—such a person's contracts are void, not voidable
   B.   **Mental Illness or Defect**—allows the person to make voidable contracts

III. Intoxicated Persons—as a general rule, an inebriated person makes voidable contracts

TRUE-FALSE: Circle true or false.

T   F   1. All persons have the legal capacity to make a valid contract.

T   F   2. Today, almost without exception, a minor's contract is valid once made.

T   F   3. It is conceivable that a court would rule school instruction, such as a college education, a necessary.

T   F   4. A minor has no power to ratify a contract while still a minor.

T   F   5. A minor may not disaffirm a contract after becoming an adult.

T   F   6. Under the U.C.C., personal property conveyed by a minor to a buyer and subsequently reconveyed by that buyer to a third person, e.g., a bona fide purchaser for value, can be recovered by the minor.

T   F   7. In contract law in the majority of the states, when age is misrepresented by a minor, the minor will be bound to the contract.

T   F   8. A mentally incompetent person cannot avoid a contract for necessaries actually furnished to that person.

T   F   9. As a general rule, if intoxication is voluntary, the intoxicated party may not avoid a contract.

T   F   10. An incompetent person's voidable contracts may not be ratified or disaffirmed even if the person becomes competent.

T   F   11. Ratification of a contract by a minor must be express to be legally binding.

T   F   12. Generally, minors are not liable for their torts.

KEY TERMS — MATCHING EXERCISE: Select the term that best completes each statement below.

1. Torts	8. Intoxicated persons	15. Restitution
2. Disaffirmance	9. Misrepresentation of age	16. Void
3. Ratification	10. Persons under guardianship	17. Adult
4. "Emancipated" minors	11. Minor	18. Contract
5. Luxury items	12. Quasi contract	19. Voidable
6. Case law	13. Capacity	20. Guardian
7. Necessaries	14. Express	

_____1. Persons whose property is supervised by court order and whose contracts are void.

_____2. Persons who are unable to understand the nature and effect of their acts or unable to act reasonably.

_____3. The return of property or the equivalent of what has been received.

_____4. The theory under which incompetent persons and minors are held contractually liable.

_____5. Acts for which minors have always been held liable as a general rule.

_____6. An act by a minor that is not allowed until majority age when a contract involves the conveyance of land.

_____7. An act that binds the minor to the contract only upon reaching majority age.

_____8. Minors who are basically on their own, free from parental control.

_____9. The kind of fraud today for which some courts are denying disaffirmance by minors.

_____10. Those things regarded as necessary to maintain oneself in a particular station of life.

_____11. Items of personal property, such as boats and TV sets, that are not considered necessities of life.

_____12. The classification of most contracts made by minors.

_____13. An infant who has not attained legal age.

_____14. A person appointed by a court to manage the property of an incompetent individual.

_____15. The classification of a contract made by a person who is under guardianship by court order.

MULTIPLE CHOICE: Select the alternative that best completes each statement below.

_____1. An item considered a necessary is (a) lodging (b) medicine (c) a textbook (d) all of the above.

_____2. Cameras, tape recorders, and the like are usually classified as (a) luxury items (b) necessaries (c) professional items (d) none of the above.

_____3. A minor may choose to approve a contract after becoming an adult by (a) disaffirmance (b) ratification (c) a loan (d) none of the above.

_____4. Under proper circumstances, which of the following would most likely be a necessary? (a) new boat (b) TV set (c) class ring (d) new suit.

_____5. Which of the following persons does not have limited contractual capacity? (a) minors (b) eccentric persons (c) incompetent persons (d) intoxicated persons.

_____6. Ratification (a) makes the contract valid and binding from the beginning (b) is final and cannot be withdrawn (c) must validate the entire contract (d) all of the above.

_____7. By the majority view, a minor who wishes to disaffirm an executed contract for the sale of a chattel must (a) pay for it (b) simply return it (c) return and pay for the use of it (d) return it in the same condition as it was received.

_____8. Based upon the principle of quasi contract, which of the following persons are liable for necessaries? (a) minors (b) incompetent persons (c) intoxicated persons (d) all of the above.

_____9. Generally, minors are liable for the tort of (a) libel (b) negligence (c) assault and battery (d) all of the above.

_____10. Ratification of a contract by an incompetent person can (a) be done at any time (b) be done when sane (c) be done only while insane (d) never be done.

_____11. An incompetent person may (a) be a person who is mentally ill (b) be a person who has a mental defect (c) ratify or disaffirm contracts when the person becomes competent (d) all of the above.

_____12. An intoxicated person (a) has contractual capacity (b) makes void contracts like a minor (c) makes voidable contracts like an incompetent person (d) none of the above.

_____13. Ratification of a minor's contract may be (a) implied (b) express (c) created by continued use of the property (d) all of the above.

CASE PROBLEMS—SHORT ESSAY ANSWERS: Read each case problem carefully. When appropriate, answer by stating a Decision for the case and by explaining the rationale — Rule of Law — relied upon to support your decision.

1. Mary is a minor. Mary looks like she is over eighteen (majority age) and tells Bob that she is twenty years old. Mary buys a motorcycle from Bob for $300. After using the motorcycle in a race over the weekend, Mary returns it to Bob and demands he return her money on the basis that she is, in fact, a minor. What result? Explain.

    Decision: _____

    _____

    Rule of Law: _____

2. Your friend's brother is unstable. He has been judged incompetent and a court has ordered a guardian appointed for him. He goes out and orders $2,000 worth of blue jeans. The merchant wants to complete the sale. How would you advise your friend? Explain.

    Decision: _____

    _____

    Rule of Law: _____

3. Charlie, at age 20, in a state where one is still a minor at 20, signs a contract to buy a new Corvette. He keeps it until he is 24, when it finally falls apart. Charlie wishes to disaffirm the contract. Can he? Explain.

Decision: _____

_____

Rule of Law: _____

4. A is intoxicated. For months B has tried to buy A's Picasso painting, but each time A has refused to sell. B again makes the offer, and A, in his inebriated condition, accepts. When A becomes sober and learns of the contract, A refuses to sell. B sues. What result?

Decision: _____

_____

Rule of Law: _____

5. Howard, a minor, has just moved into an apartment and is preparing to enter the freshman class at the University. A sales person convinces Howard to sign a contract for the purchase of cooking utensils, e.g., pots and pans. The contract reads that the purchaser (Howard) agrees the utensils are necessaries. Howard wants to disaffirm the contract. How would you advise him? Explain.

Decision: _____

_____

Rule of Law: _____

Chapter 15

CONTRACTS IN WRITING

SCOPE NOTE

Most oral contracts are fully enforceable regardless of their form. Some agreements, however, because of the perceived importance of their subject matter, must be written and signed to be enforceable. This chapter focuses on the Statute of Frauds and specific provisions of the U.C.C. that dictate those agreements that must be in writing and signed for enforcement. Parties to an otherwise valid, oral agreement that "falls within the Statute of Frauds" will most likely encounter a court refusal to enforce it. Parties entering oral agreements that fall "outside the Statute of Frauds" need not worry about lack of enforcement due to the absence of a writing, yet they should recognize the advisability of reducing their agreement to a written form to avoid conflict and confusion over the terms, conditions, and interpretations of their contract. The requirements for and exceptions to the Parol Evidence Rule are discussed.

EDUCATIONAL OBJECTIVES

1. Enumerate classes of contracts that must be written and signed to be enforced.

2. Describe the type and extent of writing required to comply with the provisions of the Statute of Frauds.

3. Identify exceptions to the general rule that contracts "within the Statute of Frauds" must be in writing and signed to be enforced.

4. Discuss those agreements that, although not required, should nevertheless be in writing.

5. Define and discuss the Parol Evidence Rule.

6. Distinguish the terms parol, parol evidence, and the Parol Evidence Rule.

7. Enumerate exceptions to the Parol Evidence Rule.

8. Explain the significance and effect of primary and secondary rules of contract interpretation.

CHAPTER OUTLINE

I. **Statute of Frauds**
   A. **Contracts Within the Statute of Frauds**—include certain oral contracts only
      1. Suretyship provision—a promise by a surety to a creditor to perform the duties of the debtor
         a. Original promise—made by a promisor to become primarily liable is not within the Statute of Frauds
         b. Main purpose doctrine—an exception to the suretyship provision
         c. Promise made to debtor—is not within the Statute
      2. Executor-administrator provision—a promise to pay personally the debts of the decedent is within the Statute
      3. Marriage provision—a promise made in consideration of marriage is within the Statute
      4. Land contract provision—a promise to transfer "any interest in land" is within the Statute
      5. One year provision—all contracts that cannot possibly be fully performed within one year are within the Statute
         a. The possibility test—can the contract possibly be performed within one year
         b. Computation of time—the year runs from the time the agreement is made
         c. Full performance by one party—makes the promise of the other party enforceable
      6. Sales of goods—the Code provides that a contract for the sale of goods over $500 is not enforceable unless in writing
         a. Admission—the Code enforces an oral contract for the sale of goods against a party who admits a contract was made
         b. Specially manufactured goods—the Code enforces an oral contract for such goods that were made for the buyer and the seller has substantially begun their manufacture
         c. Delivery or payment and acceptance—under the Code they validate the contract only for the goods that have been accepted or for which payment has been accepted
      7. Modification or rescission of contracts within the Statute of Frauds—an oral contract modifying an existing contract is unenforceable if the resulting contract is within the Statute, but an oral rescission of a written contract may be effective
   B. **Compliance With Statute of Frauds**—even though a contract is within the Statute it will be enforced if there is a sufficient writing or memorandum that complies with the requirements of the Statute of Frauds
      1. General contract provisions—the writing must specify the parties, the subject matter, the terms, and it must be signed by the party to be charged or her agent
      2. Sale of goods—the Code provisions are more liberal
   C. **Effect of Noncompliance**—the oral contracts are unenforceable
      1. Full performance—if all promises of an oral contract have been performed, the Statute no longer applies
      2. Restitution—may be recovered by a party who acted in reliance upon the contract even though it was unenforceable because of the Statute
      3. Promissory estoppel—a number of courts have used this doctrine to avoid the writing requirement of the Statute, but the use of the doctrine has been less accepted in cases for the sale of goods

II. **Parol Evidence Rule**
   A. **The Rule**—a written contract that contains the complete agreement of the parties may not be modified in any way with the use of parol (oral or written) evidence.
   B. **Situations to Which the Rule Does Not Apply**—seven exceptions are listed
   C. **Supplemental Evidence**—may be used to explain a written contract

III. Interpretation of Contracts—the determination of the meaning to be given to the written language of a contract is outside the scope of the Parol Evidence Rule; ten rules that aid interpretation are listed

TRUE-FALSE: Circle true or false.

T   F   1. Except as provided by Statute, an oral contract is just as valid and enforceable as a written one.

T   F   2. Contracts of a type or class governed by the Statute of Frauds are said to be "within" the Statute.

T   F   3. The Statute of Frauds is rendered inapplicable when the "main purpose doctrine" is available.

T   F   4. If an executor promises to pay the decedent's debt out of the executor's own pocket, it is unenforceable unless in writing and signed.

T   F   5. Only the "party to be charged, or the "party's agent," must have signed the written contract or memo in order to make it legally binding.

T   F   6. If they are to be enforced, all oral contracts must be in writing according to the Statute of Frauds.

T   F   7. Courts do not regard promises made by a surety to a debtor as being within the Statute of Frauds.

T   F   8. Mutual promises to marry do not have to be in writing according to the Statute of Frauds.

T   F   9. An oral contract to care for a handicapped person while that person attends college for the next four years is not enforceable.

T   F   10. Parol evidence consists of oral evidence only.

T   F   11. An executed (completely performed) oral contract is no longer within the Statute of Frauds.

T   F   12. The theory of the Parol Evidence Rule is that the parties will voluntarily and intentionally state in a written contract the terms to which they have agreed.

KEY TERMS — MATCHING EXERCISE: Select the term that best completes each statement below.

1. Unenforceable	8. Void	15. Enforceable
2. Parol evidence	9. "Collateral promise"	16. Promisee
3. "Main purpose"	10. Statute of Frauds	17. Executor
4. Goods	11. "Party to be charged"	18. Administrator
5. "Original promise"	12. Securities	19. Surety
6. Voidable	13. Parol Evidence Rule	20. Uniform Commercial Code
7. Parol	14. Estoppel	

_____1. The name given a promise to pay the debt of another if the debtor fails to pay.

_____2. Another name for the defendant, i.e., the person who must sign a written contract according to the Statute of Frauds.

_____3. Another name for stocks and bonds.

_____4. The term that means speech or words.

_____5. Any evidence consisting of words, spoken or written, that is not contained in a written contract.

_____6. The classification of an oral contract that is to last the lifetime of another.

_____7. The doctrine that is an exception to the section of the Statute of Frauds that deals with promises to answer for the debt of another.

_____8. Oral or written words of any prior agreement will not be permitted to vary, change, alter, or modify the terms of a written contract.

_____9. Another name for tangible (movable) personal property as defined by the U.C.C.

_____10. The classification of an oral contract that is in noncompliance with the Statute of Frauds.

_____11. The source of law that governs the enforceability of contracts for the sale of goods.

_____12. The law that requires certain types of contracts to be in a particular form to be enforceable.

_____13. The name for a person who promises a creditor to perform the obligations of a third person.

_____14. The kind of promise made by a promisor who agrees to become primarily liable for its performance.

_____15. The person named in a valid will to administer the estate of the decedent.

MULTIPLE CHOICE: Select the alternative that best completes each statement below.

_____1. The Statute of Frauds requires all contracts that cannot be performed within one year to be in writing. The year runs from the time the (a) performance is to begin (b) contract is made (c) contract is breached (d) none of the above.

_____2. The signature of the "party to be charged" (a) must be handwritten (b) must be at the bottom of the last page of the contract (c) may be typewritten or printed (d) none of the above.

_____3. The U.C.C. allows an oral contract for the sale of goods to be enforced if (a) the party defending against the contract admits it (b) the goods are to be specially manufactured (c) payment has been made and accepted (d) all of the above.

_____4. The basic difference between the "main purpose doctrine" and the "leading object rule" is (a) one of fundamental law (b) a slight variance in technique (c) nothing — they are the same (d) none of the above.

_____5. Which of the following are within the Statute of Frauds? A man promises a woman (a) an allowance to marry him (b) to convey land to her if they marry (c) to share his estate with her brother if she will marry him (d) all of the above.

_____6. Which of the following is personal property? (a) growing crops (b) land (c) buildings (d) easements.

_____7. The Parol Evidence Rule does not apply to a contract (a) that is partly oral and partly written (b) with a typographical error (c) that has ambiguous terms (d) all of the above.

_____8. If you orally contracted for the sale of goods, at what price would you become concerned with the requirements of the Statute of Frauds? (a) $5,000 (b) $500 (c) $50,000 (d) $450.

_____9. The person appointed by the court to administer the estate of a decedent who died without a will is the (a) administrator (b) executor (c) executrix (d) none of the above.

_____10. The Parol Evidence Rule does not apply to a defense to a contract of (a) fraud (b) duress (c) undue influence (d) all of the above.

_____11. The kind of promise in which the promisor is not the person who is primarily liable is (a) an original promise (b) a collateral promise (c) an objective promise (d) none of the above.

_____12. The reason a court may deem it inequitable for the Statute of Frauds to apply after reliance by the purchaser in a land sales contract is (a) hardship (b) the "part performance doctrine" (c) the "main purpose doctrine" (d) none of the above.

_____13. The Parol Evidence Rule does not apply if the written contract (a) is illegal (b) contains a clerical error (c) is subsequently and mutually rescinded (d) all of the above.

CASE PROBLEMS—SHORT ESSAY ANSWERS: Read each case problem carefully. When appropriate, answer by stating a Decision for the case and by explaining the rationale—Rule of Law — relied upon to support your decision.

1. A and B have a valid written contract. A telephones B and they mutually agree to rescind the contract. In a lawsuit between A and B, can B prevent A from introducing this oral evidence? Explain.

   Decision: _____

   _____

   Rule of Law: _____

2. A and B agree in a written memo to the sale of "some things." The writing doesn't specify the quantity of the items to be sold. Could this writing be enforced in court? Explain.

   Decision: _____

   _____

   Rule of Law: _____

3. A, a carpenter, and B, a homeowner, make an oral contract whereby B is to give A a certain tract of land in return for A's building an addition to B's house. Is this contract enforceable by A upon completion of the construction? Explain.

Decision: _____

_____

Rule of Law: _____

4. A is the only person who can use widgets. A places an oral order with XYZ Company to make 10,000 widgets at $2.00 each. Later, A refuses to accept the widgets and alleges the Uniform Commercial Code Statute of Frauds as a defense to the suit for breach of contract. Who prevails?

Decision: _____

_____

Rule of Law: _____

5. After an oral contract for the sale of a tract of land has been made, Allen writes a letter to Bernard, repeating that he will sell the land to Bernard, and Allen signs the letter. Bernard refuses to buy, and Allen sues. Bernard asserts the Statute of Frauds. Decide.

Decision: _____

_____

Rule of Law: _____

Chapter 16

THIRD PARTIES TO CONTRACTS

SCOPE NOTE

As a general rule, only the original contracting parties have rights to enforce an agreement or seek damages for its breach. In some cases, however, persons not original parties to an agreement may have enforceable rights under it. Additionally, original parties to a contract might wish to transfer to others the right to receive performance or the duty to perform contained in the original agreement. Chapter 16 addresses the type of contractual relations that create non-original-party enforceable rights and duties under a contract from the perspective of third-party beneficiary contracts as well as assignment and delegation.

EDUCATIONAL OBJECTIVES

1. Define and discuss the significance of assignment/delegation.

2. Identify classes of rights and duties that cannot be assigned or delegated.

3. Explain rules of priority controlling multiple assignment situations.

4. Differentiate important characteristics and relative advantages/disadvantages among assignment, delegation and novation.

5. Distinguish assignment/delegation from third-party beneficiary contracts.

6. Discuss differences between creditor, donee and incidental beneficiaries.

CHAPTER OUTLINE

I. **Assignment of Rights**
    A. **Law Governing Assignments**—is primarily common law but with a few Code modifications
    B. **Requirements of an Assignment**—no special words are necessary to create an assignment and consideration is not required for an effective assignment
        1. Revocability of assignments—if a contract exists between the assignor and the assignee, the assignor cannot revoke the assignment without the assent of the assignee
        2. Partial assignments — a transfer of part of the contractual rights to one or more assignees

C. **Rights That Are Assignable** — as a general rule, most contract rights are assignable
D. **Rights That Are Not Assignable** — are those to protect the obligor or the public
   1. Assignments that materially increase duty, risk or burden — are not assignable
   2. Assignments of personal rights — those of a highly personal nature are not assignable
   3. Express prohibition against assignment — is handled differently by the Code than by common law
   4. Assignments prohibited by law and public policy — regulate the assignment of certain contract rights
E. **Rights of the Assignee**
   1. Obtains rights of assignor, but no new rights
   2. Notice to the obligor of an assignment is not required
F. **Implied Warranties of Assignor** — to the assignee are listed
G. **Successive Assignments of the Same Right** — the majority rule is that the first assignee in point of time prevails over subsequent assignees

II. **Delegation of Duties**
  A. **Delegable Duties** — contract duties are generally delegable but exceptions are listed
  B. **Duties of the Parties** — a delegatee becomes liable for performance only if she assents to perform the delegated duties; however, a delegation still leaves the delegator bound to perform

III. **Third-Party Beneficiary Contracts**
  A. **Intended Beneficiary**—there are two types
   1. Donee beneficiary — is the case in which the third party receives the benefit as a gift
   2. Creditor beneficiary — is the case in which the third party is a creditor who receives the benefit to satisfy a debt
   3. Rights of intended beneficiary — are those that can be enforced
   4. Vesting of rights — states vary considerably as to when vesting takes place
  B. **Incidental Beneficiary** — is not an intended beneficiary and has no enforceable rights under the contract

TRUE-FALSE: Circle true or false

T   F   1. An effective assignment terminates the assignor's rights arising from a contract.

T   F   2. A delegation of duties is the voluntary transfer of contract rights to a third party.

T   F   3. To be valid, an assignment must be in writing.

T   F   4. Just as rights are assignable, so are duties.

T   F   5. Rights and duties of a highly personal nature cannot be assigned or delegated.

T   F   6. A valid assignment requires that notice be given to the obligor.

T   F   7. Assignments of future wages are governed by statutes that sometimes prohibit them.

T   F   8. The assignee of a contract claim has rights superior to those of the assignor.

T   F   9. An assignee will lose the rights against the debtor if the latter pays the assignor without notice of the assignment.

T   F   10. Unlike an assignment or a novation, a delegation of duties and an assumption of the delegated duties leaves the delegator and the delegatee liable for proper performance of the original contractual duties.

T   F   11. In a third-party beneficiary life insurance contract, the donee beneficiary has the right to sue and recover from the promisor (insurance company) but not from the promisee (insured).

T   F   12. In a third-party beneficiary contract, the creditor beneficiary may sue either or both the original promisor and the promisee.

KEY TERMS — MATCHING EXERCISE: Select the term that best completes each statement below.

1. Creditor beneficiary	8. Assignor	15. Successive assignments
2. Incidental beneficiary	9. Donee beneficiary	16. Obligor
3. Personal rights or services	10. Third-party beneficiary contract	17. Payment of money
4. Delegation	11. Novation	18. Delegatee
5. Delectus personae	12. An assignee in good faith who gives value	19. Consideration
6. Partial assignment	13. Intended beneficiary	20. Assignee
7. Subsequent assignee	14. Implied warranty	

_____1. A method of discharging a contract in which a third party becomes bound upon a promise to the obligee.

_____2. An assignment of parts of a claim to different assignees.

_____3. A third party designated by the two parties of a contract to receive benefits and rights from the performance of the contract.

_____4. An assignment of the same right to different persons.

_____5. A second assignee who may collect an account before the first assignee in time and keep it.

_____6. An intended beneficiary of a contract who receives the benefit of the contract as a gift.

_____7. The guarantee which the assignor who receives value makes to the assignee.

_____8. A contract in which a party promises to render a performance to a third person.

_____9. A third party who obtains possible benefits but no rights under the contract.

_____10. The transfer of contract duties to a third person.

_____11. The person who makes an assignment.

_____12. A requirement for a valid contact but not for an effective assignment.

_____13. The most common contract right that may be assigned.

_____14. An example of a contract right that is not assignable.

_____15. The person to whom a contract duty is transferred.

MULTIPLE CHOICE: Select the alternative that best completes each statement below.

_____1. Contract rights are not assignable if they (a) materially increase the risk upon the obligor (b) transfer personal contract rights (c) are prohibited by Statute (d) all of the above.

_____2. The following is not assignable (a) an option contract (b) a wage assignment (c) a partial assignment (d) an automobile liability policy.

_____3. Which of the following could be considered a personal service contract? A contract involving (a) highly skilled work (b) professional work (c) manual labor (d) all of the above.

_____4. If the delegator desires to be discharged from a duty, the delegator will have to seek which of the following from the obligee? (a) payment (b) a novation (c) another obligee (d) none of the above.

_____5. In a suit by the assignee against a debtor (obligor), the debtor may plead (a) fraud (b) failure of consideration (c) duress (d) all of the above.

_____6. A third party who benefits from the performance of a contract even though it was not the intention of the parties to the contract is (a) a creditor beneficiary (b) a donee beneficiary (c) an incidental beneficiary (d) none of the above.

_____7. An example of a third-party donee beneficiary contract is (a) a life insurance policy (b) a fire insurance policy (c) an assumption of a mortgage in a real estate purchase (d) none of the above.

_____8. Courts enforce contracts for the benefit of all of the following except (a) incidental beneficiaries (b) donee beneficiaries (c) creditor beneficiaries (d) none of the above.

_____9. According to the majority rule in the United States involving successive assignments of the same rights, which of the following prevails? The first assignee (a) to give notice (b) in point of time (c) to reassign (d) none of the above.

_____10. A subsequent assignee in good faith who gives value may prevail over the prior assignee when the subsequent assignee obtains (a) payment or satisfaction of the obligor's duty (b) a judgment against the obligor (c) a new contract with the obligor (d) all of the above.

_____11. The person to whom an assignment is made is (a) an assignor (b) an assignee (c) an obligor (d) a delegatee.

_____12. When a valid delegation and an assumption of the delegated duties have been made (a) only the delegator is liable for performance of the contractual duty (b) only the delegatee is liable for performance of the duty (c) both delegator and delegatee are liable (d) none of the above.

_____13. A delegation will not be permitted if (a) it is prohibited by Statute (b) it is prohibited by public policy (c) the duties delegated are personal (d) all of the above.

CASE PROBLEMS—SHORT ESSAY ANSWERS: Read each case problem carefully. When appropriate, answer by stating a Decision for the case and by explaining the rationale—Rule of Law — relied upon to support your decision.

1. Unknown to Y, X took out a life insurance policy naming Y, her best friend, as the beneficiary. X died and the company attempted to deny Y recovery. What result?

   Decision: _____

   _____

   Rule of Law: _____

2. For service to be done by A, B promises to purchase and deliver a new motorcycle to A. A completes the work. B refuses to buy and deliver the motorcycle. C, the exclusive motorcycle dealer (who would obviously benefit), brings suit against B. What result?

   Decision: _____

   _____

   Rule of Law: _____

3. A buys an appliance from company X on credit. A then assigns the right to the credit purchase to B. The company says that it will not honor the assignment. B sues. What result?

   Decision: _____

   _____

   Rule of Law: _____

4. E agrees to construct a swimming pool for X. E then delegates the duties to Y Swimming Pool Company. X refuses to allow Y Company to do the work. Y and E bring suit against X. What result?

   Decision: _____

   _____

   Rule of Law: _____

5. X, being an unscrupulous fellow, assigns the right to future wages first to Y and then to T. T gives notice to the employer first. Both T and Y seek to obtain the wages. Who prevails?

   Decision: _____

   _____

   Rule of Law: _____

Chapter 17

PERFORMANCE, BREACH, AND DISCHARGE

SCOPE NOTE

The cycle of the existence of a contract — formation, operation, termination — is completed in this chapter. The events, developments, and conduct that relieve parties of their contractual obligations are discussed. Also addressed is the impact the presence of conditions has on performance under the terms of the agreement.

EDUCATIONAL OBJECTIVES

1. Identify the requirements for adequate performance through payment of money.

2. Differentiate between "substantial performance" and "partial performance" both in terms of required elements and remedial options.

3. Discuss the methods and significance of termination of contracts by agreement of the parties.

4. Explain the circumstances under which termination occurs through operation of law.

5. Develop the doctrinal importance of Frustration of Purpose and Commercial Impracticability.

6. Define and discuss the significance of anticipatory repudiation.

7. Outline the problems associated with personal satisfaction as a performance evaluator.

8. Discuss the effect of impossibility of performance on contractual obligations.

9. Enumerate types of contractual conditions and their influence on the duties of parties under the agreement.

CHAPTER OUTLINE

I. **Conditions**—a condition is an event whose happening or non-happening affects a duty of performance under a contract
    A. **Express Conditions** — are explicitly set forth in language
        1. Satisfaction of a contracting party — a contracting party is not obligated to pay unless satisfied

        2. Satisfaction of a third party — a contract may provide that performance be approved by a third party

    B. **Implied-in-fact Conditions** — are understood by the parties to be part of the agreement even though they are not stated in express language

    C. **Implied-in-law Conditions** — are imposed by law in order to accomplish a just and fair result

    D. **Concurrent Conditions** — are performances by two promisors that are to take place at the same time

    E. **Conditions Precedent** — an event that must occur before performance under a contract is due

    F. **Conditions Subsequent** — is an operative event that terminates an existing duty

II. **Discharge by Performance** — the most frequent method of discharging a contract duty

III. **Discharge by Breach** — the unexcused failure of a party to perform his promise

    A. **Material Breach** — is an unjustifiable failure to perform substantially the duties promised in a contract

        1. Prevention of performance — if one party interferes with the performance of another, constituting a breach, the other party is discharged from her contract duties

        2. Perfect tender rule — the Code provides that any deviation from the promised performance in a sales contract constitutes a material breach of the contract

    B. **Substantial Performance** — essential but not complete performance

    C. **Anticipatory Repudiation** — if a party repudiates the contract in advance, the courts treat this as a breach

    D. **Material Alteration of Written Contract** — to be a discharge, a party must fraudulently and materially alter the written contract

IV. **Discharge by Agreement of the Parties**

    A. **Mutual Rescission** — an agreement between the parties to terminate their contract duties

    B. **Substituted Contracts** — the parties agree to rescind their original contract and enter into a new one

    C. **Accord and Satisfaction** — an agreement of a promisee in a contract to accept a stated performance in satisfaction of an existing contractual duty

    D. **Novation** — a substituted contract involving three parties

V. **Discharge by Operation of Law**

    A. **Impossibility** — subjective impossibility does not discharge the contractual duty but objective impossibility may

        1. Frustration of purpose — a doctrine under which a contract is discharged if supervening circumstances make impossible the fulfillment of the purpose of the contract

        2. Commercial impracticability — may excuse nonperformance according to the Restatement and the Code

    B. **Bankruptcy** — discharges a contractual duty of a debtor

    C. **Statute of Limitations** — does not discharge the duty but does bar the creditor's remedy

TRUE-FALSE: Circle true or false.

T   F   1. Discharge of a contract refers to the termination of the duties created upon the formation of the contract.

T   F   2. A condition is an event that may limit the obligation to perform a contract.

T	F	3.	There is no difference between the breach of a promise and the failure, or non-happening, of a condition; they are the same.
T	F	4.	"Provided that" is a phrase connoting an implied condition often found in a contract.
T	F	5.	The standard of satisfaction in matters involving personal taste is that of the reasonable person.
T	F	6.	A condition precedent is an event that precedes the creation of a duty of immediate performance under a contract.
T	F	7.	Once the parties to a contract agree to an accord, the contract is discharged.
T	F	8.	A mutual rescission is a contract to modify an existing contract without terminating it.
T	F	9.	Less than exact performance does not fully discharge a party to a contract.
T	F	10.	Bankruptcy and the Statute of Limitations are methods of discharging a contract by operation of law.
T	F	11.	A material breach of a contract discharges the aggrieved party from any further duty under the contract.
T	F	12.	Breach of contract is the unexcused failure of a party to perform her promise.

KEY TERMS — MATCHING EXERCISE: Select the term that best completes each statement below.

1. Novation	8. Prevention of performance	15. Accord
2. Material alteration	9. Anticipatory repudiation	16. Aggrieved person
3. Bankruptcy	10. Statute of Frauds	17. Material breach
4. Concurrent conditions	11. Statute of Limitations	18. Prohibition Statute
5. Nonmaterial breach	12. Illegality	19. Frustration of purpose doctrine
6. Condition precedent	13. Mutual rescission	20. Tender
7. Perfect tender rule	14. Satisfaction	

_____1. The position of the Code that any deviation from the promised performance in a sales contract constitutes a material breach of the contract.

_____2. An announcement prior to the date performance is due that a party will not perform.

_____3. The statute that does not discharge a contract but only acts to bar a creditor's right to bring an action.

_____4. An agreement between the parties to terminate their respective duties under the contract.

_____5. An acceptable different performance that replaces the original contractual obligation.

_____6. An agreement that involves three parties whereby one is a substitute promisee.

_____7. An act that may result in a discharge of the entire contract because of the unauthorized relevant changes by a party to the contract.

_____8. The discharge of a contract by operation of law available to a debtor.

_____9. The kind of conditions in which the contract promisors' proposed reciprocal and agreed performances are to take place at the same time.

_____10. A procedure in which one party substantially interferes with the other's performance of a contract and that acts as a discharge.

_____11. A name for the injured party who has a right to sue for breach of contract.

_____12. One example of a supervening illegality.

_____13. The kind of breach that does not discharge a contract but allows a plaintiff to recover damages.

_____14. An executory accord does not discharge a contract until this performance is completed.

_____15. The term for an attempted performance by a party who is ready, willing and able to perform.

MULTIPLE CHOICE: Select the alternative that best completes each statement below

_____1. An agreement between the parties to a contract to cancel their original contract and enter a new contract is a (a) substitution (b) novation (c) release (d) none of the above.

_____2. Where no one is able to perform the contract for reasons beyond the control of the parties, the contract is discharged due to (a) a mistake (b) impossibility (c) fraud (d) a concurrent obligation.

_____3. A material breach of contract (a) gives the aggrieved party a cause of action (b) excuses nonperformance by the aggrieved party (c) discharges the aggrieved party from any further duty to perform (d) all of the above.

_____4. The running of the Statute of Limitations on a contract between a creditor and debtor (a) discharges the debt (b) acts as an accord (c) bars the creditor's remedy (d) all of the above.

_____5. Which of the following may cause a binding promise to cease to be binding? (a) performance of the parties (b) a discharge by operation of law (c) a breach by one of the parties (d) all of the above.

_____6. A condition may be (a) express (b) implied-in-fact (c) implied-in-law (d) all of the above.

_____7. The expressions "on condition that" and "as soon as" are often part of (a) implied conditions (b) subsequent statements (c) express conditions (d) concurrent conditions.

_____8. An event that terminates the existing contractual duty of immediate performance is a (a) condition subsequent (b) condition precedent (c) concurrent condition (d) none of the above.

_____9. Tender of payment of a debt past due (a) discharges the debt (b) does not discharge the debt if the creditor refuses to accept the tender (c) makes the debt unconditional (d) none of the above.

_____10. An agreement between the parties to a contract to terminate their respective contractual duties is a (a) mutual rescission (b) material alteration (c) novation (d) none of the above.

_____11. The most frequent method of discharging a contractual duty is a discharge by (a) breach (b) performance (c) operation of law (d) impossibility.

_____12. Which of the following is not a method of discharging contractual duties by agreement of the parties? (a) novation (b) substitution (c) bankruptcy (d) rescission.

_____13. An accord and satisfaction that discharges a contract is an example of a discharge by (a) breach (b) operation of law (c) agreement (d) none of the above.

CASE PROBLEMS — SHORT ESSAY ANSWERS: Read each case problem carefully. When appropriate, answer by stating a Decision for the case and by explaining the rationale — Rule of Law — relied upon to support your decision.

1. A rents a room from B to watch the Duke of Earle ride by in a parade. B knows this is the reason. The Duke is assassinated by revolutionaries before the parade. B sues for the rent. What result?

Decision: _____

_____

Rule of Law: _____

2. Farmer A agrees to pay dentist B $500 to put braces on his son's teeth. Once the dental work is finished and instead of paying the money, A and B agree that A will butcher a cow and deliver the meat to B. The meat is delivered. Is the contract discharged? Explain.

Decision: _____

_____

Rule of Law: _____

3. X has purchased a bicycle from Y and now owes Y $150. X, Y and Z agree that Z will pay the debt and X will be discharged. If Z refuses to pay the money, can Y sue Z? Explain.

Decision: _____

_____

Rule of Law: _____

4. X employs Y to work for one year beginning March 1 and on February 28, Y refuses to begin the job. X doesn't really care and agrees. Then X hires Z. X decides in May to sue Y for damages. What result?

Decision: _____

_____

Rule of Law: _____

5. B contracts in writing to sell a car to A for $1,500. Nothing is written about time of delivery or payment. A demands the delivery of the car before payment as A needs the car now but won't be able to pay for it until later. B refuses and A sues for specific performance. What result?

Decision: _____

_____

Rule of Law: _____

Chapter 18

REMEDIES

SCOPE NOTE

Adequate performance by both parties to a contract discharges their duties. In cases where performance is inadequate — "defective" — a breach has occurred. What forms of relief both at law and in equity are available to injured parties when they are faced with performance falling short of the terms of the agreement? How do these remedies differ? When will the nonbreaching party be forced to make an election between mutually exclusive remedies?

EDUCATIONAL OBJECTIVES

1. Distinguish the various types of damages.

2. Discuss the importance of liquidated damages.

3. Enumerate the types of relief available from a court of equity and when they apply.

4. Identify the various formulas used to compute damages.

5. Explain the role and meaning of the Mitigation of Damages doctrine.

CHAPTER OUTLINE

I. **Interests Protected by Contract Remedies** — include expectation, reliance, and restitution interests

II. **Monetary Damages**
   A. **Compensatory Damages** — the right to these damages for breach of contract is always available to the injured party
   B. **Nominal Damages** — a small amount of damages fixed without regard to the amount of loss
   C. **Reliance Damages** — foreseeable loss caused by reliance upon the contract
   D. **Damages for Misrepresentation**
      1. Fraud — a party induced by fraud to enter a contract may recover general damages in a tort action

    2. Nonfraudulent misrepresentation — if the misrepresentation is neither fraudulent nor negligent, out-of-pocket damages are allowed by the Restatement

  E. **Punitive Damages** — damages awarded in cases involving willful, wanton, or malicious conduct

  F. **Liquidated Damages** — a provision in a contract by which the parties agree in advance to the damages to be paid in event of breach

  G. **Limitations on Damages** — limitations of foreseeability, certainty and mitigation have been imposed upon monetary damages

    1. Foreseeability of damages — the breaching party is not liable for loss that was not foreseeable at the time the contract was made

    2. Certainty of damages — an injured party can recover for only reasonably certain damages

    3. Mitigation of damages — the injured party cannot recover damages for loss that he could have avoided by reasonable effort and without undue risk, burden or humiliation

III. Remedies in Equity

  A. **Specific Performance** — an equity court decree that compels the defaulting party to perform her contractual duties

  B. **Injunctions** — formal court order commanding a person to refrain from doing something

IV. Restitution

  A. **Party Injured by Breach** — is entitled to restitution (a return of the consideration that was given)

  B. **Party in Default** — is entitled to restitution for any benefit she has given in excess of the loss she has caused by her breach

  C. **Statute of Frauds** — if the Statute applies, each party is entitled to restitution to the benefits conferred on the other party

  D **Voidable Contracts** — in such contracts, the party who rescinds is entitled to restitution for any benefit conferred on the other party

V. Limitations on Remedies

  A. **Election of Remedies** — a choice does not necessarily prevent a person from seeking a second remedy unless the remedies are inconsistent and the other party materially changes her position in reliance

  B. **Loss of Power of Avoidance**

    1. Affirmance — of a contract will not allow the party who affirms to later avoid the contract

    2. Delay — may cause the loss of the power of avoidance

    3. Rights of third parties — the intervening rights of third parties may limit the power of avoidance and the accompanying right to restitution

TRUE-FALSE: Circle true or false.

T   F   1. A breach of contract means a failure to perform a contract promise.

T   F   2. The injured party can always seek and obtain money damages from the wrongdoer for breach of contract.

T   F   3. The purpose of allowing damages for breach of contract is to put the injured party in as good a position as the wrongdoer.

T   F   4. A party with the power of avoidance has no time limit for rescinding a contract.

T   F   5. After learning that the goods sold to the buyer are unfit, the buyer may continue to use the goods and then sue the seller for greater damages.

T   F   6. An example of nominal damages would be a $100,000 recovery for personal injury that one suffers as a result of a traffic mishap.

T   F   7. The remedy of specific performance will generally be granted for breach of a contract for personal services.

T   F   8. Punitive damages are always recoverable for breach of contract.

T   F   9. For breach of contract, the injured party may recover consequential damages for lost profits.

T   F   10. Liquidated damages must bear a reasonable relationship to the actual or probable damage suffered for breach of a contract.

T   F   11. The purpose of restitution is to restore the injured party to the position she was in before the contract was made.

T   F   12. An injunction is the equitable remedy that compels the performance of a contract according to its terms.

KEY TERMS—MATCHING EXERCISE: Select the term that best completes each statement below.

1. Court of law	8. Special damages	15. Liquidated damages
2. Penalty	9. Nominal damages	16. Out-of-pocket damages
3. Uniform Commercial Code	10. Injunction	17. Reliance damages
4. Money damages	11. Punitive damages	18. Reformation
5. Fraud	12. Equity court	19. Benefit-of-the-bargain rule
6. Uniqueness	13. Mitigation	20. Compensatory damages
7. Specific performance	14. Restitution	

_____1. The usual judgment for breach of contract.

_____2. A recovery of $1.00 and costs.

_____3. A remedy by a court of law looking to deter future conduct.

_____4. A provision in the contract calling for payment of money in the event of breach of the contract.

_____5. When breach occurs, the plaintiff is required to lessen damages if possible.

_____6. A return of the consideration, or its value, to the aggrieved party.

_____7. The source of law that allows a defrauded party the right to rescind the contract and recover damages for breach of a contract for the sale of goods.

_____8. The court that grants the remedies of specific performance and reformation.

_____9. The characteristic of real property that allows the equity court to always grant the remedy of specific performance for breach of a sales contract.

_____10. The method the court uses to enforce a contract for an employee's exclusive personal services where damages for a breach are inadequate.

_____11. The kind of damages that protect the injured party's expectation interest.

_____12. A remedy that results in placing the injured party in as good a position as she would have been in had the contract not been made.

_____13. The damages the injured party may recover that are equal to the difference between the value of what she has received and the value of what she was given for it.

_____14. An unreasonable sum of money included as a provision of a contract that is to be paid in the event of a breach of the contract.

_____15. An equitable remedy whereby the court corrects a written contract to make it conform to the true agreement of the parties.

MULTIPLE CHOICE: Select the alternative that best completes each statement below.

_____1. A remedy for breach of contract that represents the actual dollar loss to the plaintiff is (a) specific performance (b) compensatory damages (c) restitution (d) punitive damages.

_____2. A court order conveying the title to a parcel of land from the seller to the buyer in compliance with their contractual agreement is (a) restitution (b) punitive damages (c) specific performance (d) none of the above.

_____3. Ordering a reconveyance of land would be (a) restitution (b) specific performance (c) punitive damages (d) compensatory damages.

_____4. Hadley v. Baxendale involved an issue of (a) nominal damages (b) foreseeability of injury (loss) (c) an intentional tort (d) punitive damages.

_____5. Unreasonable payment for nonperformance as expressed in the contract is deemed (a) a penalty (b) liquidated damages (c) punitive damages (d) all of the above.

_____6. A reasonable payment for nonperformance as expressed in a contract is deemed (a) a penalty (b) liquidated damages (c) punitive damages (d) all of the above.

_____7. Damages that arise directly out of the breach of contract are called (a) nominal damages (b) consequential damages (c) incidental damages (d) reliance damages.

_____8. A liquidated damages clause that becomes a penalty because it is excessive is (a) enforceable at a reasonable rate (b) unenforceable (c) enforceable (d) reasonable.

_____9.   Specific performance will be granted by an equity court when the case involves (a) a contract for personal services (b) a performance by a concert pianist (c) a unique item of property (d) none of the above.

_____10. Remedies that are mutually exclusive or inconsistent require an election of remedies. Which of the following would require the election? (a) specific performance and restitution (b) restitution and total damages (c) specific performance and compensation for incidental damages (d) only a and b above.

_____11. A contract can be avoided due to (a) lack of capacity (b) fraud (c) duress (d) all of the above.

_____12. A party who has the right and power to avoid a contract may lose that power because (a) she affirms the contract (b) she unreasonably delays in disaffirming the contract (c) rights of third parties intervene (d) all of the above.

_____13. The remedies of specific performance and injunction (a) will not be granted where there is an adequate remedy at law (b) are remedies at law (c) will be granted if the contract is created by fraud or duress (d) none of the above.

CASE PROBLEMS — SHORT ESSAY ANSWERS: Read each case problem carefully. When appropriate, answer by stating a Decision for the case and by explaining the rationale — Rule of Law — relied upon to support your decision.

1. Suppose that you own a legal gambling hall and the roulette wheel breaks down. You desperately need this machine in operation to continue business. In order to have the wheel fixed, you deliver it to Ace Repairs, hoping that they will rush it back to you. Ace takes weeks to repair the wheel. Is there any legal remedy you might pursue?

    Decision: _____

    _____

    Rule of Law: _____

2. Suppose X, a lawyer, tells A, the trusting client, that the deal X has been working on for A is all set and that all A need do is give X $5,000. As it turns out, X knowingly defrauded A. Can A get more than $5,000 damages? Explain.

    Decision: _____

    _____

    Rule of Law: _____

3. A and B have a contract whereby if one party breaches the contract, the other is entitled to $2,000. B breaches in the most minor of ways. Can A enforce the clause for the $2,000? Explain.

    Decision: _____

    _____

    Rule of Law: _____

4. A and B have a contract whereby A is to manufacture 5,000 lawnmowers for B. After 500 are built, B repudiates the contract. A pays no attention and continues to build. A then sues B. What result?

Decision: _____

_____

Rule of Law: _____

5. A offers to sell B an antique car, a one-of-a-kind rare gem. After the written contract is made, A decides not to sell. Can B force A to part with the car? Explain.

Decision: _____

_____

Rule of Law: _____

CONTRACT UNIT RESEARCH QUESTIONS: Drawing upon information contained in the text, as well as outside sources, discuss the following questions:

1. Identify five examples of oral or written contracts you have made in the past month.

2. Using either a landlord-tenant lease (contract); an insurance contract, e.g., life or car insurance; a sales contract; or a service contract, e.g., work you performed for another person, explain how the document fulfills the requirements of a valid contract and explain the terms of the agreement.

PART THREE: Agency

Chapter 19

RELATIONSHIP OF PRINCIPAL AND AGENT

SCOPE NOTE

If it were required that all commercial transactions be conducted directly between primary parties only, business would progress at a snail's pace and the marketplace process would be cumbersome. To facilitate the flow of commerce, representatives are appointed to act on behalf of others within a defined scope of authority in negotiating and finalizing business agreements covering a broad range of substantive areas. Chapter 19 introduces the law of agency, which regulates the relationship of one person (agent) acting on behalf of another (principal). The nature of the agency relationship itself, how it is created, its basic concepts and terminology, the legal identities of its originating parties, and how their rights and duties differ from other legal relationships are focused upon.

EDUCATIONAL OBJECTIVES

1. Define and discuss the benefits derived from an agency relationship.

2. Enumerate the methods for creating a valid agency relationship.

3. Explain the qualifications necessary for a principal or agent.

4. Know the source and significance of the duties and liabilities owed by agents and principals to one another.

5. Outline the tort liability of principals and agents.

6. List and explain the various ways in which an agency relationship comes to an end.

CHAPTER OUTLINE

I. **Nature of Agency** — a contractual relationship usually involving fiduciary duties
   A. **Definition** — one party (principal) engages another (agent) to act on its behalf; principal controls agent's conduct
   B. **Scope of Agency Purposes** — defined by contract, usually to facilitate conducting business
   C. **Other Legal Relations** — contrasted to agency
      1. Independent contractor — no substantial control over conduct
      2. Broker — finds buyer for property owned by another

3.   Bailee — possesses another's personal property
4.   Trustee — holds legal title to property for another's benefit
D.   **Types of Agents** — general (acts in broad capacity), special (acts in limited capacity)

II. **Creation of Agency** — to accomplish any legal purpose; contractually based
    A.   **Formalities** — generally none required unless Statute of Frauds applies; writing required for power of attorney
    B.   **Capacity**
        1.   Capacity to be a principal — general legal (contractual); voidable appointments in case of incapacity
        2.   Capacity to be an agent — generally not required since contract is between principal and third party

III. **Duties of Agent to Principal** — defined by contract; generally one of proper performance within scope of duties
    A.   **Duty of Obedience** — relevant, lawful instructions unless an emergency materially changes duties
    B.   **Duty of Diligence** — use reasonable, prudent care; principal liability under respondent superior doctrine
    C.   **Duty to Inform** — relevant, accurate, important information
    D.   **Duty to Account** — for all monies relevant to agency relationship; not co-mingle agency and personal funds
    E.   **Fiduciary Duty** — good faith and loyalty based on trust; agents cannot act for themselves
    F.   **Confidentiality** — trade secrets, customer lists, other inside information

IV. **Duties of Principal to Agent**
    A.   **Contractual Duties** — primary determiner; standard of proper performance
        1.   Compensation — reasonable amount for services
        2.   Reimbursement — reasonable expenses in carrying out proper objectives
        3.   Indemnification — for losses incurred in carrying out proper objectives
    B.   **Tort Duties** — reasonable cooperation; reasonable safety

V. **Termination of Agency** — relationship comes to an end; actual authority ceases, apparent authority may continue
    A.   **Acts of the Parties** — based on conduct of parties; notice of termination generally required
        1.   Lapse of time — specified or reasonable length of time (no time specified)
        2.   Mutual agreement of the parties — rescission
        3.   Fulfillment of purpose — proper performance
        4.   Revocation of authority — principal unilaterally ends; agent remedies, mitigation duty
        5.   Renunciation by the agent — agent unilaterally ends; principal remedies, mitigation duty
    B.   **Operation of law** — based on changed circumstances; no notice of termination required
        1.   Bankruptcy
        2.   Death
        3.   Incapacity
        4.   Change in business conditions
        5.   Loss or destruction of the subject matter
        6.   Loss of qualification of principal or agent
        7.   Disloyalty of agent
        8.   Change of law
        9.   Outbreak of war

C. **Irrevocable Agencies** — authority of agent combined with special interest or obligation
    1.   Agent has interest in the estate
    2.   Agency created for agent's benefit

TRUE-FALSE: Circle true or false.

T   F   1. Most forms of business associations, including partnerships, sole proprietorships, and corporations, are based on the general principles of agency law.

T   F   2. An agent who is a minor can only make voidable contracts on behalf of an adult, capacitated principal.

T   F   3. A person having interests adverse to that of another is generally not permitted to act as an agent for that other person.

T   F   4. Employers are generally not responsible for the torts of independent contractors committed during the course of employment.

T   F   5. The law of agency is mainly controlled by the U.C.C.

T   F   6. A fiduciary duty is one that arises out of a position of trust and confidence between persons.

T   F   7. Agents employed to sell may not become purchasers for themselves.

T   F   8. When a principal wrongfully revokes an agent's authority, the agent may recover money damages for breach of contract.

T   F   9. When an agency agreement does not mention an amount of compensation for the agent, the principal is under no obligation to pay for the agent's services.

T   F   10. The power of the principal to terminate an agency is unlimited.

T   F   11. When conducting business on behalf of a principal, an agent is usually a party to the contract entered into with the third person.

T   F   12. Agency relationships terminate when the subject of the agency (goods to be sold by an agent) are destroyed through no one's fault.

KEY TERMS — MATCHING EXERCISE: Select the term that best completes each statement.

1. Diligence	8. Infants	15. Account
2. Master	9. Gratuitous agent	16. Indemnification
3. Disloyalty	10. Independent contractor	17. Confidential
4. Rescission	11. Servant	18. Bankruptcy
5. Renunciation	12. Revocation	19. Power of attorney
6. Principal	13. Compensation	20. Reimbursement
7. Agency	14. Fiduciary	

_____1. A legal relationship under which an individual acts as the business representative of another person.

_____2. Persons who authorize others to act on their behalf.

_____3. One acting on behalf of another under an agency relationship created without consideration.

_____4. An agent's duty to perform work with reasonable care and skill.

_____5. Agent's duty to keep accurate records regarding conduct on behalf of the principal and supply such records to the principal.

_____6. A person who contracts to act for another but is not controlled by that other person in the performance of authorized acts.

_____7. A right lost by an agent who breaches a fiduciary duty.

_____8. Acts by an agent that are adverse to the principal's interest.

_____9. The withdrawal of the agent's authority by the principal to act on the latter's behalf.

_____10. Notice to the principal given by the agent that the agent wishes to discontinue the agency.

_____11. Principal's duty to pay an agent for authorized expenses paid out of the agent's own pocket.

_____12. Principal's duty to pay an agent for losses suffered by the latter while acting in an authorized manner.

_____13. A form of agency under which the agent acts as an attorney for the principal.

_____14. Information that, if disclosed, causes harm to the principal's business.

_____15. Federal court proceedings granting judicial relief to financially troubled debtors.

MULTIPLE CHOICE: Select the alternative that best completes each statement below.

_____1. Agency relationships are generally created by (a) operation of law (b) statute (c) contract (d) equitable estoppel.

_____2. Examples of information that agents are duty bound to communicate to their principals include (a) insolvency of debtors and customers of the principal (b) change of marital status of a creditor of the principal (c) change in credit rating of independent contractors (d) pending tax increases on property owned by the agent.

_____3. In most situations (a) agency contracts must be sealed and notarized to be valid (b) no specific formalities are required for valid agency contracts (c) agency contracts must be written to be enforceable (d) agency contracts must be witnessed to be valid.

_____4. All contracts made by an agent appointed by a minor principal are (a) voidable (b) valid (c) void (d) nullity.

_____5. Factors examined in distinguishing an employment from an independent contractor relationship do not include (a) method of payment (b) adoption of the Uniform Independent Contractor Code (c) length of time (d) who supplies equipment, materials and other necessities.

_____6. An agency is terminated by (a) mutual agreement of the parties (b) fulfillment of the agency's purpose (c) insanity, death or bankruptcy of either principal or agent (d) all of the above.

_____7. Which of the following are duties owed a principal by the agent? (a) to act with reasonable care (b) to act only as authorized (c) to inform the principal of all relevant information (d) all of the above.

_____8. Which of the following is not a duty an agent owes to the principal? (a) ratification (b) diligence (c) loyalty (d) accounting.

_____9. Under the Restatement, the two main elements to an agency relationship are by the principal and by the agent (a) accord/satisfaction (b) authorization/consent (c) indemnification/compensation (d) receivership/ allocation.

_____10. When the parties to an agency or the agency contract do not specify how long the agency relationship is to last, it expires (a) automatically at the end of 90 days (b) no later than two weeks after the contract is signed (c) at the end of a reasonable length of time (d) none of the above.

_____11. Tort duties owed by an employer-principal to an employee-agent include (a) insuring that work settings are hazard free (b) liability for intentional torts of employees (c) warning employees of any risks associated with the job (d) none of the above.

_____12. Duties owed by a principal to an agent that are contractual in nature include (a) obedience (b) accounting (c) indemnification (d) all of the above.

_____13. Principal Paul and Agent Abel enter an agreement whereby Abel agrees to sell, for a fee, Paul's pickle packing plants. Shortly after reaching their agreement, Paul, having inhaled excessive amounts of pickling vapor, is adjudicated mentally incompetent and Abel is confined to a hospital with a severe case of shingles. Their relationship (a) ceases through subsequent incapacity (b) continues uneffected by these tragedies (c) terminates through changed business conditions (d) ends due to changes in law.

CASE PROBLEMS — SHORT ESSAY ANSWERS: Read each case problem carefully. When appropriate, answer by stating a Decision for the case and by explaining the rationale — Rule of Law — relied upon to support your decision.

1. A promises to personally try a lawsuit for B but instead asks a fellow attorney and friend to do it because A doesn't have enough time. May A do this? Explain.

    Decision: _____

    _____

    Rule of Law: _____

2. P instructs A to buy stock in two corporations. A, instead, sells A's own stock to P at the market price without disclosing this fact to P. Can P rescind this transaction? Explain.

   Decision: _____

   _____

   Rule of Law: _____

3. A hires B to sell A's home. The market price is $50,000. B finds a buyer for $51,500 and tells A the house sold for $50,000. Can B keep the $1,500 profit on the sale? Explain.

   Decision: _____

   _____

   Rule of Law: _____

4. P authorizes A to sell one of P's valuable paintings. A sells the painting to C at a price exceptionally favorable to P. C wants another of P's paintings and is willing to pay "any price." Can A sell it to C?

   Decision: _____

   _____

   Rule of Law: _____

5. English businessperson Throckmorton contracts with Argentine businessperson Dominequez to represent Throckmorton in various business dealings in Argentina. What effect on this contract would a flare-up of British-Argentine hostilities over the Balkin Islands have? Explain.

   Decision: _____

   _____

   Rule of Law: _____

Chapter 20

RELATIONSHIP WITH THIRD PARTIES

SCOPE NOTE

Our discussion of agency law concludes by addressing the rights/duties of the originating parties to the agency relationship vis-a-vis third persons. Both contract and tort foundations for liability are focused upon. Attention is given to those situations where the agent is acting with and without the principal's authority. Also discussed are circumstances that trigger third-party liability to the originating parties.

EDUCATIONAL OBJECTIVES

1. Define and explain the nature of the principal's contractual liability to third persons.

2. Distinguish among the various types of authority bases for agent conduct.

3. Discuss when an agent may delegate authority to another and the effect of such delegation.

4. Explain the effects of termination of agency and ratification on the principal's contractual liability.

5. Develop the principal's direct and vicarious tort liability to third persons based on the authorized or unauthorized acts of the agent.

6. Know the basis for criminal liability of principals to third persons.

7. Enumerate the situations when the agent is personally liable to third persons in terms of warranty of authority, competency and existence of the principal, and disclosure of representative status.

8. Explain the breadth of agent liability for the torts committed during the agency.

CHAPTER OUTLINE

I. **Relationship of Principal and Third Parties** — third party recovery against principal for agent's acts
    A. **Contract Liability of the Principal** — party to contract made by agent within agent's scope of authority; applies to both disclosed and undisclosed principals
        1. Types of authority — scope of agent's authority

          a. Actual express authority — written or spoken
          b. Actual implied authority — reasonable inferences (incidental and customary) based on prior dealing, usage or custom
          c. Apparent authority — stems from expectations of others based on principal's words or conduct (deliberate or careless); based on agent's justifiable reliance and injury; distinguished from implied authority; prior dealings
    2. Fundamental rules of contractual liability
    3. Delegation of authority — generally no sub-agents; ministerial acts contrasted with personalized acts
    4. Effect of termination of agency upon authority — notice requirement
    5. Ratification — retroactive intentional approval of unauthorized acts; express or implied; oral or written; relation back doctrine
  B. **Tort Liability of the Principal**
    1. Direct liability of the principal — agent acting under specific direction of principal
    2. Vicarious liability of principal for authorized acts of agent — misconduct within scope of authority; nature of duties; degree of control; intent of agent; extent of departure
    3. Vicarious liability of principal for unauthorized acts of agent — misconduct beyond scope of authority (substantial detour, personal frolic)
          a. The doctrine of respondeat superior — carrying out objectives or under principal's control; cases where agent violates specific instructions
          b. Torts of independent contractor — generally not liable; principal liable in rare cases
  C. **Criminal Liability of the Principal** — generally none without participation, direction, approval of misconduct

II. Relationship of Agent and Third Persons — third party recovery against agent
  A. **Contract Liability of Agent**
    1. Disclosed principal — none since not a party
    2. Unauthorized contracts — generally not liable as a party
          a. Agent's implied warranty of authority — liable for breach of contract
          b. Misrepresentation — liable for how authority misrepresented: if innocently, then breach of warranty; if intentionally, then fraud
          c. Agent assumes liability — personal liability of agent
    3. Partially disclosed principal
          a. Liability of the parties
          b. Rights of partially disclosed principal
    4. Undisclosed principal — both agent and principal liable
    5. Non-existent or incompetent principal — agent personally liable based on implied warranty
  B. **Tort Liability of Agent** — acting outside scope of authority cuts off reimbursement rights
  C. **Rights of Agent Against Third Person** — usually no contract breach recovery

TRUE-FALSE: Circle true or false.

T   F   1. An agent can bind the principal to a contract with apparent authority.

T   F   2. Apparent authority is the same as express authority.

T   F   3. A principal may never be held criminally accountable for the acts of an agent.

T   F   4. Authority to make contracts for a principal is usually inferred from the agent's authority to conduct business for the principal.

T   F   5. Sub-agents, appointed with authority from the principal, are agents of both the principal and the agent.

T   F   6. An agent for a disclosed principal is a party to the contract made on behalf of the principal and is liable to the third person with whom the contract is made.

T   F   7. For the doctrine of respondeat superior to take effect, the agent must be acting within the normal scope of employment.

T   F   8. The principal may be liable for an agent's contracts but not for the agent's torts.

T   F   9. Ratification by a principal of an agent's unauthorized acts may occur only through express language of the principal.

T   F   10. When conduct of the parties terminates an agency, the agent's apparent authority continues with respect to some third persons until actual notice of the termination is given to them.

T   F   11. Situations of apparent authority apply to cases of both disclosed and undisclosed principals.

T   F   12. Ratification cannot occur in settings where the principal is undisclosed.

KEY TERMS—MATCHING EXERCISE: Select the term that best completes each statement below.

1. Apparent authority	8. Ratification	15. Partially disclosed
2. Vicarious	9. Delegation	16. Disclosed
3. Privity of contract	10. Contract liability	17. Actual notice
4. Actual	11. Respondeat superior	18. Constructive notice
5. Authority	12. Frolic of his/her own	19. Implied
6. Allocation	13. Undisclosed	20. Sub-agent
7. Express	14. Independent contractors	

_____1. Persons who are not employees of the parties for whom services are performed.

_____2. Spoken or written authority communicated by the principal to the agent.

_____3. Transferring to another the right or power to perform some act.

_____4. An agency in which a third party deals with the agent knowing only the existence but not the identity of the principal.

_____5. The type of liability a principal incurs when an agent commits an unauthorized negligent act while in the scope of employment.

_____6. The doctrine that makes a principal liable for the agent's torts.

_____7. The principal's confirmation or adoption of an agent's unauthorized act.

_____8. The kind of agency in which a third person believes there is no agency relationship.

_____9. A basic type of authority that is based on the consent shown by the principal to the agent.

_____10. The power of an agent to change the legal status of a principal.

_____11. Type of authority arising out of the principal's behavior that creates in another's mind the reasonable, justified belief that the agent has actual authority.

_____12. Authority arising from the statements or behavior the principal demonstrates to the agent.

_____13. A principal whose existence and identity are known by the party.

_____14. Persons acting on behalf of an agent.

_____15. Express statement to a third party of the termination of an agency relationship.

MULTIPLE CHOICE: Select the alternative that best completes each statement below.

_____1. A valid ratification (a) may stem from unauthorized acts of an agent regardless of whether the principal existed at the time of the acts (b) cannot be revoked once made (c) relates back only to the time of disclosure of the principal (d) none of the above.

_____2. Normally the principal is not liable for contracts created by an agent's acts that are (a) unauthorized (b) expressly authorized (c) actually authorized (d) implicitly authorized.

_____3. Principals adjudged liable for their agents' torts have rights of (a) equitable contribution (b) injunctive relief (c) indemnification (d) condemnation against the agents.

_____4. An agent is liable to the third person if the agent (a) acts for an undisclosed principal (b) exceeds the authority granted by the principal (c) commits a tortious act (d) all of the above.

_____5. When a third party discovers the identity of an undisclosed principal, the third party (a) may hold either the principal or agent to performance of the contract (b) may hold both liable for the contract (c) may sue and get a judgment against both principal and agent (d) none of the above.

_____6. A ratification must be (a) communicated to the agent (b) communicated to the third person (c) manifested by words (d) none of the above.

_____7. When agents falsely represent to third persons that they are authorized by the principals to make contracts for them the agents are (a) ultimately not liable (b) liable in tort (c) liable in contract (d) none of the above to the third party.

_____8. Under the Restatement, employee conduct within scope of employment includes actions (a) motivated to serve the employer (b) within set time and space limits (c) of the kind for which employees have been hired (d) all of the above.

_____9. When agents guarantee third persons that principals will carry out the terms of contracts (a) the agents are liable for nonperformance by the principals (b) only principals are liable for their nonperformance (c) no suretyship exists between the agents and third persons (d) the principals have rights of reimbursement against the agent.

_____10. Actions by an agent that make the agent liable on the contract entered into between the principal and the third party include (a) making the contract in the principal's name only (b) committing any crime (c) making the contract in the agent's name only (d) all of the above.

_____11. When a third party obtains a judgment against an agent who represents an undisclosed principal whose identity and existence have become known to the third party (a) the principal's liability remains intact (b) a right of reimbursement against the principal arises in the agent's favor (c) constructive ratification cuts off any rights the principal might have against the agent (d) none of the above.

_____12. Conditions that indicate a principal's intent to allow an agent to delegate authority to another include (a) prior dealings among the parties (b) presumption per se (c) constructive notice (d) all of the above.

_____13. Effective constructive notice is achieved through (a) radio announcements (b) statements in geographically proper newspapers of general circulation (c) billboard ads (d) handbills.

CASE PROBLEMS — SHORT ESSAY ANSWERS: Read each case problem carefully. When appropriate, answer by stating a Decision for the case and by explaining the rationale — Rule of Law — relied upon to support your decision.

1. For the past five years, agent A, acting on behalf of principal P, has purchased new model year cars from car dealership C for P's company fleet. Each year, A trades in the previous year's cars. The past year has been financially difficult for P's company so to reduce expenditures P directs A not to purchase new model year cars but to retain last year's models for at least another year. C is not aware of P's changed plans nor does A inform C of this fact when, disregarding P's instructions, A trades in the last year's models and purchases new ones. When A refuses to pay for them and C seeks payment from P, may P validly avoid payment based on the express refusal to A for the authority to make the purchases? Explain.

Decision: _____

_____

Rule of Law: _____

2. A, agent for P, is told by P to deliver an important paper to X immediately. Time is essential. Hoping to please P, A drove the company car at a high rate of speed and unfortunately struck T. Can T sue A? Explain.

Decision: _____

_____

Rule of Law: _____

3. A, an agent for disclosed principal P, makes a contract with third party T on behalf of P for the purchase of property insurance from which A will be paid $500 by P. If T breaches the contract, can A sue T? Explain.

Decision: _____

_____

Rule of Law: _____

4. In a case involving an undisclosed principal, an agent buys goods on credit but does not pay for them. Later the seller of the goods discovers the fact of the agency and the identity of the principal. The seller obtains a judgment against the principal, but the principal is insolvent. Can the seller recover from the agent? Explain.

Decision: _____

_____

Rule of Law: _____

5. P, the owner of Blackacre, hires X an independent contractor to build a hotel on P's land. When X begins to break the ground, X uses dynamite to loosen the earth. T, who lives three blocks away, has five windows broken due to the concussion from the explosions. Can T sue P even though X was an independent contractor? Explain.

Decision: _____

_____

Rule of Law: _____

AGENCY UNIT RESEARCH QUESTIONS: Drawing upon information contained in the text, as well as outside sources, discuss the following questions:

1. In what areas of our business and personal lives are we likely to encounter principles of agency law?

2. How has legislative and administrative law pre-empted certain common law agency principles? What rationale underlies these changes?

Chapter 21

INTRODUCTION TO SALES

SCOPE NOTE

We have already studied contract law. That area of the law, in addition to Article 2 of the U.C.C., controls transactions for the sale of goods. The following chapter introduces the legal intricacies associated with the law of sales and the rights and duties of the parties to a sales transaction. Knowing basic terminology, the requirements for a valid sales contract and fundamental legal doctrines that control this area of law provides the foundation for understanding the specific fields of legal inquiry that comprise the body of the law of sales. The chapter closes with an overview of the fundamental provisions of Article 2A of the Code covering the law of leases.

EDUCATIONAL OBJECTIVES

1. Distinguish between the approaches to sales contracts under common law and U.C.C. Article 2.

2. List the various Article 2 doctrines controlling sales contracts.

3. Develop the various requirements for a valid sales contract, including mutual agreement, consideration and various formality restrictions.

4. Discuss how sales contracts differ from other non-goods contracts and transactions.

5. Describe the U.C.C. provisions exclusively applicable to sales between merchants.

6. Discuss the significance of the doctrine of unconscionability in the law of sales.

7. Understand major provisions of U.C.C. Article 2A concerning leases.

CHAPTER OUTLINE

I. **Nature of Sales Contracts** — buyer and seller rights/duties associated with sales of goods
    A. **Definition** — transfer of title to goods for a price (return value)
        1. Governing law — U.C.C. Article 2 replaces common law of contracts

      2.   Nonsales transactions in goods — bailments, leases, gifts, security interests contrasted to sales

  B. **Fundamental Principles of Article 2** — guiding principles for sales contracts to facilitate commercial transactions and hold merchants to higher standards of business relations

      1.   Good faith — honesty in fact; commercial reasonableness for merchants

      2.   Unconscionability — fairness and decency over harsh, oppressive terms or conduct

         a. Procedural unconscionability — bargaining process scrutinized for improper behavior

         b. Substantive unconscionability — terms of the contract are scrutinized

      3.   Expansion of commercial practices — course of dealing, usage of trade guidelines

      4.   Sales by and between merchants — separate rules under the Code; merchant defined

      5.   Liberal administration of remedies — place nonbreaching party in as good a position as if proper performance had occurred

      6.   Freedom of contract — parties can vary Code provisions; certain standards are nondisclaimable

      7.   Validation and preservation of sales contracts — Code reduces commercial law formal requirements; focus on intent of the parties

  C. **Goods** — tangible, movable personal property; related to real property; natural resources; crops

II. **Formation of a Sales Contract** — requirements for valid, enforceable agreement.

  A. **Manifestation of Mutual Assent** — meeting of the minds

      1.   Definiteness of an offer — Code allows for reasonable indefiniteness; contractual intent controls

         a. Open price — reasonable price at delivery; good faith, reasonable

         b. Open delivery — reasonable time at seller's place of business, residence or goods

         c. Open quantity — output and requirement contracts enforced through objective standard

         d. Other open terms — Code provides various rules for payment, duration, performance issues

      2.   Irrevocable offers — option contract and firm offers; three month maximum for written assurance to keep offer made between merchants open

      3.   Variant acceptances — Code modifies common law mirror image rule; battle of forms problem

      4.   Manner of acceptance — any manner, any medium that is reasonable

      5.   Auctions — without or with reserve compared; withdrawal problem considered

  B. **Consideration** — bargain and exchange process; price (money, goods, services, land)

      1.   Contractual modifications — Code discards common law requirement of separate consideration

      2.   Discharge of claim after breach — written, signed, delivered waiver, enforceable without separate consideration

      3.   Firm offers — no consideration required

  C. **Form of the Contract**

      1.   Statute of Frauds — sale of goods for $500 or more

         a. Modification of contracts within the Statute of Frauds must be written if resulting contract is within the Statute

         b. Written compliance — more liberal than common law doctrines: sufficient writing broadly interpreted

         c. Alternative methods of compliance — sworn admittance to contract existence; oral contract for specially manufactured goods; delivered and accepted goods exception

      2.   Parol evidence — modified by course of dealing, trade usage, course of performance, evidence of additional terms

3. Seal — Code makes inoperative for sale of goods

III. Leases, U.C.C. Article 2A

A. **Defined** — transfer of possession and use of goods for consideration; contrasted to security interests under U.C.C. Article 9

B. **Default and Remedies** — Code eliminates Election of Remedy doctrine and allows cumulative remedies

C. **Consumer Leases** — definitional requirements; application of doctrine of unconscionability

D. **Finance Leases** — three-party transaction: lessor financier, lessee taker of goods, supplier of goods

TRUE-FALSE: Circle true or false.

T   F   1. Employment contracts, service contracts and insurance contracts are not covered by Article 2 of the U.C.C.

T   F   2. Contracts for the sale of goods costing $300 or more must be in writing to be enforceable.

T   F   3. Under the Code, sales contracts containing omitted terms are unenforceable due to their lack of definiteness.

T   F   4. Under the Code, merchants are held to a higher standard of commercial reasonableness than are non-merchants.

T   F   5. A written memorandum, signed by a merchant seller, confirming an earlier oral contract falling within the Statute of Frauds, binds a merchant buyer unless the latter effectively objects.

T   F   6. Retracted bids at auctions automatically revive the previously submitted bid.

T   F   7. A contract for the sale of timber to be cut and removed by purchaser is a sale of goods under the U.C.C.

T   F   8. A lease of goods is similar to a bailment.

T   F   9. Unless the parties provide otherwise, place of delivery of goods is seller's place of business.

T   F   10. According to U.C.C. provisions, sales contracts valued at $15,000 or more must be under Department of Commerce seal to be valid.

T   F   11. An exchange of goods for services is a sale.

T   F   12. As a general rule, the remedial provisions of the Code are narrowly interpreted and applied to prevent unjust enrichment to the party injured by another's breach of contract.

KEY TERMS — MATCHING EXERCISE: Select the term that best completes each statement below.

1. Option	8. Without reserve	15. Bailment
2. Mirror image rule	9. Gift	16. Waiver
3. Seller	10. Trade usage	17. Firm offer
4. Sale	11. Good faith	18. With reserve
5. Possession	12. Implied warranty	19. Lease
6. Security Agreement	13. Unconscionable	20. Trust
7. Goods	14. Merchants	

_____1. A present transfer of title to goods in exchange for a price.

_____2. Movable, tangible personal property.

_____3. The performance standard controlling parties to sales contracts on their contractual duties.

_____4. A transfer of title and possession without return consideration.

_____5. A transfer of possession to goods without a transfer of title.

_____6. A common method of doing business prevalent in a particular area of commerce.

_____7. An auction at which the auctioneer may not withdraw items put up for sale unless no bids are made.

_____8. The common law doctrine that required acceptances of offers to comply exactly with the terms of the offer.

_____9. Sales contracts that are harsh and unfair because of the unequal bargaining positions of the parties.

_____10. A contractual agreement granting a creditor the right to obtain possession of goods upon a debtor's default.

_____11. A contract binding the offeror to keep the offer open for a specific time period.

_____12. Written statement signed by non-breaching party discharging breaching party for liability for non-performance.

_____13. Transfer of possession to another for a specific time for return payment.

_____14. Irrevocable offer made by a merchant.

_____15. Auctions at which auctioneer may withdraw goods at any time until completion of the sale.

MULTIPLE CHOICE: Select the alternative that best completes each statement below.

_____1. Property included under the U.C.C.'s definition of goods includes (a) real property (b) negotiable instruments (c) growing crops (d) all of the above.

_____2. Which of the following is not a requirement for a valid consumer lease under U.C.C. Article 2A provisions? (a) merchant lessor (b) an individual lessee (c) value of the lease less than $25,000 (d) lease is primarily for business-commercial purposes.

_____3. Modifications of sales contracts must be (a) supported by consideration (b) made in good faith (c) witnessed in writing (d) all of the above to be valid under the terms of the U.C.C.

_____4. Acceptance of the terms of a sales offer may be indicated by (a) conduct (b) words (c) presumed intention (d) all of the above.

_____5. Under the Code, merchants are persons who (a) deal in certain goods (b) hold themselves out to have special knowledge peculiar to certain goods (c) employ an agent who professes to have special knowledge peculiar to goods (d) all of the above.

_____6. A pattern of business relations existing between parties often doing business with one another is called a/n (a) trade pattern (b) course of dealing (c) usage of trade (d) none of the above.

_____7. Written contractual terms intended as the final, complete agreement of the parties may not be altered, contradicted or supplemented by prior or contemporaneous agreement evidence under the (a) Parol Evidence Rule (b) Fair Interpretation doctrine (c) last in First Controlling Rule (d) none of the above.

_____8. Consideration that the buyer promises the seller in exchange for the goods is referred to as the (a) cost minus depreciation (b) price (c) appreciation (d) pledge.

_____9. The Code expressly defines unconscionability as (a) criminal dishonesty (b) fraud in execution (c) deceit (d) none of the above.

_____10. An "open-price" term in a sales contract may be filled in by (a) later agreement between the parties (b) a bailment (c) an auction (d) a conditional sale.

_____11. The Code's sales provisions (a) are mandatory and must be strictly followed by contracting parties (b) are monitored and enforced by the FTC (c) may be changed by contracting parties (d) none of the above.

_____12. The Code has changed general contract law regarding the formation of sales contracts (a) to bring more formality to this process (b) by allowing states greater freedom to apply their own rules of law (c) by favoring commercial over consumer interests (d) to modernize and promote fairness in contract law.

_____13. Under the Code, an oral contract for the sale of $850 worth of pencils is enforceable (a) if a party admits that negotiations for such a sale occurred (b) only to the extent of delivered and accepted units (c) totally as long as partial performance has occurred (d) only upon complete performance by both parties.

CASE PROBLEMS — SHORT ESSAY ANSWERS: Read each case problem carefully. Answer by stating a Decision for the case and by explaining the rationale — Rule of Law — relied upon to support your decision.

1. S, a nail wholesaler, offers to sell to B, a hardware dealer, 2 tons of nails for $600. S sends B a signed memo stating the offer will remain open for five business days. Two days later, S sends a telegram to B revoking the offer. B ignores the attempted revocation and transmits an acceptance that S refuses to honor. Do the parties have a contract? Explain.

   Decision: _____

   _____

   Rule of Law: _____

2. B enters a contract with S for the purchase of the entire production output of S's mobile home manufacturing facility from March through June. Since the exact quantity of homes to be purchased is not stated, is this contract invalid due to indefiniteness?

   Decision: _____

   _____

   Rule of Law: _____

3. A financially strapped elderly retired couple, H and W, enter an installment purchase contract with S, a door-to-door salesperson, for a dishwasher, retail value of $180, calling for four payments of $220 each. After making two installment payments, H and W become dissatisfied, not with the dishwasher, but its price. Can they withdraw from this contract with S? Why or why not?

   Decision: _____

   _____

   Rule of Law: _____

4. Penny, pet store operator, receives an offer mailed from Yummy Pet Supplies, Inc., for the sale of 6 months' supply of Yummy pet food products to be sold in Penny's store. Penny, knowing Yummy's reputation for quality, reasonably priced products, believes this pet food line will increase her business and quickly accepts Yummy's offer, adding in her acceptance letter that she'd like samples of Yummy's grooming products to examine for possible sale in her store. A few days after Penny sends her acceptance letter, she receives a call from Yale Yummy, C.E.O. of Yummy, Inc., saying he considers Penny's letter a rejection and a counter offer that he finds unpalatable and refuses to do business with her. Penny thinks she has a contract. Who wins this dispute?

   Decision: _____

   _____

   Rule of Law: _____

5. Wally Widget is the only person who would want or could use wadgets. Wally places an oral order with the Wadget Company to make 10,000 wadgets at $2.00 each. Later, Wally refuses to accept the completed wadgets and alleges the Uniform Commercial Code Statute of Frauds as a defense to the suit for breach of contract. Decide.

Decision:. _____

_____

Rule of Law: _____

Chapter 22

PERFORMANCE

SCOPE NOTE

The terms of the sales contract, as well as various provisions of the U.C.C., control the nature and interpretation of the rights/duties of the parties in performing on their sales agreement. It is the seller's obvious duty to deliver conforming goods at the proper time and location. Conversely, the buyer's self-evident duty is to accept properly tendered conforming goods and offer proper payment. The U.C.C. provisions controlling interpretation of contractual terms vis-a-vis performance give direction to how issues in this area are to be resolved. Besides outlining the broad performance rights/obligations of the parties, this chapter introduces the complex issues and resolution guidelines associated with improper performance.

EDUCATIONAL OBJECTIVES

1. Describe the "perfect tender" rule as it applies to both parties of a sales contract.

2. Discuss the seller's proper delivery obligation in terms of method, location and time.

3. Identify situations under which the seller's duties under the "perfect tender" rule are altered.

4. Explain the buyer's performance duties under the "perfect tender" rule in terms of payment and inspection.

5. Enumerate the buyer's rights upon improper delivery.

6. Define and discuss the significance of acceptance.

7. Differentiate between the buyer's right to reject and to revoke acceptance.

8. Explain the doctrine of "cure" in the context of improper performance.

9. Describe the significance of substituted performance.

10. Outline circumstances that excuse non-performance in the context of failure of conditions and damage to goods.

CHAPTER OUTLINE

I. Performance by the Seller — buyer's expectations (conforming goods are tendered) are met and contract duties are discharged; tender of delivery; entitles seller to payment; triggers buyer's acceptance duty

  A. **Time and Manner of Delivery** — reasonable time; enable buyer to take possession; held for buyer for reasonable time

  B. **Place of Tender** — seller's place of business, seller's residence, or where goods are located unless otherwise specified in contract
    1. Shipment contracts — no destination specified; seller's duties at point of shipment: delivery to carrier; make contract; notify buyer
    2. Destination contracts — specified destination point; seller's duties at destination
    3. Goods held by bailee — tender title document
    4. Goods held by seller — seller's place of business

  C. **Quality of Tender** — degree of performance that is acceptable; place/hold conforming goods; effective notice to buyer
    1. Perfect tender rule — conforming exactly to contract requirements
    2. Agreement by the parties — contractual modifications of perfect tender
    3. Cure by the seller — repair, replace, adjust price for nonconforming goods; notice of intent and delivery prior to performance date; acceptance by buyer of notice and delivery after performance date
    4. Installment contracts — test of substantial value for separate installments, impairment of specific installment or whole contract

II. Performance by the Buyer — duty to accept and pay for conforming goods at contract rate

  A. **Inspection** — reasonable time, place and method prior to payment or acceptance; at buyer's expense; preceding payment is not acceptance

  B. **Rejection** — refusal to accept (become owner) nonconforming goods; reasonable notice to seller; non-merchant contrasted to merchant's duties

  C. **Acceptance** — willingness to become owner (payment duty); implied when no rejection occurs; commercial unit

  D. **Revocation of Acceptance** — post acceptance discovery of value-impairing nonconformity; timely notice and seller's right to cure

  E. **Obligation of Payment** — at time and place of receipt; reasonable time to meet seller's demand for cash

III. Obligations of Both Parties — Code provisions for risk allocation when parties fail to mention in their agreement

  A. **Casualty to Identified Goods** — prior to acceptance (offer terminated and no contract exists) or after acceptance (risk of loss provisions from Code govern)

  B. **Non-happening of Presupposed Conditions** — discharge due to impossibility where condition is basic assumption to purpose, value of contract

  C. **Substituted Performance** — commercial impracticability triggers duty for commercially reasonable alternative

  D. **Assurance of Performance** — demand for written assurance and suspension of performance duty triggered by reasonable doubt over contract party's willingness, ability to perform

TRUE-FALSE: Circle true or false.

T   F   1. A sales contract may call for the seller to deliver goods prior to receiving payment.

T   F   2. Delivery may be tendered at any hour and conducted in any manner as the seller chooses.

T   F   3. Both parties to a sales contract are automatically excused from performance when the expressly provided for manner of delivery becomes impossible.

T   F   4. The buyer's acceptance of goods cuts off any right to reject them.

T   F   5. Parties to a sales contract may not alter the application of the perfect tender rule to their transaction through contractual provisions.

T   F   6. Unless the contract provides otherwise, payment is due at the time and place where the buyer is to receive the goods.

T   F   7. A C.O.D. shipment contract requires buyer payment for the goods prior to inspection.

T   F   8. Under the Code, acceptance of goods must always be in writing, signed by the buyer.

T   F   9. When the sales contract does not specify the location for delivery, the place for delivery is deemed the buyer's place of business.

T   F   10. When a buyer has rejected goods due to their nonconformity, the seller bears the burden of establishing that the goods conform to the contract.

T   F   11. Usually fires, strikes or lock-outs are sufficient to excuse contractual performance on the grounds of performance impossibility.

T   F   12. For a buyer to revoke acceptance, the seller's defective performance must substantially impair the value of the goods.

KEY TERMS — MATCHING EXERCISE: Select the term that best completes each statement below.

1. Shipment Contract	8. Revoke	15. Rejection
2. Seller	9. Substituted performance	16. Inspection
3. Installment contract	10. Perfect tender rule	17. Commercial impracticability
4. Possession	11. Acceptance	18. Payment
5. Cure	12. Credit sale	19. Tender
6. Commercial unit	13. Cancellation	20. Contract rate
7. Performance	14. Money damages	

_____1. The act that fulfills the expectations of the parties to their contract and discharges their contractual duties.

_____2. A sales agreement calling for delivery and payment of goods in separate lots.

_____3. A unit of goods that is a single whole for the purposes of sale, a division of which substantially impairs its identity, value or use.

_____4. The buyer's refusal to accept and make payment on non-conforming goods.

_____5. A transaction under which the buyer is not required to make payment for the goods at the time they are received.

_____6. Seller's prompt, timely delivery of conforming goods, following buyer's rightful rejection of nonconforming goods.

_____7. The obligation facing the parties to a sales contract when the agreed manner of performance has become commercially untenable without fault of either party.

_____8. A sales contract containing C.O.D., C.I.F., and C.F. delivery terms.

_____9. Duty imposed on the seller under the Code requiring tender of delivery exactly conforming to contractual terms.

_____10. Buyer's expression of willingness to become owner of goods.

_____11. Consideration buyer must give seller upon accepting commercial unit of nonconforming goods.

_____12. Buyer's pre-acceptance right to examine goods to insure that they conform to the contract.

_____13. Seller's duty to make available to the buyer conforming goods.

_____14. U.C.C. doctrine that discharges performance when unforeseen events not anticipatable by the parties make performance an extreme hardship.

_____15. Buyer's duty upon accepting conforming goods.

MULTIPLE CHOICE: Select the alternative that best completes each statement below.

_____1. When the sales contract does not mention time for delivery, the seller (a) has a reasonable time following the contractual execution to deliver the goods (b) must deliver the goods on buyer's demand (c) has no more than 60 days to deliver the goods (d) none of the above.

_____2. Following a buyer's rejection of nonconforming goods, a seller may rightfully (a) hold the buyer in breach (b) sell the goods elsewhere and thus avoid all liability to the buyer (c) rightfully refuse to reimburse the buyer for inspection expenses (d) undo the defective tender by promptly delivering conforming goods within the allowed performance time.

_____3. Under a shipment contract, the seller must (a) deliver the goods to a carrier (b) issue a document of title for the goods to the buyer (c) make a reasonable contract of cartage (d) all of the above.

_____4. To be effective, revocation of acceptance must be made (a) within a year after the goods are delivered (b) within a reasonable time after the nonconformity of the goods is discovered (c) in writing only (d) by a receiver in equity.

_____5. Merchant buyers possessing rightfully rejected goods must (a) reship them (b) resell them (c) follow the reasonable instructions of the seller concerning their disposal (d) place them in trust.

_____6. Factors relevant to the materiality of a breach of a sales contract include (a) U.C.C. definitions (b) contract subject matter (c) provisions in the constitution (d) res judicata.

_____7. Upon delivery of conforming goods, the buyer must (a) tender payment (b) issue a document of title in favor of the seller (c) warehouse the goods until the seller is paid (d) all of the above.

_____8. A buyer's right of inspection (a) can be exercised anytime (b) may not be eliminated by a clause in the contract (c) requires the buyer to bear inspection expenses (d) is usually nonexistent.

_____9. Acceptance takes place when the buyer (a) fails to reject the goods (b) informs the seller that the goods are conforming (c) tells the seller that, despite nonconformities, the goods are adequate (d) all of the above.

_____10. A sales contract containing the delivery terms "exship," "F.O.B. city of buyer," "no arrival, no sale," is a (a) substituted contract (a) destination contract (c) tendered contract (d) none of the above.

_____11. Upon delivery of nonconforming goods a buyer may (a) reject all of the goods (b) accept all of the goods (c) accept any commercial unit or units and reject the rest (d) all of the above.

_____12. Under an installment contract, when the seller has tendered nonconforming goods, the buyer (a) may reject the installment if its value is substantially impaired and the seller cannot cure the non-conformity (b) can immediately cancel the contract and hold the seller in total breach (c) has an absolute right of rejection (d) none of the above.

_____13. A sales contract is performable in installments (a) in all cases (b) only in commercial transactions between merchants (c) only if the parties so agree (d) none of the above.

CASE PROBLEMS — SHORT ESSAY ANSWERS: Read each case problem carefully. When appropriate, answer by stating a Decision for the case and by explaining the rationale — Rule of Law — relied upon to support your decision.

1. B orders two dozen personalized Halloween masks from Costume Supplies, Inc., delivery and payment at B's residence. While seller's truck is making the delivery, a flash flood strikes and sweeps the truck away. A few hours later, the truck and its driver are found, but the delivery items are a total loss. S informs B of the near tragedy and tells B, regrettably, that their contract is canceled. B, needing the masks for an upcoming party, demands that S provide substitute masks or a lawsuit will follow. Is S required to provide replacement masks as B asserts? Discuss.

   Decision: _____

   _____

   Rule of Law: _____

2. B ordered 20,000 1/2-inch bolts from S, delivery in installments of 1,000 per month in 20 different shipments. Payment was to occur on the first day of each month. On the third shipment, B is a day late in making payment. S gives immediate notice of cancellation of the entire contract. Decision for whom and why?

   Decision: _____

   _____

   Rule of Law: _____

3. Henrietta Hunter purchases a new hunting rifle from Barney's sporting goods store. An avid sportswoman, Henrietta is ready to pay top dollar for top quality. Upon unpacking the rifle and readying it for use, she notices tiny scratches on the lever and nicks in the handle. A perfectionist, Henrietta is furious and storms back to Barney's demanding a full refund. Barney refuses her request, arguing that the gun is still suitable for hunting purposes and Henrietta's dissatisfaction is over mere cosmetic blemishes. Who wins this dispute and why?

Decision: _____

_____

Rule of Law: _____

4. B, a merchant, receives a shipment of nonconforming bananas from S. B rejects them and notifies S to come and get them. S remains silent. B does nothing and the bananas spoil. In a suit by S against B for the loss of the bananas, who wins and why?

Decision: _____

_____

Rule of Law: _____

5. B and S, American business executives, enter a sales contract for 5,000 Australian widgees at 50 cents apiece, to be delivered to B's place of business no later than August 14. Diplomatic relations between America and Australia become strained. By July 21, the countries cut off diplomatic relations, call home their respective ambassadors and place an embargo on all mutual trade. When S is unable to deliver the specified widgees at the appointed time and place, B sues for breach. Who wins and why?

Decision: _____

_____

Rule of Law: _____

Chapter 23

TRANSFER OF TITLE AND RISK OF LOSS

SCOPE NOTE

Studying the legal doctrines associated with title to personal property and sales of goods is vital to understanding the law of sales. Title passage in various types of sales transactions and the factors used to determine passing of title are discussed in Chapter 23. In addition to ownership considerations, parties to sales transactions must know their rights and duties at the various stages of their business dealings. In the event of damage or destruction to goods sold, who bears the risk of loss? When may the parties to a sales transaction protect their interest in goods through insurance? The factors used in deciding risk-of-loss issues, as well as the various U.C.C. provisions controlling this area, are also examined in this chapter.

Another important aspect of the legal identities of parties to a sales transaction is knowing under what circumstances someone with less than full ownership may transfer title to purchasers of goods. What difficulties are created when an innocent buyer purchases another person's goods believing that the sale was authorized by and is made with the permission of the true owner? These issues are also addressed in Chapter 23, which develops the rules used to determine the rights of adversary parties (usually the purchaser and the original owner in cases of attempted title transfer by a non-owner of goods. The situations in which the innocent buyer prevails are discussed, as well as those cases where the original owner's title to the sold goods is protected. The chapter closes with a discussion of the rights that creditors of the seller have in the goods sold. Guidelines to purchasers from and creditors of the seller are presented to aid in determining priority of interest in these confusing transactions.

EDUCATIONAL OBJECTIVES

1. Enumerate the types of issues directly related to title location concerns.

2. Identify the rules used in determining title passage and how they are influenced by type of goods, shipment terms, the use of documents of title and other related circumstances.

3. Explain the importance of identifying goods to the contract.

4. Define and point out the significance of a buyer's "special property interest."

5. Delineate the various rules associated with determining risk of loss when no breach of contract has occurred.

6. Distinguish sale on approval from sale or return.

7. Describe how shipment terms, possession of the goods by a bailee, and breach of contract affect risk-of-loss issues.

8. Explain the legal policies in competition with one another in non-owner sales of goods.

9. Distinguish between void and voidable title transfers both at common law and under the U.C.C.

10. Define and describe the significance of a bona fide purchaser for value.

11. Discuss the treatment of an innocent buyer under the U.C.C.

12. Describe the importance of the doctrine of entrusting as developed in the U.C.C.

13. Define "bulk transfer" and list Code requirements applicable to such transactions.

14. List the type of transactions exempted from Article 6 control.

15. Discuss the effect of not complying with Article 6.

CHAPTER OUTLINE

I. **Transfer of Title and Other Property Rights** — title location important regarding replevin and conversion rights, owner liabilities and creditor rights
   A. **Passage of Title** — ownership moves from seller to buyer
      1. According to agreement between parties
      2. Physical movement of existing identified goods — at time and place seller delivers goods
         a. Shipment contracts — require/authorize seller to send goods to buyer; do not require delivery at particular destination; title passes at time and place of delivery to carrier
         b. Destination contracts — require seller to deliver goods to particular destination, title passes upon tender at destination
      3. No movement of goods — title passes upon delivery of title documents (where contract calls for such delivery) or at time and place of contracting (no documents are to be delivered)
      4. Title revests in seller — rejection or revocation of acceptance for nonconforming goods by buyer
   B. **Other Property Rights**
      1. Special property interest — buyer's non-title interest in goods identified to the contract; inspection and replevin rights; right to sue third parties
      2. Insurable interest — in seller prior to identification; in both seller and buyer upon identification; in buyer alone after title passage unless seller retains security interest
      3. Security interest — insures payment or performance of an obligation
         a. In seller — conditional sales contract; negotiable or non-negotiable bill of lading
         b. In buyer — rejection or revocation acceptance
   C. **Identification** — precedes title passage; goods linked to contract
      1. Present sale — occurs at time contract made
      2. Future sale — when goods are shipped or marked, unborn animal conceived, or crops planted
      3. Buyer has special property insurable interest; seller has insurable interest
   D. **Power to Transfer Title** — is seller rightful owner of or authorized to sell goods; problem case where seller not rightful owner of goods or authorized to sell goods (seller possesses goods of another) but retains power to transfer good title to certain buyers (good faith purchaser, buyer in ordinary course); promote certainty in marketplace

1. Void and voidable title to goods held by seller
   a. Void title — no title to goods; original owner can regain goods; bona fide purchaser does not cut off such right; fraud, duress, theft
   b. Voidable title — circumstances that may cut off former owner's right to regain goods, with bona fide purchaser retaining title: dishonored check; identity deceit; fraud; failure to pay cash in a cash agreement; indicia of ownership; minor's contracts; mistake
2. Entrusting goods to merchant — repair contracts; purchaser of goods during ordinary course of business cuts off original owner's rights to regain goods

II. Risk of Loss — whether seller or buyer bears loss for goods damaged, destroyed, or lost without either's fault between when contract entered and title/possession passes to buyer
   A. **Risk of Loss in Absence of a Breach**
      1. Agreement of the parties — contract divides, shifts risk
      2. Trial sales — buyer may return conforming goods
         a. Sale on approval — goods delivered for use; possession, not title transferred to buyer for stated period of time; seller retains title and risk of loss until buyer's approval or acceptance; buyer's notice duty; acceptance of an installment issue
         b. Sale or return — goods delivered for resale; risk of loss on buyer until title revested by return; buyers duty to act seasonably
         c. Consignment — goods delivered to merchant agent for sale; Code treats as a sale or return
      3. Contracts involving carriers — risk of loss influenced by presence of third party
         a. Shipment contracts — seller not required to deliver goods to a particular destination; risk of loss passes to buyer upon delivery of goods to carrier
         b. Destination contracts — seller required to deliver goods to a particular destination; risk of loss passes to buyer at destination upon proper tender
      4. Goods in possession of bailee — risk of loss influenced by presence of third-party goods held by bailee for delivery without being moved; risk of loss passes to buyer upon receipt of title documents or on bailee's acknowledgment
      5. All other sales — risk of loss passes to buyer at time of receipt for merchant seller, tender for non-merchant seller, or at time of contracting
   B. **Risk of Loss Where There is a Breach**
      1. Breach by seller — nonconforming goods; loss on seller until buyer accepts goods or seller has remedied defect
      2. Breach by buyer — conforming goods identified to contract; seller may treat risk of loss as resting on the buyer "for commercially reasonable time"

III. Sales of Goods in Bulk — transfer of goods, not in ordinary course of the transferor's business, of a major part of the materials, supplies, merchandise, or other inventory; fear that debtor may fraudulently liquidate assets by a bulk sale and conceal or divert the proceeds without paying creditors; Code provisions protect creditors of seller
   A. **Requirements of Article 6** — Code provisions must be met for a bulk transfer to be effective against creditors; buyers or purchasers who do not pay value or know of noncompliance take goods subject to title defect; good faith purchaser for value receive good title
   B. **Exempted Bulk Transfers** — bulk transfers that need not comply with Article 6 to be valid transfers
      1. General assignment
      2. Settlement of security interest
      3. Judicial sales
      4. Restructure sales
      5. Exempt property

6. Takeover sale
C. **Effect of Failure to Comply with Article 6** — goods still subject to claims of unpaid creditors
D. **Provisions of Revised Article 6**
E. **Application of the Proceeds** — question of what obligation transferee (purchaser) owes to transferor's (seller's) creditors
F. **Auctions and Sales** — Code requirements for valid bulk transfer sales; auctioneer liable for compliance
   1. Transferor provides sworn list of creditors and assists in preparation of a schedule of property to be sold
   2. List of creditors and schedule of property preserved for six months, available for creditor inspection, filed in public office
   3. Notice to creditors — registered or certified mail; at least 10 days before auction; states circumstances surrounding sale
   4. Net sale (auction) proceeds applied to transferor's debts

TRUE—FALSE: Circle true or false.

T   F   1. Parties to a sales contract may, by agreement, define who will assume risk of loss for damage or destruction of the goods.

T   F   2. Under the Code, buyers must own goods before they are insurable.

T   F   3. The U.C.C. does not use title location as the primary means to determine the rights of parties to a sales contract when goods are damaged.

T   F   4. The power and right to transfer title are one and the same.

T   F   5. In sales of goods by non-owners, the policies of ownership protection and marketplace stability come into conflict.

T   F   6. When a seller ships nonconforming goods to a buyer, risk of loss remains on the seller until the buyer accepts the goods.

T   F   7. Under the revised provisions of U.C.C. Article 6, buyers under bulk transfers who make good faith attempts to meet the requirements of the Article are still liable for non-compliances that occurred.

T   F   8. A bulk sale is a transfer not in the ordinary course of business.

T   F   9. Under modern law, a minor seller may avoid a sale of goods and recover them from a third-party bona fide purchaser for value.

T   F   10. A risk faced by creditors of a debtor-seller of goods in bulk is that the latter may use the bulk sale to liquidate assets and keep the sale proceeds from the creditors.

T   F   11. The bulk sales provisions of the Code are designed to protect creditors of a merchant debtor from the latter's fraud.

T   F   12. A shipment contract requires a seller to deliver goods at a specified location.

KEY TERMS — MATCHING EXERCISE: Select the term that best completes each statement below.

1. Bulk sale	8. Identification	15. C.I.F.
2. Freight forwarder	9. Entrusting	16. Sale
3. Sale or return	10. F.A.S.	17. Good faith purchaser for value
4. Initial carrier	11. Buyer in the ordinary course	18. Tender
5. Voidable title	12. Risk of loss	19. Destination
6. Bailee	13. Party intent	20. Thief
7. Security interest	14. Sale on approval	

_____1. Steps taken by the seller to choose goods that meet contractual specifications.

_____2. A transfer of goods to a merchant dealing in the type of goods transferred.

_____3. An interest in personal property that protects performance of a promised, future obligation.

_____4. A good faith purchaser for value who purchased from a merchant during normal business hours.

_____5. The interest acquired under circumstances that allow former owner-vendors to revoke a sale and recapture their prior ownership.

_____6. Burden assumed by either party to a sales contract for destruction or damage to the goods.

_____7. Transfer of title to goods under which buyer retains an option to revest title in the seller.

_____8. Controls title passage for identified, existing goods.

_____9. Transfer of goods for a period of time during which buyer determines whether or not to purchase them.

_____10. A transfer for value not in the ordinary course of business, of a substantial portion of the equipment, materials, inventory, supplies or merchandise of the business.

_____11. Someone lacking both the power and right to sell goods.

_____12. One buying goods honestly without knowledge of any title problems.

_____13. Transferring title to goods for a price.

_____14. Contract requiring seller to ship goods to a specific location.

_____15. Duty of seller to make conforming goods available to the buyer for a reasonable time and notify the buyer of this fact.

MULTIPLE CHOICE: Select the alternative that best completes each statement below.

_____1. A reason for the legal policy to protect existing ownership of goods is to (a) make transfers easier (b) protect involuntary bailees (c) ensure that people are not required to retain possession or control of goods at all times to maintain their ownership in them (d) none of the above.

_____2. The controversy that commonly follows a non-owner's sale of goods pits a (a) non-owner against an owner (b) non-owner against a good faith purchaser for value (c) good faith purchaser for value against an owner (d) none of the above.

_____3. Bulk transfers exempted from U.C.C. Article 6 coverage include (a) transfers settling a security interest (b) sales by bankruptcy trustees (c) sales by personal representatives (executor/ executrix) (d) all of the above.

_____4. Code requirements making bulk transfers valid against creditors of the bulk transferor include (a) central filing by the transferee (b) notice of the transfer by the transferee to all listed creditors of the transferor (c) a conditional pledge signed by the transferor (d) a recorded factor's lien.

_____5. When the seller alone has identified goods to the contract, other goods may be substituted by the seller until the seller (a) defaults (b) becomes insolvent (c) notifies the buyer of final identification (d) all of the above.

_____6. Persons holding void and therefore no title include (a) finders (b) bailors (c) people acquiring goods through undue influence (d) all of the above.

_____7. Examples of voidable title include acquisition through (a) mistake (b) fraud in the execution (c) sale or gift from someone under guardianship (d) all of the above.

_____8. A/n _____ is delivering personal property to an agent for sale by that person. (a) allocation (b) approval transfer (c) consignment (d) none of the above.

_____9. Under a sale on approval, the buyer's failure to reasonably notify the seller of an election to return the goods is (a) identification (b) acceptance (c) ratification (d) consignment of the goods.

_____10. Under the U.C.C., risk of loss is determined by who (a) holds title to the goods (b) has greater control over the goods (c) occupies the position of equitable receiver (d) all of the above.

_____11. The Code's approach to risk of loss is (a) a transactional approach (b) based on state-secured credit laws (c) generally outmoded and antiquated (d) none of the above.

_____12. The Code treats a consignment sale as (a) one on approval (b) a bailment (c) a sale or return (d) a lease.

_____13. Generally in cases of breach of contract, the Code places the risk of loss (a) on both parties equally (b) on the offeror (c) on the party financing the transaction (d) on the non-performing party.

CASE PROBLEMS — SHORT ESSAY ANSWERS: Read each case problem carefully. Answer by stating a Decision for the case and by explaining the rationale — Rule of Law — relied upon to support your decision.

1. A makes a bulk transfer purchase of B's goods. B failed to comply with U.C.C. provisions regulating bulk sales. B turns over the net proceeds of the sale to creditors but the amount covers only 50% of the outstanding debt. The creditors seek to avoid the transfer to A and have the goods returned. A vigorously opposes the creditor's action. Who wins this dispute?

Decision: _____

_____

Rule of Law: _____

2. B pays cash for goods purchased from S. Unable to take immediate delivery, B arranges for the goods to remain with S for a week and a half. Three days following the sale to B, S sells the same goods to C, who takes delivery. B, upon returning for delivery, learns of the sale to C and seeks to replevin the goods from C. C resists. Who has title to the goods?

Decision: _____

_____

Rule of Law: _____

3. A transfers a fur coat to retail furrier B for repair and storage. During B's regular business hours, C purchases the coat from B. What are A's rights against purchaser C? Explain.

Decision: _____

_____

Rule of Law: _____

4. Owner of grain stored in E's elevator sells the grain to B. Every bushel of grain in the elevator is covered by an outstanding negotiable document of title evidencing ownership. Upon selling the grain in the elevator, owner delivers the title document to the buyer. Shortly thereafter, the elevator burns with all contents lost. Who bears the loss for the sold grain, elevator owner, grain owner or buyer? Explain.

Decision: _____

_____

Rule of Law: _____

5. Francine goes to Mary's bridal shop to select her wedding gown. Francine chooses a gown to her liking and pays the purchase price of $1280. She leaves the gown with Mary so a train and waist ruffles can be sewn on. Mary completes her work and calls Francine telling her the dress is ready for pickup. Later that evening, vandals break into Mary's shop, causing considerable damage, including setting Francine's dress on fire, making it worthless. Advise Francine and Mary of their rights and responsibilities at this point.

Decision: _____

_____

Rule of Law: _____

Chapter 24

PRODUCT LIABILITY: WARRANTIES AND STRICT LIABILITY IN TORT

SCOPE NOTE

The purchaser of goods expects that they will conform to certain quality and title standards. When a seller's performance falls below such standards, when goods are defective, a breach of warranty usually exists making the seller liable for resulting damages. What protection is given the buyer against title/quality defects? What guarantees run to the innocent purchaser providing protection against unfair/dishonest business practices? In the following chapter, these issues are focused upon in terms of basic terminology and the principles of warranty law contained in the U.C.C. Additionally, defective products may cause personal or property damage to the buyer or other persons. Who is liable to whom for such injury, and on what basis? Chapter 24 closes with these considerations.

EDUCATIONAL OBJECTIVES

1. Identify the types of transactions to which warranty law applies.

2. Enumerate the various categories of express and implied warranties and how they are created.

3. Discuss how the "Puffing Doctrine" and the Parol Evidence Rule affect warranty protection.

4. Analyze how caveat emptor interacts with warranty liability.

5. Explain the various U.C.C. requirements for validity excluding/limiting warranty protection, both express and implied.

6. Identify the roles played by the doctrine of privity, the trade usage doctrine and the buyer's examination duty in warranty considerations.

7. Discuss the Code's application of warranty protection to third parties.

8. Identify significant changes brought to warranty law by the enactment of federal warranty legislation.

9. Explain the influence of contributory negligence and assumption of risk on warranty liability.

10. Explain strict liability and its relevance to product liability cases.

11. Outline burden of proof requirements under strict liability and demonstrate how they apply to cases of personal injury caused by defective goods.

12. Review the impact of contributory negligence and assumption of the risk in product liability cases.

CHAPTER OUTLINE

I.   **Warranties** — seller's obligation regarding satisfactory performance (quality, title, quantity, etc.) in sales of goods, action of recovery for defective products
   A.   **Types of Warranties** — created by agreement (express) or by operation of law (implied)
      1.   Warranty of title — good title; valid transfer; no encumbrances; no infringements
      2.   Express warranties — created by parties; oral or written statements of fact; basis of bargain (buyer's reliance)
         a.   No formal wording required
         b.   Puffing, sales talk (value, opinion statements) exclusion
         c.   Sales by sample, model or description
      3.   Implied warranties — created by law
         a.   Merchantability — merchant seller; fit for ordinary purpose; average quality; adequately packaged, labeled; applies to food and drink
         b.   Fitness for particular purpose — applies to any seller; seller's knowledge of buyer's purpose and buyer's reliance on seller's skill or judgment
   B.   **Obstacles to Warranty Actions** — difficulties, problems associated with claims based on warranty breach
      1.   Disclaimer or modification of warranties — defined by clauses in a contract; Code dictates validity requirements (explicit, conspicuous, timely, unequivocal)
         a.   Express exclusions — Code formalities regarding proper wording; inconsistent disclaimer not effective
         b.   Implied exclusions — conspicuous, written disclaimer including general words ("as is, with all faults")
         c.   Buyer's inspection or refusal to inspect goods — implied warranty negated for obvious defects
         d.   Conflict of warranties — intent of parties controls; guidelines for interpreting intent
         e.   Federal legislation relating to warranties of consumer products — Magnuson-Moss provisions; role of FTC; information disclosure guidelines
         f.   Course of dealing or usage of trade limitations
      2.   Privity of contract — business relationship
         a.   Horizontal privity — rights of recovery for non-contracting parties (users, bystanders) covered by the Code (family members, guests of buyer)
         b.   Vertical privity — liability of remote sellers on distribution chain (manufacturers, wholesalers)
      3.   Notice of breach — buyer's duty to seasonably notify seller of known, knowable defects
      4.   Plaintiff's conduct — as a defense to warranty-based recovery
         a.   Contributory negligence — buyer's carelessness not a defense
         b.   Voluntary assumption of risk — recognized as a valid defense; buyer uses known defective product

II. **Strict Liability in Tort** — merchant seller liability (personal injury, property damage) for defective products that are ultra-hazardous
   A.   **Nature** — applies to merchant sellers, manufacturers, lessors; contrasted to common law negligence and Code warranty liability

      1. Defective condition — plaintiff must prove existence; cause of is not material; existing when product sold
         a. Manufacturing defect — materials or assembly
         b. Design defect — lack of safety features
         c. Inadequate warning, instructions, use directions
      2. Unreasonably dangerous — ultra-hazardous defective condition; ordinary person does not expect danger from ordinary use; product cannot be made safe

B.   **Obstacles to Recovery** — problems recovering under strict liability doctrine
      1. Disclaimers and notice — contractual defenses not valid in consumer transactions; courts allow in commercial dealings
      2. Privity — standing to sue based on business relationship
         a. Horizontal privity — recovery rights in buyers, users, bystanders; broader than Code
         b. Vertical privity — liability in merchant sellers along distribution chain
      3. Plaintiff's conduct — as a defense to strict liability-based recovery
         a. Contributory negligence — generally no defense
         b. Comparative negligence — plaintiff's recovery reduced proportional to own fault
         c. Voluntary assumption of the risk — generally a valid defense; defendant's burden of proof; knowingly using defective product
         d. Misuse or abuse of the product — does plaintiff know action creates danger; is it foreseeable by seller
      4. Subsequent alteration — substantial change in product's condition (after it leaves seller) may be a defense
      5. Statute of Repose — state legislation limiting the time for which manufacturers are liable for defective products

TRUE—FALSE: Circle true or false.

T   F   1. A recent and important development in the area of products liability is the theory of strict liability in tort.

T   F   2. Sellers are always required to warrant goods they sell.

T   F   3. Extending products liability to manufacturers of goods has not reduced the liability of sellers to purchasers of defective goods.

T   F   4. All sellers impliedly warrant the merchantability of the goods they sell.

T   F   5. For the implied warranty of fitness for a particular purpose to apply, the buyer must specifically inform the seller of the express purpose for which the goods are purchased.

T   F   6. The U.C.C. reduces the controlling influence that contractual privity has in breach of warranty disputes.

T   F   7. Under the theory of strict liability in tort, a plaintiff must show how and why a product became defective to establish a recovery right.

T   F   8. Strict liability may not be disclaimed, excluded or modified by contract.

T   F   9. Manufacturers or sellers must warn purchasers of all possible hazards associated with any use of products sold.

T   F   10. Contributory negligence is not an effective defense in a suit against a seller of goods for breach of warranty.

T   F   11. Implied warranties arise by acts of parties and not through operation of law.

T   F   12. Liability for personal injuries caused by unreasonably dangerous, defective goods extends to lease transactions.

KEY TERMS—MATCHING EXERCISE: Select the term that best completes each statement below.

1. Sales acts	8. Caveat emptor	15. Magnuson-Moss Act
2. Contributory negligence	9. Express warranty	16. Trade usage
3. Comparative negligence	10. Assumption of risk	17. Sale on approval
4. Expert	11. Consumer products	18. Merchantable
5. Disclaimer	12. Inspection of goods	19. Waiver
6. Strict liability	13. By sample	20. Statutes of repose
7. Puffing	14. Privity	

_____1. Early rule of common law that placed on buyers total assumption of loss due to defective goods.

_____2. Action on the part of a buyer that nullifies the seller's implied warranty liability for obvious defects.

_____3. Statements of opinion or value made by a seller that are not a basis for warranty liability.

_____4. A seller's statement amounting to a definite assurance regarding the description, quality or condition of goods sold.

_____5. Liability without fault imposed by law as a matter of public policy in sales of defective products posing unreasonably dangerous hazards.

_____6. Voluntarily using a known defective product in the face of danger.

_____7. The contractual relationship that early common law required between a plaintiff and defendant before recovery based upon breach of warranty could be obtained.

_____8. A tort defense that completely bars plaintiffs from any recovery due to self-carelessness.

_____9. An act of Congress seeking to prevent deception and protect consumer purchasers by providing for competent product warranty information.

_____10. The tort doctrine applicable to reduce a plaintiff's damage recovery by the degree of the plaintiff's contributory fault.

_____11. One whose statements of opinion may create warranty liability.

_____12. Of fair, average and medium quality.

_____13. Regular industry customs that may create warranty liability.

_____14. Positive, explicit, unequivocal statements eliminating warranty liability.

_____15. Legislation limiting the time during which manufacturers are liable for injuries caused by products.

MULTIPLE CHOICE: Select the alternative that best completes each statement below.

_____1. The duty to warn of dangers or hazards associated with the use of products arises from (a) the duty of due care (b) specific statutory provisions (c) the spreading of the risk theory (d) none of the above.

_____2. Of the following, who is normally not subject to strict liability in tort? (a) supplier of component parts (b) manufacturer of finished goods (c) purchaser (d) retailer.

_____3. Under the Code, liability of the seller for express warranty is made dependent on whether the statement in question was (a) the basis for the bargain (b) a repudiation of the contract (c) the basis for damages (d) made with the necessary intent.

_____4. The Code's extension of seller warranty applies to (a) employees of the buyer (b) household guests of the buyer (c) guest passengers in the buyer's car (d) all of the above.

_____5. A defense in tort that may be successfully used by the seller against an injured buyer of defective goods in a breach of warranty suit is (a) assumption of the risk (b) res ipsa loquitur (c) contributory negligence (d) equitable cloture.

_____6. Sellers of products are liable for injuries that result from (a) any misuse of a product (b) unanticipatable product abuse (c) foreseeable misuse of a product (d) all of the above.

_____7. Which of the following is not a required element of proof for strict liability under Section 402A, Restatement of Torts, Second Edition? (a) merchant seller (b) life expectancy of product (c) defective condition (d) unchanged condition of the product.

_____8. Implied warranties are excludable by (a) the words "as is" (b) usage of trade (c) course of dealing (d) all of the above.

_____9. The implied warranty of merchantability speaks to goods being (a) safe from any defect (b) suitable for any purpose (c) adequately labeled, packaged and contained (d) all of the above.

_____10. Warranties of quality under the Code generally do not apply to sales of (a) land (b) services (c) stocks (d) all of the above.

_____11. Situations where title warranties do not run with the transaction include (a) sheriff's sales (b) foreclosure sales (c) judicial sales (d) all of the above.

_____12. To maintain a warranty action, a buyer must prove (a) the seller has been notified of the breach; (b) no contributory negligence occurred; (c) the seller was a merchant (d) all of the above.

_____13. _____ privity concerns sellers in the product distribution chain with whom the buyer did not deal (a) equitable (b) vertical (c) horizontal (d) constructive.

CASE PROBLEMS — SHORT ESSAY ANSWERS: Read each case problem carefully. Answer by stating a Decision for the case and by explaining the rationale — Rule of Law — relied upon to support your decision.

1. B, a sportsperson, purchases a handwarmer from a non-merchant neighbor, M. B carries the handwarmer in a coat pocket while hunting and suffers burns when the handwarmer explodes. May B bring suit against M using a strict liability theory for the injuries caused by the defective handwarmer? Explain.

   Decision: _____

   _____

   Rule of Law: _____

2. B buys a used car from S, a used car dealer. B drives the car for two days when suddenly, all four wheels fall off and the steering mechanism collapses. What rights has B against S? Discuss.

   Decision: _____

   _____

   Rule of Law: _____

3. B purchases a bottle of hair coloring. The label contains a conspicuously typed and displayed caution: "WARNING. Always make a patch test before using this product." B applies the coloring, according to its directions, to a table top in an attempt to remove a water stain. The next day, the table is ruined. B sues the manufacturer for the damages to the table. Who prevails and why?

   Decision: _____

   _____

   Rule of Law: _____

4. B purchased 40 lbs. of 1/8" steel rods cut to six-foot lengths. The contract price was $800. When the rods arrived, B accepted them. Sometime later, B discovers that some of the rods are not 1/8" and others are more than six feet. B sues for breach of warranty. The value of the rods accepted was $700. Their value, had they conformed to the contract, would have been $1000. What is the level of B's damages? Explain.

   Decision: _____

   _____

   Rule of Law: _____

5. While eating pieces of fried chicken at Chuck's Chicken Coop, customer C chokes on a chicken bone which becomes stuck in her throat. C sues restaurant owner B for her injuries, arguing that the presence of the inedible bone was a breach of the implied warranties of fitness and merchantability. Evaluate C's argument.

   Decision: _____

   _____

   Rule of Law: _____

Chapter 25

REMEDIES

SCOPE NOTE

Chapter 25 brings to a close our study of the law of sales and its related fields of inquiry by addressing the issues related to inadequate performance under the sales contract. The breadth of remedies made available under the U.C.C. to a non-breaching party are outlined. The purpose of the Code's remedy variety is to enable the non-breaching party to gain the position they would have occupied had the breaching party performed properly. It is vitally important to note the key factors associated with a breach that dictate which particular choice of remedies will be available and efficacious to the innocent, non-breaching party.

EDUCATIONAL OBJECTIVES

1. Describe the pre-acceptance remedies made available to both non-breaching buyer and seller.

2. Outline the pre-acceptance breaching party's rights and duties.

3. Explain the non-breaching party's choice of remedies following acceptance.

4. Define and discuss the implications of anticipatory repudiation.

5. Identify how insolvency of the breaching party affects the choice-of-remedies question.

6. Discuss choice-of-remedy issues in the context of installment contract.

7. Define liquidated damages vis-a-vis the ability of the parties to limit or expand their choice of remedies in the agreement.

8. Evaluate the role of equity in enforcing sales contracts.

CHAPTER OUTLINE

I. **Remedies of the Seller** — triggered by buyer's contract breach (wrongful rejection, wrongful revocation of acceptance, refusal to make payment, repudiation); tied to possession, type and time of breach
   A. **To Withhold Delivery of the Goods** — goods in seller's or warehouser's possession

1. Installment contract — whole contract impaired
2. Buyer's insolvency — demand for cash

B. **To Stop Delivery of the Goods** — goods in carrier's possession; timely notice; cut off by buyer receipt, negotiation of title document

C. **To Identify Goods to the Contract** — follows buyer's anticipatory repudiation; good faith; commercial reasonableness duties

D. **To Resell the Goods and Recover Damages** — good faith commercial reasonable duties; difference between contract price and resale price plus incidental damages, seller not liable for profit

E. **To Recover Damages for Non-acceptance or Repudiation** — market price/contract price difference is standard measure

F. **To Recover the Price** — buyer has accepted goods; no ready resale market; no other adequate damages remedy

G. **To Recover Incidental Damages** — commercially reasonable expenses triggered by buyer's breach

H. **To Cancel the Contract** — terminate agreement and recover damages

I. **To Reclaim the Goods Upon Buyer's Insolvency** — within 10 days after receipt of goods or any time if buyer made fraudulent written assurances of solvency within three months prior to delivery; cut off by buyer's lienors, good faith purchasers or buyers in the ordinary course of business

II. **Remedies of the Buyer** — triggered by seller's wrongful default (failure to deliver conforming goods); duty to act seasonably

A. **To Cancel the Contract** — notice requirement; further performance excused

B. **To Recover Payments Made**

C. **To Cover** — contract for substituted goods; difference between cover costs and original contract price

D. **To Recover Damages for Non-delivery or Repudiation** — difference between market price and contract price

E. **To Recover Identified Goods upon the Seller's Insolvency** — based on buyer's special property interest; full or partial payment by buyer

F. **To Sue for Replevin** — recover goods in seller's possession; goods identified to contract, no adequate cover opportunity

G. **To Sue for Specific Performance** — goods are unique; money damages not effective

H. **To Enforce a Security Interest in the Goods** — to extent of payment made; buyer has possession

I. **To Recover Damages for Breach in Regard to Accepted Goods** — difference between value in defective condition and value as warranted; following acceptance of nonconforming goods and timely notice to seller

J. **To Recover Incidental Damages** — any reasonable expenses in undoing loss from breach

K. **To Recover Consequential Damages** — resulting losses (property or personal) of which seller had notice

III. **Contractual Provisions Affecting Remedies** — Code allows parties to exclude, modify or limit remedies

A. **Liquidation or Limitation of Damages** — contract specifies amount or measure of damages: reasonable approximation of actual loss standard

B. **Modification or Limitation of Remedy by Agreement** — parties may expand or restrict U.C.C. designated remedies; exclusive remedy provision; limited by doctrine of unconscionability

TRUE—FALSE: Circle true or false.

T   F   1. An unpaid seller, faced with a buyer's material breach of the contract or insolvency may properly withhold or stop delivery of the goods.

T   F   2. When a buyer has breached the sales contract, the seller may resell the goods at either a public or private sale.

T   F   3. A bona fide purchaser at a resale takes title to the goods subject to the superior interests of the original buyer when the seller fails to properly notify the breaching original buyer of the time, date and location of the resale.

T   F   4. Failure of a buyer to "cover" upon the seller's breach will bar the buyer from seeking other remedies.

T   F   5. A buyer acquires a special property interest in existing goods when they are identified to the contract.

T   F   6. A provision in a sales contract providing for liquidated damages is void per se.

T   F   7. A sales contract may validly limit consequential damages for commercial loss.

T   F   8. The Code places a four-year statute of limitations for sales contracts breaches commencing at the time the non-breaching party learned of the breach.

T   F   9. An unpaid seller may reclaim goods delivered to a buyer any time after the seller has learned of the buyer's insolvency.

T   F   10. The Code has adopted the common law approach to specific performance.

T   F   11. The goal of Code remedy provisions is to place the non-breaching party in as good a position as if the breaching party had properly performed.

T   F   12. The Code uses both equity and bankruptcy definitions of insolvency.

KEY TERMS — MATCHING EXERCISE: Select the term that best completes each statement below.

1. Equitable insolvency	8. Liquidated damages	15. Dilatory
2. "Cover"	9. Cancellation	16. Punitive damages
3. Bankruptcy insolvency	10. Reclamation	17. Profit
4. Specific performance	11. Highest standard of care	18. Election of remedies
5. Consequential damages	12. Incidental damages	19. Commercial reasonableness
6. Replevin	13. Public sale	20. Breach
7. Penalty	14. Speculative damages	

_____1. Inability to meet debts as they come due.

_____2. Resale of goods at which a non-breaching, unpaid seller may be a purchaser.

_____3. The buyer's remedy to purchase substitute goods elsewhere following the seller's failure to perform properly.

_____4. Remedy available for injury resulting to a person or property caused by breach of warranty.

_____5. An action to recover goods in the possession of and wrongfully withheld by another.

_____6. A provision in a sales contract calling for liquidated damages at an unacceptably high level.

_____7. The non-breaching party's termination of the contract in response to the breaching party's failure of performance.

_____8. Unpaid seller's right to retake goods from an insolvent buyer.

_____9. Commercially reasonable expenses incurred by a seller in connection with the remedies available following a buyer's breach.

_____10. Buyer's equitable remedy compelling seller to deliver conforming goods as described in the sales contract.

_____11. Failure of a contracting party to properly perform contractual duties.

_____12. Seller's remedy when the market price/contract price difference fails to place seller in as good a position as if buyer had performed properly.

_____13. Damages generally not recoverable under the Code.

_____14. Standard merchants must follow when deciding whether to finish manufacturing goods or cease manufacturing or sell the partially finished goods for scrap value.

_____15. Common law doctrine requiring non-breaching party to choose a single remedy to the exclusion of all others.

MULTIPLE CHOICE: Select the alternative that best completes each statement below.

_____1. A seller's right to stop delivery ceases when (a) a carrier acknowledges that goods are held for the seller (b) a bailee acknowledges that goods are held for the buyer (c) goods are rejected by the buyer (d) all of the above.

_____2. A seller may recover as damages against a breaching buyer (a) the difference between the market price and the contract price plus incidental damages (b) the profit that would have been received had the deal gone through plus incidental damages (c) liquidated damages as provided for in the contract (d) any of the above.

_____3. A buyer may exercise a right of cover when (a) conforming goods have been wrongfully rejected (b) the seller has made proper delivery of conforming goods (c) the seller has repudiated the sales contract (d) the buyer has improperly revoked acceptance.

_____4. Identification of goods to the contract may be made by (a) the seller only (b) the buyer only (c) either the seller or buyer (d) the court after an action at law has been brought.

_____5. A sales contract between buyer and seller may (a) not limit a remedy provided for by the Code (b) provide for fewer remedies than those specified in the Code (c) allow for penalties in lieu of stipulated damages (d) none of the above.

_____6. In deciding whether to liquidate goods through public or private sale, a seller (a) must follow normal trade practices and usage (b) need not be concerned about the nature of the goods (c) is generally free to make the choice without any restrictions (d) must follow Code provisions exactly and is allowed no deviation.

_____7. Upon cancellation of a sales contract, (a) the canceling party's duty of future performance is discharged (b) all security interests in the goods are voided (c) a trustee in bankruptcy is treated as an assignee of the contract (d) none of the above.

_____8. A seller's reclamation right is always subject to (a) the buyer's business partners (b) an equitable receiver (c) a buyer in the ordinary course of business from the non-performing purchaser (d) a bank.

_____9. Following buyer's breach, an unpaid seller may recover the contract price when the (a) buyer has rejected the goods (b) goods are damaged and the risk of loss remains with the seller (c) goods are identified to the contract and they have no resale market value (d) none of the above.

_____10. Insolvency for the purposes of federal bankruptcy law occurs when (a) a receiver is appointed to take control of the debtor's assets (b) the debtor's total liabilities exceed total assets (c) the debtor has stopped making payments on debts during the normal course of business (d) a fraudulent conveyance has been made.

_____11. When the buyer has breached the sales contract, the seller _____ unfinished goods (a) may cease manufacture and resell them for scrap (b) may finish their manufacture and identify them to the contract (c) must use reasonable judgment to minimize losses (d) all of the above.

_____12. When liquidated damages are provided for they must be (a) provable through appraisal (b) commensurate with the anticipated or actual losses (c) no more than $500 (d) supported by affidavits of value.

_____13. A buyer who has "covered" the seller's breach may recover (a) all losses (b) the difference between the cost of "cover" and the contract price plus incidental or consequential damages (c) b above minus expenses saved as a result of the seller's breach (d) none of the above.

CASE PROBLEMS — SHORT ESSAY ANSWERS: Read each case problem carefully. When appropriate, answer by stating a Decision for the case and by explaining the rationale — Rule of Law — relied upon to support your decision.

1. B breaches a sales contract and S elects to resell the goods. The contract price called for a $10,000 payment from B. The resale realized $18,000 for S. In a suit by B against S for the excess above the contract price, what might B recover and why?

Decision: _____

_____

Rule of Law: _____

2. B ordered $10,000 worth of grade A grotaberries from S. On May 1, S shipped grade A wingaberries that were rightfully rejected by B. The following day, B bought grade A grotaberries on the open market from another supplier for $9,000. In a suit against S for the breach, what are the damages recoverable by B? Explain

Decision: _____

_____

Rule of Law: _____

3. B enters a contract with S for the sale of $10,000 worth of feather dusters. The dusters were labeled with B's name at S's warehouse. On July 10, B makes a $2,500 advance to S. A day later, B learns that S is insolvent. Fearing a loss of both the money and the goods, B seeks your advice. What should be done to protect B's interests?

Decision: _____

_____

Rule of Law: _____

4. B receives a shipment of nails from a building materials supplier S that are nonconforming to the contract. B had made a down payment of $200 on the contract. B writes to S and notifies S of an intent to reject the nails. Three months pass without B receiving any reply from S. What may B do? Discuss.

Decision: _____

_____

Rule of Law: _____

5. Art dealer A contracts with art collector C to purchase one of C's Rembrandt paintings. Later, because of the painting's sentimental value, C repudiates the contract. In a suit by A against C, what remedy will A most likely seek? Explain.

Decision: _____

_____

Rule of Law: _____

SALES UNIT RESEARCH QUESTIONS: Drawing upon information contained in the text, as well as outside sources, discuss the following questions.

1. In response to performance breakdowns in new cars, some states have adopted what is popularly known as new car Lemon Laws. Explain the rationale for these laws and identify their significant provisions. What are the advantages and disadvantages of these laws? Does your state have such a law? Explain why you support or oppose your state's position on this issue?

2. In the past two decades, the incidence of product liability lawsuits has grown dramatically. What factors have contributed to this litigation "explosion?" What beneficial and negative consequences flow from this development? What changes in the law, as well as management policies and practices, have been/should be made to meet financial burdens created by the increased incidence of product liability lawsuits?

PART FIVE: Commercial Paper

Chapter 26

FORM AND CONTENT

SCOPE NOTE

Commercial paper occupies a crucial position in today's marketplace. Commerce moves on written contracts to pay sums of money that pass for and are accepted as money in most marketplace transactions. This chapter introduces the law regulating the issuance and use of commercial paper. The development of the law of commercial paper is traced and the most commonly used forms of commercial paper are explained. Also discussed is the key concept of negotiability. The terminology and rules addressed in Chapter 26 form a useful basis for understanding the subsequent chapters on commercial paper law.

EDUCATIONAL OBJECTIVES

1. Explain the importance and function of commercial paper in today's business.

2. Compare creating commercial paper performance duties to contractual performance duties.

3. Define and discuss the significance of negotiability.

4. Identify the essential elements of a negotiable instrument.

5. Differentiate contract assignment from negotiating commercial paper.

6. Discuss the effect on negotiability of various provisions/omissions in a written promise to pay.

7. Distinguish the essential characteristics of the various forms of negotiable commercial paper.

8. Identify the rights/duties of parties under the various types of commercial paper.

CHAPTER OUTLINE

I. **Negotiability** — commercial paper (notes, drafts, checks) passes for money: convenience; safety; facilitates credit extension for business financing

II. Types of Commercial Paper — depends on number, status of parties, and statements made on instrument
   A.   **Order to Pay** — three-party instrument: drawer; drawee; payee
       1. Drafts — time; sight; bank; trade acceptance
       2. Checks — drawer has funds deposited in drawee; special type of draft
   B.   **Promises to Pay** — two-party instrument; maker, payee
       1. Notes — collateral, installment, mortgage
       2. Certificates of deposit — bank acknowledges money received, makes repayment promise

III. Form of Commercial Paper — requirements for validity and negotiability on the face of the document
   A.   **Writing** — form or type not important
   B.   **Signed** — any authorized means; placement not crucial; by maker or drawer; intentionally made
   C.   **Promise (note) or Order (draft) to Pay** — more than request, authorization or acknowledgment; drawee must be identified
   D.   **Unconditional** — payment rights clear from face of document without reservation or contingency
       1. Statements making paper conditional and non-negotiable
          a. Payment subject to, governed by another agreement
          b. Payment out of specific fund or from specific source
       2. Statements not making paper conditional
          a. Reference to transaction creating instrument
          b. Reference to separate agreement, prepayment, payment acceleration, security interest or fund source
   E.   **Sum Certain in Money**
       1. Money — official medium of exchange; commodity payment makes non-negotiable
       2. Sum certain — present value known from face of document; not effected by interest rate, installment statements so long as reasonably definite
   F.   **No Other Promise or Order** — acts additional to payment; makes document non-negotiable unless related to payment security
   G.   **Payable on Demand or at a Definite Time** — no time designated (on demand, at sight) for demand paper
       1. Time paper includes payment
          a. "On or before"
          b. At a fixed period after a stated date
          c. At a fixed period after sight
          d. At a definite time subject to acceleration
          e. At a definite time subject to extension
       2. Payable upon occurrence of an uncertain act or event — not at a definite time; makes non-negotiable
   H.   **Payable to Order or to Bearer** — words of negotiability
       1. Payable to order — named persons, trust, fund, officer, partnership
       2. Payable to bearer — no payee designated (cash, bearer, etc.)
   I.   **Terms and Omissions and Their Effect on Negotiability**
       1. Absence of statement of consideration — no effect
       2. Absence of statement of where the instrument is drawn or payable — no effect
       3. Sealed instruments — no effect
       4. Dating of the instrument — undated; incorrectly dated; post or antedated — no effect

5. Incomplete instruments — awaits authorized completion; unauthorized completion is material alteration

6. Ambiguous instruments — construed to favor negotiability; draft or note; words and figures conflict

J.   **Non-complying Instrument** — transferable, enforceable contract

TRUE—FALSE: Circle true or false.

T   F   1. A promise to pay out of a specific fund is conditional and renders commercial paper non-negotiable.

T   F   2. An acceleration clause in commercial paper destroys negotiability because of the uncertainty of the due date.

T   F   3. A certificate of deposit is a written receipt for deposited money with a financial institution that the latter promises to pay out at some future date.

T   F   4. The location of a maker's signature on a promissory note affects its enforceability and negotiability.

T   F   5. The U.C.C. requires that for commercial paper to be negotiable, it must be payable on demand or at a definite time.

T   F   6. Antedating or postdating commercial paper destroys its negotiability.

T   F   7. Failure to state on commercial paper its place for payment does not automatically destroy negotiability.

T   F   8. Omitting the words "order," "bearer" or their equivalent makes a note non-negotiable.

T   F   9. A note payable, "Sixty days after Maker's death," is negotiable under the U.C.C.

T   F   10. Commercial paper made payable "to order of cash" is a bearer instrument.

T   F   11. The negotiability of an instrument must be determined on its face without further inspection, inquiry or reference to another source.

T   F   12. A bank draft is a form of promissory note.

KEY TERMS — MATCHING EXERCISE: Select the term that best completes each statement below.

1. Trade acceptance	8. Negotiability	15. Drawee
2. Money	9. Credit device	16. Variable interest rate
3. Acceleration	10. Assignment	17. Promissory note
4. Time draft	11. Sum certain	18. Check
5. Sight drafts	12. Cashier's check	19. Time paper
6. Installment	13. Collateral note	20. Barter
7. Bearer	14. Non-negotiable	

_____1. Instruments payable immediately upon presentation to the drawee.

_____2. A medium of exchange adopted by a government as its currency.

_____3. An instrument payable only upon the occurrence of a future, uncertain event or act.

_____4. A check drawn by a bank on itself payable to the order of a named payee.

_____5. A three-party instrument payable on a specific future date.

_____6. A legal concept that allows written documents to be easily used as money substitute forms of payment.

_____7. The determinable minimum payment to be made on commercial paper.

_____8. The person ordered to pay a draft.

_____9. A clause that gives a payee the right to demand payment before a note is mature.

_____10. An instrument drawn by the seller of goods on their purchaser made payable to the seller.

_____11. A use for negotiable instruments other than as a substitute for money.

_____12. A two-party negotiable instrument.

_____13. Instruments payable at a definite time.

_____14. Provision in commercial paper judicially interpreted to make the instrument nonnegotiable.

_____15. The most common form of commercial paper.

MULTIPLE CHOICE: Select the alternative that best completes each statement below.

_____1. An order to pay a sum certain is conditional if an instrument (a) states its consideration (b) specifies it is subject to another agreement (c) indicates it is secured by a mortgage (d) refers to the transaction that created it.

_____2. The signature of the maker of a note may be (a) under an assumed name (b) a thumb print (c) made by an authorized agent (d) all of the above.

_____3. The primary obligor on a promissory note is the (a) acceptor (b) cosigner (c) payee (d) none of the above.

_____4. An instrument that is an order by one party upon another party to pay a third party is a (a) promissory note (b) draft (c) bond (d) collateral note.

_____5. Negotiability of an instrument is adversely affected by (a) not dating the instrument (b) a clause authorizing payment in goods (c) a clause providing for extension of the maturity date (d) its being under seal.

_____6. To be negotiable, commercial paper must be (a) signed by its maker (b) an unconditional promise to pay a sum certain (c) payable on demand or at a definite time (d) all of the above.

_____7. Negotiability applies to (a) warehouse receipts (b) investment securities (c) bills of lading (d) all of the above.

_____8. The various types of commercial paper are generally called (a) instruments (b) documents of title (c) payment contracts (d) none of the above.

_____9. An undated instrument made payable "two days after the date" (a) is negotiable (b) lacks consideration (c) is not negotiable (d) is complete on its face.

_____10. Commercial paper that does not specify a payment date is (a) demand paper (b) non-negotiable (c) fatally incomplete (d) all of the above.

_____11. Which of the following is not a type of commercial paper? (a) certificate of deposit (b) bill of lading (c) draft (d) promissory note.

_____12. The bank upon which a check is drawn is the (a) drawer (b) drawee (c) payee (d) accommodation party.

_____13. An instrument payable to "John Doe, County Collector of Cook County" is payable (a) to order (b) to bearer (c) on condition (d) to accommodation.

CASE PROBLEMS — SHORT ESSAY ANSWERS: Read each case problem carefully. When appropriate, answer by stating a Decision for the case and by explaining the rationale — Rule of Law — relied upon to support your decision.

1. B purchases a television set from S and executes a 30 day note that reads, "nine hundred ($90) dollar purchase price." S accepts the note and is later faced with B asserting the $90 is the cost of the transaction. B steadfastly refuses to pay $900. S sues B for the $810 difference. Who wins the dispute?

Decision: _____

_____

Rule of Law: _____

2. M executes a promissory note payable to P in 25 days. The note contains a provision allowing M to extend the maturity date for an additional fifteen days. What effect does the extension option have on the note's negotiability? Explain.

Decision: _____

_____

Rule of Law: _____

3. M's 90 day $100 note at 6% interest, payable to P, provides for the addition of collection costs to the amount due if the holder has to resort to legal procedures for collection. Is this a negotiable instrument? Explain.

Decision: _____

_____

Rule of Law: _____

4. M executes a promissory note by typing the necessary information on a sheet of paper and signing it with a rubber stamp. Has the note been properly signed? Discuss.

Decision: _____

_____

Rule of Law: _____

5. M writes out in longhand, with an affixed signature, "I owe C $150," and dates the instrument. C transfers the memorandum to D to discharge a debt C owed D. Does D have an enforceable right of payment against M? Explain.

Decision: _____

_____

Rule of Law: _____

Chapter 27

TRANSFER

SCOPE NOTE

Usually a negotiable instrument will have a useful life extending beyond the transaction that created it. The first taker of commercial paper most likely will transfer it to another person. The process followed in effectively transferring the rights/duties contained in negotiable instruments to other parties is discussed in the following chapter. Requirements for a valid transfer—negotiation—are explained in Chapter 27 in relation to the different types of commercial paper.

EDUCATIONAL OBJECTIVES

1. Distinguish the definitional elements and effects of transfer by assignment from those of negotiation.

2. Identify the various types of indorsement and their respective uses.

3. Summarize the rights/duties of the parties to an indorsement.

CHAPTER OUTLINE

I. **Transfer and Negotiation** — assignment (non-negotiable paper; transferee not a holder); contrasted to negotiation (negotiable paper makes transferee a holder); by delivery for bearer paper or delivery and indorsement for order paper. Delivery: actual, constructive, transfer of possession

II. **Indorsements** — transferor's signature; type determines right and duties of parties; indorser secondarily liable to holder
   A. **Method of Indorsement** — formalities; affects how instrument is transferred but not its negotiability
      1. Written by holder or agent
      2. On instrument or attached paper
      3. Transfers full value, partial assignment if less
      4. Words of negotiability not required
      5. Not affected by assignment, waiver, disclaimer, conditional, guarantee wording
      6. Payee must indorse if written to order of named payee
      7. Transferee may request transferor's indorsement for bearer paper

B. **Blank Indorsements** — mere signature; bearer paper; controls negotiation method; negotiable by delivery; converts order paper to bearer paper

C. **Special Indorsements** — signature and specified payee; order paper; controls negotiation method; negotiable by delivery and indorsement; converts bearer paper to order paper

D. **Restrictive Indorsements** — restrictions on indorsee's payment rights; controls indorser's payment liability; no effect on maker/drawer liability; no effect on negotiability; contrasted to non-restrictive
1. Conditional indorsements — payment subject to an event
2. Indorsements prohibiting further transfer — unrestricted
3. Indorsements for deposit or collection — in banking process
4. Indorsements in trust — first taker must comply with

E. **Qualified Indorsements** — "without recourse"; limits indorser's liability; contrasted to unqualified indorsements

F. **Negotiations Subject to Rescission** — negotiation valid even though transaction is void or voidable

TRUE—FALSE: Circle true or false.

T F 1. A finder of lost bearer commercial paper can become a holder.

T F 2. An indorsement "pay to the order of Mary" is a blank indorsement.

T F 3. The usual way to disclaim indorser's liability is to add the words "without recourse" along with the indorser's signature.

T F 4. The transferee of an instrument can be a holder either by negotiation or by assignment.

T F 5. Trust indorsements make the indorser a fiduciary.

T F 6. Under the U.C.C., a properly worded restrictive indorsement may prevent further transfer or negotiation of the instrument.

T F 7. A conditional indorsement is a type of restrictive indorsement.

T F 8. A blank indorsement transforms a bearer instrument into an order instrument.

T F 9. An indorsement "for collection" places the instrument within the banking system for deposit or collection.

T F 10. A qualified indorsement terminates negotiability and stops further negotiation of the paper.

T F 11. Absent any agreement of assignment, it is presumed that in transfers for value, the parties intend for a negotiation to occur.

T F 12. It is preferable from the transferee's standpoint to take an instrument by assignment and not by negotiation.

KEY TERMS — MATCHING EXERCISE: Select the term that best completes each statement below.

1. Holder	8. Payor	15. Negotiation
2. Shelter rule	9. Qualified	16. Order paper
3. Transfer	10. Conditional indorsement	17. Equitable
4. Blank	11. Collection indorsement	18. Assignment
5. Signature	12. Trust indorsement	19. Warranty
6. Assignee	13. Special indorsement	20. Restrictive
7. Bearer paper	14. Allonge	

_____1. An indorsement bearing only the indorser's signature, designating no indorsee.

_____2. A separate document containing an indorsement firmly affixed to commercial paper.

_____3. Simplest form of indorsement.

_____4. One possessing commercial paper drawn, issued or indorsed to the possessor, the possessor's order, or in blank.

_____5. Transferring commercial paper that makes the transferee a holder.

_____6. An act specifying the person to whom or to whose order an instrument is payable.

_____7. An act that makes the rights of an indorsee subject to the occurrence of a certain event.

_____8. The legal doctrine granting a non-holder transferee the rights of a holder if the transferee takes the instrument from a holder in due course.

_____9. Indorsing an instrument with the words "payment to A for B."

_____10. Commercial paper transferred by possession alone, making it equivalent to cash.

_____11. Transferring of commercial paper by which the transferee does not become a holder.

_____12. A "for deposit only" indorsement.

_____13. Commercial paper that must be indorsed for proper transfer.

_____14. Transferee of commercial paper who is not a holder.

_____15. Liability of the indorser that is not affected by a qualified indorsement.

MULTIPLE CHOICE: Select the alternative that best completes each statement below.

_____1. Transferring non-negotiable commercial paper operates as a/n (a) negotiation (b) indorsement (c) accommodation (d) assignment.

_____2. An indorsement reading "Pay Sue only" is treated as a/n (a) conditional indorsement (b) assignment (c) unrestricted indorsement (d) subsequent cancellation by the Code.

_____3. All indorsements disclose the (a) type of interest transferred (b) liability of the indorser (c) method of subsequent negotiation (d) all of the above.

_____4. Fraud (a) has no effect on a properly negotiated instrument (b) invalidates negotiation (c) prevents the transferee from becoming a holder (d) makes an instrument void.

_____5. An indorsement must always be (a) in ink (b) witnessed by at least two other people (c) either written on the instrument or on an allonge (d) written twice wherever used.

_____6. When the payee of a check simply signs a name on the back of the check without anything more, the indorsement is (a) special, qualified and nonrestrictive (b) blank, unqualified and nonrestrictive (c) conditional, special and in trust (d) none of the above.

_____7. When an instrument has been made payable to the order of its holder and the holder's name is misspelled, the holder may (a) do nothing since all rights have ceased (b) bring suit and recover against the indorsee (c) legally and equitably change their name for the purpose of securing the instrument (d) indorse the instrument in the misspelled name, in their own name or both.

_____8. Indorsements may be (a) equitable or civil (b) restrictive or nonrestrictive (c) logical or sequential (d) chronological or baited.

_____9. An indorsement containing the words "without recourse" is a/n (a) blank (b) qualified (c) Drach (d) unqualified.

_____10. An unqualified indorser guarantees (a) payment only if specific conditions have been met (b) that value has been given for the instrument (c) payment on the instrument (d) that all persons named on the instrument had good title.

_____11. Generally, subject to specified exception, the transfer of an instrument vests in the transferee (a) only those rights the transferor has (b) no new rights (c) fifty percent of the transferor's rights (d) none of the above.

_____12. An order instrument (a) may never be changed to bearer paper (b) may be changed to bearer paper by a blank indorsement (c) may be changed to bearer paper only if done within 24 hours after receipt (d) none of the above.

_____13. The words "Pay Alex" (a) are sufficient to make an instrument negotiable (b) fail the specificity test for valid indorsement (c) make an instrument bearer paper (d) are sufficient to make an order indorsement.

CASE PROBLEMS — SHORT ESSAY ANSWERS: Read each case problem carefully. When appropriate, answer by stating a Decision for the case and by explaining the rationale — Rule of Law — relied upon to support your decision.

1. X issued a note "payable to the order of Y" Y indorses the note "Pay to Z only if Safe-Way Airlines Flight 602 arrives at Hollman Field by 2:30 p.m., August 23, 1980." On August 20th, 1980, Z presents the note to X for payment. X refuses to honor the note, arguing the controlling influence of Y's indorsement. Z sues X for wrongful dishonor of the note. What result?

   Decision: _____

   _____

   Rule of Law: _____

2. X indorses a $1,000 note, "Pay Y $650 of this note." What is the effect of this indorsement? Explain.

   Decision: _____

   _____

   Rule of Law: _____

3. M executes a $500 note "payable to bearer" and delivers it to P. P indorses the note "Pay to the order of X." Sometime later, P loses the note and F finds it. F presents the note to M for payment. Must M honor Fs presentment? Explain.

   Decision: _____

   _____

   Rule of Law: _____

4. T steals a $250 bearer note from P. T sells the note to B who presents it for payment. Is B rightfully entitled to payment?

   Decision: _____

   _____

   Rule of Law: _____

5. A indorses an instrument to B in blank. Assuming B is the holder, what can B do to prevent the instrument from being treated as cash? Discuss.

   Decision: _____

   _____

   Rule of Law: _____

Chapter 28

HOLDER IN DUE COURSE

SCOPE NOTE

As a general rule of contract law, assigning rights under a contract not only creates in the assignee the same rights held by the assignor but also exposes the assignee to liability on the defenses to performance that could have been validly asserted against the assignor. This latter fact, in the marketplace of commercial paper, would constitute a substantial cloud on the marketability and usefulness of these instruments. Chapter 28 addresses the circumstances under which this vulnerability of the taker of a negotiable instrument is removed, thus enhancing the transferability of the instrument. The Holder in Due Course doctrine is focused upon. How must a taker of a negotiable instrument acquire it to achieve holder in due course status? What are the benefits of such status? Under what circumstances may a holder in due course still face non-payment vulnerability? These are the type of issues that are the focus of discussion in the following chapter.

EDUCATIONAL OBJECTIVES

1. Identify and discuss the significance of the requirements that must be met to acquire holder in due course status.

2. Explain situations where, even though holder in due course requisites have been met, the status will be denied the holder.

3. Define and discuss the significance of the Shelter Rule.

4. Distinguish the definitional elements of the two major classes of payment defenses.

5. Enumerate the payment defenses effective only against "ordinary" holders.

6. List and understand the importance of payment defenses assertable against all holders of commercial paper.

7. Know the types of contracts that make a holder in due course vulnerable to personal defenses.

CHAPTER OUTLINE

I. **Requirements of a Holder in Due Course** — created by due negotiation of commercial paper; transferee's rights greater than transferor's (obligor may use only real defenses against recipient); contrasted to assignment: transferee's rights; available defenses; non-negotiable paper
   A. **Holder** — transferee with payment rights
   B. **Value** — to extent of consideration actually given (gift, executory promise); purchase of limited interest; past antecedent debt; security for present loan
   C. **Good Faith** — honesty in fact; no actual knowledge of a defense at time of acquisition
   D. **Lack of Defect Notice** — at time of acquisition: actual knowledge; implied knowledge (reason to know from facts, circumstances)
      1. Notice an instrument is overdue — time paper (expired, overdue) or demand paper (reasonable time); acceleration of payment effect
      2. Notice an instrument has been dishonored — payment refusal
      3. Notice of a claim or defense — defect knowable from paper (incomplete, forgery, alteration) or surrounding circumstances (breach of fiduciary duty, title defect, discharge); knowledge not sufficient to place purchaser on notice of claim or defense
         a. Antedated, postdated paper
         b. Paper accompanied by separate agreement
         c. Accommodation signature
         d. Completion of incomplete instrument
         e. Negotiation by a fiduciary
         f. Interest payment default

II. **Holder in Due Course Status** — protected rights to payment superior to former owners of paper
   A. **A Payee May Be a Holder in Due Course** — payee not a party to the issuance of note
   B. **The Shelter Rule** — holder not qualifying as an HDC acquires such rights through a prior HDC; facilitates free negotiability of commercial paper
   C. **Special Circumstances Denying Holder in Due Course Status** — HDC status denied, transferred due to misconduct (participant to fraud, theft, other illegality); non-HDC cannot become HDC by reacquiring paper from HDC

III. **The Preferred Position of a Holder in Due Course** — party obligated to make payment seeks to avoid payment obligation; HDC payment rights superior to former owners
   A. **Real Defenses** — effective against any holder including HDC; usually stems from a void transaction
      1. Minority — as a simple contract defense; state law controls
      2. Void obligations — stemming from illegal transaction, incapacity, extreme duress; state law controls
      3. Fraud in the execution — deception regarding nature of the document; doctrine of estoppel in cases of negligent contribution
      4. Discharge in bankruptcy
      5. Discharge of which the holder has notice
      6. Forgery and unauthorized signature — doctrine of estoppel in cases of negligent contribution
      7. Material alteration — changes obligations of parties (number, relationship); unauthorized completion exception
      8. Statute of Limitations
   B. **Personal Defenses** — not effective against commercial HDC; simple contract defenses not listed above (fraudulent inducement, lack of consideration, theft of bearer paper, non-delivery, slight duress)

IV. Procedure in Recovering on Instrument
   A. Enforcing altered paper according to original terms
   B. Enforcing incomplete paper to completed terms

V. Limitations Upon Holder in Due Course Rights — state and federal law restricting availability of HDC status in consumer credit transactions; FTC notice rule — holder takes subject to claims and defenses (HDC doctrine not applicable to consumer credit transactions)

TRUE OR FALSE: Circle true or false.

T   F   1. The U.C.C.'s definition of good faith stresses honesty-in-fact under a transaction.

T   F   2. An example of failure to give value for the purposes of determining holder in due course status occurs when a holder of an instrument gives it to another person.

T   F   3. Value for the purposes of negotiable instrument law is the same as consideration in the law of contracts.

T   F   4. According to the U.C.C., one who takes a postdated check has notice of a claim or defense and therefore can never become a holder in due course.

T   F   5. The Code does not specify what is reasonable time for the purposes of determining whether a note is overdue.

T   F   6. The U.C.C. specifically states when minority is available as a defense on an instrument and under what circumstances it may be claimed.

T   F   7. Under the Code, holders give value when commercial paper is received as payment of or security for antecedent debts.

T   F   8. A person whose signature has been forged on an instrument is usually liable for payment to holders in due course.

T   F   9. Under the Code, a reasonable time for presentment on a check is 30 days.

T   F   10. The FTC has changed the effect of the holder in due course doctrine in consumer credit transactions.

T   F   11. One who takes an instrument knowing that all previous parties have been discharged may still acquire the status of holder in due course.

T   F   12. A transferee of stolen commercial paper who takes from the person who stole the instrument cannot become a holder in due course.

KEY TERMS — MATCHING EXERCISE: Select the term that best completes each statement below.

1. Shelter Rule	8. Acceleration	15. Cancellation
2. Subjective	9. Void	16. Material alteration
3. Forgery	10. Ratification	17. Dishonor
4. Holder	11. Real	18. Negotiability
5. Objective	12. Bankruptcy	19. Holder in due course
6. Fraud in the execution	13. Personal	20. Certification
7. Estoppel	14. Valid	

_____1. The possessor of a negotiable note who, by its terms, is entitled to payment.

_____2. The test for good faith adopted by the Code.

_____3. Doctrine making signer liable on the instrument even though their signature is forged.

_____4. The act of affixing another person's signature to an instrument without actual, apparent or implied authority.

_____5. Factual misrepresentation inducing a party to sign a note without knowing or having an opportunity to know its nature or material terms.

_____6. Defenses effective against all holders except those in due course.

_____7. Process by which an unauthorized signature is transformed into a valid one.

_____8. Defenses available against any holder, including one in due course.

_____9. Doctrine that transforms a non-due-course holder into a holder in due course if they have taken the instrument from a holder in due course.

_____10. Insolvency proceedings that can operate to discharge a party from any liability on a note to all holders, including those in due course.

_____11. Transferee of negotiable commercial paper who takes instrument for value in good faith and without notice of dishonor, outdatedness or defenses to payment.

_____12. Changing the rights and responsibilities of parties to commercial paper.

_____13. Concept that facilitates free flow of commercial paper.

_____14. Type of contractual obligation giving rise to commercial paper that triggers valid payment defenses against a holder in due course.

MULTIPLE CHOICE: Select the alternative that best completes each statement below.

_____1. Methods of acquiring commercial paper that preclude the transferee from becoming a holder in due course include (a) purchase at a judicial sale (b) acquisition through legal process (c) purchase at a non-regular bulk transaction (d) all of the above.

_____2. Personal defenses include (a) fraud in the inducement (b) forgery (c) bankruptcy discharge (d) all of the above.

_____3. According to the U.C.C., notice of an event is (a) actual awareness of it (b) notification of it (c) reason to know of it (d) all of the above.

_____4. The purpose of the Shelter Rule is to (a) provide marketability of commercial paper to holders in due course (b) guarantee rights of cloture to holders of commercial paper (c) protect interests of all transferees of commercial paper (d) guard against the hardships associated with equitable discharge.

_____5. Real defenses include (a) duress making the transaction void (b) minority (c) fraud in the execution (d) all of the above.

_____6. Material alteration discharges a party on the note when (a) it is made for any purpose (b) done with intent to defraud (c) it specifies payment more than 25 days after the initial payment date (d) done for no value.

_____7. To qualify as a holder in due course, a transferee must acquire an instrument (a) for no value (b) hold possession of it for at least ninety days (c) without notice of certain specified matters (d) for the purpose of subsequent transfer to an heir.

_____8. Signing a negotiable instrument by carbon copy in the induced belief that only an autograph is being given is an example of (a) failure of consideration (b) fraud in the execution (c) non-delivery (d) fraud in the inducement.

_____9. The effect of the FTC rule applying to consumer credit transactions is to make transferees of negotiable paper associated with the transaction (a) holders in due course (b) trustees (c) receivers (d) assignees.

_____10. Shortening the time for payment on a note by operation of a provision in the note is (a) ademption (b) abatement (c) acceleration (d) none of the above.

_____11. Which of the following does not constitute value given? (a) an executory promise (b) a check as security for a debt (c) a check as payment for a debt (d) exchanging negotiable instruments.

_____12. A _____ is protection against liability: (a) claim (b) defense (c) allonge (d) privilege.

_____13. The doctrine that prevents someone from asserting a defense to liability because their conduct caused another person to change their position to their own loss or hardship is (a) negligence (b) lache (c) estoppel (d) trust.

CASE PROBLEMS — SHORT ESSAY ANSWERS: Read each case problem carefully. When appropriate, answer by stating a Decision for the case and by explaining the rationale — Rule of Law — relied upon to support your decision.

1. M issues a $1,000 note payable to P and delivers it. P negotiates the note to H who promises to pay $850 for it by the end of the month, which H does. On payment of the $850, what rights to payment has H acquired, the original value of $1,000 or the $850 that was paid? Explain.

Decision: _____

_____

Rule of Law: _____

2. P fraudulently induces M to execute a $1,000 note payable to P. Following delivery of the instrument, P negotiates the note to holder in due course H, who in turn renegotiates the note back to P. Has P acquired the status of a holder in due course? Discuss.

Decision: _____

_____

Rule of Law: _____

3. M buys a new car with a note payable to seller S reading "thirty-five hundred dollars ($350)." S changes the figure to $3,500 and negotiates the note to H, who attempts to collect from M. M refuses to make payment asserting material alteration by S. Who wins this dispute and why?

Decision: _____

_____

Rule of Law: _____

4. M draws a check on bank B payable to P. P presents the check to bank B for payment. Shortly before a teller at bank B cashes the check, bank B learns that M has issued a stop payment notice due to fraud. Has bank B acquired notice sufficient to preclude it from becoming a holder in due course?

Decision: _____

_____

Rule of Law: _____

5. B purchases for home use, on an $850 installment contract, a riding mower from S. As part of the transaction, B issues a $750 note payable to S for the balance remaining after B's $100 down payment. S negotiates the note to holder in due course H. After three weeks of frustrating, breakdown-ridden use of the new mower, marred by S's refusal to service the defects, B revokes acceptance of the mower and notifies H that the note is being canceled. H refuses to accept B's cancellation, asserting that as a holder in due course the defense of defective goods is not valid against him. Is H correct?

Decision: _____

_____

Rule of Law: _____

Chapter 29

LIABILITIES OF PARTIES

SCOPE NOTE

Payment on commercial paper is the eventual goal of the parties utilizing it. A basic rule regarding payment liability is that no one faces a duty of payment unless their signature appears on the instrument. But, with all names that might appear on an instrument after a number of negotiations, how is the order of payment obligation determined? In Chapter 29, the rules controlling liability for payment are developed. Special attention must be given to the type of instrument used and the relation of the parties to that instrument.

EDUCATIONAL OBJECTIVES

1. Differentiate primary from secondary parties.

2. Identify the types of commercial paper in which the payment obligation is triggered by acceptance.

3. Outline the procedure for acceptance.

4. List the various conditions that must be met, and their respective procedures, before secondary parties are liable on the instrument.

5. Discuss when the conditions precedent for secondary party liability are waived or excused.

6. Explain the meaning and significance of accommodation parties.

7. Distinguish transfer and presentment warranties and explain party liability for breach of those warranties.

8. Explain the effect on payment liability of the problem of conversion.

9. Enumerate the various circumstances that terminate a party's payment obligations on the instrument.

CHAPTER OUTLINE

I. **Contractual Liability** — based on agreement of parties, authorized signature
    A. **Signature** — on commercial paper required for liability; any intended mark, symbol
        1. Authorized signatures — agent, maker, indorser, drawer, principal

2. Unauthorized signatures — forger, agent has liability; ratification and estoppel exceptions
B. **Liability of Primary Parties** — based on authorized signatures; unconditional payment obligation
   1. Makers of notes — payment according to terms; admits payee's existence and authority to indorse; liable for completion of incomplete note but not material alteration
   2. Acceptors of drafts — similar to makers; drawee's acceptance (signed, written promise to honor)
     a. Check certification — discharges drawer, prior indorser
     b. Bank not obligated to certify
     c. Acceptance changing draft terms — holder's refusal; holder's assent
     d. Payment according to terms upon acceptance
C. **Liability of Secondary Parties** — conditional liability based on certain preconditions; liable only when primary parties don't pay
   1. Indorsers and drawers — liability follows order of signatures
   2. Conditions precedent to liability — triggers secondary party contractual liability
     a. Presentment — demand for payment or acceptance against payor (maker, drawee)
       1) Time of presentment — on specific date; reasonable time after sight or issuance; reasonable time after acceleration; reasonable time after liability arises. Reasonable time based on type of paper, trade practices
       2) Check reasonable time — 30 days for drawer, 7 days for indorser liability
     b. Dishonor — refusal to pay or accept; holder recourse against drawer, indorser
     c. Notice of dishonor — midnight deadline rule for banks, other persons; any reasonable manner; from holder to drawer, indorsers
     d. Protest — certified dishonor in cases of foreign drafts; separate document attached to paper
     e. Delay in presentment, notice, or protest excused
     f. Presentment notice or protest excused or waived ("collection guaranteed") — no control over delay; words on instrument
   3. Disclaimer by secondary parties — qualified indorsement (without recourse); warranty liability remains
D. **Liability of Accommodation Parties** — status of accommodating party (signing without consideration in any capacity to lend name to another party); surety liability — recourse against accommodated party
E. **Liability for Conversion** — wrongful payment (on forgery); refusal to pay or return; face amount liability

II. Liability Based on Warranty — exists without preconditions
A. **Warranties on Transfer** — made by transferor for value; liability breadth depends on type of transfer: delivery alone to transferee; delivery with indorsement to any subsequent good faith holder
   1. Good title — rightful transfer
   2. Signatures genuine and authorized
   3. No material alteration
   4. No valid defenses against transferor
   5. No knowledge of insolvency proceedings
B. **Warranties on Presentment** — made by person obtaining payment or acceptance
   1. Good title
   2. Genuineness of signature of maker and drawer — HDC exception
   3. No material alteration — HDC exception

III. Termination of Liability — discharge of payment obligation except against HDC
    A.   **Payment or Satisfaction** — discharges paying party except bad faith restrictive indorsement violations
    B.   **Tender of Full Payment** — discharges interest, court costs, attorneys fees; holder's refusal discharges parties with recourse against tenderor
    C.   **Cancellation and Renunciation** — issue of intent; acts against paper; separate signed writing; surrender of paper to obligor
    D.   **Impairment of Recourse or Collateral** — release or agreement not to sue; suspension of enforcement; jeopardizes value of collateral; express reservation of rights
    E.   **Other Methods of Discharge**
        1. Fraudulent, material alteration — discharges all parties whose contracts are changed
        2. Re-acquisition by prior holder — intervening parties
        3. Unexcused delay, presentment, notice or protest — discharges indorser and drawer to extent of loss caused
        4. Contractual discharge — drawer and indorsers not assenting to acceptance varying draft terms
        5. Certification by holder — drawer and all prior indorsers

TRUE—FALSE: Circle true or false.

T   F   1. Generally a person is not contractually liable on commercial paper unless the person's signature appears on the instrument.

T   F   2. The two recognized types of payment liability for commercial paper are contractual and warranty.

T   F   3. When a check is certified at the request of the holder, the drawer is discharged but not indorsers.

T   F   4. Presentment for payment is prerequisite for a primary party to be liable on a negotiable instrument.

T   F   5. Presentment of an uncertified check should be made within thirty days after its date of issuance in order to hold the drawer of the check liable.

T   F   6. Presentment of an uncertified check should be made within seven days after an indorsement in order to hold the indorser liable.

T   F   7. Notice of dishonor of an instrument must be given in writing.

T   F   8. Someone whose own negligence substantially contributed to their unauthorized signature appearing on an instrument can be liable for payment.

T   F   9. Transfer warranties run to any subsequent good faith holder of the instrument when transfer is by delivery alone without indorsement.

T   F   10. Transferors of negotiable instruments warrant that they have no knowledge of insolvency proceedings pending against the maker, acceptor or drawer of an instrument.

T   F   11. Under the Code, the requirements of presentment and notice of dishonor may be waived.

T   F   12. When a forged instrument has been paid by the drawee, the loss can be shifted to the drawer by charging the latter's account.

KEY TERMS — MATCHING EXERCISE: Select the term that best completes each statement below.

1. Drawer	8. Acceptance	15. Secondary
2. Conversion	9. Protest	16. Primary
3. Drawee	10. Signature	17. Renunciation
4. Certification	11. Dishonor	18. Warranty
5. Acceptor	12. Insolvency proceedings	19. Disclosure
6. Presentment	13. Payment	20. Ratification
7. Accommodation parties	14. Cancellation	

_____1. The promise of a bank to honor a check when it is subsequently presented for payment.

_____2. The drawee bank's refusal to pay the amount stated on a check.

_____3. An act by the holder discharging all parties to an instrument.

_____4. The act that makes the drawee of a draft primarily liable.

_____5. Notice of dishonor made under the hand and seal of a notary public.

_____6. Persons who sign a negotiable instrument for the purpose of lending their credit to another party on the note.

_____7. The tort of wrongfully exercising dominion over another's personal property.

_____8. The demand made by a holder on the maker or drawee for acceptance or payment of the instrument.

_____9. The most obvious way for a party to discharge liability on an instrument.

_____10. A situation totally excusing presentment but not notice or protest.

_____11. Liability imposed on signers and non-signers of commercial paper as a result of the transfer, payment or acceptance of the instrument.

_____12. The type of payment obligation assumed by makers of promissory notes and acceptors of drafts.

_____13. Someone secondarily liable for payment on a check.

_____14. Indicating the intent to accept and be bound by another's unauthorized signature.

_____15. Written statement by a holder giving up right of payment.

MULTIPLE CHOICE: Select the alternative that best completes each statement below.

_____1. Indorsers and drawers of checks have _____ liability for payment (a) primary (b) no (c) secondary (d) tertiary.

_____2. Acceptance of an instrument is effective only when (a) it is in the drawee's own handwriting (b) it is oral (c) it is made within 14 days after issuance (d) none of the above.

_____3. The conditions precedent to the liability of secondary parties do not include (a) protest (b) default (c) notice of dishonor (d) presentment.

_____4. The proper person to make a protest is (a) a bank cashier (b) a United States consul (c) any police officer (d) an equitable receiver.

_____5. Notice of dishonor must be given by a bank on or before midnight (a) on the day of dishonor (b) three days after dishonor (c) on the next banking day following receipt of a dishonor notice (d) within 24 hours after certification.

_____6. To assure that acceptance will be proper, the drawee may require (a) reasonable identification of the person making presentment (b) proof of mature indorsement (c) notice of dishonor (d) certification of protest.

_____7. Examples of conversion include (a) waiver of presentment (b) adoption by protest (c) payment on an instrument bearing a forged indorsement (d) none of the above.

_____8. Check drawers and indorsers may avoid their usual secondary contractual payment obligation by making or indorsing the paper (a) without recourse (b) as accommodation parties (c) without certification (d) none of the above.

_____9. Any mark, made in any manner, that indicates a present intent to validate commercial paper is a (a) protest (b) signature (c) contribution (d) payment.

_____10. Methods by which a party's liability on an instrument may be discharged include (a) material alteration (b) unexcused delay in presentment (c) notice of dishonor (d) all of the above.

_____11. Examples of unauthorized signatures include (a) using rubberized stamps (b) mechanized signatures (c) an agent exceeding authority (d) all of the above.

_____12. Code warranties running with the sale of commercial paper include (a) drawee and payee warranties (b) presenter and transferor warranties (c) statutory and judicial warranties (d) none of the above.

_____13. When bearer paper is transferred by delivery alone, the transferor warrants to all subsequent holders (a) nothing, since warranties in the case run only to an immediate transferee (b) good title (c) no defense (d) no dishonor.

CASE PROBLEMS — SHORT ESSAY ANSWERS: Read each case problem carefully. When appropriate, answer by stating a Decision for the case and by explaining the rationale — Rule of Law — relied upon to support your decision.

1. A maintains a checking account at XYZ Bank, having $1,000 on deposit. A draws a check for $500 in favor of M. A has the check certified by the bank and gives it to M. Before M presents the check for payment, XYZ Bank ceases operations due to insolvency. When M makes presentment for payment, the bank refuses to pay. What can M do? Explain.

Decision: _____

_____

Rule of Law: _____

2. A makes a promissory note in favor of B payable at State Bank in 60 days at 10% interest per month. After 60 days, A is willing and able to pay the note at the bank. B takes a round-the-world tour for a year while the interest builds on the note. A asks your advice about liability on the note and interest. Explain.

Decision: _____

_____

Rule of Law: _____

3. H holds a draft payable at the Trust Bank main office. H meets an official of the drawee on the street and requests payment. The official refuses and says it must be paid at the specified location. Is this a dishonor? Explain.

Decision: _____

_____

Rule of Law: _____

4. M, executing an instrument on behalf of P, signs it "M, as agent" without naming P. The instrument is negotiated to H who seeks payment from M. Who is liable on this document? Explain.

Decision: _____

_____

Rule of Law: _____

5. M executes a note payable to P for $800. P raises the amount to $1,800 and negotiates it to holder in due course H. H presents the note for payment to M who pays the $1,800. Discovering the error a short time later, M seeks reimbursement of the $1,000 overpayment from H. H refuses to pay. Who wins? Explain.

Decision: _____

_____

Rule of Law: _____

Chapter 30

BANK DEPOSITS, COLLECTIONS, AND FUNDS TRANSFERS

SCOPE NOTE

In the past four chapters we have looked at the life cycle of commercial paper—from the drafting of the instrument, through its transfer, to discharge of its parties. This chapter completes the cycle by addressing the procedures attendant to lodging one type of commercial paper—the check—within its payment process—the banking system. Attention is given to the rights and obligations of the various banks along the chain of payment, as well as to the parties to the instrument as controlled by Article 4 of the U.C.C. The discussion closes with an examination of the laws regulating electronic fund transfers.

EDUCATIONAL OBJECTIVES

1. Discuss the collection process and the relationship of payor and collecting banks.

2. Describe the contractual relationship between a bank and its customers.

3. Explain bank liability for wrongfully dishonoring a check.

4. Identify the methods for and effect of stopping payment.

5. Develop the meaning and importance of a customer's duty to inspect monthly statements.

6. Outline bank alternatives upon the death or incompetence of a customer.

7. Enumerate the requisites for and effect of final payment.

8. Explain the importance of electronic fund transfers.

9. Outline the major provisions of the Electronic Fund Transfer Act.

10. Understand the scope, importance and provisions of U.C.C. Article 4A.

CHAPTER OUTLINE

I.   Collection of Items — check clearing, payment procedure to facilitate manageable money flow; deferred posting
   A.   **Collecting Banks** — non-payor bank handling check: depository, clearinghouse, intermediary banks
      1.   Duty of care — handle check properly; liable to depositor for breach
      2.   Duty to act seasonably — midnight deadline rule; "banking day" defined
      3.   Indorsements — typical banking stream indorsements
      4.   Warranties — similar to presentment, transfer warranties
      5.   Final payment — cash; completed posting to drawer's account; unrevoked provisional settlement; cuts off stop order rights
   B.   **Payor Banks** — drawee bank obligated to make payment (sorting, proving, posting or return of items)
      1.   Time limits — over-the-counter presentment; provisional settlement
      2.   Payment order — bank convenience dictates order
      3.   Collection when drawer, payee have accounts at same bank contrasted to differing banks

II. Payor Bank and its Customer
   A.   **Payment of an Item** — out of customer account; insufficient funds; customer indebtedness; stale checks (6-month rule); wrongful dishonor (sufficient funds, check not stale) problems (bank liability for proximately caused damages)
   B.   **Stop Payment Orders** — reasonable time to comply and wrongful payment problems
      1.   Customer's right and notification duty—oral (14-day rule) or written (6-month rule)
      2.   Nondisclaimable bank liability for wrongful payment — customer's loss
      3.   Not effective for certified checks
      4.   Drawer liability to HDC
   C.   **Bank's Subrogation Rights on Improper Payment** — situations of forged signatures, material alterations, forged indorsements: reimburse customer and seek recovery from wrongdoer; doctrine of estoppel against customer for negligence or failure to properly notify bank
   D.   **Customer's Death or Incompetence** — payment until: notice and reasonable opportunity to act upon incapacity adjudication; 10 days after knowledge of death unless effective stop order by interested party
   E.   **Customer's Duties** — reasonable care: examine statements, discover and report errors, forgeries; act promptly; customer recovery rights against bank cut off by expiration of notice deadlines and estoppel

III. Electronic Fund Transfer — computer technology replacing checks
   A.   **Types of Transfers**
      1.   Automated teller machines
      2.   Point of sale systems
      3.   Direct deposits and withdrawals
      4.   Pay-by-phone systems
      5.   Wholesale electronic funds transfers
   B.   **Electronic Fund Transfer Act**
      1.   Disclosure
      2.   Documentation and periodic statements
      3.   Preauthorized transfers
      4.   Error resolution
      5.   Consumer liability

      6. Liability of financial institution
  C. **U.C.C. Article 4A**
      1. Payment order
      2. Parties
      3. Exclusions
      4. Acceptance
      5. Payment order errors

TRUE—FALSE: Circle true or false.

T   F   1. Article 4A of the U.C.C. covers both debit and credit transactions.

T   F   2. Under the Code, deposits made by check are available for immediate drawing by the depositing customer.

T   F   3. Holders of checks have no right to force drawee banks to pay them even when sufficient funds are in the drawer's account to cover the checks.

T   F   4. Any day a bank is open constitutes a banking day.

T   F   5. A stop payment order is never renewable.

T   F   6. A bank may continue to certify or pay checks drawn by a deceased customer for up to ten days after the customer's death, regardless of the bank knowing of the death.

T   F   7. The customer bears a duty of reasonably prompt and careful examination of both the account statements and the paid items made available by the bank.

T   F   8. There are no exceptions to the "midnight deadline" rule in determining whether a bank has acted seasonably.

T   F   9. When an item received by a depository bank has no indorsement, the only recourse open to the bank is to return the item to its customer.

T   F   10. Projections are that electronic fund transfers will replace checks as primary vehicles of payment in commerce.

T   F   11. Collecting banks must use extraordinary care in handling items transferred to it for collection.

T   F   12. A collecting bank has the duty to act seasonably.

KEY TERMS — MATCHING EXERCISE: Select the term that best completes each statement below.

1. Depository	8. Point of sale transfer	15. Stop payment order
2. Float	9. Two years	16. Agency
3. Payor	10. Check	17. Clearinghouse
4. Banking day	11. Pay any bank	18. Nonconsumer electronic transfers
5. Intermediate	12. Collection guaranteed	19. Examination and notice
6. Posting	13. Provisional	20. One year
7. Midnight deadline	14. Final payment	

_____1. The bank at which an item is presented for credit to the payee's account.

_____2. The bank on which an item is drawn.

_____3. The type of initial credit given to a bank's customer before an item is finally paid.

_____4. The concept underlying the determination of whether a bank has met its duty to act seasonably.

_____5. Terminal point in the collection process constituting the turnaround point from which the proceeds of the item begin their return flow.

_____6. A statement countermanding the drawer's order to the bank authorizing it to pay a certain sum of money and charge the amount to the drawer's account.

_____7. An automatic transfer of funds from a bank to a merchant completed through machines at the merchant's place of business.

_____8. The normal indorsement made when a bank forwards an item for collection.

_____9. The term describing a check drawer's use of funds between time of issuance of and final payment on the check.

_____10. The procedure followed by the payor bank in deciding to pay an item and making a record of the payment.

_____11. A group of banks cooperating together to settle accounts with one another on a daily basis.

_____12. Time period in which a customer must report alterations or unauthorized signatures after statements or items are made available to preserve rights against a bank.

_____13. The exclusive focus of U.C.C. Article 4A.

_____14. Relationship between collecting banks and owner of an instrument pending final settlement.

_____15. General duties of bank customers regarding their own accounts.

MULTIPLE CHOICE: Select the alternative that best completes each statement below.

_____1. Customers or collecting banks transferring items in return for settlement or consideration warrant that (a) signatures on the instrument are genuine and authorized (b) no parties in the collection chain have filed for bankruptcy (c) no restrictive endorsements have been made (d) all of the above.

_____2. Reasons why a bank would dishonor a check and return the item include (a) the drawer not holding an account at the bank (b) a forged signature on the item (c) insufficient funds in the drawer's account (d) all of the above.

_____3. Electronic fund transfers are preferred over checks because they (a) eliminate the check drawer's float of funds (b) reduce the time and expense of processing checks (c) both a and b (d) neither a nor b.

_____4. Items received after the cutoff hour fixed by the bank for receipt of such items may be treated as having been received at (a) the beginning of the day of actual receipt (b) the opening of the day after the next banking day (c) the opening of the next banking day (d) none of the above.

_____5. A payor bank is under no obligation to pay an uncertified check that is over (a) six weeks old (b) six months old (c) sixty days old (d) none of the above.

_____6. Steps involved in posting an item include (a) appointing a receiver (b) freezing the drawer's assets (c) verifying a signature (d) all of the above.

_____7. Where the customer's account is not sufficient to pay all items presented, the bank must charge them against the account (a) in the order of their arrival (b) in any order deemed reasonable by the bank (c) in reverse order of their arrival (d) according to their date of issuance.

_____8. When a customer believes that a monthly statement from their bank contains errors, the customer must notify the bank within ___ days of the error (a) 60 (b) 30 (c) 45 (d) 14.

_____9. The steps taken by a bank in presenting an item for collection include (a) choosing a reasonable method of forwarding the item (b) acting within a reasonable time after receipt of the item (c) careful routing of the item (d) all of the above.

_____10. When a bank mistakenly pays a check over a customer's valid stop order, it is liable to the customer for the (a) customer's losses resulting from the payment (b) amount of the payment (c) incidental loss to the bank (d) none of the above.

_____11. Electronic transfers not regulated by E.F.T.A. include transactions between (a) businesses (b) financial institutions (c) businesses and financial institutions (d) all of the above.

_____12. Situations in which a financial institution is not liable for E.F.T. errors include (a) employee negligence (b) equipment failure (c) customer account subject to legal process (d) all of the above.

_____13. The type of relationship between collecting banks and an owner of an item after final settlement is (a) agency (b) debtor-creditor (c) conservatorship (d) none of the above.

CASE PROBLEMS — SHORT ESSAY ANSWERS: Read each case problem carefully. When appropriate, answer by stating a Decision for the case and by explaining the rationale — Rule of Law — relied upon to support your decision.

1. A issues a $750 check to B drawn on A's $600 account with bank C. C honors the item when presented for payment and charges A's account. The bank then seeks the $150 difference from A, plus service charges for the overdraft created. A refuses to pay, maintaining that it was the bank's obligation to dishonor the check since it knew sufficient funds were lacking to cover it. Who wins this dispute? Explain.

Decision: _____

_____

Rule of Law: _____

2. Cathy Consumer, short of cash, decides to withdraw money from her bank account by using her bank card at an automated teller. She discovers, however, that both the bank card and her PIN card are missing from her purse. Searching at home, in her car, at friends' houses and at work leads to nothing. She cannot find the card anywhere. Meanwhile, Frank Fraud, having found Cathy's cards, has made $200 in withdrawals from her account. To what extent, if at all, is Cathy liable for these withdrawals?

Decision: _____

_____

Rule of Law: _____

3. B purchases $20,000 worth of lumber from S, for use in homes B is constructing, with a check drawn on B's $40,000 checking account at PQR Bank. S negotiates the check to holder in due course, H. Much of the lumber B received from S is rotten so B notifies PQR Bank to stop payment. H presents B's $20,000 check for payment, and the bank honors the stop payment notice. What may H do to realize payment on the item? Explain.

Decision: _____

_____

Rule of Law: _____

4. A presents an item to bank R for collection at 2:30 on Friday afternoon. The bank has a 2:00 p.m. cut-off time. On the following Wednesday, bank R forwards the item for collection. The person who was ultimately liable for the item files a bankruptcy petition one day before the item is presented to the person for payment. A claims the bank did not act seasonably. Decide.

Decision: _____

_____

Rule of Law: _____

5. Millionaire spendthrift D issues a check drawn on an account with bank P payable to R for $10,000. Two days earlier, D's relatives had instituted an incompetency proceeding against D seeking to remove his financial responsibility. The court declares D incompetent a day before R presents the $10,000 check to bank P for payment. Unaware of D's adjudication of incompetence, bank P honors the check and charges D's account. The relatives learn of this fact and bring suit against the bank for wrongful payment. Who wins? Explain.

Decision: _____

_____

Rule of Law: _____

COMMERCIAL PAPER UNIT RESEARCH QUESTIONS: Drawing upon information contained in the text, as well as outside sources, discuss the following questions:

1. What effects have advancements in computer technology had on the principles and practice of negotiable instruments law? What changes have occurred/need to occur in the law to accommodate further developments in computer technology and vice versa?

2. Over the past years, Congress has enacted major changes in banking and savings and loan laws. What developments were these new laws intended to meet? Discuss the major provisions of these laws, and the rationale underlying them. How effective have these laws been? Do they need modifying? Explain.

PART SIX: Partnerships

Chapter 31

NATURE AND FORMATION

SCOPE NOTE

Businesses are usually organized in one of three different forms: a sole proprietorship, a partnership, or a corporation. Chapters 31 through 34 develop the law of partnerships and limited partnerships and Chapters 35 through 38 discuss corporate law.

The basis for the discussion of the law of partnership is the Uniform Partnership Act. In Chapter 31, the legal principles associated with the nature and formation of a partnership, we focus our attention on the character of the property interest related to a partnership, and the comparative advantages and disadvantages associated with this form of business organization.

EDUCATIONAL OBJECTIVES

1. Define and discuss the criteria for determining partnership existence.

2. Contrast the types of partnerships and partners.

3. Explain the substantive and procedural requirements for establishing a partnership.

4. Discuss the nature of the property interest held by a partnership.

5. Understand the theories and principles of partnership law included in the Articles of Partnership.

6. Develop the importance of contract law in the formation of a partnership.

CHAPTER OUTLINE

I. **Nature of Partnership**
   A. **Definition** — a partnership is an association of two or more persons as co-owners to carry on a business for profit

B. **Entity Theory** — a legal entity is a unit with the capacity of possessing legal rights and being subject to legal duties
    1. Partnership as a legal entity — the UPA recognizes a partnership as a legal entity distinct from its members for some purposes
    2. Partnership as a legal aggregate — a partnership is an aggregate for some purposes and thus it cannot sue nor be sued in the firm name unless a statute allows it
C. **Types of Partners** — numerous types are listed

II. Formation of a Partnership

A. **Articles of Partnership** — is a written agreement creating a partnership
    1. Statute of Frauds — does not usually apply to a contract for the formation of a partnership and thus no writing is required to create one unless the partnership is to continue for more than one year
    2. Firm name — there are some restrictions on the choice of a name for the partnership
B. **Tests of Partnership Existence** — consists of three components, all of which must be met
    1. Association — the partnership must have two or more persons who agree to be partners
    2. Business for profit — for a partnership to exist, there must be a business for profit in addition to the co-ownership of property
    3. Co-ownership — of a business is essential for the existence of a partnership
C. **Partnership Capital and Property** — total money and property contributed by the partners is the partnership capital, while the sum of all of the partnership assets, including capital, is the partnership property
D. **Rights in Specific Partnership Property** — is in the form of ownership called a tenancy in partnership and each partner is a tenant in partnership
E. **Partner's Interest in the Partnership** — is defined as her share of the profits and surplus
    1. Assignability — a partner may sell or assign her interest in the partnership, but this does not cause dissolution and the new owner or assignee does not become a partner
    2. Creditors' rights — a partner's interest is subject to the claims of that partner's creditors who may obtain a charging order (a type of judicial lien) against the partner's interest

TRUE-FALSE: Circle true or false.

T   F   1. Partnerships pay Federal income tax on the profits they acquire.

T   F   2. Generally, a partnership cannot sue or be sued in its own name in the absence of a permissive statute.

T   F   3. A judgment creditor of a partnership can demand payment of the entire amount of the debt from any one of the partners.

T   F   4. A partnership cannot acquire title to real property in its own name.

T   F   5. A partnership must be organized as a business for profit.

T   F   6. The fact that two or more persons own property jointly in itself establishes a partnership.

T   F   7. Unless each partner takes an active part in the management of the firm, a partnership does not exist.

T   F   8. The Statute of Frauds does not specifically cover contracts for the establishment of a partnership.

T	F	9. Under common law, a partnership was considered an entity.
T	F	10. The Uniform Partnership Act (U.P.A.) is a primary source of partnership law in all states except Louisiana.
T	F	11. A partner may not sell or assign her interest in the partnership.
T	F	12. A partner's interest in the partnership is subject to the claims of that partner's individual creditors.

KEY TERMS — MATCHING EXERCISE: Select the term that best completes each statement below.

1. Partnership	8. Capacity	15. Equitable partner
2. Capital	9. Secret partner	16. Partnership agreement
3. Sole proprietorship	10. Legal entity	17. Surplus
4. Ostensible partner	11. Joint stock company	18. Charging order
5. General partner	12. Subpartner	19. Statute of Frauds
6. Nominal partner	13. Partnership property	20. Joint venture
7. Limited partner	14. Silent partner	

_____1. The sum of all of the partnership assets.

_____2. A person who is not a partner but who is entitled to share profits of a partnership.

_____3. A group of persons acting as co-owners to carry on a business for profit.

_____4. Another name for a partner by estoppel.

_____5. Partners who are liable for a firm's debt only to the extent of their own capital contributions.

_____6. A unit that has the acknowledged capacity to possess legal rights and to be subject to legal duties.

_____7. A real partner who plays no part in the management of the business.

_____8. A key factor determining whether a natural person may become part of a partnership.

_____9. Form of business organization in which one person operates the enterprise alone.

_____10. Aggregate total of money and property committed to the operation of a business enterprise.

_____11. A form of business association, not a partnership, organized to accomplish a single business transaction.

_____12. Another name for the articles of partnership that creates the partnership.

_____13. A type of judicial lien a creditor may obtain against a partner's interest.

_____14. A partner who has unlimited liability for partnership debts, full management powers, and who shares in the profits.

_____15. A partner whose membership in the partnership is not disclosed to the public.

MULTIPLE CHOICE: Select the alternative that best completes each statement below.

_____1. Title to real property that becomes a partnership asset may be conveyed (a) in the name of the partnership according to the U.P.A. (b) only to an individual partner (c) only in the names of all the partners (d) none of the above.

_____2. Which of the following is not a test for determining the existence of a partnership? (a) co-ownership (b) conducting a business (c) profit sharing (d) business experience.

_____3. One of the following could be a partnership: a (a) medical clinic (b) political organization (c) literary society (d) charitable foundation.

_____4. A real partner, who is both a silent and a secret partner, is called a (a) dormant partner (b) special partner (c) subpartner (d) nominal partner.

_____5. Sharing of profits, sharing of losses, and the right to manage and control the business are specific tests for determining (a) proprietorship (b) co-ownership (c) corporate existence (d) all of the above.

_____6. The capacity in which partners hold themselves out to the world is as an (a) equitable shareholder (b) investor (c) agent (d) irrevocable donee.

_____7. The partnership name (a) must include the name of all the partners (b) may be a fictitious name (c) must include the name of at least one of the partners (d) may be the same name as an existing corporation.

_____8. The Uniform Partnership Act holds that no inference that a partnership exists can be made where profits are received in payment of (a) a debt (b) wages (c) an interest on a loan (d) all of the above.

_____9. Contributions by a partner to the partnership may include (a) services (b) property (c) money (d) all of the above.

_____10. The capacity in which the Internal Revenue Service views a partnership is as (a) an entity (b) a nontaxable proprietorship (c) an aggregate (d) none the above.

_____11. The Uniform Partnership Act broadly defines "person" to include (a) individuals (b) partnerships (c) corporations (d) all of the above.

_____12. The formation of a partnership may result from (a) an oral or written agreement between the parties (b) an informal arrangement (c) the conduct of the parties (d) all of the above.

_____13. An enforceable agreement can provide for all of the following except (a) any conceivable arrangement of capital investment and profit distribution (b) continuity of the partnership in the event of one member's death or retirement (c) the oral formation of a partnership that is to last for five years (d) none of the above.

CASE PROBLEMS — SHORT ESSAY ANSWERS: Read each case problem carefully. When appropriate, answer by stating a Decision for the case and by explaining the rationale — Rule of Law — relied upon to support your decision.

1. A and B are nieces of X. X dies and under a will leaves apartment buildings to A and B as tenants in common. A and B continue to manage and lease the apartments cooperatively. At the end of each year, A and B split the profits from the rents collected. Do A and B have a partnership? Explain.

   Decision: _____

   _____

   Rule of Law: _____

2. A and B are partners. C, with A's and B's knowledge, agrees to represent himself as another member of the partnership to X. On the basis of C's representation, X loans a large sum of money to the partnership of A and B. Can X force C to contribute to the repayment of the loan? Explain.

   Decision: _____

   _____

   Rule of Law: _____

3. A has been declared a mentally incompetent person by a court decision, and the judge has appointed a guardian for A. If A enters into a partnership agreement with B, does a partnership exist? Explain.

   Decision: _____

   _____

   Rule of Law: _____

4. A, B and C are partners. All three share in the profits and losses of the business, but only A and B manage the business. In addition, C's membership in the business is not disclosed to the public. What type of partner is C? Explain.

   Decision: _____

   _____

   Rule of Law: _____

5. A, B and C are members of a partnership. They have orally contracted to form their partnership and to continue its business for five years. Is their contract to form a partnership enforceable? Explain.

   Decision: _____

   _____

   Rule of Law: _____

Chapter 32

DUTIES, RIGHTS AND LIABILITIES

SCOPE NOTE

Chapter 32 continues our discussion of partnership law. The chapter examines the legal doctrines and principles that control the operations of a partnership. What are the rights/duties existing among the members of the partnership? What are the rights/duties of people doing business with the enterprise? These and other topics are the primary themes of Chapter 32.

EDUCATIONAL OBJECTIVES

1. Trace the various categories of partnership authority and discuss the extent of responsibilities associated with each.

2. Explain the liability of partners in terms of contract, tort and agency theories.

3. Define and discuss the significance of a partnership by estoppel.

4. Understand the nature and substance of duties partners owe one another.

5. Outline the specific rights partners have with one another.

CHAPTER OUTLINE

I. **Relationships Among Partners**
   A. **Duties Among Partners** — the legal duties imposed upon partners are listed below
      1. Fiduciary duty — each partner owes a duty of absolute and utmost good faith and loyalty to his partners
      2. Duty of obedience — each partner must act in obedience to the partnership agreement
      3. Duty of care — each partner owes a duty of faithful service to the best of her ability to the partnership
   B. **Rights Among Partners** — provided by law are listed below
      1. Right to share in distributions — transfers of partnership property from the partnership to the partners

a. Right to share in profits — each partner is entitled to a share of the profits
b. Right to return of capital — after all partnership creditors are paid, each partner is repaid her capital contribution
c. Right to return of advances — if a partner makes loans to the firm, she is entitled to repayment plus interest
d. Right to compensation — generally, no partner is entitled to payment for acting in the partnership business
2. Right to participate in management — each partner has an equal voice in management
3. Right to choose associates — no person can become a partner without the consent of all the partners
4. Enforcement rights — the law provides partners with the means to enforce rights and duties
a. Right to information and inspection of the books — is a right of each partner
b. Right to an account — may lead to an accounting, which is an equitable proceeding for a comprehensive and effective settlement of all partnership affairs

II. Relationship Between Partners and Third Parties
A. **Contracts of Partnership** — the act of every partner binds the partnership to transactions within the scope of partnership business unless the partner does not have actual or apparent authority
1. Authority to bind partnership — a partner may bind the firm by her act if she has any of the kinds of authority listed below
a. Actual express authority — may be oral or written and it is usually included in the partnership agreement
b. Actual implied authority — is authority that is reasonably deduced from the partnership nature or terms of the partnership agreement
c. Apparent authority — is authority that may be reasonably considered to exist by a third person who has no knowledge or notice of the lack of actual authority
2. Partnership by estoppel — imposes partnership duties and liabilities upon a person who is not a partner but who has either represented herself or consented to be represented as a partner
B. **Torts and Crimes of Partnership** — a partnership is liable for any loss or injury caused by a wrongful act or omission of any partner while acting within the ordinary course of the business or with authority of the co-partners; a partner is not criminally liable for the crimes of her partners unless she authorized or participated in them
C. **Admissions of and Notice to a Partner** — admissions by a partner may be used as evidence against the partnership and notice to any partner of any matter relating to the firm's affairs binds the partnership
D. **Liability of Incoming Partner** — a person admitted as a partner into an existing partnership is liable for all of the obligations of the partnership arising before her admission, but this liability may be satisfied only out of partnership property

TRUE—FALSE: Circle true or false.

T   F   1. Each partner owes a duty of good faith and loyalty to the other partners.

T   F   2. Upon termination of the partnership, partners are entitled to the return of their capital contributions after all debts have been paid.

T   F   3. Generally, when partners are repaid their capital contributions, they also receive interest on the contribution.

T   F   4. In most cases, the proportion in which partners bear business losses depends on their relative capital contributions.

T   F   5. An incoming partner has unlimited liability for all obligations arising after the partner's admission.

T   F   6. Partners who loan money to the partnership beyond their capital contribution become creditors of the firm.

T   F   7. Generally, a partner is entitled to compensation for services performed for the firm.

T   F   8. In an action on tort liability, the plaintiff must sue all the partners jointly.

T   F   9. A partnership is not bound by notice to a partner of a matter relating to partnership affairs since such notice must be given to all partners.

T   F   10. Much of the law of partnership is based on the law of agency.

T   F   11. If a partner has neither actual authority nor apparent authority, the partnership is bound only if it ratifies the act of the partner.

T   F   12. Any lawsuit based upon breach of contract brought against the partners must name all the partners as defendants.

KEY TERMS—MATCHING EXERCISE: Select the term that best completes each statement below.

1. Indemnification	8. Delectus personae	15. Partnership by estoppel
2. Unlimited personal liability	9. Court of equity	16. Contributory negligence
3. Agency law	10. Change in membership	17. Advances
4. Express authority	11. Fiduciary	18. Ratification
5. Limited personal liability	12. Apparent authority	19. Duty of obedience
6. Distribution	13. Court of law	20. Culpable negligence
7. Formal account	14. Implied authority	

_____1. A principle that establishes the right of persons to select their own partners.

_____2. The right one partner who pays partnership debts has against the other non-paying partners.

_____3. The liability of a general partner.

_____4. A major basis for partnership law and liability.

_____5. Actual partnership authority that is oral or written.

_____6. The court in which a partner sues for an accounting.

_____7. The partnership created when persons not partners hold themselves out as partners.

_____8. Partnership authority reasonably deduced from the partnership itself or from the relations of the partners.

_____9. The relationship of trust and confidence existing between partners.

_____10. A transfer of partnership property from the partnership to a partner.

_____11. A type of negligence somewhat less than gross negligence.

_____12. Another name for loans a partner makes to the partnership.

_____13. A detailed statement of financial transactions.

_____14. An act that requires the consent of all of the partners.

_____15. The duty violated by a partner who extends credit to her relatives using partnership funds.

MULTIPLE CHOICE: Select the alternative that best completes each statement below.

_____1. Upon termination of a solvent partnership, partners are entitled to the (a) return of their capital contributions (b) interest on their capital contributions by right of implication (c) repayment of their loans to the partnership without interest (d) none of the above.

_____2. Decisions that require unanimous agreement of the partners include (a) disposal of the good will of the business (b) adding a new partner (c) submitting a dispute to arbitration (d) all of the above.

_____3. The duties of a partner include the duty of (a) care (b) loyalty (c) obedience (d) all of the above.

_____4. Authority of a partner to act that is specifically provided for in the partnership agreement is (a) apparent (b) equitable (c) express (d) apportioned.

_____5. A partner does have implied authority to (a) hire employees (b) fire employees (c) purchase property for the business (d) all of the above.

_____6. A partner does not have apparent authority to (a) pay individual debts out of partnership assets (b) indorse checks (c) give warranties in selling goods (d) enter into contracts for advertising.

_____7. The rights of a partner do not include the right to (a) compensation for performing partnership business (b) payment of a debt to a partner before payment to creditors of the partnership (c) add a friend or relative to the partnership without consent of all the partners (d) all of the above.

_____8. Liability of general partners for valid partnership contracts is (a) limited personal liability (b) joint liability (c) joint and several liability (d) none of the above.

_____9. Liability of general partners for torts of a partner or an employee doing company business is (a) limited personal liability (b) joint liability (c) joint and several liability (d) none of the above.

_____10. The rights of a partner include the right to (a) share profits (b) participate in managing the business (c) a repayment of capital contributions (d) all of the above.

_____11. A partner may not (a) compete with the partnership business (b) acquire for himself a partnership asset (c) make a profit from the partnership business other than his agreed compensation (d) all of the above.

_____12. A partner must manage the partnership business without (a) any negligence (b) culpable negligence (c) ordinary negligence (d) all of the above.

_____13. A partner's form of ownership of specific partnership property is a (a) joint tenancy (b) tenancy in common (c) tenancy in partnership (d) none of the above.

CASE PROBLEMS — SHORT ESSAY ANSWERS: Read each case problem carefully. When appropriate, answer by stating a Decision for the case and by explaining the rationale — Rule of Law — relied upon to support your decision.

1. Floral Designs is a partnership among A, B and C. A sells his partnership interest to P, who alleges that as a result of the purchase, she is now a co-partner with B and C. Accordingly, she demands a voice in managing the firm, and B and C refuse. P threatens suit. Who wins? Explain.

Decision: _____

_____

Rule of Law: _____

2. Futuristic Concepts is a partnership owned by P, B and Q, who have provided in the Articles of Partnership that profits should be shared equally. P and B decide to change the method of sharing profits. Q finds the change in method unacceptable and demands that the original equal-share method be retained. P and B resist, asserting "majority rules." What result? Explain.

Decision: _____

_____

Rule of Law: _____

3. While acting for the partnership, A completes a business transaction that nets the firm over $50,000. A demands payment for the work or an increase in the partnership profits. The other partners refuse. What result? Explain.

Decision: _____

_____

Rule of Law: _____

4. Without authority from her co-partners B and C, A assigns a truck owned by the firm to Z, a creditor of the partnership. Z demands the truck. The partners refuse to relinquish it. Who prevails? Explain.

Decision: _____

_____

Rule of Law: _____

5. A, B and C are partners. B is wrongfully excluded from the management of the partnership business. B commences a lawsuit against the partnership seeking damages. Is B entitled to this remedy? Explain.

Decision: _____

_____

Rule of Law: _____

Chapter 33

DISSOLUTION, WINDING UP AND TERMINATION

SCOPE NOTE

Chapter 33 continues our discussion of partnership law. The chapter examines the legal doctrines and principles that control the operations and termination of a partnership. What happens when a partnership ends? These and other topics dealing with the management and dissolution of the partnership are the primary themes of Chapter 33.

EDUCATIONAL OBJECTIVES

1. Trace the various categories of partnership authority and discuss the extent of responsibilities associated with each upon dissolution and termination of the partnership.

2. Define and discuss dissolution and its causes.

3. Explain and discuss the rights of partnership creditors.

4. Outline the specific rights partners have during and after dissolution.

5. Contrast partnership dissolutions harmonious with and contravening to the partnership contract.

6. Discuss procedures associated with "winding up" a partnership in the context of insolvent and solvent enterprises.

7. Develop the significance of continuing a partnership as opposed to termination.

CHAPTER OUTLINE

I. Dissolution
    A. Causes of Dissolution
        1. Dissolution by act of the partners — a partner always has the power but not always the right to dissolve the partnership by her own acts

    2. Dissolution by operation of law — death, bankruptcy, or subsequent illegality dissolve the partnership

    3. Dissolution by court order — four ways are listed that cause dissolution by a court order

  B. **Effects of Dissolution**

    1. Authority — dissolution terminates actual authority of a partner to act for the partnership, but apparent authority persists

    2. Existing liability — dissolution does not itself discharge the existing liability of any partner

II. Winding Up

  A. **The Right to Wind Up** — belongs to any partner upon dissolution

  B. **Distribution of Assets** — assets are reduced to cash and distributed to creditors and then to partners

    1. Solvent partnership — assets of the partnership are greater than its liabilities

    2. Insolvent partnership — liabilities to creditors are greater than the assets of the partnership

    3. Contribution of partner upon insolvency — generally, partners contribute equally to the losses of the partnership

  C. **Marshaling of Assets** — segregating partnership assets and liabilities from those of the individual partners

III. Continuation after Dissolution

  A. **Right to Continue Partnership** — three rights are listed

    1. Continuation after wrongful dissolution — a partner who wrongfully withdraws cannot force liquidation

    2. Continuation after expulsion — an expelled partner cannot force liquidation

    3. Continuation agreement of the partners — is the best and most reliable way of preserving a partnership after dissolution

  B. **Rights of Creditors** — are listed whenever a change in the membership of the partnership occurs

TRUE—FALSE: Circle true or false.

T   F   1. Partners owe one another fiduciary duties of good faith and loyalty.

T   F   2. Upon termination of the partnership, partners are entitled to the return of their capital contributions after all debts have been paid.

T   F   3. Upon dissolution, the partnership is terminated.

T   F   4. The proportion in which partners bear business losses depends on their relative capital contributions.

T   F   5. Dissolution may occur by acts of the partners or by operation of law.

T   F   6. Partners who loan money to the partnership beyond their capital contribution become creditors of the firm but their claims are secondary to the claims of other creditors of the partnership.

T   F   7. A partnership is dissolved any time its membership changes, but a continuation agreement can preserve a partnership business after dissolution.

T   F   8. Upon dissolution, the existing liability of all partners to creditors and other third parties is discharged.

T   F   9. A partner who wrongfully withdraws from a partnership can force the liquidation of the firm.

T   F   10. A partner expelled from the partnership pursuant to the terms of the partnership contract cannot force the liquidation of the enterprise.

T   F   11. Termination of a partnership occurs when the process of winding up has been completed.

T   F   12. A partner always has the power and the right to dissolve the partnership by his own actions.

KEY TERMS — MATCHING EXERCISE: Select the term that best completes each statement below.

1. Contribution	8. Winding up	15. Partnership by estoppel
2. Bankruptcy	9. Continuation	16. Actual notice
3. Novation	10. Change in membership	17. Solvent partnership
4. Marshaling	11. Fiduciary	18. Trustee
5. Dissolution by operation of law	12. Dissolution by court order	19. Insolvent partnership
6. Termination	13. Apparent authority	20. Constructive notice
7. Dissolution by act of the partners	14. Actual authority	

_____1. The process of liquidating a partnership.

_____2. The right one partner who pays all the partnership debts has against the other non-paying partners.

_____3. The change in the relationship of partners resulting when one partner withdraws from the operation of the business.

_____4. An agreement among a retiring partner, continuing partners, and creditors whereby the retiring partner may be discharged from existing liabilities.

_____5. Segregating and separating assets and liabilities of a partnership from those of the respective partners.

_____6. An agreement used to guarantee the ongoing operations of a partnership following the death, disability or retirement of a partner.

_____7. Dissolution caused by death of a partner.

_____8. Partnership authority that terminates upon dissolution.

_____9. The relationship of trust and confidence existing between partners.

_____10. The final state in ending the existence of a partnership.

_____11. The type of notice a withdrawing partner makes by newspaper publication that may protect her from further liability of the firm.

_____12. The type of notice a withdrawing partner must give to creditors of the partnership prior to dissolution.

_____13. Dissolution caused by the adjudicated incompetence of a partner.

_____14. Partnership authority that continues upon dissolution unless proper notice of the dissolution is given to third parties.

_____15. A partnership in which the partnership assets exceed the partnership liabilities (debts) to creditors.

MULTIPLE CHOICE: Select the alternative that best completes each statement below.

_____1. Upon termination of a solvent partnership, partners are entitled to the (a) return of their capital contributions (b) interest on their capital contributions by right of implication (c) repayment of their loans before payment to creditors (d) none of the above.

_____2. Dissolution occurs by (a) court order (b) an act of the partners (c) operation of law (d) all of the above.

_____3. An act that dissolves a partnership by operation of law is (a) an agreement of the parties (b) the bankruptcy of a partner (c) the proper expulsion of a partner (d) all of the above.

_____4. Upon dissolution, the type of authority of a partner that binds the partnership for acts for the business unless notice of the dissolution is given to third parties is (a) apparent (b) equitable (c) actual (d) apportioned.

_____5. Which of the following does not occur during the winding up period of a partnership? (a) the termination of the partners' liabilities (b) the payment of creditors (c) the distribution of assets (d) the collection of debts.

_____6. Dissolution by act of the partners occurs when a (a) partner withdraws (b) partner dies (c) judge dissolves the partnership (d) partner becomes insane.

_____7. Under the UPA, a partner has the right to liquidate the partnership except when (a) contrary to the partnership contract (b) that partner has been properly expelled (c) there is unanimous agreement for continuation (d) all of the above.

_____8. When membership of a partnership changes, (a) default occurs (b) the partnership is dissolved (c) estoppel bars further withdrawal of other partners (d) none of the above.

_____9. A court will order the dissolution of a partnership if (a) a partner is incompetent (b) a partner is guilty of conduct prejudicial to the business (c) the business cannot operate profitably (d) all of the above.

_____10. Placing an advertisement in a newspaper of general circulation calling attention to the dissolution of a named partnership is called (a) actual notice (b) equitable notice (c) notice by attention (d) constructive notice.

_____11. Continuation agreements that allow partnerships to continue business after dissolution are (a) the best and most reliable way to preserve a partnership (b) used to insure continuity after a partner's death (c) used to insure continuity after a partner's retirement (d) all of the above.

_____12. Under Federal bankruptcy law, the person who is appointed to administer the assets of the partnership is the (a) general partner (b) marshal (c) trustee (d) none of the above.

_____13. Which of the following is not a stage that leads to the extinction of a partnership? (a) dissolution (b) distribution (c) liquidation (d) termination.

CASE PROBLEMS — SHORT ESSAY ANSWERS: Read each case problem carefully. When appropriate, answer by stating a Decision for the case and by explaining the rationale — Rule of Law — relied upon to support your decision.

1. X, Y and Z are partners. Z wants to retire from the firm (partnership) and terminate her liability to existing creditors of the partnership. X and Y want to continue the partnership business. Are these desires possible? Explain.

Decision: _____

_____

Rule of Law: _____

2. In question 1 above, how can Z, the retiring partner, protect herself against liability on contracts that are entered into by the partnership subsequent to her withdrawal? Explain.

Decision: _____

_____

Rule of Law: _____

3. A, B and C are partners. Each originally contributed $5,000 to the partnership. If, after dissolution and liquidation, the firm's assets are $100,000 and its debts owed to creditors are $40,000, how much will be C's share of the assets if according to the partnership contract they are to be divided equally among the partners? Explain.

Decision: _____

_____

Rule of Law: _____

4. Without authority from his co-partners, B and C, and in breach of their partnership agreement, A assigns a truck owned by the firm to Z, an individual creditor of A. Z demands the truck. The partners B and C refuse to relinquish it. Can the partnership be dissolved? Explain.

   Decision: _____

   _____

   Rule of Law: _____

5. A, B and C are partners. With A's and B's consent, C retires. Pursuant to their agreement, A and B agree to assume all the old debts and obligations of the firm and proceed with the accounting and dissolution. X, a creditor of the firm before dissolution, has a debt that A and B cannot satisfy, so X sues C. C refuses to pay X, arguing the controlling influence of C's agreement with A and B. Who prevails? Explain.

   Decision: _____

   _____

   Rule of Law: _____

Chapter 34

LIMITED PARTNERSHIPS

SCOPE NOTE

Chapter 34 ends our discussion of partnership law with a review of one of the fastest growing forms of partnership: the limited partnership. This chapter identifies the rights/duties that exist among the members of the limited partnership, explains the procedures for the formation and dissolution of the limited partnership, and discusses the advantages/disadvantages of this partnership as well as other forms of business associations, e.g., the business trust, mining partnerships, and joint ventures.

EDUCATIONAL OBJECTIVES

1. Discuss the criteria for the formation and dissolution of a limited partnership.

2. Explain the liability of limited partners concerning torts or contracts of the partnership.

3. Discuss the rights and duties of limited partners.

4. Identify the advantages and disadvantages of other forms of business associations, e.g., mining partnerships, joint ventures, business trusts, etc.

CHAPTER OUTLINE

I. Limited Partnerships
    A.   **Definition** — a partnership formed by two or more persons under the laws of a state and having at least one general partner and one limited partner
    B.   **Formation** — requires substantial compliance with the limited partnership statute
        1. Filing of certificate of the limited partnership with the Secretary of State is required
        2. Name of the limited partnership may not contain the surname of the limited partner in most cases
        3. Contributions may be in the form of cash, property or services
        4. Defective formation — the limited partnership is formed when the certificate is filed; if not done or done improperly, liability of the limited partners may be in jeopardy
        5. Foreign limited partnerships are considered foreign in any state in which they have not been formed

C. **Rights**
 1. Control is in the hands of the general partners
 2. Voting rights — the partnership agreement may grant voting rights to some or all of the general or limited partners
 3. Choice of associates — no partner can be added without the consent of all partners
 4. Withdrawal — the certificate determines the right and method of withdrawal, although a general partner may withdraw at any time by giving written notice to the other partners
 5. Assignment of partnership interest — the interest is the partner's share in the profits and her right to distribution of partnership assets
 6. Profit and loss sharing — is allocated among the partners, except limited partners who are generally not liable for losses beyond their contribution of capital
 7. Distributions — of assets are shared by partners as provided in their partnership agreement
 8. Loans — all partners may be secured or unsecured creditors of the partnership
 9. Information — all records must be kept at the partnership office and each partner has the right to inspect the records
 10. Derivative actions — limited partners may sue on behalf of the partnership if general partners refuse to bring the action
D. **Duties and Liabilities**
 1. Duties — general partners have a fiduciary duty to limited and other general partners
 2. Liabilities — limited partners have limited personal liability
E. **Dissolution**
 1. Causes — limited partners do not have the right to dissolve the partnership, but four causes are listed
 2. Winding up — generally this is done by the general partners
 3. Distribution of assets — the priorities in distributing the assets of a limited partnership are listed

II. Other Types of Unincorporated Business Associations
 A. **Joint Venture** — a form of temporary partnership to carry out a particular business enterprise for profit
 B. **Limited Liability Company** — is a non-corporate form of business organization in which all of its owners have limited liability
 C. **Joint Stock Company** — a form of general partnership that is a cross between a corporation and a partnership
 D. **Mining Partnerships** — an association of owners of the mineral rights in land
 E. **Limited Partnership Associations** — a legal hybrid but called a partnership association
 F. **Business Trusts** — a transfer of the legal title of specific real property to one person for the use and benefit of another

TRUE—FALSE: Circle true or false.

T   F   1. The amount of capital invested in limited partnerships has declined substantially since 1916.

T   F   2. The major advantage of limited partnerships is that the sale of such partnerships is not subject to governmental regulations.

T   F   3. Members of a limited partnership association are not personally liable for the debts of the association.

T   F   4. One difference between a mining partnership and a general partnership is that death of a mining partner does not dissolve the mining partnership.

T   F   5. The causes of dissolution and the priorities in the distribution of assets are the same for the limited partnership as they are for the general partnership.

T   F   6. A general partner has a fiduciary duty to the limited partners, but it is unclear whether the limited partners have a fiduciary duty to the general partners.

T   F   7. A general partnership and a limited partnership have the same formal requirements for their formation.

T   F   8. The personal liability of a limited partner for partnership debts is limited to the amount of capital the limited partner has contributed.

T   F   9. A limited partner has no right to participate in the management of the limited partnership.

T   F   10. Limited partners always share the profits of the limited partnership equally.

T   F   11. Today, a promise by a limited partner to contribute to the limited partnership is not enforceable unless it is written and signed.

T   F   12. Unlike a corporation, a joint stock company is formed by contract and not by state authority.

KEY TERMS — MATCHING EXERCISE: Select the term that best completes each statement below.

1. General partnership	8. Foreign limited partnership	15. Mining partnership
2. Joint venture	9. Massachusetts trust	16. Assignor
3. Limited personal liability	10. Certificate of limited partnership	17. Equity participant
4. Fiduciary duty	11. Constructive trust	18. Attorney General
5. Limited partnership	12. Assignee	19. Secretary of State
6. Dissolution	13. Joint stock company	20. Assignment
7. Capital contribution	14. Limited partnership associations	

_____1. A partnership composed of one or more general partners and one or more limited partners.

_____2. A kind of limited partnership that cannot enforce actions in a state's courts for business transactions until it registers.

_____3. The first step in the extinguishment of a general or limited partnership.

_____4. Another name for a business trust that has the power to own and sell real estate.

_____5. The document that is filed in the Secretary of State's office in the state in which the limited partnership has its principal office.

_____6. Another name for a joint stock association that is formed by contract and not by state authority.

_____7. The type of partnership in which death or insanity of a partner causes dissolution of the partnership.

_____8. A form of business association organized to carry out a single business operation for profit.

_____9. The extent or the amount of liability of a limited partner for losses of the partnership.

_____10. An association of several owners of the mineral rights in land for the purpose of extracting the minerals for profit.

_____11. A method a partner can use to transfer her partnership interest.

_____12. The kind of obligation a general partner owes a limited partner.

_____13. The person to whom a limited partner may transfer her partnership interest.

_____14. The person who contributes to the capital of a business in a good faith but erroneous effort to become a limited partner.

_____15. The office or person with whom a foreign limited partnership must register before transacting any business in a state.

MULTIPLE CHOICE: Select the alternative that best completes each statement below.

_____1. Generally, death of a limited or mining partner dissolves the following (a) a mining partnership (b) a limited partnership (c) a foreign limited partnership (d) none of the above.

_____2. Which of the following uniform laws governs the creation and operation of limited partnerships? (a) U.P.A. (b) U.L.P.A. (c) R.U.L.P.A. (d) all of the above.

_____3. Both general and limited partners (a) have limited personal liability (b) have the right to manage the partnership (c) must unanimously consent to add a partner to the partnership (d) all of the above.

_____4. A basic difference between a general partnership and a limited partnership is (a) a statute must exist that provides for the formation of the limited partnership (b) the limited partnership must comply with statutory requirements (c) the limited partners' liability is limited to their capital contributions (d) all of the above.

_____5. The uniform laws provide that a limited partner shall have the same rights as a general partner to (a) inspect the partnership books (b) copy records of the firm's business (c) obtain tax returns of the limited partnership (d) all of the above.

_____6. Failure of a limited partnership to comply with the statutory requirements for its formation may result in (a) a name change of the firm (b) the loss of limited liability for the limited partners (c) the loss of the limited partner's right to manage the partnership (d) all of the above.

_____7. Which of the following is a legal entity that resembles a corporation but whose members are not personally liable for its debts? (a) mining partnership (b) joint stock company (c) limited partnership association (d) business trust.

_____8. In a business trust, the person who has the responsibility of managing the trust is the (a) trustee (b) beneficiary (c) limited partner (d) joint venturer.

_____9. Death or bankruptcy (a) of a limited partner dissolves the partnership (b) of a general partner dissolves the partnership (c) never has any effect on the limited partnership (d) none of the above.

_____10. Limited partners (a) must share the profits of the partnership equally (b) must receive the return of their capital contributions at the same time (c) may contribute cash, property or services under the revised act (d) all of the above.

_____11. A limited partnership requires that (a) all partners be limited partners (b) the number of limited and general partners be equal (c) the partnership be created according to statutory law (d) none of the above.

_____12. If the surname of a limited partner is used in the partnership name, the limited partner (a) is entitled to a higher percentage of the partnership profits (b) may participate in the management of the partnership (c) may be liable to creditors who are unaware of the limited partnership (d) all of the above.

_____13. A joint venture (a) is another name for a limited partnership (b) generally lasts indefinitely (c) is governed by the law of corporations (d) is organized to carry out a particular business enterprise for profit.

CASE PROBLEMS — SHORT ESSAY ANSWERS: Read each case problem carefully. When appropriate, answer by stating a Decision for the case and by explaining the rationale — Rule of Law — relied upon to support your decision.

1. For 1993, XYZ Limited Partnership has a $50,000 loss. Carol is a limited partner of the firm. Must Carol pay for a share of this loss from her personal assets? Explain.

Decision: _____

_____

Rule of Law: _____

2. A and B form a limited partnership. A is the general partner; B is the limited partner. The name of their company is A and B Partnership. C agrees to make a loan to the partnership. If the partnership defaults on this loan, whom can C sue? Explain.

Decision: _____

_____

Rule of Law: _____

3. A, B and C are members of a limited partnership. A is the limited partner. They buy a large tract of land surrounding a lake, subdivide it, and begin selling the lots at a generous profit. If A dies, is the limited partnership dissolved? Explain.

Decision: _____

_____

Rule of Law: _____

4. A, B and C form a limited partnership. A and B want to add D to the partnership as a new general partner. Can this be done? Explain.

Decision: _____

_____

Rule of Law: _____

5. Bob, Carol, Ted and Alice agree to form a limited partnership. They are prepared to execute and sign a certificate but are unsure what is required by the Uniform Limited Partnership Act. Explain to them what the certificate of limited partnership contains.

Decision: _____

_____

Rule of Law: _____

PARTNERSHIP UNIT RESEARCH QUESTIONS: Drawing upon information contained in the text, as well as outside sources, discuss the following questions:

1. You and your best friend want to form a business. The form of business enterprise the two of you select is a partnership. Although partnerships may be created by an oral agreement, you prefer a written partnership agreement.
   A. Explain the steps and processes you would complete to establish a formal partnership.
   B. Include in your explanation a sample partnership agreement (articles of partnership) that would be appropriate for your business.

2. Denny and Forrest are partners in a corner grocery store. Forrest makes some bad personal investments and has to file for bankruptcy. What effect will this have on the partnership? Explain. What would be the advantage if the above business was a corporation and an owner (stockholder) had to file for personal bankruptcy? Would this effect the other stockholders? Explain?

PART SEVEN: Corporations

Chapter 35

NATURE, FORMATION AND POWERS

SCOPE NOTE

The most common form of business organization among modern industrial businesses is the corporation. It is a major institution of the private sector. In today's economy, corporations occupy a significant position as employers, taxpayers, and primary participants in the flow of goods and services constituting G.D.P. How did this form of business organization evolve? Why is it so popular in certain sectors of the marketplace? These and other related concerns are the subject of Chapters 35-38. In these chapters, the law of corporations is discussed, including its basic doctrines, principles and terminology.

Chapter 35 focuses upon what corporations are, the functions they perform, how they are created, and the types of powers they can hold. This chapter serves as a general introduction to corporate law that can help in understanding the subsequent chapters that address particular aspects of a corporation's operational identity.

EDUCATIONAL OBJECTIVES

1. Define and explain the basic characteristics of a corporation.

2. Trace the historical development of corporations.

3. Compare the advantages/disadvantages of the corporate form of business organization.

4. Outline the various rights/duties associated with a corporate legal identity.

5. Differentiate among the various kinds of corporations.

6. Enumerate the substantive and procedural formalities associated with effectively establishing a corporation.

7. Understand the consequences of ineffective formation of a corporation.

8. Identify the meaning and importance of the phrase "piercing the corporate veil."

9. Discuss the sources, nature and kinds of operational powers a corporation holds.

10. Define and develop the importance of "ultra vires."

11. Know the tort and criminal liability of a corporation.

CHAPTER OUTLINE

I. Nature of Corporations
A. Corporate Attributes
1. Legal entity — makes the corporation separate and apart from its shareholders with rights and liabilities entirely distinct from theirs and it allows the corporation to sue or be sued
2. Creature of the state — a corporation must be formed by compliance with a state incorporation statute
3. Limited liability — means the shareholders are not personally liable for corporate debts
4. Free transferability of corporate shares — may be done by sale, gift, or pledge
5. Perpetual existence — is common and included in the articles of incorporation.
6. Centralized management — the shareholders elect the board of directors, who manage the business
7. As a person — a corporation is considered a person under most of the Federal Constitution Amendments
8. As a citizen — a corporation is considered a citizen of the state of its incorporation and of the state of its principal place of business

B. Classification of Corporations
1. Public or private — a corporation is formed for both purposes
2. Profit or nonprofit — a corporation is formed for profit or for charitable, educational, or scientific (nonprofit) purposes
3. Domestic or foreign — it is domestic in the state in which it is incorporated and foreign in all others
4. Publicly held or closely held — a corporation owned by a large number of persons is publicly held; if owned by a small number of persons is closely held
5. Subchapter S corporation — is taxed like a partnership
6. Professional corporation — a corporation formed by duly licensed professionals

II. Formation of a Corporation
A. Organizing the Corporation
1. Promoters — persons who originate and organize the corporation
   a. Promoters' contracts — contracts created by promoters before the corporation is formed
   b. Promoters' fiduciary duty — is due to the fiduciary relationship among themselves as well as to the corporation, its subscribers, and its initial shareholders
2. Subscribers — the persons who offer to purchase capital stock in a corporation yet to be formed
3. Selection of state for incorporation — generally is the state in which the corporation intends to be located and do business

B. Formalities of Incorporation
1. Selection of name — it must contain a word or words that indicate it is a corporation
2. Incorporators — persons who sign and file the articles of incorporation
3. Articles of incorporation — the charter or basic governing document of the corporation
4. Organizational meeting — the first meeting to adopt corporate bylaws and elect officers
5. Bylaws — the rules that govern the internal management of the corporation

III. Recognition or Disregard of Corporateness
A. Defective Incorporation
1. Common law approach— a defectively formed corporation was accorded corporate attributes
   a. Corporation de Jure — a corporation formed in substantial compliance with the statute
   b. Corporation de Facto — a corporation not formed in compliance with the statute but is recognized as a corporation

       c. Corporation by Estoppel — estoppel does not create a corporation
       d. Defective corporation — the courts deny the associates the benefits of incorporation
    2. Statutory approach — if the articles are filed, that is generally conclusive proof of proper incorporation under the statute

  B. **Piercing the Corporate Veil**
    1. Closely held corporations — its shareholders may relax the traditional corporate formalities without courts piercing the veil
    2. Parent-subsidiary — courts will pierce the corporate veil and hold the parent liable for the debts of its subsidiary under certain circumstances

IV. Corporate Powers
  A. **Sources of Corporate Powers**
    1. Statutory powers — provided by the Revised Act are listed
    2. Express charter powers — are stated in the articles of incorporation
    3. Implied powers — exist by reasonable inference of the statute or the charter

  B. **Ultra Vires Acts**
    1. Effect of Ultra Vires Acts — most statutes abolish the defense of ultra vires in an action by or against a corporation
    2. Remedies for Ultra Vires Acts — three remedies are possible under the Revised Act

  C. **Liability for Torts and Crimes** — a corporation is liable for the torts committed by its agents in the course of their employment, and it may be convicted of a criminal offense for the conduct of its employees (officers or directors)

TRUE—FALSE: Circle true or false.

T   F   1. A corporation incorporated under the laws of one state is known as a foreign corporation in other states.

T   F   2. If the sole shareholder of a corporation willfully destroys corporate property by fire, the doctrine of "piercing the corporate veil" will protect the fire insurance company.

T   F   3. A corporation can have its principal place of business in one state and be incorporated under the laws of another state.

T   F   4. A corporation is "de jure" if it has failed to meet some of the technical requirements for incorporation.

T   F   5. The powers of a corporation are limited to the express powers granted either in its charter or by the statutes of its state of incorporation.

T   F   6. A corporation is liable for the torts of its agents and employees while they are engaged in company business.

T   F   7. A corporation may be formed only by substantial compliance with a state incorporation statute.

T   F   8. A corporation is a legal entity, and therefore it is liable for its debts.

T   F   9. A shareholder of a corporation is the owner and an agent of the corporation.

T   F   10. Title to corporate property belongs to the shareholders.

T   F   11. A transfer of corporate stock by gift or sale from one shareholder to another causes dissolution of the corporation.

T   F   12. A corporation may be incorporated in one state and conduct all or most of its operations in another state.

KEY TERMS — MATCHING EXERCISE: Select the term that best completes each statement below.

1. Perpetual	8. Incorporator	15. "Inc." or "Ltd."
2. De jure	9. Respondeat superior	16. Officers
3. Limited liability	10. Subscriber	17. Dividends
4. De facto	11. Diversity of citizenship	18. Closely held corporation
5. Charter	12. Bylaws	19. Municipal corporation
6. Pierce the corporate veil	13. Unlimited liability	20. Board of directors
7. Promoter	14. Ultra vires	

_____1. The kind of liability shareholders usually have.

_____2. A corporation organized substantially in compliance with the statutes.

_____3. Another name for the articles of incorporation, which authorizes a corporation to do business.

_____4. The procedure a court uses to disregard the corporate entity when it is wrongfully used to avoid personal accountability.

_____5. The person who signs and files the articles of incorporation.

_____6. The person who may be individually liable for contracts made prior to the corporation's existence.

_____7. Corporate acts that are beyond the scope of its powers.

_____8. The rules and regulations that govern a corporation's internal management.

_____9. The doctrine that imposes liability on a corporation for the torts committed by its agents and employees during their employment.

_____10. The term that signifies that the parties to a lawsuit are from different states.

_____11. Payments made to shareholders from profits of the corporation.

_____12. A corporation owned by a small number of persons such as a family or friends.

_____13. The potential lifetime of a corporation.

_____14. Another name for a public corporation.

_____15. The individuals appointed to run the operations of a corporation on a day-to-day basis.

MULTIPLE CHOICE: Select the alternative that best completes each statement below.

_____1. The person who offers to buy stock in a nonexisting corporation is a (a) promoter (b) incorporator (c) subscriber (d) none of the above.

_____2. The debts of a corporation are satisfied from (a) assets of the corporation (b) a shareholder's personal assets (c) an incorporator's personal assets (d) all of the above.

_____3. A shareholder is (a) a principal of the corporation (b) an agent of the corporation (c) liable only for corporation torts (d) none of the above.

_____4. Most incorporation statutes require that a corporation name (a) not be the same as the name of an existing corporation doing business within the state (b) contain wording that indicates it is a corporation (c) both A and B (d) none of the above.

_____5. A promoter's profits may be allowed if they are (a) disclosed to the corporation (b) relatively small (c) secret (d) none of the above.

_____6. A corporation whose existence cannot be challenged by the state is a (a) corporation de facto (b) corporation by estoppel (c) corporation de jure (d) none of the above.

_____7. A corporation derives all of its power and its existence from (a) its charter (b) the state (c) the articles of incorporation (d) the bylaws.

_____8. Today, a corporation cannot be guilty of a crime (a) because it is impossible for it to have a guilty mind (b) because it is impossible to imprison a corporation (c) because it is an artificial "person" (d) the statement is false.

_____9. An ultra vires act by the corporation may be remedied by (a) an injunction brought by a shareholder (b) a representative suit by shareholders for the corporation against the officers (c) a proceeding to dissolve or enjoin the corporation brought by the Attorney General of the state (d) all of the above.

_____10. Generally, all of the following are proper names for a corporation except (a) Johnson and Son, Inc. (b) Merry Widow Corporation (c) A. B. Lincoln and Company (d) T. F. Elliot, Ltd.

_____11. The existence of a corporation is terminated by the (a) death of a shareholder (b) withdrawal or retirement of a director (c) addition of a new officer (d) none of the above.

_____12. Corporations may be classified as (a) public or private (b) profit or nonprofit (c) domestic or foreign (d) all of the above.

_____13. The following individuals need not be shareholders of the corporation (a) officers of the corporation (b) creditors of the corporation (c) members of the corporation's board of directors (d) all of the above.

CASE PROBLEMS — SHORT ESSAY ANSWERS: Read each case problem carefully. When appropriate, answer by stating a Decision for the case and by explaining the rationale — Rule of Law — relied upon to support your decision.

1. A, B and C plan to go into business together. A and B have limited assets. C is very wealthy. Would it be advantageous for C to insist upon a corporation? Explain.

   Decision: _____

   _____

   Rule of Law: _____

2. A bartender of an incorporated tavern illegally sells liquor to a minor. The act is a crime under the state law. If the bartender is a nonowner, can the tavern be criminally prosecuted for the illegal sale? Explain.

   Decision: _____

   _____

   Rule of Law: _____

3. A promoter contracts with B to engage B to manage ABC Corporation upon its incorporation. The directors of ABC Corporation refuse to accept the terms of the contract, and B refuses to be employed by ABC Corporation except on the terms of the contract with the promoter. What are B's rights? Explain.

   Decision: _____

   _____

   Rule of Law: _____

4. X, a promoter of a corporation created to do business as a shopping center, collects a 20% commission on the sale of land to the corporation. X does not inform the directors of the corporation. Can X keep the commission? Explain.

   Decision: _____

   _____

   Rule of Law: _____

5. A, B and C hire attorney Y to incorporate their dry-cleaning partnership. All formal steps for incorporation are taken except publication of the articles in a legal newspaper and filing of the articles with the Register of Deeds in the county of the corporation's principal place of business. A, B and C rely on Y to take all necessary steps and believe the procedures have been completed. Thereafter, a customer is seriously injured by dry-cleaning fumes. Can the customer sue A, B and C personally on the theory that the corporation is not validly formed and A, B and C are still operating as partners? Explain.

Decision: _____

_____

Rule of Law: _____

Chapter 36

FINANCIAL STRUCTURE

SCOPE NOTE

In Chapter 36, the financial structure of a corporation is discussed. The legal concepts and rules relating to corporate funding, stocks and bonds, payment of dividends, and transfer of ownership of shares are focused upon.

EDUCATIONAL OBJECTIVES

1. Identify the use and types of debt securities used as a source of corporate funds.

2. Distinguish among the various classes of stock commonly used in corporate financing.

3. Develop the difference between "par" and "no par" value.

4. Discuss the procedures related to issuing, redeeming, canceling and acquiring stock.

5. Explain the nature of the shareholder's dividend rights and liabilities.

6. Differentiate among the several types of dividends.

7. Understand the dividend declaration and payment process.

8. Identify what is meant by wrongful and illegal dividends.

9. Contrast the methods of marketing shares of stock.

10. List the warranties that run with a transfer of shares.

11. Develop the consequences of wrongful indorsement of lost or stolen securities.

12. Explain the securities registration process.

CHAPTER OUTLINE

I. Debt Securities
A. **Authority to Issue Debt Securities** — also called bonds, is a sole responsibility of the board of directors

B. **Types of Debt Securities**
1. Unsecured bonds — or debentures, have only the obligation of the corporation backing them
2. Secured bonds — are creditor claims enforceable against general corporate assets and also as a lien on specific corporate property
3. Income bonds — are debt securities that condition the payment of interest on corporate earnings
4. Convertible bonds — may be exchanged for other securities at a specified ratio
5. Callable bonds — are bonds that are subject to redemption

II. Equity Securities
A. **Issuance of Shares**
1. Authority to issue — is within the articles of incorporation
2. Preemptive rights — a shareholder's right to purchase a proportionate part of a new share issue
3. Amount of consideration for shares — depends on the type of shares being issued
   a. Par value stock — may be issued for any amount set by the directors or shareholders, but not less than par
   b. No par value stock — may be issued for any amount
   c. Treasury stock — shares that have been issued and then reacquired by the corporation, and may be sold for any amount
4. Payment for shares — depends on two issues
   a. Type of consideration — may include cash, property, or services but not promissory notes or future services. The Revised Act allows future services and notes
   b. Valuation of consideration — exchanged for shares; is determined by the directors
6. Liability for shares — a shareholder's only liability is to pay to the corporation the full consideration for the shares issued

B. **Classes of Shares**
1. Common stock — frequently the only class of stock issued with no special contract rights or preferences
2. Preferred stock — has superior contract rights to common stock over dividends and assets upon liquidation
   a. Dividend preferences — means that preferred shareholders will receive full dividends before any are paid to common stockholders
   b. Liquidation preferences — after creditors are paid, preferred stockholders usually receive assets ahead of common stockholders
   c. Additional rights and limitations — preferred stock may have these
3. Stock rights — rights of existing shareholders to purchase corporate shares of a specific class or classes

III. Dividends and Other Distributions
A. **Types of Dividends and Other Distributions**
1. Cash dividends — most common type of dividend
2. Property dividends — a dividend of property
3. Stock dividends — a ratable distribution of additional shares to the shareholders
4. Stock splits — each of the issued and outstanding shares is split into a greater number of shares
5. Liquidating dividends — a distribution of capital assets to shareholders upon termination
6. Redemption of shares — the option of the corporation to repurchase its own shares
7. Acquisition of shares — a corporation may acquire its own shares, called treasury shares

B. **Legal Restrictions on Dividends and Other Distributions**
  1. Definitions — legal concepts and finance terms concerning corporation assets are defined
  2. Legal restrictions on cash dividends
      a. Earned surplus test — some states permit dividends to be paid only from earned surplus
      b. Surplus test — a number of states permit dividends out of earned or capital surplus
      c. Net asset test — the MBCA, as amended in 1980, and the Revised Act use this test
  3. Legal restrictions on liquidating distributions — states usually permit distributions, or dividends, in partial liquidation from capital surplus
  4. Legal restrictions on redemption and acquisition of shares — redemption and the purchase of its own shares may not be made at a time when the corporation is insolvent or when the purchase would make it insolvent
C. **Declaration and Payment of Distributions** — is accomplished at the direction of the board of directors
  1. Shareholder's right to compel a dividend — is done by a suit in equity seeking an injunction
  2. Effect of declaration — once a cash dividend is declared, it cannot be rescinded
D. **Liability for Improper Dividends and Distributions** — the Revised Act imposes personal liability upon the directors to the corporation and to its creditors

IV. **Transfer of Investment Securities**
A. **Ownership of Securities**
  1. Record of ownership — shares represented by certificates or uncertificated shares are registered on books (records) kept for that purpose
  2. Duty of issuer to register transfer of security — the issuing corporation has this duty and to then issue new certificates to the new owner under certain conditions
  3. Lost, destroyed, or stolen certificated securities — under any of these conditions, the owner is entitled to a new certificate if other requirements are met
B. **Transfer of Securities**
  1. Restrictions on transfer — are seldom made, but if they exist, they are included in the articles or bylaws
  2. Statute of Frauds — a contract for the sale of securities is not enforceable unless it satisfies the Statute of Frauds
  3. Manner of transfer — includes methods of transferring certificated and uncertificated securities
  4. Bona fide purchasers — good faith purchasers for value whose transfer rights are included
  5. Transfer warranties — given to a purchaser for value are listed
  6. Forged or unauthorized indorsement — the owner of certificated securities is not deprived of title by a transfer bearing a forged or unauthorized indorsement

TRUE—FALSE: Circle true or false.

T   F   1. Common and preferred stock are examples of debt investment securities.

T   F   2. Common stock shareholders generally bear the heaviest loss if a corporation fails.

T   F   3. A corporation's board of directors and shareholders share the responsibility for declaring dividends.

T   F   4. The current profits or net earnings of a corporation are the only lawful source of corporate dividends.

T   F   5. Generally, a stock dividend increases the shareholder's relative interest in the net worth of the corporation.

T   F   6. The purchaser of a bond issued by a corporation becomes an owner of the corporation like a shareholder.

T   F   7. Preferred shareholders have priority to the assets of the corporation over creditors of the corporation.

T   F   8. A shareholder has no right to transfer shares of stock by sale or gift.

T   F   9. The buyer of a security bearing a forged indorsement does not acquire title to the security (stock).

T   F   10. A corporation that issues stock is under a duty to register transfers of its certificated stock and to issue new stock certificates to the new owner.

T   F   11. Modern statutes expressly authorize the articles of incorporation to deny or limit a shareholder's preemptive rights.

T   F   12. A stock split is a ratable distribution of additional shares of the capital stock of the corporation to its shareholders.

KEY TERMS — MATCHING EXERCISE: Select the term that best completes each statement below.

1. Indorsement	8. Blue Sky laws	15. Liquidating dividend
2. Negotiation and transfer	9. Preemptive rights	16. Debentures
3. Model Act	10. Equity securities	17. Prospectus
4. "An appropriate person"	11. No par stock	18. Distribution
5. Bona fide purchaser	12. Par value stock	19. Stock split
6. U.C.C. Article 8	13. Nimble dividend	20. Treasury stock
7. Stock certificate	14. Cumulative dividend	

_____1. The evidence of a shareholder's interest in a corporation.

_____2. The statute containing the rules applicable to stock transfer.

_____3. The procedure that enables the bona fide purchaser (transferee) of stock to take title free of adverse claims not noted on the stock certificate.

_____4. The person specified in the stock certificate or entitled to it by special indorsement who may transfer the registered stock by indorsing and delivering it.

_____5. The state statute that regulates the issuance and sale of corporate securities.

_____6. A transferee of stock who is a purchaser for value in good faith.

_____7. Stock in which the stated value is found in the articles of incorporation.

_____8. A shareholder's right to purchase a pro rata share of every new offering of stock by the corporation.

_____9. A source for financing corporations that includes common stock.

_____10. The dividend paid to preferred shareholders for all arrearages on their stock before any dividends are paid on the common stock.

_____11. Stock of a corporation that has been issued and subsequently reacquired by the corporation.

_____12. Another name for unsecured bonds.

_____13. A written offer made by corporations to interest people in buying stock.

_____14. A direct or indirect transfer of money or other property by a corporation to its shareholders in respect of any of its shares.

_____15. The breakup of outstanding shares of corporate stock into a greater number of shares, each representing a smaller interest in the corporation.

MULTIPLE CHOICE: Select the alternative that best completes each statement below.

_____1. The duty to register a transfer of securities and issue new certificates to the new owner is performed by the (a) shareholders (b) promoters (c) incorporators (d) corporation.

_____2. Valid consideration for the issuance of shares of a corporation generally includes (a) cash (b) property (c) services to the corporation (d) all of the above.

_____3. In all states, cash dividends may be paid from (a) stated capital (b) earned surplus (c) capital surplus (d) any surplus.

_____4. Preferred shareholders may be entitled to (a) liens on corporate assets (b) cumulative dividends (c) rights superior to creditors (d) none of the above.

_____5. The board of directors who vote for or assent to the distribution of an illegal dividend are (a) not liable to the corporation (b) liable only in equity (c) liable only to creditors (d) personally liable to the corporation.

_____6. When an unsuspecting shareholder receives an illegal dividend from a solvent corporation, the majority rule is the shareholder (a) may keep the dividend (b) must refund the dividend (c) may be sued by creditors of the corporation (d) none of the above.

_____7. The transferee of stock is a bona fide purchaser if (a) the transferee pays value in good faith (b) the transferee has no notice of any adverse claim (c) the certificate is properly indorsed (d) all of the above.

_____8. The shareholder is entitled to a new stock certificate if the original is (a) lost (b) destroyed (c) stolen (d) all of the above.

_____9. If an innocent purchaser of a stock certificate bearing a forged indorsement resells the certificate to a bona fide purchaser, legal right to the shares belongs to the (a) innocent purchaser (b) bona fide purchaser (c) original owner whose signature was forged (d) none of the above.

_____10. Only shareholders on the corporate record books can (a) vote (b) receive dividends (c) receive reports of corporate assets and finances (d) all of the above.

_____11. The term that constitutes the entire surplus of a corporation other than its earned surplus is (a) stated capital (b) net assets (c) capital surplus (d) none of the above.

_____12. Dividends are (a) prohibited from being paid if the corporation is insolvent (b) declared and distributed by the officers of the corporation (c) in the form of cash or stock but not other kinds of property (d) none of the above.

_____13. A contract for the sale of stock is enforceable if (a) it is written and signed by the parties (b) it satisfies the requirements of the Statute of Frauds (c) an admission is made in court that a contract exists (d) all of the above.

CASE PROBLEMS — SHORT ESSAY ANSWERS: Read each case problem carefully. When appropriate, answer by stating a Decision for the case and by explaining the rationale — Rule of Law — relied upon to support your decision.

1. The board of directors of XYZ Corporation issues 100 shares of no par stock valued at $10,000 to A and B in exchange for land valued in good faith by all parties to be worth $10,000. XYZ goes bankrupt and the land is sold for $6,000. Can A and B be held liable for the balance of $4,000 by the corporation's creditors? Explain.

Decision: _____

_____

Rule of Law: _____

2. The XYZ Corporation intends to redeem its preferred stock. The company has $10,000 in cash, and it intends to use it to redeem part of its outstanding $100 par stock. Several creditors of XYZ seek to enjoin the redemption alleging that XYZ will have no money with which to pay its debts. Can the corporation redeem the stock? Explain.

Decision: _____

_____

Rule of Law: _____

3. XYZ Corporation declared a cash dividend on common stock. Before the dividend was paid, the board of directors voted to revoke the dividend on grounds that, due to changed circumstances, the corporation needed the funds. Can holders of the common stock force the company to pay the dividend? Explain.

Decision: _____

_____

Rule of Law: _____

4. A was an innocent purchaser of a stock certificate bearing a forged indorsement. A sells the certificate to B, a bona fide purchaser. B discovers the forgery and sues A for the value B paid A. What result? Explain.

Decision: _____

_____

Rule of Law: _____

5. A, the bona fide purchaser of an unauthorized indorsed stock certificate, receives from B Corporation a newly reregistered certificate. B Corporation discovers the improper indorsement and wishes to cancel A's ownership. What result? Explain.

Decision: _____

_____

Rule of Law: _____

Chapter 37

MANAGEMENT STRUCTURE

SCOPE NOTE

This chapter develops the nature of the relationship between a corporation, its directors, officers, and shareholders. What role do shareholders play in setting corporate policy? Particular attention is paid to the management functions of corporations. Who performs these functions? What is the source and nature of their authority? What limitations are placed on such authority? How is corporate policy established and executed? These and related issues are the focus of attention in Chapter 37 in its development of the rules and doctrines that control the management area of corporate law.

EDUCATIONAL OBJECTIVES

1. Identify and explain the rights and liabilities of shareholders.

2. Discuss proxy, cumulative, and trust voting.

3. Understand the nature and function of a board of directors.

4. Identify the qualifications for service on and the process of appointment to a board of directors.

5. Discuss the scope of powers/responsibilities held by corporate directors and explain the purpose of board meetings.

6. Know what management powers are delegated to corporate officers and outline the process of delegation.

7. List corporate officers and explain their responsibilities and basis for authority.

8. Outline the selection/removal procedure for corporate officers as well as how they are compensated.

9. Enumerate the kinds of duties and standard of care to which corporate officers are held.

CHAPTER OUTLINE

I. **Corporate Governance**

II. **Role of Shareholders**
    A. **Voting Rights of Shareholders**
        1. Shareholder meetings — shareholders may vote at both annual and special shareholder meetings
        2. Quorum and voting — generally, a majority of shares entitled to vote constitutes a quorum
        3. Election of directors — is the voting right of the shareholders, usually one vote per share
        4. Removal of directors — by a majority vote, shareholders may remove any director or the entire board
        5. Approval of fundamental changes — like amendments to the articles of incorporation, these require shareholder approval
        6. Concentrations of voting power
            a. Proxies — a shareholder may vote either in person or by written proxy
            b. Voting trusts — are devices designed to concentrate corporate control in one or more persons
            c. Shareholder voting agreements — shareholders may agree in advance to vote in a specific manner for the election or removal of directors or other matters
    B. **Enforcement Rights of Shareholders**
        1. Right to inspect books and records — is a right of shareholders if for a proper purpose
        2. Shareholder suits — the ultimate recourse is a shareholder's suit against or on behalf of the corporation
            a. Direct suits — are brought to enforce a shareholder's claim against the corporation
            b. Derivative suits — are brought by one or more shareholders on behalf of the corporation
        3. Shareholder's right to dissent — concerns certain corporate actions such as mergers

III. **Role of Directors and Officers**
    A. **Function of the Board of Directors**
        1. Selection and removal of officers — the directors hire and can fire the officers
        2. Capital structure — and the financial policy of the corporation are determined by the directors
        3. Fundamental changes — such as making, amending, and repealing bylaws are decided by the directors, unless reserved to the shareholders by the articles of incorporation
        4. Dividends — are declared by the directors, including the amount and type of dividends
        5. Management compensation — for both officers and directors is determined by the directors
    B. **Election, Number, and Tenure of Directors**
        1. Election, number, and tenure of directors — directors are elected at annual meetings of the shareholders and hold office for one year. State statutes usually set the number
        2. Vacancies and removal of directors — a vacancy may be filled by a majority vote of the remaining directors while removal is done by the shareholders' vote
        3. Compensation of directors — Revised Act authorizes the board to fix the compensation for directors
    C. **Exercise of Directors' Functions**
        1. Quorum and voting — a majority of the directors is a quorum, and it is necessary for a vote in most states
        2. Action taken without a meeting — requires written consent of all the directors
        3. Delegation of board powers — may be done by a majority vote of the full board of directors
        4. Directors' inspection rights — include the right to inspect corporate books and records

D. **Officers**
   1. Selection and removal of officers — is done by the directors
   2. Role of officers
      a. President — the principal executive officer
      b. Vice-President — serves in the absence of the President
      c. Secretary — keeps minutes, is custodian of the corporate records and stock transfer books
      d. Treasurer — has custody and is responsible for all funds and securities of the corporation
   3. Authority of officers
      a. Actual express authority — arises from the incorporation statute, the articles, the bylaws, and resolutions of the directors
      b. Actual implied authority — officers have this authority to do what is reasonably necessary
      c. Apparent authority — arises when a third party relies on the fact that an officer has exercised the same authority in the past
      d. Ratification — a corporation may ratify the unauthorized acts of its officers

E. **Duties of Directors and Officers**
   1. Duty of obedience — directors and officers must act within their authority
   2. Duty of diligence — they must exercise ordinary care and prudence
      a. Reliance upon others — they are permitted to entrust important work to others
      b. Business judgment rule — precludes imposing liability upon the directors for honest mistakes of judgment
   3. Duty of loyalty — they owe a fiduciary duty to the corporation and its shareholders
      a. Conflict of interests — today, a contract between officers or directors and the corporation may be upheld under certain safeguards
      b. Loans to directors — by the corporation are not permitted without shareholder authorization
      c. Corporate opportunity — directors and officers may not usurp any corporation opportunity
      d. Transactions in shares — the issue of shares at favorable prices to management could constitute a breach of the fiduciary duty
      e. Duty not to compete — directors and officers may not compete with the corporation
   4. Indemnification of Directors and Officers — a corporation may indemnify a director or officer for liability incurred if he acted in good faith and he was not adjudged negligent or liable for misconduct
   5. Liability Limitation Statutes — forty states have authorized corporations, with shareholder approval, to limit or eliminate the liability of directors in some instances

TRUE-FALSE: Circle true or false.

T   F   1. Bylaws may require a number greater than a simple majority of the directors for a quorum in order to transact corporate business.

T   F   2. Shareholders elect the corporation's board of directors who manage the business of the corporation.

T   F   3. Because they are so important to a publicly held corporation, directors are usually full-time employees who owe a fiduciary duty to the shareholders.

T   F   4. The bylaws of a corporation set forth the duties of each officer of the corporation.

T   F   5. Under the Revised Act, one person may be both the president and secretary of a corporation.

T   F   6. Each corporation must comply with rigid common law requirements establishing the qualifications of directors.

T   F   7. Although officers and directors are generally free from personal liability on contracts of the corporation, they are personally liable for breaching any duty they owe to the corporation and shareholders.

T   F   8. According to the Revised Act, a vacancy on the board of directors may be filled by a majority vote of the remaining directors.

T   F   9. Shareholders and directors generally do not have the right to inspect the books of the corporation.

T   F   10. Cumulative voting works to the advantage of the majority shareholders.

T   F   11. The vast majority of corporations are closely held corporations.

T   F   12. Directors and officers of a corporation may not engage in their own private business interests during their tenure with the corporation.

KEY TERMS — MATCHING EXERCISE: Select the term that best completes each statement below.

1. Liability of directors	8. Fiduciary duty	15. Direct suit
2. Voting trust	9. Majority	16. Business judgment rule
3. Short-swing	10. Derivative suit	17. Secretary
4. Honorarium	11. Conflict of interest	18. Proxy
5. Bylaws	12. Interlocking directorate	19. Treasurer
6. Insider	13. Void	20. President
7. Quorum	14. Cumulative voting	

_____1. An action taken by a shareholder to enforce the right to inspect corporate books.

_____2. The small fee paid a director for attendance at meetings.

_____3. The essence of this obligation is the subordination of self-interest to the interest of the corporation.

_____4. The shareholder's remedy for breach of fiduciary duty by a director.

_____5. The problem of involvement when a contract is made between a director and the corporation.

_____6. The term that describes two corporations having common directors.

_____7. The number of directors usually necessary for a quorum.

_____8. An officer or director who has advance information not available to the public that may affect the future market value of stock.

_____9. A written agreement created when one or more shareholders transfer their shares to a trustee who is authorized to vote the shares.

_____10. The voting procedure that may allow a minority shareholder to obtain minority representation on the board of directors.

_____11. The principle that courts will not substitute their judgment for a good faith decision by the directors or officers of a corporation.

_____12. The principal executive officer of the corporation.

_____13. The minimum number of members necessary to be present at a meeting in order to transact business.

_____14. A shareholder's authorization to an agent to vote her shares at a particular meeting.

_____15. Rules adopted by a corporation to manage its internal affairs.

MULTIPLE CHOICE: Select the alternative that best completes each statement below.

_____1. Because of their positions of trust and loyalty, directors can best be described as (a) fiduciaries (b) trustees (c) salespersons (d) none of the above.

_____2. Generally, a corporation has the following officers, a (a) president (b) secretary (c) treasurer (d) all of the above.

_____3. Typically, bylaws include (a) the time and place of shareholders' meetings (b) the qualifications of directors (c) the number of directors needed for a quorum (d) all of the above.

_____4. Directors are most often elected for a term of (a) 3 years (b) 6 years (c) 5 years (d) 1 year.

_____5. A method of ridding the corporation of a poor director is (a) firing the director (b) removal by vote of the shareholders (c) removal by a quorum of the other directors (d) none of the above.

_____6. Officers of a corporation are (a) appointed by the shareholders (b) removed by the shareholders (c) agents of the corporation (d) all of the above.

_____7. The majority of the members of the board of directors constitutes a (a) quorum (b) bylaw directorate (c) proxy (d) all of the above.

_____8. Director power might include (a) fixing the selling price of newly issued shares (b) amending the bylaws (c) initiating merger proceedings (d) all of the above.

_____9. In an election of directors of a corporation, cumulative voting allows a (a) shareholder to distribute votes among many candidates (b) shareholder to give all votes to one candidate (c) minority shareholder to obtain minority representation on the board if a certain minimum number of shares are owned (d) all of the above.

_____10. In relation to other contracts, courts subject contracts between corporations with interlocking directorates to (a) more scrutiny (b) less scrutiny (c) the same scrutiny as other corporations' contracts (d) no scrutiny since such contracts are void.

_____11. A closely held corporation has (a) a small number of shareholders (b) no ready market for its shares (c) shareholders who are often also the corporation's directors and officers (d) all of the above.

_____12. The only potential personal liability a shareholder may have would be liability for (a) defective incorporation (b) disregard of corporateness (c) receipt of improper distributions (d) all of the above.

_____13. The duties the directors and officers of a corporation are required to perform include the duties of (a) obedience (b) diligence (c) loyalty (d) all of the above.

CASE PROBLEMS — SHORT ESSAY ANSWERS: Read each case problem carefully. When appropriate, answer by stating a Decision for the case and by explaining the rationale — Rule of Law — relied upon to support your decision.

1. In a corporation with cumulative voting, X has only ten shares. Each share has one vote. There are three directors to be elected. Explain the possible voting methods X can follow.

   Decision: _____

   _____

   Rule of Law: _____

2. If A, as president of B Corporation, learns of a good buy in land that the corporation expected to buy and would use profitably, can A buy the land personally without informing the corporation? Explain.

   Decision: _____

   _____

   Rule of Law: _____

3. All the directors of X Corporation vote to convey, by deed, corporate land to Z. Each of the directors votes separately on the matter without a board meeting. Is such a vote binding on the corporation? Explain.

   Decision: _____

   _____

   Rule of Law: _____

4. X, director of Y Corporation, using X's best judgment, convinces the corporation to enter into a contract with Z Corporation. Y Corporation loses a lot of money on the contract. The shareholders bring suit against X for the loss. What result?

Decision: _____

_____

Rule of Law: _____

5. X, an out-of-state director of Y Corporation, has not attended a directors' meeting for five years. The corporation suffers serious losses, and the shareholders seek to hold X liable. What result?

Decision: _____

_____

Rule of Law: _____

Chapter 38

FUNDAMENTAL CHANGES

SCOPE NOTE

Chapter 38 brings our discussion of corporation law to a close. The chapter focuses on laws regulating the amending of the corporation's charter, the termination of the corporation's existence, and cases where independent business enterprises seek to join forces. Why would individual corporate enterprises wish to combine operations? What forms of combination are recognized by the law? How and why would a corporation terminate its existence? How are corporations regulated by the respective states in which they operate? These and other pertinent concerns complete our study of corporate law.

EDUCATIONAL OBJECTIVES

1. Discuss the methods and procedures for amending a corporation's charter.

2. Distinguish between the processes related to, the reasons for, and the effect of consolidation and merger.

3. Discuss shareholder rights/remedies related to opposing corporate combinations.

4. Contrast voluntary and involuntary dissolution procedures and their related effects.

CHAPTER OUTLINE

I. **Charter Amendments**
   A. **Approval by Directors and Shareholders** — the board of directors adopts a resolution setting forth the proposed amendment that then must be approved by a majority vote of the shareholders
   B. **Approval by Directors** — the Revised Act permits directors to adopt certain amendments without shareholder action

II. **Combinations**
   A. **Purchase or Lease of All or Substantially All of the Assets** — of another corporation results in no change in the legal personality of either corporation

        1.   Regular course of business — if sale or lease is in this manner, approval of the directors is required but not of the shareholders

        2.   Other than in regular course of business — the sale or lease also requires approval of the shareholders

  B.   **Purchase of Shares** — an alternative to the purchase of the assets of another corporation

        1.   Sale of control — the courts require that such sales be made with due care

        2.   Tender offer — another method of purchasing shares of another corporation

  C.   **Compulsory Share Exchange** — a method of share acquisition that is compulsory on all owners of the acquired shares

  D.   **Merger** — of two or more corporations is the combination of all of their assets

  E.   **Consolidation** — combines the assets of two or more corporations in which title is taken by a newly created corporation

  F.   **Going Private Transactions** — a corporate combination that makes a publicly held corporation a private one

        1.   Cash-out combinations — used to eliminate minority shareholders by forcing them to accept cash or property for their shares

        2.   Management buy-out — a transaction by which existing management increases its ownership of a corporation and eliminates its public shareholders

  G.   **Dissenting Shareholders** — a shareholder's statutory right to dissent and receive payment for her shares when she objects to fundamental changes in the corporation

        1.   Transactions giving rise to dissenters' rights — examples are listed

        2.   Procedure — the corporation must notify the shareholders of the dissenter's rights before the vote is taken on the corporate action

        3.   Appraisal remedy — payment by the corporation of the fair value of the dissenters' shares plus interest

III. Dissolution

  A. **Voluntary Dissolution** — effected by a resolution of the board with the approval of a majority of the shareholders

  B. **Involuntary Dissolution** — effected by administrative dissolution or by judicial dissolution

  C. **Administrative Dissolution** — commenced by the Secretary of State

  D. **Judicial Dissolution** — may be brought by the state, a shareholder, or a creditor

IV. Liquidation — the winding up of the corporation's affairs and liquidation of its assets

V. Protection of Creditors — the statutory safeguards for creditors after dissolution of the corporation

TRUE—FALSE: Circle true or false.

T   F   1. It is illegal for one corporation to acquire all the assets, including the good will, of another corporation.

T   F   2. The purchase of all the assets of one corporation by another completely alters the legal existence of both.

T   F   3. Unlike a sale, mergers require one corporation to cease existence.

T   F   4. The surviving corporation in a merger assumes the merged corporation's debts and liabilities.

T   F   5. The dissenting shareholders in a merger have no recourse.

T   F   6. Dissolution terminates the corporation's existence and requires the corporation to liquidate its assets.

T   F   7. Shareholders of each corporation in a consolidation must receive new stock of the same class from the newly formed corporation.

T   F   8. Fundamental changes, such as amendments to the articles of incorporation, generally require the approval of the corporation's shareholders.

T   F   9. Dissenting shareholders in a merger or consolidation must notify the corporation in writing of their objections and of their demand for payment for their stock.

T   F   10. Involuntary liquidation of a corporation is usually conducted by the corporation's board of directors.

T   F   11. According to the Revised Act, all amendments to a corporation's articles of incorporation require shareholders' approval.

T   F   12. If acts of the directors are illegal or fraudulent, the shareholders may bring a court action for dissolution of the corporation.

KEY TERMS — MATCHING EXERCISE: Select the term that best completes each statement below.

1. Parent corporation	8. Dissenting shareholder	15. Appraisal remedy
2. Consolidation	9. Fair value	16. Leveraged buyouts
3. Merger	10. Preferred shareholder	17. Involuntary dissolution
4. Subsidiary corporation	11. Voluntary dissolution	18. Secretary of State
5. Par value	12. Short-form merger	19. Articles of Incorporation
6. Dissolution	13. Liquidation	20. Tender offer
7. Creditors	14. Interstate	

_____1. A combination of corporations leaving one survivor.

_____2. A combination of corporations leaving no survivors but instead a new corporation.

_____3. The right of dissenting shareholders to recover the fair value of their shares.

_____4. The name of a corporation owned or acquired by another corporation.

_____5. The value of the stock to which a dissenting shareholder is entitled.

_____6. The method of stopping the continuation of a corporation's business.

_____7. The persons who have the superior right to the corporate assets upon its dissolution.

_____8.   A shareholder who does not agree with a plan of merger.

_____9.   The kind of combination when a corporation owns at least 90% of the outstanding shares of another corporation (called a subsidiary) and combines the subsidiary into itself.

_____10.   The procedure for turning into cash all assets for distribution first to the creditors of a corporation.

_____11.   A general invitation to all the shareholders of a target company to offer their shares for sale at a specified price.

_____12.   Another name for management buyouts that make extensive use of borrowed funds.

_____13.   The name of a corporation that acquires another corporation.

_____14.   Dissolution of a corporation without court action.

_____15.   Dissolution by a court action brought by a creditor who shows that the corporation is unable to pay its debts as they become due.

MULTIPLE CHOICE: Select the alternative that best completes each statement below.

_____1.   Which of the following requires shareholder approval? (a) the amendment of the corporate charter (b) merger (c) consolidation (d) all of the above.

_____2.   The Revised Act permits the board of directors to adopt certain amendments without shareholder approval such as (a) making minor name changes (b) extending the duration of the corporation (c) splitting authorized shares if the corporation has only one class of shares (d) all of the above.

_____3.   Dissolution (a) does not terminate the corporation's existence (b) requires the corporation to wind up its affairs (c) requires liquidation of the corporation's assets (d) all of the above.

_____4.   Annual reports of a corporation must be delivered to the (a) county recorder (b) board of directors (c) Attorney General (d) Secretary of State.

_____5.   Dissolution by court action may be brought by shareholders when acts of the directors are (a) illegal (b) oppressive (c) fraudulent (d) all of the above.

_____6.   Dissolution of a corporation (a) may be voluntary or involuntary (b) does not terminate the corporation's existence (c) requires that the corporation wind up its affairs and liquidate its assets (d) all of the above.

_____7.   Involuntary judicial dissolution of a corporation may be commenced by (a) creditors (b) the State (c) shareholders (d) all of the above.

_____8.   Statutory provisions governing dissolution (a) do not preserve creditor claims against the corporation (b) require mailing of notice to known creditors (c) do not require notice of any kind (d) none of the above.

_____9. A corporation may be dissolved involuntarily if it failed to (a) pay its franchise taxes (b) extend its duration that now has expired (c) appoint and maintain a registered agent in the state in the prescribed time (d) all of the above.

_____10. A resolution adopted by the board of directors is required for a (a) merger (b) consolidation (c) compulsory share exchange between corporations (d) all of the above.

_____11. The procedural acts in amending a corporation's charter include the (a) vote of the shareholders (b) vote of the board of directors (c) filing of the articles of amendment (d) all of the above.

_____12. The directors of a corporation may adopt certain amendments to the articles of incorporation without shareholder approval except an amendment that (a) makes a minor name change (b) changes the voting rights of shareholders (c) extends the duration of the corporation (d) none of the above.

_____13. Shareholder approval is not required for (a) a merger (b) the sale of corporate assets in the usual and regular course of business (c) a consolidation (d) all of the above.

CASE PROBLEMS — SHORT ESSAY ANSWERS: Read each case problem carefully. When appropriate, answer by stating a Decision for the case and by explaining the rationale — Rule of Law — relied upon to support your decision.

1. X Corporation is dissolved by act of the legislature and A, as a creditor, wants to know what A's rights are to the assets. Explain.

   Decision: _____

   _____

   Rule of Law: _____

2. Abby is a dissenting shareholder to a merger between corporations X and Y. Abby wants nothing to do with the new corporation and wishes to get her money back. The state in which both corporations are located follows the Revised Act. Abby does nothing for 45 days, then seeks payment for the shares. Is Abby entitled to payment? Explain.

   Decision: _____

   _____

   Rule of Law: _____

3. A "short-form merger" takes place between parent Corporation X and subsidiary Corporation Y. Do the dissenting shareholders of each corporation have the right to an appraisal remedy? Explain.

   Decision: _____

   _____

   Rule of Law: _____

4. A, a director with X Corporation, and B, a director of Y Corporation, believe that their corporations are too much alike and that something ought to be done to eliminate their competition. What possible steps might be taken?

Decision: _____

_____

Rule of Law: _____

5. X Corporation is a parent corporation to its subsidiary Y after a compulsory share exchange. Y owes A and B large sums of money but refuses to pay them after becoming the subsidiary. Can A and B sue Y Corporation? Explain.

Decision: _____

_____

Rule of Law: _____

PARTNERSHIP AND CORPORATION UNIT RESEARCH QUESTIONS: Drawing upon information contained in the text, as well as outside sources, discuss the following questions:

1. Assume you want to go into business. Your choice this time for the form of business organization is a corporation.
   a.   Trace the steps and explain the process necessary to incorporate the business.
   b.   Explain the differences between a corporation and a general partnership and those between a corporation and a limited partnership.
   c.   List the advantages and disadvantages of selecting a corporation as the choice for the business enterprise rather than a partnership.

2. Since you have chosen to form a corporation, it is necessary for you to create articles of incorporation, hold the first organization or board of directors meeting, and adopt bylaws. Draft examples of the documents, including minutes of the organization meeting, necessary for the formation and operation of your corporation.

Chapter 39

SECURED TRANSACTIONS IN PERSONAL PROPERTY

SCOPE NOTE

In today's marketplace, purchasers neither expect nor are they expected to pay fully for the goods, services, land or money that they plan to buy. When a seller/lender (creditor) performs completely for a buyer (debtor) who, in return, only partially performs, the unexecuted balance of the buyer's performance is called credit. The importance of such arrangements — promised future performance in exchange for present full performance — is reflected in the hundreds of billions of dollars of outstanding commercial and consumer credit. The person who has extended trust (credit) faces a risk of loss through debtor nonpayment. Chapter 39 examines the general principles and basic vocabulary associated with creditors protecting their position against nonpayment losses and obtaining a status superior to other creditors of and buyers from the debtor through security devices. The advantages of such secured credit over unsecured credit are discussed.

EDUCATIONAL OBJECTIVES

1. Identify the sources of law that control the issuance and maintenance of secured debt.

2. Explain the requirements for creating a valid security agreement in personal property.

3. Define and discuss the importance of a purchase money security interest.

4. Understand the significance of perfecting personal property security interests.

5. Outline the requirements for validly perfecting a security interest in personal property.

6. Distinguish among the various classifications of personal property in relation to attachment and perfection.

7. Explain the rules for determining priorities among conflicting interests, secured and unsecured creditors, purchasers, bailees, etc. in common collateral.

8. Discuss the rights/duties of the parties upon debtor default.

CHAPTER OUTLINE

I. Essentials of Secured Transactions
  A. **Governing Law** — U.C.C. Article 9
  B. **Contractual Base** — agreement, value and collateral; transaction intended as security
  C. **Definitions** — basic terminology
    1. Security interest — personal property securing debt payments
    2. Secured party — creditor holding security interest
    3. Debtor — owes payment
    4. Security agreement — contract creating security interest
    5. Collateral — property subject to security interest
    6. Financing statement — document giving notice of security interest
    7. Attachment — creating security interest
    8. Perfection — protecting security interest

II. Classification of Collateral — determines how to properly secure an interest
  A. **Goods** — movable tangibles; based on primary use
    1. Consumer goods — personal, family, household
    2. Equipment — business, professional
    3. Farm products — farming operations
    4. Inventory — held for sale or manufacturing
    5. Fixtures — attached to land or building
    6. Proceeds — money from sale of collateral
  B. **Indispensable Paper**
    1. Chattel paper — written document evidencing debt and security interest
    2. Instruments — commercial paper evidencing debt but no security interest
    3. Documents — bill of lading, warehouse receipt, evidencing ownership in goods
  C. **Intangibles** — not evidenced by indispensable paper
    1. Contract rights and accounts — right to payment not evidenced by instrument or paper
    2. General intangibles — catch-all category covering all other property not listed above

III. Attachment — elements necessary to create security interest; designates property for debt satisfaction upon nonpayment (default)
  A. **Value** — given by secured party; contractual consideration
  B. **Debtor's Rights in Collateral**
  C. **Security Agreement** — written document; identifies collateral; debtor signature
    1. Consumer goods — nonpurchase money household goods restriction
    2. After-acquired property — floating lien concept
    3. Proceeds — sale of collateral
    4. Future advances

IV. Perfection — protecting security interest against competing interests (subsequent creditors and purchasers), method determined by type and use of collateral and debtor status
  A. **Filing a Financial Statement** — document describing collateral, debt and identifying parties, notice of interest; sets competing claim priority
    1. Location — central (Secretary of State) or local (county residence or collateral location) depending on type of collateral
    2. Improper filing — generally ineffective
    3. Subsequent change of information — location of use changes; intra or interstate change
    4. Duration — initial 5 years plus 60 days renewable through continuation statement
    5. Required for nonpossessory collateral

    B.   **Possession** — pledge of goods or instrument
       1. Collateral held by creditor
       2. Filing grace period (21 days) prior to receipt or following release
    C.   **Automatic Perfection** — occurs upon attachment
       1. Purchase money security interest in consumer goods — goods acquired with extended credit from lender or seller
       2. Temporary perfection — grace period (usually 21 days) for filing; negotiable instruments

V. **Priorities of Secured Creditors** — ranking of competing interests in same collateral; original secured party vis-a-vis subsequent creditors and purchasers
    A.   **Against Unsecured Creditors** — secured prevails
    B.   **Against Other Secured Creditors** — special rules for fixtures, cases of accession, reacquired goods, finished products
       1. Perfected versus unperfected — perfected prevails
       2. Perfected versus unperfected — first perfected prevails
       3. Unperfected versus unperfected — first to attach prevails
    C.   **Against Buyers**
       1. Buyers in the ordinary course of business — eliminates inventory security interest
       2. Buyers of consumer goods — eliminates unfiled PMSI
       3. Purchasers of intangibles — generally eliminates earlier security interests
          a. Chattel paper, instruments or securities
          b. Instruments, documents — HDC eliminates earlier perfected security interest
       4. Other buyers — interest in identifiable sale proceeds; additional filing not necessary if covered in original financing statement
    D.   **Against Trustee in Bankruptcy**
       1. Perfected interest protected; unperfected security interest may be subordinated
       2. Preferential transfer avoidance
    E.   **Against Lien Creditors** — creditors with unsatisfied judgment execute against debtor property
       1. Judicial lien — perfected security interest preceeding judgment prevails; unperfected security interest subordinated
       2. Common law, statutory mechanics' liens — perfected security interest subordinated during lien holder's possession of collateral

VI.   **Default** — Rights/Duties/Remedies upon unexcused nonpayment; creditor option to enforce contract or seek judgment on debt; debtor due process protection
    A.   **Take possession of collateral** — breach of peace limitations; undisclaimable reasonable care duty
       1. Debtor's duty to assemble and make collateral avoidable
       2. Debtor bears expenses and risk of accidental loss
    B.   **Sale of collateral** — commercial reasonableness duty
       1. Public or private — creditor may be purchaser
       2. Notice duty — exceptions for perishables, recognized market, rapid value decline
       3. Debtor deficiency, creditor surplus liability
       4. 90 day rule for consumer goods, 60% of purchase price paid
    C.   **Retention of collateral** — strict foreclosure
       1. Prohibited — 60% purchase price rule
       2. Notice requirement — written objection forces sale
    D.   **Debtor's Rights** — redemption; forced sale
       1. Redemption — regain goods by paying debts plus expenses; cut off by sale
       2. Forced sale — automatic or through written objection or court order

E. **Distribution of Sale Proceeds**
   1. Reasonable expenses
   2. Debt balance
   3. Subordinated creditors
   4. Creditor liable for surplus
   5. Debtor liable for deficiency — statutory limitations

TRUE—FALSE: Circle true or false.

T   F   1. An obligation to pay money owed to another must be secured before it is valid and enforceable.

T   F   2. The Code defines "goods" as movable tangible personal property at the time of attachment.

T   F   3. A perfected security interest is not valid and enforceable against a trustee of a debtor in bankruptcy.

T   F   4. A security interest may be perfected by filing a financial statement or taking possession of the collateral.

T   F   5. Most states require the filing of a financing statement to perfect a security interest in a motor vehicle.

T   F   6. Perfection of a purchase money security interest in consumer goods occurs without having to file a financing statement.

T   F   7. Examples of "general intangibles" that meet the Code's classification of collateral are good will, patent rights and contractual performance rights.

T   F   8. A debtor has an absolute, unwaivable right of redemption that may be exercised at any time.

T   F   9. Consumer goods are purchased primarily for personal, family, or household use.

T   F   10. A goal of Article 9 of the U.C.C. is to reduce the cost associated with and foster the use of secured financing in commercial and consumer transactions.

T   F   11. For a security interest to attach, the security agreement must refer to and describe the transaction that gave rise to the debt.

T   F   12. A financing statement that has not been filed in the proper location is always ineffective against competing security interests.

KEY TERMS — MATCHING EXERCISE: Select the term that best completes each statement below.

1. Financing statement	8. Attachment	15. Chattel paper
2. Fixture	9. Perfection	16. Secured party
3. Inventory	10. Field warehousing	17. Floating lien
4. Contract rights	11. Foreclosure	18. Redemption
5. Equipment	12. Account	19. Debt
6. General intangibles	13. After acquired property	20. Pledge
7. Collateral	14. Mechanics lien	

_____1. Goods bought for business or professional use.

_____2. Property that is subject to a security interest.

_____3. The act of making a valid security interest in property enforceable against other creditors of a debtor.

_____4. An inventory financing arrangement allowing debtor access to pledged goods that remain under the secured creditor's control.

_____5. A document filed to create a public record of the existence of a security interest in identified goods.

_____6. Property not presently owned by a debtor that might be obtained in the future.

_____7. The act of creating a valid enforceable security interest.

_____8. Personal property so firmly attached to a building that it is considered part of it.

_____9. A payment right for sold or leased goods not evidenced by an "instrument."

_____10. Property held for sale or lease, including raw materials, items used in business or a manufacturer's materials.

_____11. Duty to pay money or perform an act that is owed to another.

_____12. Lender, seller or other person who owns a security interest in collateral.

_____13. Written document evidencing both an obligation to pay money and security interest in specific goods.

_____14. Delivery of personal property to secure payment of a debt.

_____15. Debtor's right to pay off a default on a debt and regain an interest in collateral.

MULTIPLE CHOICE: Select the alternative that best completes each statement below.

_____1. Priority among competing secured interests in common collateral is governed by (a) state legislation (b) the FTC (c) Article 9 of the U.C.C. (d) the equitable doctrine of laches.

_____2. One who owes payment or performance on an obligation is the (a) secured party (b) debtor (c) attacher (d) perfector.

_____3. Under the Code's classification of collateral, goods are divided into (a) inventory (b) equipment (c) farm products (d) all of the above.

_____4. A security agreement is enforceable between the parties upon (a) perfection (b) attachment (c) filing (d) registering.

_____5. One who acquires title to property free of either known or unknown perfected security interests is a (a) trustee in bankruptcy (b) lien creditor (c) buyer in the ordinary course of business (d) all of the above.

_____6. A secured transaction involves (a) a money payment obligation (b) creditor interest in specific property of the debtor (c) securing payment on the debt (d) all of the above.

_____7. Priority among competing unperfected security interests in common collateral rests on (a) order of attachment (b) location of collateral (c) time of filing (d) type of collateral.

_____8. A financing statement is automatically effective for a period of (a) 4 years (b) 8 years (c) 5 years (d) 10 years from the filing date.

_____9. When two security interests, both perfected by filing, are held by different creditors in the same collateral, priority is determined by (a) time of attachment (b) type of collateral (c) place of filing (d) time of filing.

_____10. The information required in a financing statement for it to be effective includes (a) the details of the sales transaction creating the debt (b) a description of the collateral (c) co-signature of the debtor's spouse (d) all of the above.

_____11. Examples of value as defined by the Code include (a) an antecedent debt (b) contractual consideration (c) a binding credit extension commitment (d) all of the above.

_____12. _____ extends the time period over which a financing statement is effective. (a) continuation statement (b) termination notice (c) release statement (d) filing statement.

_____13. Examples of lien creditors include (a) secured creditors (b) holders of pledges (c) trustees in bankruptcy (d) all of the above.

CASE PROBLEMS — SHORT ESSAY ANSWERS: Read each problem carefully. When appropriate, answer by stating a Decision for the case and by explaining the rationale — Rule of Law — relied upon to support your decision.

1. Merchant seller S sold goods to buyer B under a conditional sales contract. Buyer took the goods home but later stopped making payments on the contract. S asserts a right to take possession of the goods. Buyer resists. Who wins this dispute and why?

   Decision: _____

   _____

   Rule of Law: _____

2. Lawyer L receives a $1,500 loan from bank B. As collateral for the loan, L lists an office library, calling it inventory since the books are continually used. B questions this classification and believes it is improper. What advice can you give?

   Decision: _____

   _____

   Rule of Law: _____

3. Re-read case problem #2. Assume L sells the library to Bev Bookbuyer for $1,000. B seeks to claim the money, but L resists, arguing that B's interest was in the books, not money. Advise B.

   Decision: _____

   _____

   Rule of Law: _____

4. Borrower B grants lender L a security interest in a sculpture that B owns for $3,500 that L advances to B. A financing statement is executed and filed by L. Sometime later, B pledges the sculpture to C for an additional $1,500. B defaults on both loans. Who has priority to the sculpture? Explain.

   Decision: _____

   _____

   Rule of Law: _____

5. B, an automobile assembly line worker, purchases from S a $2,500 TV/stereo entertainment unit under a conditional sales contract. S retains a purchase money security interest in the unit. After properly making 17 of the 25 $100 monthly payments called for in the contract, B, laid off from the assembly plant, is unable to make any further payments and defaults on the contract. S repossesses the unit with the intent to retain it as full satisfaction on the debt and so informs B. B believes S's actions are improper but S disagrees. Who is right? Explain.

Decision: _____

_____

Rule of Law: _____

Chapter 40

SURETYSHIP

SCOPE NOTE

Chapter 40 continues our discussion of security interests in personal property. It focuses on debt enforcement against third party cosigners of the debt payment obligation following debtor default. This area of law, called suretyship, is an alternative to the debt enforcement provisions of U.C.C. Article 9. Suretyship law is a non-Code, nonproprietary method of creating and enforcing security interests presuming a three-party secured transaction: the creditor; the debtor; and one or more parties promising to make payment on the debt if the debtor does not. The terminology, controlling doctrines, and enforcement steps of surety law are examined in Chapter 40.

EDUCATIONAL OBJECTIVES

1. Identify and define the parties involved in a suretyship transaction.

2. Differentiate a strict surety from a guarantor and discuss what significance this difference has under the Statute of Frauds.

3. Explain how surety contracts are created.

4. List various payment defenses available to sureties.

5. Discuss alternative courses of action open to sureties upon making debt payments.

CHAPTER OUTLINE

I. **Nature and Formation** — contractually based creditor protection (third party agrees to debt payment)
   A. **Types of Payment Guaranty Contracts** — for return value or gratuitous
      1. Surety — creditor protection
        a. Primary, concurrent, joint obligor on debt-creating contract
        b. Statute of Frauds not applicable
      2. Guarantor — creditor protection
        a. Secondary, conditional payment liability following default and notice of; not a party to debt-creating contract
        b. Statute of Frauds applicable

3. Indemnity — two-party (debtor, insurer) debtor protection. Debtor pays premium for insurer to assume nonpayment risk

B. **Formation** — debtor, creditor and third-party agreement; Statute of Frauds might apply

II. Rights of Surety — against creditor or debtor

A. **Exoneration** — against debtor to compel payment; based on court order; against creditor to extent of collateral value

B. **Reimbursement** — against debtor for payment of debt; actual amount paid; not until debt due

C. **Subrogation** — takes creditor's rights against debtor upon debt payment; enforces security interest; prevents creditor release of collateral; assumes debtor rights against creditor

D. **Contribution** — against co-sureties following full payment; equal share rule and recovery of disproportionate payment share; time extension, release may discharge co-sureties

III. Creditor Rights

A. **Proceed Against Debtor or Third Party, Regardless of Collateral**

B. **Notice Not Generally Required** — delay of required notice may discharge surety

C. **Joint/Several Liability Among Co-sureties**

D. **Prevent Surety from Releasing, Impairing Collateral**

IV. Defenses of Surety — discharge payment obligation; asserted by surety

A. **Personal Defenses of Principal Debtor**

1. Not available to surety: incapacity, bankruptcy, statute of limitations, debtor misconduct
2. Available to surety: mistake, fraud, duress, illegality, undue influence, failure of consideration

B. **Personal Defenses of Surety** — fraud, material alteration, general release, contract breach, payment of debt, surety contract invalid, surety's claim against creditor, time extension

C. **Defenses of Both Surety and Principal Debtor** — forgery, material alteration, debt payment, failure of original contract

TRUE—FALSE: Circle true or false.

T   F   1. When property covered by an existing mortgage, is sold to a purchaser who acquires the property "subject to" the existing mortgage, the purchaser becomes a surety on the mortgage.

T   F   2. Suretyships may be created with any contractual wording conveying such intent of the parties.

T   F   3. Gratuitous surety relationships are binding on the parties involved.

T   F   4. The surety's obligation to pay the creditor is discharged when the principal debtor is a minor or incapacitated due to a mental condition.

T   F   5. Failure of the creditor to disclose immaterial facts to the surety is usually not fraud.

T   F   6. When the debtor's offer of payment is refused by the creditor, both the debtor and the surety are discharged from further obligations under the contract.

T   F   7. A surety is not obligated to make payment to a creditor when the latter, without the surety's consent, releases the principal debtor from the contract and makes no effort to reserve payment rights against the surety.

T   F   8. Upon the principal debtor's default, the surety's only recourse is to sue the debtor for the damages caused by the nonpayment.

T   F   9. In co-suretyships, one of the sureties may be liable for the full debt to the creditor.

T   F   10. Absent special circumstances or contractual arrangements to the contrary, sureties may not reduce payments to creditors by the amount of the claims debtors might have against the creditors.

T   F   11. The obligations owed the creditor by the principal debtor and the surety are contractually based.

T   F   12. When a material modification occurs without surety approval, uncompensated sureties are usually discharged from their debt payment obligation only if the modification jeopardizes their rights.

KEY TERMS — MATCHING EXERCISE: Select the term that best completes each statement below.

1. Fidelity bond	8. Exoneration	15. Conditional guarantor
2. Reimbursement	9. Money judgment	16. Statute of Frauds
3. Uniform Commercial Code	10. Subrogation	17. Payment
4. Personal	11. Performance bond	18. Bailbond
5. Substantive law	12. Main purpose doctrine	19. Estoppel
6. Surety	13. Contribution	20. Assumption of mortgage
7. Injunction	14. Official bond	

_____1. One promising to pay the debts of another.

_____2. One answering for another's debts only after the creditor has exhausted legal remedies against the debtor.

_____3. A specialized surety relationship designed to protect employers from the losses caused by dishonest employees.

_____4. A specialized surety relationship securing compliance with provisions of construction and building contracts.

_____5. Surety's right against a defaulting debtor upon the former's payment of the debt to the creditor.

_____6. Non-payment defenses that may be used only by either the principal debtor or the surety but not both.

_____7. The process under which the surety "steps into the creditor's shoes" following payment by the surety.

_____8. An exception to the general rule that the Statute of Frauds applies to suretyships.

_____9. The debt-paying surety's right against co-sureties when the former has paid more than their proportionate share of the debt.

_____10. Money that a public officer must deposit to ensure proper performance of certain duties.

_____11. Purchasing property subject to an outstanding mortgage by which the purchaser becomes the principal debtor and the seller becomes a surety.

_____12. Requires surety contracts to be in writing to be enforced.

_____13. Right of surety to require the principal debtor to make payment to the creditor when the debt is due.

_____14. An act that discharges both the surety and principal debtor.

_____15. A judicial bond in criminal proceedings.

MULTIPLE CHOICE: Select the alternative that best completes each statement below.

_____1. Situations in which surety relationships are usually created include (a) contracts involving minors (b) debts where security interests are readily available (c) pledges (d) all of the above.

_____2. A surety relationship does not typically involve a/n (a) creditor (b) investor (c) debtor (d) none of the above.

_____3. Surety rights against the principal debtor on the latter's default do not include (a) subrogation (b) contribution (c) partition (d) exoneration.

_____4. Suretyships arise from (a) contract law (b) tort law (c) public policy considerations (d) Constitutional law.

_____5. _____ of the contract is conduct between the principal debtor and the creditor that results in discharge of the surety's contractual duties. (a) execution (b) reimbursement (c) apportionment (d) modification.

_____6. Acts by the creditor that discharge payment obligations for both the principal debtor and the surety include (a) forgery (b) fraud (c) coercion (d) all of the above.

_____7. Substantial changes in important contractual terms made by one or more parties to the contract is (a) spoilation (b) material alteration (c) substitution (d) none of the above.

_____8. Examples of specialized surety relationships include (a) equitable suretyships (b) constructive suretyships (c) judicial bonds (d) all of the above.

_____9. Elements required for a valid suretyship include (a) capacity of the parties (b) an incidental third-party beneficiary (c) notarization (d) all of the above.

_____10. Refusal by the creditor to accept the debtor's offer of payment (a) constitutes a breach of fiduciary duty (b) often leads to criminal inditements (c) is usually grounds for defamation liability (d) terminates interest accruing on the debt.

_____11. Defenses discharging both the debtor's and surety's payment obligation include (a) impossibility of performance of debtor's contract (b) mental incompetence of debtor (c) extension of debt maturity (d) all of the above.

_____12. Surety relationships are used to (a) obtain credit (b) reduce risk of default (c) all of the above.

_____13. Defenses to payment that only the surety can assert include (a) creditor fraud against the surety (b) the surety's incapacity (c) failure of consideration (d) all of the above.

CASE PROBLEMS — SHORT ESSAY ANSWERS: Read each case problem carefully. When appropriate, answer by stating a Decision for the case and by explaining the rationale — Rule of Law — relied upon to support your decision.

1. Dean Debtor has obtained an $1850 loan from Casper Creditor. Their agreement, cosigned by Samantha Surety, calls for ten $185 monthly payments, final payment to be made no later than December of that year. Falling on financial hard times, Dean approaches Casper to extend the final payment date to March of the following year. Casper agrees. What effect does their action have on Samantha's payment obligations under the contract? Explain.

   Decision: _____

   _____

   Rule of Law: _____

2. Ben Borrower needs a quick loan for a down payment on a stereo/TV home entertainment center. He obtains a loan from Lenny's Loans, Inc. with the understanding that if Ben defaults, Lenny can seek payment from Ben's buddy Beatrice. Beatrice orally agrees to the arrangement but does not sign the contract. Both Ben and Beatrice assure Lenny not to worry since Beatrice's word is "good as gold." Sometime later, Ben stops making monthly payments on the contract and Lenny seeks payment from Beatrice. Is her promise enforceable? Discuss.

   Decision: _____

   _____

   Rule of Law: _____

3. Danny Debtor owes Cindy Creditor $18,800 in three separate loans, one for $9,000, another for $5,400, and a third for $4,400. On the $5,400 debt, Cecil Surety has cosigned as a co-debtor. Danny makes a $2,700 payment on his account with Cindy, including no instructions on how she is to apply the money. Cindy applies the payment to the $9,000 loan and seeks payment of the $5,400 from Cecil. He refuses to make payment, arguing that the $2,700 should be applied to the $5,400 debt and that he is liable for only $2,700. Who wins this dispute and why?

   Decision: _____

   _____

   Rule of Law: _____

4. Charlie Creditor lends $2,100 to Debbie Debtor. Cosigning the agreement is Salvatore Surety. Under the agreement, Debbie has pledged a $2,500 diamond broach to Charlie to secure her payment obligation. The broach is a family heirloom and when other family members learn of Debbie's action, they approach Charlie requesting his release of the broach. Sympathetic to their wishes, he agrees. What effect, if any, does this action have on Sal's suretyship status? Explain.

Decision: _____

_____

Rule of Law: _____

5. Ray Ramshackle, president of Ramshackle Construction, Inc., obtains a $425,000 loan from Cityville Bank to keep his floundering enterprise afloat. Cosigning the note is Sally Surety. Ray's business finally sinks and he files bankruptcy. Cityville seeks payment from Sally, who asserts Ray's discharge in bankruptcy as a defense to her payment. Who prevails and why?

Decision: _____

_____

Rule of Law: _____

Chapter 41

BANKRUPTCY

SCOPE NOTE

Debtors encountering financial problems that prevent timely and proper debt payments have several options to resolve their troubles. Some debt resolution methods involve informal agreements between a debtor and creditors. Others take the shape of formal judicial proceedings under state insolvency laws. When all attempts to reach agreement between debtors and creditors fail, federal bankruptcy is an option. Chapter 41 examines these choices with special emphasis on the historical development, substance and procedure of contemporary bankruptcy laws. The terminology and the legal principles associated with the three types of bankruptcy proceedings (liquidation, reorganization and debt adjustments) are examined.

EDUCATIONAL OBJECTIVES

1. Differentiate among the various non-bankruptcy forms of debt resolution.

2. Distinguish pre-judgment creditor remedies from post-judgment ones.

3. Explain the commencement procedures for voluntary and involuntary bankruptcy proceedings.

4. Trace the steps in a typical debtor liquidation proceeding.

5. Outline the duties of the parties associated with debtor liquidation proceedings.

6. Contrast the rights of secured and unsecured creditors as well as priority and non-priority claims under federal bankruptcy.

7. Discuss how the debtor's estate may be enlarged or reduced in size and value by the conduct of creditors and the trustee.

8. List non-dischargeable debts and explain the significance of discharge and debtor denial of discharge.

9. Explain the grounds and procedure for Chapter 11 corporate reorganization plans.

10. Describe Chapters 12 and 13 debt adjustment processes and explain their debtor/creditor benefits.

244

CHAPTER OUTLINE

I. **Federal Bankruptcy Law** — constitutionally based equitable treatment of creditors; allowing honest debtor a new start through liquidation or rehabilitation
   A. **Legislative Basis**
      1. Acts of 1898, 1938
      2. Reform Act of 1978 — modernize, streamline procedure; better protection for consumer debtor; creates new court, judges and trustees
      3. 1986 Reform Act
         a. Reorganizes structure, duties of trustees and judges
         b. Provides for family farm debt adjustment
   B. **Case Administration (Chapter 3)** — debtor's finances before federal court
      1. Commencement of the case — debtor/creditor seeks help
         a. Voluntary petitions — debtor (any person) takes initiative; files asset/liability schedule, creditor list, statement of affairs, exemption claim. Exclusions — financial institution, railroad, insurance company
         b. Involuntary petitions — creditors take initiative; not applicable against farmers, charities. Unsecured, noncontingent claims of $5,000 (3 creditors if 12 or more, 1 if less than 12)
      2. Automatic stays — upon petition being filed; halts creditor enforcement actions against debtor
      3. Trustees — administers debtor's finances (collect, sell assets, pay creditors); court appointed, creditor-selected estate representative
      4. Meeting of creditors — prove claims; examine debtor; establish committee
   C. **Creditors, the Debtor, and the Estate (Chapter 5)**
      1. Creditors
         a. Proof of claims — 6 month filing period; excluded claims include unenforceable ones, unmatured interest, excessive insider/attorney fees, certain landlord claims
         b. Secured claims — protection of security interest; unsecured for debt balance exceeding collateral value
         c. Priority of claims — full payment of certain debts in specified order (administration expenses, gap creditors, wages, employee benefits, consumer purchase prepayment, taxes)
         d. Subordination of claims — trustee discretion to promote fair, equitable distribution among equal priority claims; court decides payment order
      2. Debtors
         a. Debtor's duties — cooperation (surrender property, attend meetings, obey court orders); file proper documents; claim exempt property
         b. Debtor's exemptions — protected assets not subject to creditor claim; state or federal designation; personal, business assets; public assistance monies; homestead
         c. Discharge — relief from debt enforcement; debtor "misconduct" denies discharge; certain debts not discharged (taxes, child support, alimony, unscheduled claims, fraud, malicious tort, student loans, fiduciary tort, debtor reaffirmation of discharged debt)
      3. Estate — debtor's assets, legal, equitable, tangible, intangible; 180 days after acquired property provision; sales generated proceeds; products
         a. Trustee as lien creditor — estate enlarging (judicial lien enforcement, unperfected security interest), avoidance, voidable transfer avoidance
         b. Voidable preference avoidance — preferential (unfair) creditor payment (90 days, antecedent debt, debtor insolvency, undue creditor benefits)
         c. Fraudulent transfer avoidance — intent of debtor, one year time limitation, debtor insolvency, inexcusable deficient return value
         d. Statutory liens

D. **Liquidation (Chapter 7)** — debtor's finances terminated; new financial life commenced
    1. Proceedings — not commenceable by parties excluded from voluntary filing
    2. Distribution of the estate — payment order (secured creditor, priority creditor, unsecured creditor, balance to debtor)
    3. Discharge — denial, revocation based on debtor status, debtor "misconduct"

E. **Reorganization (Chapter 11)** — revival, continued operation of financially distressed business
    1. Proceedings — voluntary or involuntary except investment brokers, railroad. Debtor retains property possession, operates business
    2. Plan of reorganization — initiated by debtor, creditor, shareholders or trustee
       a. Unsecured creditor consultation with trustee
       b. Contents — class claim designation; equal treatment of claims; execution procedure
    3. Acceptance of plan — by class of claims, class of interests
    4. Confirmation of plan — court approval based upon good faith, feasibility, cash payments, creditor acceptance
    5. Effect of reorganization — binding on creditor and debtor discharged
    6. Conversion to liquidation if justified

F. **Adjustment of Debts of Individuals (Chapter 13)** — court supervised debt restructuring, repayment plan
    1. Proceedings — individual, business; regular income; unsecured debt under $100,000, secured debt under $350,000
    2. The plan — 3-year payment schedule extendible to 5 years; debtor filed; approved by secured creditors. Future income to trustee; full payment to priority claims; equal payment to claims within a class
    3. Confirmation — fair, reasonable and feasible; court approval. In creditor best interest
    4. Discharge — successful completion of plan; convertible to liquidation. Chapter 7 six year sale not applicable

G. **Adjustment of Debts of Farmers (Chapter 12)** — similar to Chapter 13
    1. Proceeding — 50% gross income from farming; $1.5 million gross debt ceiling; 80% debt from farming operations
    2. Plan, confirmation, discharge similar to Chapter 13

II. **Creditor's Rights and Debtor Relief Outside of Bankruptcy** — contractually, statutorily based debt payment; restructuring policies and practices

A. **Creditor's Rights**— debt enforcement, property preservation options; obtain court control over debtor assets to preserve debt payment
    1. Pre-judgment remedies — attachment (property in debtor's hands); garnishment (debtor property in third-party hands)
    2. Post-judgment remedies — exempt property excluded
       a. Writ of execution — demand payment; sale of seized property
       b. Obtaining additional property for debt balance deficiency (supplementary proceedings, garnishment)

B. **Debtor's Relief** — debt restructuring options; contract or statute based
    1. Compositions — contract; partial payment of each claim discharges full debt; nonparty creditor claims remain enforceable
    2. Assignments for benefit of creditors — contract based; property transfer to trustee for claims payment; debt balance not discharged
    3. Statutory assignments — combination of common law assignment and composition
    4. Equity receiverships — court-appointed third party takes control of debtor property. Property sale, business operation, preserve assets

TRUE—FALSE: Circle true or false.

T	F	1. State courts have exclusive jurisdiction over bankruptcy proceedings.

T	F	2. A debtor need not be insolvent to file for voluntary bankruptcy.

T	F	3. All creditors of a debtor share equally in the assets of a debtor discharged in bankruptcy.

T	F	4. A debtor in bankruptcy has a choice of claiming exemptions either under federal bankruptcy law or state law.

T	F	5. Both intentional and negligent tort claims are nondischargeable in bankruptcy.

T	F	6. Creditor claims of equal statutory priority must always be dealt with equally by the bankruptcy court with no claim receiving priority over the others.

T	F	7. In cases of involuntary bankruptcy, a debtor must owe claims totaling at least $15,000 before a petition may be filed.

T	F	8. Not all cases of corporate rehabilitation under Chapter 11 will result in the court appointing a trustee to administer the proceedings.

T	F	9. The only-once-every-six-years limitation for Chapter 7 proceedings does not always apply to cases of wage-earner debtor-adjustment proceedings.

T	F	10. A successfully contested involuntary bankruptcy petition resulting in dismissal of the proceedings may lead to creditor liability for the costs, expenses and damages incurred by the debtor in attacking the petition.

T	F	11. Bankruptcy discharge of a debt does not extinguish any security interest held against the debt.

T	F	12. Once a Chapter 13 debt adjustment has been confirmed, it can only be changed upon a petition brought by secured creditors.

KEY TERMS—MATCHING EXERCISE: Select the term that best completes each statement below.

1. Estate	8. Attachment	15. Reorganization
2. Exemptions	9. Trustee	16. Discharge
3. Composition	10. Bank	17. Confirmation
4. Receiver	11. Straight bankruptcy	18. Writ of execution
5. Priority claim	12. Debt	19. Judicial lien
6. Preference	13. Referee	20. Claim
7. Garnishment	14. Assignment	

_____1. A specific sum of money owed to another person.

_____2. A contract between a debtor and creditors providing for the pro rata sharing of the creditors in the debtor's assets as satisfaction on the creditors claims.

_____3. One who gathers and protects assets of a debtor under an action in equity.

_____4. Termination and liquidation of a debtor's financial life.

_____5. Claims that must be fully satisfied before payment may be made to other creditors.

_____6. Aggregate equitable and legal property interests of the debtor when bankruptcy proceedings are commenced.

_____7. Assets that a bankrupt debtor retains title to that are beyond the reach of creditors.

_____8. A statutory debt satisfaction proceeding used to seize property of the debtor in the possession of another person.

_____9. Bankruptcy proceedings that provide an opportunity for a financially distressed business to preserve its existence by eliminating poor management policies, practices and personnel.

_____10. A debt enforcement process by which property of the debtor is taken into court custody and applied towards payment.

_____11. Right to payment enforceable against a bankruptcy debtor.

_____12. Release from payment obligation through bankruptcy procedure for certain debts.

_____13. Creditor's interest in debtor's property obtained through judicial process to secure payment on a debt.

_____14. Court approval of a plan for reorganization.

_____15. Document obtained by judgment creditor, served on the debtor by a sheriff ordering payment of the judgment debt.

MULTIPLE CHOICE: Select the alternative that best completes each statement below.

_____1. The two types of petitions used for commencing bankruptcy proceedings are (a) equitable and legal (b) jurisdictional and stipulatory (c) voluntary and involuntary (d) none of the above.

_____2. Examples of unallowable claims are (a) ones for matured interest (b) those that are not enforceable against the debtor (c) reasonable attorney's fees (d) all of the above.

_____3. Which of the following is not a definitional element of a voidable preference (a) a property transfer made within 90 days of filing a bankruptcy petition (b) intent to defraud creditors (c) insolvency of the debtor (d) payment on a debt owing before the transfer.

_____4. The party whose duty is to gather, liquidate and distribute the assets of the debtor is the (a) trustee (b) referee (c) creditor (d) none of the above.

_____5. The purpose of bankruptcy is to (a) make equitable payments to creditors (b) discharge a debtor from unmeetable debts (c) enable a debtor to start a new financial life (d) all of the above.

_____6. A fraudulent conveyance requires (a) an intent to prefer one creditor over another (b) insolvency of the debtor (c) a transfer of property for little or no return value (d) payment on an antecedent debt.

_____7. Of the following claims, which are nondischargeable? (a) alimony payments (b) non-scheduled debts where the creditor had notice of the bankruptcy proceedings (c) payments made subject to a preferential transfer (d) moneys owed to foreign officials.

_____8. A debtor in bankruptcy must (a) file a joint stipulation with the spouse (b) post a bond with the court amounting to no less than 20% of the aggregate value of all claims owed at time of filing (c) submit a statement of personal preference to the referee (d) file a schedule of assets and liabilities.

_____9. Requirements for a reorganization plan to be confirmed by the court include (a) filing with the Secretaries of State for the residences of the creditors (b) feasibility of the plan (c) the plan providing for a minimal 45% return on a claim for each creditor (d) all of the above.

_____10. Under a plan of reorganization, creditors with rights of priority to have claims fully satisfied in cash are (a) business partners of the debtor (b) secured creditors (c) employees with wages owing (d) tax officials.

_____11. _____ occurs when a debtor voluntarily transfers property to a trustee with the understanding that these assets are to be used for payment on all debts then owing: (a) fiduciary trust (b) general assignment (c) extension (d) consolidation loan.

_____12. Requirements for the validity of a Chapter 11 reorganization plan include (a) stating how each class of creditor interests/claims will be treated (b) insuring that all claims and interests share assets equally (c) notarized appraisal of the debtor's net worth (d) none of the above.

_____13. Automatic stays terminate when (a) the debtor is discharged (b) a case is closed (c) a case is dismissed (d) all of the above.

CASE PROBLEMS — SHORT ESSAY ANSWERS: Read each case problem carefully. When appropriate, answer by stating a Decision for the case and by explaining the rationale — Rule of Law — relied upon to support your decision.

1. Sara Student, finishing her last year of medical school, is worried about the $8,500 in student loans she has outstanding. She seeks advice from her first-year law-school friend, Darence Clarrow, who assures Sarah that if she files for bankruptcy, "all her financial troubles will be over." Is Mr. Clarrow correct? Discuss.

Decision: _____

_____

Rule of Law: _____

2. D, recently discharged in bankruptcy, starts receiving calls from Ajax Appliance who urges D to reaffirm the $1,600 debt D had owed Ajax prior to the proceedings. D, worried about the "dire consequences" that Ajax had been referring to in the calls, decides to enter an agreement with Ajax for full payment on the debt. Is this contract with Ajax, who had notice of D's bankruptcy proceedings, enforceable? Explain.

Decision: _____

_____

Rule of Law: _____

3. D has fallen upon complete financial disaster. With an estate valued at $45,000, D files a Chapter 7 petition listing the following creditors: a $17,000 debt to Creditor One, $10,000 of which is secured; $8,000 in back wages to Creditor Two; $6,000 in unpaid income taxes to the federal government, Creditor Three; a $12,000 unsecured negligence judgment to Creditor Four who has filed this claim with the court; an unsecured $11,000 breach of contract judgment to Creditor Five who has also filed a claim; and a $10,000 unsecured loan from D's in-laws who have not filed their claim although they had notice of the proceedings. List how D's $45,000 will be distributed among these creditors.

Decision: _____

_____

Rule of Law: _____

4. Doodles Dingle, his finances in a shambles ($23,000 in liabilities, $4,200 in assets), is spending sleepless nights worrying over the creditor calls that constantly hound him. Having had enough, Doodles files for bankruptcy. At the creditor's meetings it is discovered that eight months prior to Doodles' filing, he had given his sister, Daphne, a $5,200 boat and his brother, Darby, a $7,500 car, both with the understanding that the property would be returned to Doodles when his financial woes were ended. Discuss the significance of Mr. Dingle's transfers.

Decision: _____

_____

Rule of Law: _____

5. Paddywack has over $120,000 tied up in his Knick-Knack Estates realty business. He also has debts of $100,000. With an intent to prefer various creditors over others, Paddywack transfers property worth $15,000 to those creditors. The other creditors ask your advice. Discuss the significance of Paddywack's transfers.

Decision: _____

_____

Rule of Law: _____

DEBTOR AND CREDITOR RELATIONS RESEARCH QUESTIONS: Drawing upon information contained in the text, as well as outside sources, discuss the following questions.

1. Research your State's law on exempt property. Compare Federal exemptions with your state's exemptions. If you were to file for bankruptcy, which exemption path would you choose and why ?

2. Over the past few years, three major corporate reorganizations, based on similar financial scenarios, have occurred — Texaco, A.H. Robins and Johns-Mansville cases. What do these cases have in common? Why did these firms choose bankruptcy as a solution to their problems? Is this a proper use of bankruptcy law?

PART NINE: Regulation of Business

Chapter 42

PROTECTION OF INTELLECTUAL PROPERTY

SCOPE NOTE

Since the late 19th century, the controlling influence of the "laissez-faire" philosophy defining the appropriate role of government vis-a-vis business has declined. In response to various private sector developments (anti-competitive practices, deception and fraud), the Federal government has undertaken an increasingly active role in regulating business practices that undermine fair, open, and honest competition. Chapter 42 examines the statutes, administrative regulations, and court rulings that define, proscribe and redress false, deceptive and unfair trade practices in the area of protecting intellectual property rights, including trade secrets, trade symbols, copyrights and patents.

EDUCATIONAL OBJECTIVES

1. Evaluate the policy considerations underlying proscription of false, deceptive and unfair commercial practices relating to intellectual property rights.

2. Explain common law doctrines and legislation protecting and regressing infringements on trade secrets, trade symbols and trade names.

3. Describe the purpose and protection process associated with copyright and patent laws.

CHAPTER OUTLINE

I. **Intellectual Property** — promote and protect research and innovation: new products, services
   A. **Trade Secrets** — commercially valuable secret information (formula, process, lists, etc.)
      1. Employee's duty not to reveal — ends on employment termination unless contract restriction
      2. Misappropriation — employee breaches loyalty duty; competitor espionage
   B. **Trade Symbols** — Lanham Act registration protection

       1. Types of trade symbols — distinctive identification of goods, services
       2. Registration process — U.S. Patent Office
       3. Infringement and remedies — civil and criminal sanctions
  C. **Trade Names** — words and names not within Lanham Act coverage
  D. **Copyrights** — original works of art, literature, expression of ideas; exclusive publication rights
       1. Procedure — federal control; protection covers author's life plus 50 years
       2. Limited use — compulsory license and fair use rules
       3. Ownership transferable
       4. Infringement and remedies — civil and criminal sanctions
  E. **Patents** — inventor's exclusive ownership (limited monopoly); nonrenewable 17-year period
       1. Patentability — useful, new and not obvious
       2. Procedure — federal registration with U.S. Patent Office
       3. Infringement — direct, indirect, contributory
       4. Remedies — money damages and injunctive relief

TRUE—FALSE: Circle true or false.

T   F   1. The law of unfair competition concerns business practices that disrupt protected intellectual property interests.

T   F   2. Employees have a duty not to reveal their employer's secrets to competitors.

T   F   3. A copyright lasts for a period of 17 years from the date of first publication.

T   F   4. Exclusive monopoly rights exist at the time a patent seeker files an application with the Patent Office.

T   F   5. Descriptive, personal and generic words and names may be protected as trade names.

T   F   6. For a violation of copyright law to occur, the infringement of the exclusively protected right must be intentional.

T   F   7. Patent protection is not renewable.

T   F   8. Computer programs are not copyrightable under federal laws.

T   F   9. Forces, substances and conditions of nature are not patentable.

T   F   10. Copyright protection applies to new ideas or concepts.

T   F   11. Trade symbol infringement does not require proof of intentionally caused or actual confusion.

T   F   12. The owner of a collective mark is either the producer of the goods or service provider.

KEY TERMS—MATCHING EXERCISE: Select the term wthat best completes each statement below.

1. Misappropriation	8. Sherman Act	15. Trade name
2. Palming off	9. Certification mark	16. Compulsory license
3. Trade secret	10. Abandonment	17. Collective mark
4. Trademark	11. Vertical	18. Works for hire
5. Publication	12. Allonge	19. Service mark
6. Lanham Act	13. Cease & desist order	20. Direct infringer
7. Copyright	14. Infringement	

_____1. Unconsented to interference with protected intellectual property interests.

_____2. Wrongfully using a trade secret.

_____3. Business, vocation or occupation identification.

_____4. Indicates origin, material or quality of goods.

_____5. Falsely representing one's products as those of another.

_____6. Protection given authors of original creative works including music, novels, plays, paintings and sculptures.

_____7. A distinguishing symbol identifying tangible goods or products but not services.

_____8. Trademark owner's failure to properly use the mark.

_____9. Federal legislation providing for protective registration of trade symbols.

_____10. Confidential information essential to the successful operation of a business.

_____11. Indication of trade union or association membership.

_____12. An unauthorized user, seller or maker of a patented invention.

_____13. Doctrine providing for copyright ownership to be held by non-authors of creative works.

_____14. Symbol identifying and distinguishing one's services from others.

_____15. Permission to make limited use of copyrighted material, usually accompanied by payment of royalties.

MULTIPLE CHOICE: Select the alternative that best completes each statement below

_____1. A process for protecting new distinctive fruits and vegetables is (a) presently nonexistent (b) called a plant patent (c) expressly banned by the Berne Convention (d) none of the above.

_____2. Trade secrets include (a) customer lists (b) product formulas (c) production methods (d) all of the above.

_____3. _____ meaning refers to the special significance acquired by descriptive, generic words through continued, extensive use connected to specific goods and services. (a) primary (b) popular (c) secondary (d) equitable

_____4. Symbols that are denied protection under Federal registration include (a) titles of TV shows (b) insignia of the United States (c) identification of how products are manufactured (d) all of the above.

_____5. One who actively encourages another to commit a patent infringement is referred to as a/n _____ infringer. (a) indirect (b) contributory (c) direct (d) equitable.

_____6. Unfair trade practices include (a) competitive advertising (b) registering trademarks (c) betrayal of trade secrets (d) free competition in the marketplace.

_____7. For a patent to be issued, a patent application must contain a/n (a) judicial certification of ownership (b) profit projection and market allocation (c) claims statement and specification (d) all of the above.

_____8. Remedies for unintentional violations of the Lanham Act include (a) a profit accounting (b) treble money damages (c) fine and/or imprisonment (d) all of the above.

_____9. To accomplish a valid transfer of copyright ownership, _____ is required. (a) consideration (b) a writing signed by the copyright owner (c) recording (d) all of the above.

_____10. _____ is the doctrine that allows reproduction of copyrighted works for the purpose of criticism, news reporting, teaching, comment or research without an infringement occurring. (a) Fair Use (b) Main Purpose (c) Reasonable Decency (d) Good Faith.

_____11. "U.L." is an example of a (a) service mark (b) tradename (c) collective mark (d) certification mark.

_____12. Patentability depends on the (a) dollar value (b) growth potential (c) newness and usefulness (d) none of the above.

_____13. Sanctions for Patent Act violations do not include (a) attorneys fees (b) fine or imprisonment (c) treble money damages (d) injunctions.

CASE PROBLEMS — SHORT ESSAY ANSWERS: Read each case problem carefully. When appropriate, answer by stating a Decision for the case and by explaining the rationale — Rule of Law — relied upon to support your decision.

1. Lanny Lantern comes up with a new design for battery-powered portable lamps. Searching for a name to attract and build sales as well as differentiate his product from that of competitors, Lanny coins the phrase, Portalantern. Lanny attempts to register this as a trademark. Will he be successful?

Decision: _____

_____

Rule of Law: _____

2. A and B have been long-time employees of Toys Manufacturing Company. During their employment, they have acquired highly technical skills and knowledge. A competitor of Toys Company—Playthings, Inc. — offers A and B higher paying jobs if they leave Toys. Their employment contracts with Toys contain no clause prohibiting employment with a competitor. What, if anything, may Toys Mfg. Co. do to prevent A and B from using the trade secrets of Toys when they go to work for Playthings, Inc.? Explain.

Decision: _____

_____

Rule of Law: _____

3. Following years of expensive, painstaking research, Dr. Science has discovered a cure for the common cold: a strain of bacteria living in the nodules on the backs of Australian green toads. Excited over potential profits and benefits for humans, Dr. Science is asked whether he intends to patent his discovery. Is his reply, "You bet," legally sound? Explain.

Decision: _____

_____

Rule of Law: _____

4. Elsie and Elmer Eskimo of Arctic Circle, Alaska, win $22 million in the Alaska lottery. They move south with their fortune to Guelph, North Dakota. Enjoying the warm climate and cultural wonders of their new home, the Eskimos co-author a book discussing the splendors of Guelph. They apply for and receive, but never register, a copyright for their publication. A few years later, another book, Guelph, North Dakota: Paradise Found, is released by Puffer Publishers. The Eskimos, believing the similarities between this book and their earlier work are more than coincidental, sue the authors of the new book for $1.5 million, alleging copyright infringement. Who prevails and why?

Decision: _____

_____

Rule of Law: _____

5. Home Products, Inc., markets their shaving cream under the name "Clean and Smooth." Over the past year, sales of the product have slipped substantially. To boost sales, Home launches a nationwide advertising campaign asserting that "Clean and Smooth" bears the American Association of Shaving Cream Producers (which does not exist) seal of hygienic purity. Cans of "Clean and Smooth" are marked with a circled "P" to indicate such approval. C&S sales jump 200% within months after the first ads appear. Competitors of Home Products, concerned over declining shaving cream sales, seek your advice. You tell them?

Decision: _____

_____

Rule of Law: _____

Chapter 43

ANTITRUST

SCOPE NOTE

America's economic philosophy is based on the belief that the public interest (product, service, prices, quality, availability and innovation) is best served through free and open competition in the marketplace. Concentration of business power in the hands of a few, through combinations and monopolies, is considered an unacceptable threat to the benefits of free, open trade. This chapter examines the law of trade regulation designed to deter monopolistic practices or other activities that constitute unreasonable restraints on trade. The sources of antitrust laws, the types of activities prohibited, and the role of Federal courts, administrative agencies, and state laws in promoting free competition in interstate commerce are discussed.

EDUCATIONAL OBJECTIVES

1. Evaluate the policy underlying laws proscribing "trusts" and "combinations" that threaten free and open competition.

2. Identify the types of business practices prohibited under Sections 1 and 2 of the Sherman Antitrust Act.

3. Define and develop the importance of the "rule of reason" test.

4. Differentiate the types of activities considered inherently anti-competitive under the Sherman Act.

5. Distinguish among the tests used to determine "monopolization" under the Sherman Act.

6. List the types of acts prohibited under the Clayton Act.

7. Explain how the Robinson-Patman Act strengthened government regulation of anti-competitive business practices.

8. Discuss the role of the FTC in promoting fair, open, honest and free competition.

CHAPTER OUTLINE

I. **Sherman Antitrust Act** — written in general terms; promotes free and open competition, prevents unfair concentrations of economic power: Section 1 - Restraints of Trade; Section 2 - Monopolies
   A. **Restraints of Trade** — unilateral or group-based contracts, conspiracies, combination to reduce competition, control market
      1. Tests — restrictive agreement; wrongful purpose; substantial anti-competitive effect, interstate commerce
         a. Rule of Reason — degree of anti-competitive effect: significant (illegal); insignificant (not illegal)
         b. Per Se violations — conclusive presumption of illegality regardless of motive, impact; agreement has no redeeming value
      2. Examples of per se violations
         a. Price fixing — price reasonableness, negative effect of price competition are not defenses
         b. Market allocations and territory restraints
            1) Horizontal — same market level competitors; competition increase, no defense.
            2) Vertical — not illegal; dealer/distributor restrictions from manufacturer.
         c. Boycotts — refusal to conduct business, deal
            1) Individual — not illegal for manufacturer to cut out retail seller not adhering to set price; linking wholesalers to resale price maintenance plan is illegal.
            2) Group — agreements to cut out specific firm or ones on a list are illegal
         d. Production control plan
         e. Tying arrangements — coercive reciprocal exclusive dealing
      3. Standing to sue — Justice Department; injured parties; state Attorneys General.
      4. Enforcement — criminal (fine/imprisonment) and civil (treble damages, injunction) sanctions
   B. **Monopolies** — price controls, competition exclusion
      1. Monopolization — monopoly power and market share
         a. Courts decide relevant market
         b. Cross elasticity test — interchangeable goods, same purposes
         c. Product price changes compared to sales responsiveness
         d. Nonstandardized product price production control exclusion
      2. Attempts to monopolize — issue of intent, chances for success; proving conspiracy, combination precludes market scope issue

II. **Clayton Act** — specific practices prohibited
   A. **Tying, Exclusive Dealing Contracts** — restricts dealing with competitor
      1. Goods only sold to certain buyer
      2. Goods sold only if buyer purchases other products from seller
      3. Indicators of illegality — tied items; market domination by seller; tied item readily available
      4. Defenses — separation impractical; product integrity and goodwill
   B. **Mergers, Acquisitions** — stock/asset (Cellar-Kefauver Amendment) purchase reducing competition in line of commerce, area of country
      1. Types — merger, consolidation, parent/subsidiary
      2. Economic categories — horizontal (same level competitor absorbed); vertical (different level, different function noncompetitor absorbed); conglomerate (neither of above)
      3. Establishing merger effect — probability of competition reduction, monopoly creation
         a. Present, future, competition patterns
         b. Substantial market — position of parties, degree of concentration relative to product, geographic markets

4. Justice Department 30-day notice — if acquiree has at least $10 million annual sales and acquirer has $100 million
        5. Failing company defense
    C. **Interlocking Directorates** — same persons on different boards of directors, interstate commerce, over $10 million total capital among the companies.

III. **Robinson-Patman Act** — overcome Clayton Act price discrimination deficiencies (local focus); protect small retailers competitively disadvantaged by chain store distribution, direct volume buying practices
    A. **Price Discrimination** (reduces competition, creates monopoly) prohibited
        1. Price differences among different purchasers of identical products
        2. Price differences across geographic areas
        3. Compensation for unrendered services — promotional allowances, facilities, commissions
    B. **Injury levels** — primary (direct competitor); secondary (competitors of favored customer); tertiary (competitors of favored customer's customer)
    C. **Recognized defenses** — good faith, commercially reasonable business practices explain price differences
        1. Cost justification — manufacturing, selling, delivery cost differences
        2. Changing conditions — perishables, business discontinuance, obsolescence affect market, demand for product
        3. Meeting competition — matching competition price reduction

IV. **Federal Trade Commission Act** — consumer division enforces prohibitions against unfair, deceptive acts/practices
    A. **FTC co-authority to enforce antitrust laws**
    B. **Prohibited Practices**
        1. Unfair — false advertising; shipping unordered goods; scare sale tactics; inducing employee disloyalty
        2. Deceptive — quality endorsement, testimonial misrepresentation; pricing policies (false savings claims); confusion regarding guarantees; trademark misappropriation
    C. **Enforcement**
        1. Rule-making authority
        2. Sanctions — civil (damages, cease and desist orders); criminal (fines)

TRUE—FALSE: Circle true or false.

T   F   1. Court decisions have had a major impact on defining what constitutes Sherman Act Section 1 violations since that Section is broadly worded.

T   F   2. For business practices to constitute prohibited monopolization attempts, both an intent to monopolize and a probability of success must be shown.

T   F   3. Violations of the Clayton Act are punished with criminal penalties.

T   F   4. A major objective of the Sherman Act is to promote free, open competition in the marketplace.

T   F   5. Price differentials are always Robinson-Patman violations regardless of whether they are based on cost savings or attempts to match competition prices.

T   F   6. Generally, monopolization by itself is sufficient to constitute a violation of the Sherman Act.

T   F   7. The FTC is responsible for promoting fair, honest, competitive practices in commerce.

T   F   8. A victim of a violation of the Sherman Antitrust Act is allowed to recover no more than twice the amount of actual loss suffered from the violation.

T   F   9. The U.S. Supreme Court has ruled that present/wholly owned subsidiary trade restraints are not Sherman Act violations.

T   F   10. Horticulture, labor and agricultural organizations are specifically subject to antitrust regulation by the Clayton Act.

T   F   11. The primary goal of antitrust law is to promote and protect free, fair and open competition in the marketplace.

T   F   12. Unilateral conduct by a single business can constitute an illegal restraint of trade under Section 1 of the Sherman Act.

KEY TERMS—MATCHING EXERCISE: Select the term that best completes each statement below.

1. Disparagement	8. Sherman Act	15. Per se violations
2. Conglomerate merger	9. Rule of reason	16. Cost justification
3. Exclusive dealing contracts	10. Horizontal	17. National Cooperative Research Act
4. Boycott	11. Vertical merger	18. Robinson-Patman Act
5. Interlocking directorate	12. Market allocations	19. Injunction
6. Market share	13. Cease and desist order	20. Retail price maintenance
7. Monopoly power	14. Tying arrangements	

_____1. Business arrangements that prevent buyers from doing business with competitors of a seller.

_____2. Ability of an enterprise to control prices or access to a marketplace.

_____3. Business arrangements considered automatic violations of antitrust laws.

_____4. Doctrine stating that only business arrangements that create unreasonable restraints of trade are violations of the Sherman Antitrust Act.

_____5. Business contracts that require a purchaser to buy more than one product from the seller.

_____6. Directives calling for an immediate halt to business practices and agreements that violate antitrust laws.

_____7. Refusal to do business with someone.

_____8. Antitrust violations involving restraint of trade agreements among competing retailers.

_____9. A test to determine whether an enterprise's control of a market is monopolistic based on product and geographic factors.

_____10. Illegal restraints of trade involving collaboration among competing enterprises to refrain from competition in specified markets.

_____11. Law passed by Congress to promote new technology research and development through joint ventures.

_____12. Manufacturers setting the prices at which retailers must sell products.

_____13. Defense to alleged Robinson-Patman violations based on documented cost differences among competing buyers.

_____14. A company purchasing one of its customers or suppliers.

_____15. Control over competing enterprises concentrated in a few persons or a small group.

MULTIPLE CHOICE: Select the alternative that best completes each statement below.

_____1. The Clayton Act, as amended, prohibits interlocking directorates in corporations that are (a) in direct competition (b) aggregately capitalized to the extent of 10 million dollars or more (c) engaged in interstate commerce (d) all of the above.

_____2. FTC remedial options include (a) contribution (b) corrective advertising (c) receivership (d) all of the above.

_____3. Which of the following types of business transactions is a "per se" violation of Antitrust Statutes? (a) floating contracts (b) territorial allocation of markets (c) unilateral boycotts (d) none of the above.

_____4. The Federal Trade Commission was established to (a) enforce state bankruptcy acts (b) draft a model antitrust code (c) supplement the Sherman and Clayton Antitrust Acts (d) enforce Fair Trade Statutes.

_____5. _____ refers to the area in which a firm sells its products or services. (a) geographic market (b) concentrated share (c) product market (d) none of the above.

_____6. Acquisition of the stock or assets of a competing company is referred to as a/n (a) vertical merger (b) conglomerate merger (c) horizontal merger (d) none of the above.

_____7. The FTC investigates (a) false or misleading advertising (b) stock swindles (c) fraudulent equitable receiverships (d) all of the above.

_____8. Which of the following acts prohibits price discrimination: (a) Lanham Act (b) Federal Trade Act (c) Robinson-Patman Act (d) Unfair Sales Act.

_____9. Restraints of trade among businesses at different distribution levels are labeled (a) triangular (b) vertical (c) multiple (d) equitable antitrust violations.

_____10. _____ injuries are Clayton Act Section 2 violations that cause harm to a seller's competitors. (a) tertiary (b) unconscionable (c) secondary line (d) primary line.

_____11. Factors assessed in determining geographic market share include (a) transportation costs (b) competitive product quality (c) marketplace efficiencies (d) all of the above.

_____12. Examples of "unfair conduct" under Section 2 of the Sherman Act include (a) technological advances (b) research and development efficiencies (c) activities intended to exclude competition (d) none of the above.

_____13. Antitrust law examines _____ to determine whether a merger violates antitrust. (a) absolute size of merged entry (b) size of merged firm relative to geographic and/or product market share (c) degree of unfair conduct (d) none of the above.

CASE PROBLEMS — SHORT ESSAY ANSWERS: Read each case problem carefully. When appropriate, answer by stating a Decision for the case and by explaining the rationale — Rule of Law — relied upon to support your decision.

1. Super Oil Company has contracts with its independent retail stations requiring them to purchase and sell only the Super Oil line of tires, batteries and auto accessories. Discuss the validity of this business arrangement.

    Decision: _____

    _____

    Rule of Law: _____

2. Whiskey, Inc., a liquor distributor, affixes a price tag to every bottle leaving its plant and requires all retailers handling its products to sell at the stated price. Discuss the significance of this business relationship.

    Decision: _____

    _____

    Rule of Law: _____

3. Home Furnishing, Inc., a retail furniture store, entered into an agreement with its supplier to sell Home Furnishing's inventory at prices below what the supplier was charging other retail furniture outlets in the same area. Learning of Home Furnishing's contract with the supplier, competitors argued that the agreement violated antitrust laws. Are they correct? Discuss.

    Decision: _____

    _____

    Rule of Law: _____

4. Pewtrid Paints, Inc., a manufacturer and retailer of paint products, is conducting a special advertising promotion offering one gallon of paint "free" with every two gallons purchased. The regular price of the paint is $9.99 a gallon. During this advertising campaign, Pewtrid raised its prices to $13.99 a gallon. Is this a violation of the FTC Act? Explain.

Decision: _____

_____

Rule of Law: _____

5. Metropolis County Bar Association issued a minimum fees schedule to its member attorneys requiring all members to abide by the schedule or face "disciplinary" action. Does this action constitute a violation of the Sherman Act? Discuss.

Decision: _____

_____

Rule of Law: _____

Chapter 44

CONSUMER PROTECTION

SCOPE NOTE

Over the past few decades, law has shown an increased concern for recognizing and protecting the rights of consumer purchasers. At state and federal levels, legislation, court decisions, and administrative rulings have assumed greater importance in equalizing the relationship between buyers and sellers in the consumer marketplace. Today's consumers are less at the mercy of caveat emptor (let the buyer beware) when they enter the marketplace. They have greater security in knowing that their contractual expectations will be satisfactorily met. Chapter 44 offers an overview of significant federal legislation designed to advance and protect the rights of purchasers at various stages and in certain types of consumer transactions. The policy underlying the statutes discussed is to recognize and give legal meaning to the various rights consumers assert under the "Consumer Bill of Rights": right to safety; right to information; right to recovery; right to fairness; and right to satisfactory fulfillment of contractual expectations. Chapter 44 develops the legal doctrines and principles of consumer protection in the context of credit transactions, real estate purchases, warranty coverage, safety, deceptive selling tactics and equality of bargaining positions.

EDUCATIONAL OBJECTIVES

1. Evaluate the policy underlying the emergence and growth of consumer protection laws.

2. Discuss the role of the Federal Trade Commission in controlling and preventing deceptive trade tactics and abusive, unfair warranty coverage practices.

3. Define, discuss the importance of, and identify significant provisions within the Consumer Credit Protection Act.

4. Explain the purpose and effects of the Equal Credit Opportunity Act, the Fair Credit Billing Act, the Fair Credit Reporting Act, the Fair Debt Collection Practices Act, and the Consumer Product Safety Act.

CHAPTER OUTLINE

I. **Unfair and Deceptive Trade Practices**— Federal Trade Commission
   A. **Legislation enforced** — FTC Act; Magnuson-Moss Warranty Act; Consumer Protection Act
   B. **Regulatory power** — prevent unfair competition; unfair and deceptive trade practices affecting interstate commerce

1. Fraud, misrepresentation, deception
2. Cliffdale test — material statement, practice, omission likely to mislead reasonably acting consumer
3. Issues trade rules — substantive law appealable to circuit court; HDC rule; home solicitation sales cancellation
   C. **Enforcement** — cease and desist order; affirmative disclosure; corrective advertising; multiple product order; injunction; fines

II. Consumer Purchases
A. **Consumer Warranty Act (Magnuson-Moss)** — FTC enforced
   1. Coverage — written warranties for consumer products over $5
   2. Regulation — no warranty requirements; written warranty must meet information, disclosure requirements
      a. Full, conspicuous, understandable disclosure of crucial terms
      b. Designation "full" or "limited" — for goods at least $10
         1) "Full" — no implied warranty limitation; repair, refund or replacement duty; no consequential damages limitation
         2) "Limited" — implied warranty limitable to duration
      c. No implied warranty disclaimer
      d. Promote informal dispute settlement
B. **Rights of Rescission** — contract cancellation within certain time period
   1. Door-to-door sales — state and federal law
   2. Lien against debtor's home — CCPA
   3. Land purchases — Interstate Land Disclosure Act

III. Consumer Credit
A. **Uniform Consumer Credit Code** — unify state credit legislation; similar to Truth in Lending; regulates home solicitation sales: 3-day cancellation right; wage assignment, referral schemes prohibited; balloon payment refinancing; deficiency judgment restriction
B. **Market Access** — Equal Credit Opportunity Act as part of CCPA; enforced by FTC
   1. Prohibited credit discrimination — race, religion, nationality, age, sex, marital status, public assistance
   2. Married women protections
   3. Prohibited inquiries related to loan application
   4. Written disclosure of credit denial
C. **Disclosure Requirements**
   1. Truth in Lending Act — part of CCPA; Federal Reserve Board enforcement (Regulation Z); pre-empts less stringent state law
      a. Coverage — nonbusiness real estate, consumer purchases under $25,000
      b. Credit cost disclosure — four installment rule; APR figure
      c. Open/closed ended credit distinctions
      d. Cancellation right — creditor lien against debtor's home
   2. Fair Credit Billing Act — part of CCPA; promote debtor fair treatment by billing creditor; dispute resolution method: consumer written notice of billing error; no creditor retaliation, collection, reporting of disputed debt; discounts for cash purchases
   3. Real Estate Settlement Act — cost, material terms, disclosure; restrictions — referral schemes; fees for unperformed services; taxes and insurance deposits
D. **Contract Terms** — State usury restrictions; FTC holder in due course rule

IV. Consumer Credit Fraud
   A. **Credit Card Fraud Act** — part of CCPA; card issuer restrictions; no unsolicited distributions. Unauthorized use liability limit — $50 ceiling; proper notification eliminates liability; no liability for unaccepted card
   B. **Fair Credit Reporting Act** — part of CCPA; enforced by FTC
      1. Ensure accurate, complete, updated credit information
      2. Application — merchant credit information compilers and dispensers; credit, employment insurance users. User, reporter, disclosure duties
      3. Debtor rights — name of user, reporter; access to file; removal of inaccurate, unverifiable information; contributions to file
      4. Mandatory file deletion — outdated information
   C. **Creditor Remedies** — rights/duties following debtor default
      1. Wage assignment restrictions
      2. Garnishment restrictions — 25% of disposable income; no job loss; hearing required
      3. Repossession restrictions — anti-deficiency judgment; 60% of loan price paid
      4. Payment acceleration restrictions
      5. Fair Debt Collection Practice Act — prevent unfair, abusive, fraudulent debt collection

V. Consumer Health and Safety
   A. **Consumer Product Safety Commission** — issues and enforces rules preventing manufacture and sale of defective or unsafe goods
      1. Legislation enforced — Consumer Product Safety Act; Hazardous Substance Act; Flammable Fabrics Act; poison prevention, packaging; refrigerator safety
      2. Regulatory powers — producer, distributor, retailer
         a. Set mandatory safety standards — unreasonable injury risk in design, materials, construction, packaging, labeling
         b. Ban further sale — cannot be made safe
         c. Accident records maintained — safety information
         d. Remedies — public notice; injunctions; recalls; repair/replacement/refund
      3. Violations — civil and criminal sanctions

TRUE—FALSE: Circle true or false.

T   F   1. Lack of coordination and inconsistent consumer laws among the states create few problems and complications for interstate businesses.

T   F   2. Under Federal warranty law, written warranties may not disclaim implied warranty protection.

T   F   3. A Sears credit card, a Texaco credit card, and an American Express credit card are examples of open-ended credit accounts.

T   F   4. When a credit card is lost, the card issuer must be notified within 24 hours of the loss, otherwise the card owner will be liable for all purchases made by the finder.

T   F   5. The doctrine of caveat emptor is a long-standing, fundamental doctrine of the American free enterprise system that controls today's consumer marketplace.

T   F   6. The Warner-Lambert case illustrates the FTC's power to order corrective advertising.

T   F   7. The two basic elements of a credit transaction that must be disclosed to the borrower by the lender are loan repayment terms and the cost of the loan.

T   F   8. A secured creditor may repossess the goods sold from a defaulting debtor-purchaser and retain them as full satisfaction on the debt under all circumstances.

T   F   9. Federal warranty regulations require that written warranty protection be given to buyers in all consumer sales over $50 in value.

T   F   10. Under federal legislation, advertisements and other promotional communications need not result in actual deception to amount to prohibited misleading or false statements.

T   F   11. The FTC Act contains provisions that specifically define what constitutes unfair or deceptive practices.

T   F   12. The Home Equity Loan Consumer Protection Act includes second homes and vacation homes under its definition of principal dwelling.

KEY TERMS - MATCHING EXERCISE: Select the term that best completes each statement below.

1. Equal Credit Opportunity Act	8. Magnuson-Moss Act	15. Interstate Land Sales Full Disclosure Act
2. Foreclosure	9. Fair Debt Collection Practices Act	16. Full
3. Waiver of abatement	10. Cease and desist order	17. Truth in Lending
4. Affirmative disclosure	11. Hazardous Product Act	18. Fair Credit Reporting Act
5. Closed-ended	12. Consumer transaction	19. Community Reinvestment Act
6. Rebate	13. Fair Credit Billing Act	20. Limited
7. Federal Trade Commission	14. Consumer Product Safety Act	

_____1. A single transaction issuance of non-revolving credit for a specific period of time.

_____2. A federal agency responsible for investigating unfair, deceptive fraudulent and misleading business practices.

_____3. Federal legislation designed to prevent deception and unfairness in consumer product warranties.

_____4. Federal legislation requiring that "statements of record" be filed in certain sales of unimproved land.

_____5. Federal legislation designed to end abusive, unfair debt enforcement tactics used by collection agencies.

_____6. A purchase of goods, services or credit for family, household or personal use.

_____7. A directive requiring businesses to halt deceptive or unfair practices.

_____8. Federal legislation enacted to protect purchasers of consumer goods from hazards associated with defective goods.

_____9. An FTC remedial device requiring advertisers to include in ad copy factual statements that reduce the likelihood of deception or misrepresentation.

_____10. Federal legislation prohibiting discriminatory extensions of credit.

_____11. Federal legislation designed to promote money expenditures in the geographic areas served by financial institutions.

_____12. Warranty granting purchaser rights of refund or replacement for unrepairable defects as well as no-cost repair services.

_____13. Federal legislation requiring the disclosure of consumer credit costs

_____14. Federal legislation designed to eliminate various problems associated with credit billing errors.

_____15. Federal legislation designed to insure accuracy and updatedness of consumer credit information.

MULTIPLE CHOICE: Select the alternative that best completes each statement below.

_____1. The total charges payable to the creditor by the debtor in a consumer credit transaction is called a (a) carrying charge (b) lender's fee (c) finance charge (d) credit fee.

_____2. Purchasers of consumer credit who use their homes as collateral in the consumer transaction may effectively cancel the security interest (a) by telephone (b) in writing if done within three days after the transaction (c) only with the consent of the credit extender (d) none of the above.

_____3. The goals of Truth in Lending include: (a) promoting competition among credit extenders (b) facilitating comparison shopping for credit terms (c) increasing stability in the consumer credit marketplace (d) all of the above.

_____4. The cost of consumer credit must be expressed in an (a) annual percentage rate (b) appraisal fee ratio (c) allocated monthly formula (d) appreciated rate schedule.

_____5. Appeals from FTC orders are taken to (a) Federal District Court (b) U.S. Supreme Court (c) U.S. Court of Appeals (d) Federal Court of Claims.

_____6. Federal law provides for a three-day cooling-off period in (a) purchases of all major appliances (b) door-to-door sales over $25 in value (c) car sales over $6,000 (d) none of the above.

_____7. Federal warranty law requires that written warranties (a) be written in plain language (b) contain the description label "full" or "limited" (c) explain informal dispute settlement procedures (d) all of the above.

_____8. State legislation granting new car buyers refund or replacement rights for unrepairable defects is called (a) lemon (b) equitable allocation (b) (c) lime aid (d) perpetuity laws.

_____9. Federal consumer credit protection legislation was designed to (a) restrict access to consumer credit as an anti-inflation measure (b) promote fair and accurate reporting of credit information (c) broaden debt enforcement remedies available to a creditor (d) remove unduly burdensome legal regulation of credit contract terms.

_____10. Information available to a consumer under the Fair Credit Reporting Act includes (a) the actual contents of a credit report file (b) the names of people from whom information was obtained (c) the source of the information (d) all of the above.

_____11. General nonfactual statements of opinion that the FTC does not consider unfair or deceptive are called (a) disclosures (b) puffery (c) warranties (d) disclaimers.

_____12. A Federal consumer protection agency with authority to regulate misbranded and adulterated products is the (a) National Safety Council (b) Wholesome Food Association (c) Safe Products Council (d) Food and Drug Administration.

_____13. The Real Estate Settlement Procedures Act (a) seeks to provide residential home purchasers accurate cost information regarding home purchases (b) grants home buyers a three day cooling off period to insure satisfaction with a home purchase (c) places a ceiling on mortgage interest rates (d) all of the above.

CASE PROBLEMS — SHORT ESSAY ANSWERS: Read each case problem carefully. When appropriate, answer by stating a Decision for the case and by explaining the rationale — Rule of Law — relied upon to support your decision.

1. Jackson was sent an unrequested credit card from Plakton Petroleum Corporation as part of a promotional campaign. The card was stolen from Jackson's mailbox. The thief made purchases of $250 with the card. When Plakton sends Jackson a monthly statement containing the $250 in charges, what amount will Jackson be responsible for? Explain.

Decision: _____

_____

Rule of Law: _____

2. P bought $850 worth of furniture from S under an installment vendor credit contract. P is unable to make the fifth $85 monthly payment and enters a wage assignment agreement with S. S notifies P's employer E to apply a percentage of P's wages to the debt. E, greatly upset over the bookkeeping complications the wage assignment might cause, threatens to discharge P unless the debt to S is quickly paid off. Are E's actions legal?

Decision: _____

_____

Rule of Law: _____

3. B purchased a new car from car dealer C. Under the terms of the credit agreement, B was to make 35 $160 monthly payments. A final monthly payment of $1,600 was called for to complete the purchase. If B falls on financial hard times and cannot make the final $1,600 payment, does B lose the car? Discuss.

Decision: _____

_____

Rule of Law: _____

4. B purchases a lawnmower from S for $450. The written contract contains a clause stating that no warranties, express or implied, run with the sale. After two weeks of use, the mower breaks down. Has B any recourse through the Magnuson-Moss Act against S? Explain.

Decision: _____

_____

Rule of Law: _____

5. New York married couple H and W receives a promotional flyer in the mail from Desert Land Sales Corp. of Arizona. The flyer advertises undeveloped one-acre sites as part of a 250-acre residential development in Suntown, Arizona. H and W, deciding the deal and its terms are quite appealing, sign for the purchase of one site. Other than the sales contract itself, H and W were given no other printed materials from Desert Land prior to or following their signing of the contract. Seven months after entering the agreement with Desert Land, H and W are laid off from work. Unable to make payment on their contract with Desert Land, they seek your advice. What will you tell them?

Decision: _____

_____

Rule of Law: _____

Chapter 45

EMPLOYMENT LAW

SCOPE NOTE

Chapter 45 examines state and federal laws that direct and control crucial aspects of employer-employee relations. Prior to the onset of the industrial revolution, most issues related to working conditions and employment practices were dealt with through criminal, contract and tort law. As American society changed following the industrial revolution, the personal relationship that characterized pre-industrial employer-employee relations was no longer an effective regulatory mechanism. The need arose for a more formal system of intervention to resolve the problems of labor-management relations, job injuries, unemployment and other issues. This chapter discusses these laws and their goals to promote employee safety, nondiscriminatory employment practices, equality of bargaining power, and "civilized" work settings.

EDUCATIONAL OBJECTIVES

1. Evaluate the policies underlying labor relations law.

2. Explain the scope and purpose of federal regulations on labor-management relations in the context of unionization and collective bargaining.

3. Discuss the breadth of applicability of federal laws prohibiting discriminatory employment practices.

4. Outline state and federal laws dealing with worker safety issues, worker and unemployment compensation, job security and decent working conditions.

CHAPTER OUTLINE

I.   Labor Laws — fair, stable labor/management relations; contrasted to 19th century legal position
    A.   **Norris-La Guardia Act** — nonviolent labor dispute defined; injunctions limited; yellow dog contracts prohibited
    B.   **National Labor Relations Act** — federal support for collective bargaining and right to unionize; employer unfair labor practices; creates NLRB and dispute-settling process; outlines union election process
    C.   **Labor-Management Relations Act** — employer free speech; ends closed shop; creates cooling off period; validates right-to-work laws; creates Federal Mediation Service; defines union unfair labor practices

    D.   **Labor-Management Reporting and Disclosure Act** — defines corrupt union practices; creates union member Bill of Rights; mandates democratization of internal union procedures

II.   Employment Discrimination Law

    A.   **Equal Pay Act** — prohibits gender-based salary discrimination; recognizes seniority/merit systems, work quality/quantity defenses to unequal pay

    B.   **Civil Rights Acts of 1964 and 1991** — prohibits race, religion, national origin, sex-based job discrimination
        1.   Discrimination — proof of improper employer intent not required
            a. EEOC enforcement authority
            b. Coverage exceptions — less than 75 workers; valid seniority/merit system; bona fide occupational qualification; valid ability testing
            c. Creates affirmative action program
            d. Examples of discrimination — disparate treatment, effects of past discrimination, disparate impact
        2.   Reverse discrimination — remedies past under-representation
        3.   Sexual harassment — respondeat superior doctrine applied to employer; basis for job decision; offensive work atmosphere standards
        4.   Comparable worth — respond to Equal Pay Act deficiencies (female work underpaid, undervalued); validation guidelines for equating job categories

    C.   **Age Discrimination in Employment Act** — prohibits employer age discrimination for 40 and older workers
        1.   Labor Department enforcement
        2.   Coverage limitations
        3.   Seniority, bona fide job qualification defenses

    D.   **Handicap Discrimination**
        1.   1973 Rehabilation Act
        2.   1990 Americans With Disabilities Act
        3.   1974 Veterans Readjustment Act

    E.   **Executive Order** — affirmative action for federal contractors

III. Employee Protection

    A.   **Employee Termination at Will** — restrictions on employer discretion, freedom in firing
        1.   Statutory limitations — retaliatory discharge, specified protected rights, just cause limit
        2.   Judicial limitations — contract (implied good faith, just cause), tort, public-policy based

    B.   **Occupational Safety and Health Act** — workplace safety (reduce job accidents); OSHA inspection and investigation of work hazards; compliance standards; worker rights; employer record keeping

    C.   **Workers' Compensation** — strict liability based; common law defenses ended
        1.   Worker, family compensation (lost income, disability benefits) for job-related injuries
        2.   Cash payment — specific amount for certain injuries; unspecified amount for general lost earning power

    D.   **Social Security and Unemployment Insurance**

    E.   **Fair Labor Standards Act** — hours, wages, age and hazard restrictions

    F.   **Employee Privacy**

    G.   **Drug and Alcohol Testing**

    H.   **Worker Adjustment and Retraining Notification Act**

    I.   **Family and Medical Leave Act**

TRUE—FALSE: Circle true or false.

T   F   1. Workers taking leaves of absence due to family health crises or births/adoptions cannot be summarily fired for having taken such a leave.

T   F   2. In applying Equal Pay Act provisions to litigation, courts have interpreted "equal work" to mean identical work and not substantially equal work.

T   F   3. The Norris-La Guardia Act specifically authorized Federal courts to employ injunctive relief in all types of labor disputes.

T   F   4. The Labor-Management Reporting and Disclosure Act outlines a union bill of rights in attempting to bring more democratic practices to unions.

T   F   5. The 1991 Civil Rights Act limits recovery of compensatory and punitive damages to only cases of racial discrimination.

T   F   6. Federal legislation prohibiting discriminatory employment practices applies only to businesses with gross capitalization over $3,500,000.

T   F   7. Federal law prohibits mandatory retirement for employees under 70.

T   F   8. Worker's Compensation Statutes eliminate traditional common law defenses in claims brought by injured employees.

T   F   9. The Fair Labor Standards Act prohibits employment of 14 to 18 year olds in non-farm hazardous job settings.

T   F   10. Workers in the private sector receive broad protection against workplace alcohol/drug testing program abuses under the comprehensive Federal Uniform Substance Abuse Testing Act.

T   F   11. Generally, employers are liable for sexual harassment committed by employees only when they know or should have known of the harassment incidents.

T   F   12. The Occupational Safety and Health Act specifically pre-empts state regulation of work setting safety issues leaving states with little regulatory authority.

KEY TERMS—MATCHING EXERCISE: Select the term that best completes each statement below.

1. Estoppel	8. Worker Adjustment and Retraining Notification Act	15. Affirmative action
2. Fair Labor Standards Act	9. Taft-Hartley Act	16. Yellow dog contract
3. Norris-LaGuardia	10. OSHA	17. Reverse discrimination
4. Labor dispute	11. NLRB	18. Employment at will
5. Renunciation	12. Reagan Act	19. Comparable worth
6. Workers' Compensation laws	13. Social Security	20. Union shop
7. Wagner Act	14. Fiduciary	

_____1. Controversies over employment terms and conditions or union representation.

_____2. Federal legislation intended to protect unionization and collective bargaining efforts of employees.

_____3. Federal agency responsible for enforcing employee rights under the Wagner Act.

_____4. Federal legislation designed to prevent various union unfair labor practices.

_____5. Employment programs focused on actively recruiting minority employees.

_____6. Federal legislation enacted to promote safe and healthy working conditions.

_____7. Federal legislation requiring 60 days advance notice of plant closing or extensive layoffs.

_____8. Congressional legislation establishing minimum hourly wage schedules.

_____9. Federal law providing retirement, death and disability benefits to workers.

_____10. State statutes creating commissions to administer injured-employee damages claims.

_____11. Employer/employee agreements prohibiting employees from joining or forming a union.

_____12. Work setting in which non-union members can be hired but must join the union representing other employees to continue on the job.

_____13. Description of employer affirmative action plans emphasizing racial or gender factors in hiring or promoting to achieve greater balance in formally secured jobs.

_____14. Concept stressing that wage scales among various jobs should be based on objectively grounded rating systems or performance assessments free of possible sex bias.

_____15. Common law doctrine allowing employers to hire employees at their own, generally unlimited, discretion.

MULTIPLE CHOICE: Select the alternative that best completes each statement below.

_____1. Present day statutory regulations of employment settings focus on (a) safety and health issues (b) discrimination (c) labor-management relations (d) all of the above.

_____2. Unfair labor practices by management include (a) mandatory dress codes (b) discrimination against non-union workers (c) refusal to bargain in good faith (d) all of the above.

_____3. Congressional legislation aimed at ending corrupt labor union practices was the (a) Landrum-Griffin Act (b) Fair Labor Standards Act (c) Norris-La Guardia Act (d) Fair Dealing Compliance Act.

_____4. Which of the following is an acceptable pay differential basis under the Equal Pay Act (a) worker's sex (b) worker's age (c) worker's productivity level (d) none of the above.

_____5. _____ is responsible for enforcing federal anti-discrimination laws (a) FTC (b) EEOC (c) FAA (d) none of the above.

_____6. Federal law allows for discriminatory employment practices based on (a) seniority (b) job qualifications (c) ability tests (d) all of the above.

_____7. The ADA allows screening out of handicapped workers through job selection/qualification criteria and testing programs if (a) reasonable accommodation of a particular handicap is impossible (b) such discrimination comforts to standards set by the Uniform Job Discrimination Code (c) a majority of the workplace employees approve (d) all of the above.

_____8. Common law based injured employee actions are founded on a/n _____ theory of recovery (a) strict liability (b) nuisance (c) negligence (d) agency.

_____9. Federal law requires overtime payment when more than (a) eight hours is worked in a single day (b) 40 hours is worked in a single week (c) 25 hours is worked in a three-day period (d) none of the above.

_____10. Federal unemployment insurance laws are administered by (a) state programs (b) federal courts (c) Office of Unemployment Compensation (d) administrative tribunals.

_____11. _____ are state statutes prohibiting union shop agreements (a) Closed Shop Acts (b) Fair Employment laws (c) Yellow Dog Contract laws (d) Right to Work laws.

_____12. Employers can fire employees for (a) trying to form a union (b) missed work days due to jury duty (c) reporting an OSHA violation (d) none of the above.

_____13. Union activity amounting to unfair labor practices includes (a) informational leafleting (b) enforcing union shop agreements (c) "feather bedding" (d) all of the above.

CASE PROBLEMS — SHORT ESSAY ANSWERS: Read each case problem carefully. When appropriate, answer by stating a Decision for the case and by explaining the rationale — Rule of Law — relied upon to support your decision.

1. Square Deal Lumber Yard employs male and female workers of all ages in various jobs. The male stock clerks at Square Deal learn that they receive less pay than female yard attendants. The stock clerks argue that this amounts to a violation of the Equal Pay Act. Are they correct? Explain.

Decision: _____

_____

Rule of Law: _____

2. Aerospace Industries, Inc. puts out a hiring call for trained, experienced retrofitters. Chuck Campion, a 25-year-old certified retrofitter with four years work experience, applies for the job. He is turned down, the personnel department explaining that no one under 30 will be hired for the jobs. Chuck files a claim against the company arguing violation of federal age discrimination laws. Who wins the dispute and why?

Decision: _____

_____

Rule of Law: _____

3. Fortisque Thistlemeyer, president and founder of Thistle Theatrical Productions, Inc., is embroiled in bitter contract negotiations with the union representing his employees. A bargaining impasse has been reached regarding overtime work on national holidays. The union threatens to strike if an accommodation cannot be reached. Fortisque, an outspoken, anti-union hard-liner, blasts the union as a collection of heartless, money-sucking, dishonest ingrates. The union files an unfair labor practices charge against him. Who prevails? Discuss.

Decision: _____

_____

Rule of Law: _____

4. Charlene Carlisle, a storage drum loader at Petro Processors for the past four years, has just been fired. Her employment record is spotless. Petro unloads, stores and ships hazardous chemical wastes generated by chemical manufacturers. OSHA regulations require workers at Petro to be provided adequate protective goggles, masks, gloves, and outer garments to insure no health-endangering employee exposure to the toxins Petro handles. A truckload of dioxin-contaminated wastes arrives at Petro. The manager requests that it be unloaded but Charlene, unable to find a proper mask, refused, citing health and safety hazards as her reason. The manager ordered Charlene to unload the truck or "face the consequences." She refused and was fired. She alleges violation of OSHA regulations and the company denies it. What outcome?

Decision: _____

_____

Rule of Law: _____

5. Folsum Meatpacking, Inc. is entering its third month of a particularly bitter labor dispute. Its workers are beginning their second month of a strike. In an effort to induce the company to settle, the union, which also represents workers at other meatpacking houses in the area, tells those members not to handle any meat from shippers or ranchers who do business with Folsum. Folsum alleges that the union's activity is an unfair labor practice but the union asserts "just tough business tactics." Who is right?

Decision: _____

_____

Rule of Law: _____

Chapter 46

SECURITIES REGULATION

SCOPE NOTE

In response to problems of fraud and inaccurate information in securities transactions, state and federal legislatures have passed laws to protect investors from possible loss caused by these abuses. Chapter 46 focuses on securities regulation at the federal level and traces the Federal government's involvement in controlling the securities marketplace from the early 1930s to the present. The discussion addresses the basic doctrines, principles and terminology that define and control the rights/duties of people engaged in trading investment securities. Also dealt with are the nature and extent of liability for violations of Federal securities laws.

EDUCATIONAL OBJECTIVES

1. Identify the scope, purpose and major provisions of the Securities Act of 1933.

2. Outline the important procedural requirements under the 1933 Act.

3. Distinguish among the various transactions and the types of securities given exemption from coverage under the 1933 Act.

4. Explain the nature and breadth of liability for violations of the 1933 Act.

5. Identify the scope, purpose and major provisions of the Securities Exchange Act of 1934.

6. Discuss the extent of regulatory authority held by the SEC.

7. Know the purpose and significance of the Foreign Corrupt Practices Act of 1977.

CHAPTER OUTLINE

I. Purpose of Regulation
    A. **Promote Full, Accurate Financial Information Disclosure**
    B. **Prevent Fraud**

II. The Securities Act of 1933 — registration of securities held for public sale; SEC administered
    A.   **Definition of a Security** — notes, bonds, stocks as investment (profit expectation from effort of others); money risked in business managed by others
    B.   **Registration of Securities** — prerequisite for public sale (primary distribution)
        1.   Statement filed with SEC for review
        2.   Content — business, property description; management information; significant provisions; financial disclosure verified by CPA
        3.   Deficiencies — informal letter process clears correctable problems; hearing and stop order for uncorrectable problems
    C.   **Prospectus** — disclosure statement similar to registration furnished to prospective investors
    D.   **Review Process** — pre-filing, waiting, post-filing periods
    E.   **Special Cases** — normal filing process not completely followed
        1.   Integrated disclosure — coordinated, simplified filing under '33 and '34 Acts
        2.   Shelf registrations — continued sales without refiling under Rule 415
    F.   **Exempt Securities** — securities sold without following statement filing process
        1.   Regulation A — short form; $15 million maximum within 12-month period
        2.   Intrastate issues — parties in one state; no resale for 9 months
        3.   Short-term commercial paper
        4.   Other exempt securities — government issues; bank securities; insurance policies; religious and charity securities
    G.   **Exempt Transactions** — sales, issuances not subject to normal statement filing process
        1.   Private placements — fewer than 35 investors; no publicity; accredited, experienced investors; resale limitation
        2.   Limited offers not exceeding $5 million — unlimited accredited investors
        3.   Limited offers not exceeding $1 million — no public offer; noninvestment co-issuers
        4.   Limited offers solely to accredited investors
        5.   Resales of restricted securities — miscellaneous restrictions
    H.   **Liability Based on Statute Violations** — investor recovery against signers, directors, partners, certifying experts
        1.   Types of violations
            a. Unregistered sales — absolute liability
            b. False registration statements — material omissions, misstatements
        2.   Defenses — due diligence (reasonable conduct, relying on expert's financial inquiry), no causation (immateriality, no losses, investor knowledge)
        3.   Anti-fraud provision
        4.   Criminal sanctions — willful violations

III. The Securities Exchange Act of 1934 — regulate public trading (secondary distribution); SEC-administered
    A.   **Registration (once for entire stock class) and Periodic Reporting Requirements** — listing registration of brokers, security markets
        1.   Coverage — publicly held companies; national stock exchanges; over-the-counter market
        2.   Reporting — annual, quarterly, periodic
    B.   **Anti-fraud Provision** — using mails, interstate commerce to promote fraud
        1.   Section 10b-5 — prevent any false statements, fraud
        2.   Requisites of Rule 10b-5 — party misconduct for registered, unregistered securities. Knowingly made material, false statement; investor reliance
        3.   Insider trading — recipients of sensitive information prohibited from trading prior to public disclosure

C. **Short-Swing Profits** — Section 16b, Rule 10b-5 differences; corporate, investor profit recovery for insider trading
D. **Proxy Solicitations** — shareholder delegating voting rights to another
   1. Disclosure of material information
   2. Statement filing with SEC
E. **Tender Offers** — take over proposal of equity securities at stated price; disclosure registration requirements
   1. 5% Disclosure Reporting Rule — fund source; purpose and plans of takeover, shares owned
   2. Defensive tactics — 10-day response period; shareholder 7-day withdrawal period
   3. State regulation purpose; validation by U.S. Supreme Court
F. **Foreign Corrupt Practices Act**
   1. Accounting requirements — internal reporting, record-keeping procedures; adoption of GAAP
   2. Anti-bribery provisions — undue influence on foreign government officials by business persons
   3. Criminal sanctions or fines, imprisonment

TRUE—FALSE: Circle true or false.

T   F   1. Federal laws have exclusive jurisdiction over regulating sales of securities.

T   F   2. The SEC uses registration documents to evaluate the soundness and potential for profit of investment opportunities.

T   F   3. New SEC registration and reporting regulations are designed to aid small businesses to compete more effectively in public financial markets.

T   F   4. Liability for selling unregistered securities that are required to be registered under federal law is absolute, there being no defense for the violation.

T   F   5. Anti-fraud provisions of the 1933 Securities Act apply only to intrastate sales of securities.

T   F   6. Securities sales with a value not exceeding $5 million dollars may be made over any 12-month period and the sales require only that an offering statement be filed with the SEC.

T   F   7. Once an issuer has filed registration documents, no additional filing is required to update the initial registration.

T   F   8. A major objective of federal laws focused on preventing fraud in securities transactions is to promote and preserve public confidence in the securities market.

T   F   9. The Foreign Corrupt Practices Act attempts to prevent bribery of foreign governments and officials by U.S. corporations.

T   F   10. Under federal laws, the term "security" is limited in its definition to include only stocks and bonds.

T   F   11. The primary goal of the Truth in Securities Act registration requirements is to reveal to potential investors material information that can assist them in assessing the worthiness of an investment opportunity.

T   F   12. A security issue offered and sold only to purchasers residing in a single state by an issuer residing and doing business in the same state is exempt from registration requirements under the 1933 Act.

KEY TERMS—MATCHING EXERCISE: Select the term that best completes each statement below.

1. Short-term commercial paper	8. Proxy	15. Securities Act of 1933
2. Da Ma Doctrine	9. Private placements	16. Restricted
3. Insider	10. Accredited investor	17. Integrated disclosure
4. Intrastate	11. Exemption	18. Affiliate
5. Registration	12. Prospectus	19. Porcupine provisions
6. Poison pill	13. Constructive disclosure	20. Securities Exchange Commission
7. Tender offer	14. Reasonable diligence	

_____1. Federal legislation enacted to prevent fraud and promote accessible, truthful information in securities sales.

_____2. The act required of some securities sellers by which information is disclosed to potential investors.

_____3. Documents distributed to potential investors containing required disclosure information.

_____4. Notes, drafts or other working capital issuances with maturity dates of nine months or less.

_____5. One having knowledge of nonpublic, confidential and material information related to the value of a security.

_____6. A general invitation to all shareholders of a company to purchase their shares at a specified price.

_____7. A signed written statement, issued by a shareholder, granting authority to another to vote the signer's stock.

_____8. Defensive strategy based on conditional stock rights making attempted hostile takeover prohibitively expensive.

_____9. Exempted security transactions by an issuer that do not involve a public offering.

_____10. Banks, insurance companies and investment firms purchasing securities sold under the private placement provisions of securities regulations.

_____11. Governmental agency primarily responsible for enforcing Federal securities laws.

_____12. Descriptor for the three-tiered registration system adopted to reduce duplication of effort in complying with requirements under the 1933 and 1934 Acts.

_____13. Securities sold under such registration transaction exemptions as private placements, accredited investor limited offer, or limited offers under $ 1 million.

_____14. One who controls, is controlled by, or is under common control with an issuer.

_____15. Restrictive corporate bylaws intended to repel hostile takeovers.

MULTIPLE CHOICE: Select the alternative that best completes each statement below.

_____1. The anti-fraud sections of the Truth in Securities Act (a) apply to securities transactions in interstate commerce (b) impose only criminal sanctions for their violations (c) cover only securities sales that are exempt from registration (d) none of the above.

_____2. The date a registration statement becomes effective is _____ after filing (a) 2 months (b) 2 weeks (c) 20 days (d) 1 month.

_____3. Of the following, which is not information that must be disclosed on securities registration forms? (a) description of the business of the registrant (b) certified financial statements (c) management information (d) accounting procedures used by registrant.

_____4. Transactions exempted from registration under the 1933 Act include limited offers (a) solely to accredited investors (b) not exceeding $10 million (c) public displacements (d) all of the above.

_____5. Securities exempt from registration include those (a) from domestic banks (b) sold by domestic governments (c) involving short-term commitments (d) all of the above.

_____6. A/n _____ involves an investment for profit derived from the management efforts of others (a) debt (b) lease (c) security (d) gift

_____7. Enforcement options related to Federal securities laws include (a) criminal sanctions (b) administrative remedies (c) civil liability (d) all of the above.

_____8. A defense to an action based on untrue statements contained in a registration statement is (a) due diligence (b) innocent mistake (c) subjective honesty (d) capitalized equity.

_____9. Persons who receive nonpublic material investment information from insiders are referred to as (a) co-conspirators (b) accomplices (c) tippees (d) none of the above

_____10. The Securities Exchange Act of 1934 applies primarily to (a) bankruptcy trust securities (b) secondary securities distributions (c) equitable receiverships (d) none of the above.

_____11. Tender offers must be kept open for at least (a) 2 weeks (b) 2 months (c) 30 days (d) 20 days.

_____12. Actions taken by the target company to oppose a hostile takeover attempt include (a) white knight strategy (b) stock repurchasing by insiders (c) reincorporation in states having anti-takeover laws (d) none of the above.

_____13. Recent U.S. Supreme Court rulings have (a) upheld state anti-hostile-takeover laws (b) ruled that the Williams Act exclusively pre-empts state action (c) held golden parachute agreements as unconstitutional (d) none of the above.

CASE PROBLEMS — SHORT ESSAY ANSWERS: Read each case problem carefully. When appropriate, answer by stating a Decision for the case and by explaining the rationale — Rule of Law — relied upon to support your decision.

1. Ajax, Inc., seeking to raise capital, issued $500,000 in securities during the past year. Regardless of whether this issue was subject to state laws, was it entirely exempt from Federal regulation. Discuss.

    Decision: _____

    _____

    Rule of Law: _____

2. Brown, president of Waylay, Inc., owns 25% of that corporation's stock, which is registered with the SEC. On October 25th, Brown purchases Waylay securities, which increases his share of ownership to 30%. The following January, Brown sells some of his Waylay shares reducing his ownership to 22%. What liability does Brown face for the profits from these transactions? Explain.

    Decision: _____

    _____

    Rule of Law: _____

3. World Food, Inc. is a non-profit organization distributing American crop surpluses to underdeveloped nations facing food shortages. To expand its operation, World Food issues $250,000 worth of securities. Must this issue be registered with the SEC?

    Decision: _____

    _____

    Rule of Law: _____

4. Explorations, Inc., to capitalize its development of a natural gas field, registers with the SEC to sell $3.5 million in securities. In its registration statement and prospectus, Explorations lists Sammy Maudlin and Edith Pringle, famous stars from the entertainment world, as members of its board of directors. Investor I, reviewing Explorations' registration statement and prospectus, in which the working life of the gas field is stated to be at least 25 years, decides to purchase $20,000 of Explorations' stock issue. The venture eventually turns sour as Explorations discovers that the fields actually have a producing life of just over 10 years, too short a period to make the development profitable. Explorations abandons the project. Investor I, remembering the statements made in the prospectus, sues for return of his investment

alleging fraud. Named as defendants in the suit are Sammy and Edith who claim no liability since they had no "hands-on" management responsibilities with Explorations. Is I entitled to a return of his $20,000 and are Maudlin and Pringle accountable for it? Discuss.

Decision: _____

_____

Rule of Law: _____

5. XYZ Corporation, with assets totaling $850,000, needs additional capital to finance an expansion of its operations The board of directors decides to promote an issue of $300,000 in equity securities to raise the necessary capital. At the time of this issue, XYZ has 230 shareholders owning this class of securities. Must XYZ register the securities it plans to sell if it anticipates trading them over the counter?

Decision: _____

_____

Rule of Law: _____

Chapter 47

ACCOUNTANTS' LEGAL LIABILITY

SCOPE NOTE

Accountants face possible civil and criminal liability stemming from the work they perform for others This chapter examines common law and statutory bases for such liability: to whom are accountants liable; what defenses may be asserted; what are the rights/duties flowing between accountants, clients and the general public. These are the new major issues addressed in Chapter 47.

EDUCATIONAL OBJECTIVES

1. Explain contractually based accountant liability.

2. Distinguish between tort and criminal bases for accountant liability.

3. Discuss controversial issues related to client access to accountant working papers.

4. Develop the importance of client-accountant communication privileges.

5. Outline accountant liability under Federal securities and tax laws.

CHAPTER OUTLINE

I. **Common Law** — liability for improper performance
   A. **Contract Liability** — agreement defines rights and duties
      1. Duty of proper performance — expressly stated contract terms; implied professional competence
      2. No legal advice beyond accounting function
      3. Material breach — cuts off compensation rights; liable to third-party beneficiary (intended work product recipient)
   B. **Tort Liability** — professional misconduct; no strict liability basis (not accuracy insurer)
      1. Negligence based — ordinary reasonable, prudence standard
      2. Fraud based — deliberate (actual), reckless (constructive) incompetence
      3. Third-party liability — expansion to reasonably foreseeable plaintiffs (excluding investors and general public)
   C. **Criminal Liability** — fraud; tax and securities laws violations

     D.   **Client Information** — accountant as independent contractor with non-delegatable duties
         1. Working papers — owned by accountant; disclosed to client; confidential, nondisclosable to nonclients. Disclosure exception — client consent; court order; required under professional rules
         2. Accountant-client privilege — not generally recognized; client information subject to legal process

II. Federal Securities Law — liability for violations

     A.   **Securities Act of 1933** — material, false, misleading information (omissions) in financial statement
         1. Privity no defense — broad investor liability (any innocently relying stock purchaser)
         2. Due diligence defense
         3. Duty of care extends to registration statement effectiveness date
         4. Criminal sanctions for willful violation
     B.   **Securities Exchange Act of 1934** — false financial statement detrimentally relied on
         1. Liability to any stock purchaser relying on statement filed with SEC
         2. Defense of good faith and no knowledge of falsity
         3. Criminal sanctions for willful violation

TRUE—FALSE: Circle true or false.

T   F   1. Accountants provide financial information important in economic resource allocation decisions.

T   F   2. In the relationship with the client, an accountant is responsible for performing only to the level of competence explicitly provided for in the contract.

T   F   3. Accountants are generally not liable for insuring the absolute accuracy of their reports.

T   F   4. Most states employ the primary benefit test in deciding the extent of negligence-based accountant liability to third parties.

T   F   5. Accountant criminal liability is mainly based upon federal securities and tax laws.

T   F   6. Accountants are usually allowed to argue client-plaintiff contributory negligence in defending against malpractice claims.

T   F   7. The confidentiality of accountant-client communications is not a privilege recognized under either state or federal law.

T   F   8. To maintain a civil action against an accountant under Section 11 of the 1933 Security Exchange Act, the plaintiff must establish both privity and reliance.

T   F   9. Accountants are not civilly liable under Section 18 of the 1934 Securities Exchange Act if their actions are without knowledge of untrue statements and based on good-faith motivation.

T   F   10. Accountants are always liable for releasing information obtained from clients without their consent.

T   F   11. Accountant liability for services performed is based partly on federal securities laws.

T   F   12. The standard of competence applied when an accountant contractually agrees to conduct an audit to find embezzlement is Generally Accepted Auditing Standards.

KEY TERMS—MATCHING EXERCISE: Select the term that best completes each statement below.

1. Fraud	8. Private interest	15. Scienter
2. Due diligence	9. Third-party beneficiary	16. Willful violation
3. Tort	10. Statute of limitations	17. Accountant
4. Privileged communication	11. Material breach	18. Foreseen user
5. Interpretation	12. Negligence	19. Estoppel
6. Trespass	13. Working papers	20. Judgment errors
7. Privity	14. Substantial performance	

_____1. Non-contractual party intended by the contracting parties to receive a direct, primary benefit under the contract.

_____2. Contractual non-performance that terminates an accountant's right to compensation.

_____3. Failure to use the care of a reasonably competent accountant.

_____4. Contractual doctrine limiting accountant liability to persons with whom a business relationship (clients) had been established.

_____5. Accountant's defense to civil liability under Section 11 of the 1933 Securities Exchange Act.

_____6. Intentional or knowingly wrongful conduct.

_____7. Civil wrong, not a contractual breach, triggering a right of compensatory recovery in the victim.

_____8. Accountant's records, including data-gathering process followed, information obtained, and conclusion drawn therefrom.

_____9. Confidential information that witnesses or others may rightfully refuse to release based on the nature of a relationship existing with the person providing the information.

_____10. False material statement of fact issued with deceitful intent.

_____11. Accountant misconduct that triggers criminal liability under federal securities law.

_____12. One who provides reliable financial information to assist the decision making of others.

_____13. Test for negligence-based accountant-third-party liability applied to persons accountants know will use their work product.

_____14. Accountant behavior that triggers a right to compensation for services less damages for losses caused by less-than-complete performance.

_____15. Accountant misconduct triggering no liability so long as professional duties were performed with care.

MULTIPLE CHOICE: Select the alternative that best completes each statement below.

_____1. Which of the following is not a basis for accountant legal liability under state law (a) criminal codes (b) tort law (c) constitutional clauses (d) contract law.

_____2. The basis for tort liability applied to accountants in performing their professional services includes (a) negligence and fraud (b) strict liability and promissory estoppel (c) administrative construction and offsetting partition (d) all of the above.

_____3. Essential elements of a fraud-based cause of action do not include (a) justifiable reliance (b) false statement of fact (c) knowledge of falsity (d) undue influence.

_____4. Misconduct that is the basis for accountant criminal liability under state law includes (a) breach of fiduciary relationship (b) perjury (c) coercion (d) none of the above.

_____5. Criminal liability for accountants under federal tax laws includes (a) forgery (b) material alteration of accounting records (c) intentional assistance of a client to prepare false tax returns (d) all of the above.

_____6. Accountant-client confidentiality issues arise in (a) tax disputes (b) civil cases (c) criminal litigation (d) all of the above.

_____7. Accountant liability for false financial information contained in registration statements filed under Section 11 of the 1933 Securities Exchange Act is based on (a) careless audit procedures (b) failure to register working papers (c) confidential meetings with clients (d) all of the above.

_____8. Accountants should not release confidential information drawn from client meetings unless (a) a conflict of interest exists (b) directed to do so by a court order (c) specifically provided for by enabling legislation (d) all of the above.

_____9. The test for accountant negligence under Section 11 of the 1933 Securities Exchange Act is (a) breach of a fiduciary duty (b) based on trustee duties of care (c) failure to act as prudent people would in managing their own property (d) none of the above.

_____10. Which of the following is not a valid requirement for an accountant-client contract (a) fiduciary relationship (b) mutual agreement (c) capacity (d) consideration.

_____11. _____ is accountant misconduct that triggers liability to anyone whom the accountant should have foreseen would have relied on the information and would be hurt through such reliance (a) negligence (b) chemical dependence (c) perjury (d) fraud.

_____12. An accountant cannot disclose information contained in working papers without (a) payment from the information seeker (b) first filing the papers with the Secretary of State in the client's state of residence (c) client consent or a court order (d) none of the above.

_____13. _____ is based upon an accountant's reasonable belief that financial statements accompanying a client's SEC registration statement contained accurate, true and complete information at the date the registration became effective. (a) GAAS defense (b) due diligence defense (c) statutory compliance defense (d) none of the above.

CASE PROBLEMS — SHORT ESSAY ANSWERS: Read each case problem carefully. When appropriate, answer by stating a Decision for the case and by explaining the rationale — Rule of Law — relied upon to support your decision.

1. Client contracts with accountant to audit client's business and submit a final annual report by May 15th. Accountant, in accepting the terms of the agreement, assures client that no trouble will be encountered in meeting the completion date. Client is relieved to hear this and repeats the importance of having the audit completed by May 15th since annual reports must be distributed to stockholders by May 20th. During the audit, accountant experiences various unexpected misfortunes: employee illnesses; equipment failure; unavailable records; weather-related delays. By May 8th, accountant is less than half through with the audit and May 15th appears an unrealistic goal. What are the rights and liabilities of the parties if May 15th passes with no annual report completed? Explain.

   Decision: _____

   _____

   Rule of Law: _____

2. In conducting the above audit, accountant discovers various unexplainable discrepancies in client's records. Upon notifying client of this fact, accountant is assured that these are mere "entry oversights" that will "balance out when the audit is completed." Trusting client's word, accountant makes no further inquiries. Sometime later, accountant receives an anonymous tip that client and other company directors are siphoning funds from the company. Accountant does not pursue the matter, completes the audit and submits the final annual report pointing out the strong financial health of client's company. Relying upon the data, statements and conclusions in the report, various present stockholders in client's company increase their holdings. Shortly thereafter, the SEC files fraud, theft and swindling charges against client and the firm for embezzlement and falsely representing stock value. Client's company collapses, with most stockholders incurring heavy losses. Some stockholders sue accountant for compensatory and punitive damages in an attempt to recapture their losses. Who prevails and why?

   Decision: _____

   _____

   Rule of Law: _____

3. Pursuant to the SEC prosecution mentioned above, client subpoenas accountant working papers to examine for possible evidentiary benefit. Accountant refuses and client sues. Discuss who wins and why.

   Decision: _____

   _____

   Rule of Law: _____

4. Reread question 1. Assume that instead of a scheduled May 15th completion date that is crucial to client, May 15th is merely referred to as a convenient completion date. By May 16th, accountant has 80% of the final report completed and requires two additional days for finishing. What are the rights and liabilities of the parties at this point?

Decision: _____

_____

Rule of Law: _____

5. In the federal government's prosecution of client mentioned in question 2, accountant is called to testify against client. Accountant refuses, alleging that an accountant-client privilege makes all communications between accountant and a client confidential. The judge threatens accountant with contempt unless the information is released. Who wins this dispute and why?

Decision: _____

_____

Rule of Law: _____

Chapter 48

INTERNATIONAL BUSINESS LAW

SCOPE NOTE

Today's marketplace is increasingly global in nature. Transnational business, commercial activity conducted across national boundaries, is commonplace. The flow of goods, services, technology, credit and information in an international marketplace requires an understanding of legal principles and processes beyond that of the U.S. alone. Knowledge of international legal systems, doctrines and procedures associated with worldwide trade and commerce is important. Chapter 48 examines that area of law dealing with multinational business activities. The controlling principles, purposes, organizations and business relationships relating to international law are discussed in the context of the reality of a contemporary global economy.

EDUCATIONAL OBJECTIVES

1. Understand the importance of the international legal business environment.

2. Explain the authority and functions of the International Court of Justice and Regional Trade Communities.

3. Discuss the role of treaties in multinational business relations.

4. Know the significance of jurisdiction over foreign government action by differentiating the doctrines of Sovereign Immunity and Act of State.

5. Delineate the risks of and protection against governments taking over foreign investment property.

6. Outline crucial aspects, complications and problems associated with multinational commercial activity in the context of: (a) trade relations; (b) labor force; (c) investment financing and payments; (d) contract negotiations; and (e) American antitrust laws.

7. Identify and distinguish among the various forms of transnational enterprises including: (a) direct export sales; (b) foreign agents; (c) distributorships; (d) licensing; (e) joint ventures; and (f) wholly owned subsidiaries.

CHAPTER OUTLINE

I. International Environment — scope of international law; general unenforceability of international law
- A. **International Court of Justice** — judiciary branch of U.N.; parties are nations; voluntary submission to jurisdiction; no formal decision enforcement mechanism
- B. **Regional Trade Communities** — organizations focusing on international commerce; voluntary nation membership; facilitate trade, common economic goals; Common Market example
- C. **International Treaties** — Presidential initiative with Senate approval; GATT example (facilitate international trade through trade barrier removal, most-favored status, free-trade areas, etc.)

II. Jurisdiction over Actions of Foreign Governments — breadth and restrictions on nation's authority over foreign nation, foreign citizens
- A. **Sovereign Immunity** — degree of legal accountability of foreign nation under Foreign Sovereign Immunity Act
- B. **Act of State Doctrine** — courts take "hands off" position regarding foreign government activity; exceptions include waiver of defense, commercial activities
- C. **Taking Foreign Investment Property** — government seizure of foreign-owned assets, property (expropriation contrasted to confiscation); protection through insurance

III. Transacting Business Abroad — breadth and legal controls on foreign commercial activity
- A. **Trade Flow** — purpose, effect of tariff and nontariff trade barriers and export controls
- B. **Labor Flow** — purpose, use of passports, visas and other people-moving regulations
- C. **Capital Flow** — function of IMF in managing international monetary issues and problems; use and importance of regional banks and letters of credit
- D. **International Contract** — legal issues surrounding formation, interpretation and enforcement of international contracts; important risk-reduction clauses; authority of C.I.S.G. over international sales of goods
- E. **Antitrust Laws** — regulatory effect of Sherman Antitrust Act on foreign commercial activity

IV. Forms of Multinational Enterprises — factors considered in choosing, types of international business ventures
- A. **Direct Export Sales**
- B. **Foreign Agents** — purpose and characteristics
- C. **Distributorship** — contrasted to agency
- D. **Licensing** — application to intellectual property transactions; importance of royalties and franchising
- E. **Joint Venture** — coordinated commercial activity; limitations to protect domestic business
- F. **Wholly Owned Subsidiary** — situations where desirable and useful

TRUE—FALSE: Circle true or false.

T   F   1. Generally speaking, expropriations are considered violations of international law while confiscations are not.

T   F   2. Under contemporary policies, the sovereign immunity doctrine applies only to public acts.

T   F   3. GATT favors import quotas as the preferred method to protect domestic businesses.

T   F   4. Validly entered and approved treaties are considered the law of the land carrying the legal force of Federal legislation.

T   F   5. The Common Market is an example of a joint venture.

T   F   6. Judges sitting on the International Court of Justice are elected by the U.N. General Assembly and Security Council.

T   F   7. A significant advantage associated with the wholly owned subsidiary approach to conducting transnational business is the retention of control and authority this approach affords overall aspects of the commercial activity undertaken.

T   F   8. Using direct export sales as a method of conducting international business carries the most risk of committing antitrust violations.

T   F   9. When the C.I.S.G. and U.C.C. are in conflict, the latter prevails.

T   F   10. International law, in contrast to domestic law, is generally not readily enforceable.

T   F   11. The Foreign Sovereign Immunities Act allows for jurisdiction of U.S. courts over foreign commercial activity.

T   F   12. In cases of transnational commercial activity carried out through agency relationships, the agent typically acquires title to the goods bought and sold.

KEY TERMS—MATCHING EXERCISE: Select the term that best completes each statement below.

1. Customs certificate	8. European Economic Community	15. Export control
2. Joint venture	9. Treaty	16. International Court of Justice
3. Favored nation status	10. Tariff	17. Confiscation
4. Visa	11. General Agreement on Trade & Tariffs	18. International law
5. Distributorship	12. Letter of credit	19. Licensing
6. Sovereign immunity	13. Acts of State	20. Multinational enterprise
7. Passport	14. Expropriation	

_____1. Doctrine protecting foreign countries from application of host country laws.

_____2. Multinational agreement intended to remove trade barriers between countries and enhance international trade relations.

_____3. Agreement between countries to accomplish common, desirable goals.

_____4. Judicial branch of the United Nations.

_____5. Law relating to activities, relations between countries.

_____6. Doctrine limiting extent of host country judicial intervention in internal foreign government actions.

_____7. Government seizure of foreign-owned property for a public purpose accompanied by just compensation.

_____8. Government tax on imports or exports to protect domestic business.

_____9. Government restrictions on goods flowing out of a country.

_____10. Individual companies from different countries coordinating commercial activity to achieve a common goal.

_____11. Sale of intellectual property rights to foreign companies for use in foreign markets.

_____12. Business conducting commercial activity in foreign countries.

_____13. Commitment from purchaser's bank to pay seller of goods or services upon happening of specified conditions.

_____14. Document from customs officials clearing goods for export.

_____15. Government issued document allowing foreigners to enter a country for specific purposes or a limited time period.

MULTIPLE CHOICE: Select the alternative that best completes each statement below.

_____1. Nontariff barriers used by countries to protect and promote domestic industries include (a) export controls (b) import quotas (c) streamlined customs procedures (d) all of the above.

_____2. _____ occurs when governments take control over foreign owned property without returning just compensation or for a nonpublic purpose. (a) expropriation (b) equitable cloture (c) confiscation (d) liquidation

_____3. Under U.S. law, the Act of State doctrine does not apply to (a) waivers of the defense (b) property claims based on alleged improper confiscation by a third nation (c) business conducted by a foreign government (d) all of the above.

_____4. Public activities undertaken by governments to which the Sovereign Immunity doctrine applies are (a) restrictions on natural resource use (b) military equipment purchases (c) buying stock in an American corporation (d) none of the above.

_____5. The effectiveness of the International Court of Justice is limited since (a) its decisions are enforceable only through criminal sanctions (b) jurisdiction is limited to disputes between private parties (c) it has authority only over parties who voluntarily submit to its jurisdiction and agree to abide by its ruling (d) no provisions are made for exercising advisory jurisdiction.

_____6. Under a/n _____ form of multinational business relationship, the foreign business representative acquires ownership in the goods received. (a) agency (b) distributorship (c) wholly owned subsidiary (d) licensing

_____7. _____ is a type of licensing arrangement tied to specific limitations. (a) franchising (b) partitioning (c) joint partnership (d) none of the above

_____8. The _____ was created in part to help reduce foreign currency exchange limitations that hinder the development of international trade. (a) United Nations Bank (b) International Trade Bank (c) World Financial Federation (d) International Monetary Fund.

_____9. Problems unique to transnational business agreements include (a) contract negotiations (b) mutually acceptable terms of agreement (c) language and currency differences (d) all of the above.

_____10. Factors influencing which type of business organization should be chosen to undertake multinational business transactions include (a) limitations imposed by a host country (b) financing considerations (c) taxation issues (d) all of the above.

_____11. A contractual clause defining the rights of parties to a multinational business transaction upon the occurrence of an unforeseeable natural disaster or political crisis is called a/n _____ clause. (a) liquidated risk (b) force majeure (c) assumption of risk (d) equitable apportionment.

_____12. The type of business relationship readily suited to limited involvement in an international market is (a) agency (b) joint venture (c) distributorship (d) wholly owned subsidiary.

_____13. International courts _____ jurisdiction to resolve disputes. (a) have compulsory (b) have no (c) voluntarily accepted by the parties to a dispute have (d) have U.N. required.

CASE PROBLEMS — SHORT ESSAY ANSWERS: Read each case problem carefully. When appropriate, answer by stating a Decision for the case and by explaining the rationale — Rule of Law — relied upon to support your decision.

1. Glewbenstein, a tiny country between France and Spain, is home to the Glewbenstein tree, whose sap is renown for its natural adhesive qualities. The Ministry of Science for Glewbenstein, in conjunction with the Economic Development Ministry, undertakes an extensive research program to determine the feasibility of developing industrial-strength adhesive products from the sap. The experimental results prove quite promising. Lacking extensive capital reserves, production capacity or management expertise within the country, the Ministry for Economic Development seeks foreign investors and businesses to develop a Glewbenstein glue industry. Several parties express an interest and it appears a deal will soon be struck. Glewbenstein officials, concerned that the company that emerges from the agreement remain under Glewbenstinian control, come to you for help in achieving that goal. What advice do you give them?

Decision: _____

_____

Rule of Law: _____

2. Mediterranean Moods, Inc., a Spanish cosmetics and perfume company, and Splendid Scents of York, Pennsylvania, are competitors in the international perfume market. Desiring to protect their respective market shares, the two companies enter a reciprocal import/export restriction contract, agreeing to eliminate all direct competition between them in their home countries. What is the legal status of that agreement under American law?

Decision: _____

_____

Rule of Law: _____

3. Monaco Enterprises, Inc., a gambling education program owned and operated by the government of Monaco, guarantees that program enrollees, using the expertise gained through the course, will become "instant winners." The $350, three-day seminar attracts many customers during its American tour. Grumblings from program graduates are soon heard, however, expressing general dissatisfaction over the level of skill and strategy presented in the course, arguing that it amounts to no more than a basic introductory, how-to course on typical gambling games. Many commence civil actions against Monaco Enterprises, Inc., in various state courts, seeking restitution of their enrollment fees based on false advertising and breach of an express warranty of "instant winners." The Monaco government moves to dismiss these lawsuits on grounds of sovereign immunity. Is the defense likely to prevail on this argument?

Decision: _____

_____

Rule of Law: _____

4. Re-read question # 1. Assume that a French bank and an Italian industrialist are interested in undertaking such an enterprise. They, along with representatives from the Glewbenstein Ministry of Economic Development, commence contract negotiations. Realizing the need for an international law business expert, the parties seek your advice regarding contract form and content to provide for complications and problems associated with multinational commercial ventures. What do you tell them.

Decision: _____

_____

Rule of Law: _____

5. Re-read question #2. Could the parties seek an advisory opinion regarding the legality of their agreement from the International Court of Justice? Explain.

Decision: _____

_____

Rule of Law: _____

REGULATION OF BUSINESS RESEARCH QUESTIONS: Drawing upon information contained in the text, as well as outside sources, discuss the following questions.

1. Two controversial areas of employment law are AIDS- and drug-testing of employees. What legal issues surround such testing programs? Explain the rationale underlying employer and employee perspectives on these tests. How does Federal law deal with such testing programs? How do your state laws deal with this controversy?

2. Two developments in the area of corporate mergers have been hostile takeovers and junk-bond-financed leveraged buyouts. Identify and explain arguments supporting and opposing these types of mergers. What role should law play in response to these developments? What approach have your state's laws taken?

PART TEN: Property

Chapter 49

INTRODUCTION TO PROPERTY AND PROPERTY INSURANCE

SCOPE NOTE

Property rights, along with life and liberty, are among the most highly valued elements of our legal identities. English and American law view property rights as a fundamental component of a society governed by a system of laws. In the following chapters, we discuss the general principles and basic concepts of the American system of property law. What is property? What are the various categories of property interests? What limitations are placed on property ownership rights/duties? How does one acquire ownership to property? These and other concerns are the focus of attention in the upcoming materials.

Chapter 49 concludes by examining the basic principles and terminology of property insurance law—the nature and function of insurance, as well as the regulation of the conduct and the contract of the insurance parties. The types of property interests that can be insured against loss are focused upon.

EDUCATIONAL OBJECTIVES

1. Explain what is meant by the term "property."

2. Contrast the basic categories of property.

3. Develop the benefits/burdens of property ownership.

4. Distinguish between acquiring title to personal property by sale and by gift.

5. Compare title through accession with title by confusion.

6. Differentiate among taking possession of lost, abandoned and mislaid property.

7. Describe the rules governing the law of fixtures.

8. Define insurance and discuss the role it plays in our lives.

9. Describe how the insurance industry is regulated.

297

10. Distinguish characteristics of the various types of insurance companies.

11. Contrast the various types of property insurance.

12. Outline the requirements for and the steps involved in creating a valid, enforceable insurance contract.

13. Apply the Insurable Interest doctrine to the various types of property insurance coverage.

14. Differentiate between waiver, estoppel, representations and warranties as they affect forfeiture and avoidance of an insurance contract.

15. Explain the rules controlling party performance and termination of the insurance contract.

CHAPTER OUTLINE

I. **Introduction to Property** — legally protected rights excluding personal liberty
    A. **Kinds of property** — properly classified
        1. Tangible and intangible — extent of physical concrete form; possessability
        2. Real and personal — land and attached items or freely movable, unattached items.
        3. Fixtures — attached (immovable) items to land, buildings
            a. Tests for — degree of attachment, ease of removability; adaptability of use purpose; intention of parties
            b. Significance — taxes; mortgage interests; transfer of land; landlord-tenant disputes
    B. **Incidents of Property Ownership** — rights/duties flowing with ownership; controlling law: location (land), or domicile (personal property)
        1. Transfer of property during life — deed and other formalities required for real property contrasted to personal property informality (bill of sale)
        2. Devolution of title on death of owner — probating decedent's estate
        3. Taxation — sales, property, death, etc., taxes influenced by classification

II. **Personal Property** — U.C.C. provisions govern sales of goods, investment securities, commercial paper, secured transactions
    A. **Transfer of Title**
        1. By sale — tangibles and intangibles; title in exchange for price
        2. By gift — no return consideration; contrast inter vivos with causa mortis
            a. Delivery — actual v. constructive, symbolic
            b. Intent — donor's purpose of no return value
            c. Acceptance — donee's willing, voluntary receipt
            d. Enforceability — executory v. executed
        3. By will or descent — follows owner's death
        4. By accession — owner's rights to value increase; identity changes (new form); innocent v. wrongful taking — title passage and compensatory damages
        5. By confusion — fungibles (identical goods) intermixed; innocent v. wrongful intermixing - title passage and bearing risk of loss
        6. By possession — finder of lost/mislaid property situations; abandonment
    B. **Concurrent Ownership** — single item owned by more than one person

III. **Nature of Insurance**
    A. **Fire and Property Insurance** — protects the owner of real or personal property against loss from fire and other perils
    B. **Title Insurance** — protects against loss from defects in the title to real property or due to liens on the property

IV. Nature of Insurance Contracts

A. **Offer and Acceptance** — the basic principles of contract law apply to insurance policies and it is the insured who makes the offer that can be accepted by the insurance company

B. **Insurable Interest** — this concept's purpose is to eliminate gambling and lessen the moral hazard
   1. Property insurance — ownership creates an insurable interest in the property.
   2. Life insurance — close relatives, creditors, and business associates or employers may take out insurance on another's life.

C. **Premiums** — the money paid by the insured to the company for the insurance protection.

D. **Defenses of the Insurer** — three closely related defenses are listed to induce an insurer to enter into a contract
   1. Misrepresentation — a false statement made by or on behalf of an applicant for insurance to induce an insurer to enter into a contract
   2. Breach of warranty — in insurance contracts, warranties operate as conditions that must exist before the contract is effective
   3. Concealment — the failure of an applicant for insurance to disclose material facts that the insurer does not know

E. **Waiver and Estoppel** — waiver is the intentional relinquishment of a known right; estoppel means that a person is prevented by his own conduct from asserting a position inconsistent with his acts

F. **Termination** — most contracts of insurance are performed and thus the insurer's obligations are terminated

TRUE—FALSE: Circle true or false.

T   F   1. Generally, "property" means those legally protected rights or interests a person holds in physical things and objects.

T   F   2. The basic principles of contract law apply to insurance policies.

T   F   3. The recipient of a gift is referred to as the donor.

T   F   4. An innocent converter who changes the identity of another's personal property acquires title thereto if the value of the property has been substantially increased.

T   F   5. When identical goods of two different owners are accidentally intermixed, all loss falls on the person who caused the "confusion."

T   F   6. To rescind an insurance contract for nonfraudulent misrepresentation, all premiums paid by the insured must be returned by the insurer.

T   F   7. An owner of land on which lost property is discovered through excavation generally has a superior claim to what is found over the finder.

T   F   8. Gratuitous promises to make gifts are usually not enforceable.

T   F   9. When a tenant builds a brick fireplace attached to the living room wall of a leased house, the fireplace can usually be removed by the tenant upon the expiration of the lease.

T   F   10. Transferring title to personal property is generally less formalized and ritualized than real property title transfers.

T   F   11. A representation by an applicant for insurance is generally not a part of the insurance contract.

T   F   12. Generally, intention of parties expressed in an agreement is the controlling factor determining whether an article of personal property is a fixture.

KEY TERMS — MATCHING EXERCISE: Select the term that best completes each statement below.

1. Accession	8. Co-tenants	15. Friendly
2. Estoppel	9. Real	16. Constructive
3. Attachment	10. Deed	17. Personal liberty
4. Fixture	11. Tangible	18. Movability
5. Binder	12. Intangible	19. Premium
6. Conveyance	13. Donor	20. Concealment
7. Gift	14. Personal property	

_____1. An act transforming personal property into real property.

_____2. A transfer of property without an exchange for return value.

_____3. A category of property that includes land and all items thereon.

_____4. Property that cannot be reduced to physical possession.

_____5. Personal property that is attached to land or a building.

_____6. Document used by an agent that makes the insurance coverage effective immediately.

_____7. Two or more people who hold title to real or personal property concurrently.

_____8. Property that can be reduced to physical possession.

_____9. The doctrine giving an owner of property all that is added to or produced from the property.

_____10. The kind of fire that fire insurance policies do not cover.

_____11. A principal characteristic of personal property.

_____12. Type of delivery where the subject of a gift is incapable of actual delivery and is accomplished by delivering a symbol of ownership.

_____13. The failure of an applicant for insurance to disclose material facts that the insurer does not know.

_____14. A legally protected interest — a right — not falling within the definition of property.

_____15. The consideration given in exchange for insurance coverage.

MULTIPLE CHOICE: Select the alternative that best completes each statement below.

_____1. A method used to increase coverage of a fire insurance policy to include benefits not provided in the standard policy is (a) a binder (b) an indorsement (c) a waiver (d) none of the above.

_____2. A/n _____ gift is one that is conditional and made in contemplation of the donor's impending death. (a) inter vivos (b) equitable (c) in perpetuity (d) causa mortis.

_____3. When A gives B the key to A's safe deposit box at Friendly Full Service Bank, telling B that the contents of the box are now B's, A has delivered the safe deposit box to B. (a) constructively (b) actually (c) equitably (d) allocated.

_____4. Requirements for a valid gift include (a) donor's payment (b) revocability by a trustee (c) acceptance by the donee (d) all of the above.

_____5. An $8,000 fire insurance policy covers a $10,000 building, and there is an 80% co-insurance clause. If there is total destruction, the insured's recovery is (a) $8,000 (b) $2,000 (c) $10,000 (d) $6,400.

_____6. The insurable interest for property insurance must exist at the time (a) the property loss occurs (b) the policy is taken out (c) the property is purchased (d) none of the above.

_____7. Defenses an insurance company can assert to an insurance contract include (a) breach of warranty (b) concealment (c) misrepresentation (d) all of the above.

_____8. Personal property is a fixture if it (a) has become part of land (b) cannot be removed without material injury (c) is intended to be a fixture by parties (d) all of the above.

_____9. "Trade fixtures" are removable by a tenant (a) provided no material injury will result to the building or land (b) at any time (c) only before the lease has expired (d) only with the consent of the landlord.

_____10. Conflicts over who has superior rights to claim a fixture as theirs commonly arise between (a) Federal and State officials (b) intestate and testate heirs (c) landlords and tenants (d) bailors and bailees.

_____11. Major concepts underlying America's system of property include (a) emphasis on public ownership (b) constitutional protections of ownership (c) roots in French civil law (d) all of the above.

_____12. Examples of intangible property include (a) patent rights (b) commercial paper (c) mortgages (d) all of the above.

_____13. Where found property is classified _____, the owner of the premises where the property was found prevails over the finder. (a) mislaid (b) abandoned (c) lost (d) none of the above.

CASE PROBLEMS — SHORT ESSAY ANSWERS: Read each case problem carefully When appropriate, answer by stating a Decision for the case and by explaining the rationale — Rule of Law — relied upon to support your decision.

1. While strolling through the park one day, Ragmuffin comes upon a pile of fabric pieces, in assorted sizes and colors. Believing the pieces of cloth discarded junk, Ragmuffin gathers it up, takes it home and sews a beautiful coat of many colors. The fabric actually belonged to Josephine Forgetful who had lost the pieces while picnicking the day before. She lays claim to Ragmuffin's coat and sues to gain possession. Who wins? Explain.

   Decision: _____

   _____

   Rule of Law: _____

2. Generous Gene, desiring to share material wealth with others less fortunate, issues three $250,000 money orders to strangers Sam, Sean and Sallie and delivers them. Gene hears nothing from the three for six months. In the seventh month, Gene receives Sam's returned money order, which had never been deposited, with a note from Sam saying he had taken a vow of poverty and must refuse Gene's generosity. Gene's budget and accounting schedules will be substantially unsettled if the money is refused by Sam. Gene sues Sam to force him to take it. Who prevails and why?

   Decision: _____

   _____

   Rule of Law: _____

3. While eating lunch at Smith's restaurant, Brown finds a ring on the floor. Brown gives the ring to Smith to hold in case the true owner returns. When the true owner cannot be found, Brown demands the return of the ring. Smith refuses and Brown sues Smith for the ring. Who prevails?

   Decision: _____

   _____

   Rule of Law: _____

4. Audrey has a $30,000 face value policy on her $50,000 house. A devastating fire totally destroys the house. Does Audrey recover for her loss? How much? Explain.

   Decision: _____

   _____

   Rule of Law: _____

5. Homeowners H and W sell their home to purchasers M and F. The purchase agreement makes no mention of what appliances are to be sold along with the sale of the house. H and W believe that no appliances will be sold while M and F believe that most of the household appliances will be sold along with the house. Acting on their belief, H and W remove a stereo home entertainment center bricked into the fireplace wall of the family room, a combination stove/oven built into the center of the kitchen, and a lighted, 100 gallon aquarium mounted in the wall of the sunken living room. Finding these items absent when they take possession, M and F demand their return but H and W refuse. Who has superior claim to these missing items?

Decision: _____

_____

Rule of Law: _____

Chapter 50

BAILMENTS AND DOCUMENTS OF TITLE

SCOPE NOTE

Transferring possession of goods (without title) is an everyday occurrence. "May I borrow a cup of sugar" illustrates the pervasive influence bailments have in our private and public lives. This chapter focuses upon the rights and obligations between parties to a bailment — situations where one has entrusted possession of personal property to another. Explained in Chapter 50 are the general types of bailments recognized by law, how bailments are created and the rules of liability applied to the various types of bailment. Also discussed in the chapter are two special cases of bailments: freight transporters and lodging operators. What are the legal dynamics surrounding hotelkeeper/guest relationships, as well as owners and storers/carriers of goods. The chapter closes with an examination of the types, functions and transferability of documents of title, instruments used to transfer ownership of goods when the actual transfer of the goods is cumbersome and inconvenient.

EDUCATIONAL OBJECTIVES

1. Define and discuss the importance of bailments.

2. Identify characteristics of a bailment that distinguish it from other property transactions.

3. Differentiate the rights/duties of parties to a bailment associated with the various types of bailments.

4. Describe classes of bailments and the related degrees of care required by the parties associated with them.

5. Distinguish among common possessory liens on personal property.

6. Identify the type of and rationale for a hotelkeeper's protective duty to guests and their property.

7. Discuss the differences between common law and statutory definitions of hotelkeeper liability.

8. Explain definitional and liability differences between private and common carriers of goods.

9. Outline the breadth of and defenses to common carrier liability for freight damage during transit as well as warehousers liability for stored goods.

10. Discuss the role played by title documents in sales transactions.

11. Identify the two most common documents of title used in sales of goods and the rights/duties of parties under those documents.

12. Discuss the significance of negotiability and the rights/duties of the parties related to the process of "due negotiation."

CHAPTER OUTLINE

I. **Bailments** — transfer of possession of personal property without title for specific purpose
  A. **Parties** — transferor (bailor), transferee (bailee)
  B. **Types of Bailments** — who benefits from the relationship; how bailment created; express (contract); implied (operation of law)
    1. Sole benefit of bailor — storing, taking care of, repairing as a favor; no consideration
    2. Sole benefit of bailee — lending property as a favor; no consideration
    3. Mutual benefit of both parties — common, commercial repair, service, rental contracts
  B. **Essential Elements of a Bailment** — requirements for creating valid bailment relationship
    1. Delivery of possession — bailee exercises control; bailee does not acquire title
    2. Personal property — tangible
    3. Possession for a determinable time — contrasted to sales (property kept indefinitely) and other title transfers (finder of abandoned property, gift donor)
    4. Restoration of possession to the bailor — at end of bailment; bailment terminates by mutual assent, breach, destruction of property
  C. **Rights and Duties of Bailor and Bailee**
    1. Bailee's duty to exercise due care — degree of care required to protect goods; determined by type of bailment: mutual benefit (reasonable prudent person); sole benefit of bailee (high degree of care); sole benefit of bailor (slight care)
    2. Bailee's absolute liability — return undamaged property; negligence presumption against bailee; liability for misdelivery; duty to fulfill contractual purpose (unauthorized use problems), damages (retail replacement value) for loss; effect of liability disclaimers
    3. Bailee's rights to compensation — reasonable payment for work in connection with bailment; based upon express, implied agreement
  D. **Special Types of Bailment**
    1. Pledges — personal property transferred to secure a debt
    2. Warehousing — storage of goods; warehouse receipts
    3. Carriers of goods — common/private carrier distinction; consignor/consignee distinction; bill of lading
      a. Duty to carry — to public (common carrier) or to contract party (private carrier)
      b. Liability for loss or damage — private carrier (negligence standard) v. public carrier (strict liability except in special cases)
      c. Duty to deliver to the right person
      d. Commencement of duties — delivery to carrier, loading goods
      e. Termination of duties — unloading, notice, inspection
    4. Innkeepers — liability for damage or loss
      a. Common law — strict liability except for specific exceptions
      b. Statutory — liability avoidance by providing sale and posting notice of liability limitation for "nonsafeable" articles

II. **Documents of Title** — written document representing ownership in goods; issued by, addressed to bailee holding goods

A.   **Types of Documents of Title** — goods being shipped or stored
  1. Warehouse receipts — goods in storage; issued by merchant warehouser
    a. Duties of warehouseman — reasonable care to prevent loss, damage
    b. Lien of warehouseman — against goods for payment of storage fees; enforceable through sale of goods
  2. Bills of lading — goods being shipped; issued by merchant carrier
    a. Duties of issuer of bill of lading — delivery as per terms of document
    b. Through bills of lading — connecting carriers situations; liability for loss or damage
    c. Lien of carrier — against goods for payment of transit fees; enforceable through sale
B.   **Negotiability of Documents of Title** — negotiable (to order of, to bearer) contrasted with non-negotiable (specifically named recipient)
  1. Due negotiation — purchaser for value, in good faith, without notice, in regular course of business
  2. Rights acquired by due negotiation — transferee acquires transferor's rights or greater (from terms in the document itself); assignee obtains only those rights held by assignor
  3. Rights acquired in the absence of due negotiation — transferor's rights only defeatable by creditors, buyers in ordinary course of business
  4. Warranties — genuineness; no knowledge of defect; rightful negotiation
  5. Ineffective documents of title — ownership in goods not obtainable through wrongful delivery (theft situations)
  6. Lost or missing documents of title — issuance of substitute document through court order

TRUE—FALSE: Circle true or false.

T   F   1. A negotiable bill of lading provides for the delivery of goods to the bearer or to the order of the named person.

T   F   2. Carriers have a lien for unpaid charges that may be enforced by public or private sale of the goods shipped.

T   F   3. Warehousemen are statutorily prohibited from limiting their liability through contractual provisions.

T   F   4. Finders of abandoned property and donees of gifts are bailees.

T   F   5. A bailment presumes separation of ownership and possession between different people.

T   F   6. When bailed goods are destroyed, the law presumes that the bailor negligently caused the damage.

T   F   7. An owner of a document of title has ownership of the goods covered only if accompanied by actual, physical possession of the goods.

T   F   8. Both private and common carriers have an absolute duty to deliver goods to the correct person.

T   F   9. A warehouseman has no separate, enforceable right against goods to secure and enforce payment for services.

T   F   10. Extraordinary bailees are generally insurers of the safety of the goods bailed.

T   F   11. The carrier of goods subject to a bearer or order title document has no further liability under the shipping contract once the goods are delivered at the destination point, regardless of whether the carrier obtains possession of the document.

T   F   12. Naming in a negotiable title document the person to receive notice upon the arrival of goods does not limit the document's negotiability.

KEY TERMS—MATCHING EXERCISE: Select the term that best completes each statement below.

1. Extraordinary	8. Possession	15. Negotiation
2. Warehouser	9. Common	16. Non-negotiable
3. Bailee	10. Custody	17. Good faith purchaser
4. Consignee	11. Bailment	18. Document of title
5. Lease	12. Pledge	19. Negotiable
6. Bill of Lading	13. Private carrier	20. Through bills
7. Abandoned	14. Common carrier	

_____1. The person to whom goods are to be delivered by a carrier.

_____2. The relationship created when a person parks a car in a parking lot, pays a charge, receives a ticket, locks the car and takes the keys.

_____3. The person to whom property is transferred under a bailment.

_____4. Title document issued by a carrier or transporter of goods.

_____5. A bailment for the purpose of securing payment on a debt.

_____6. A transaction in which possession of personal property is delivered without a transfer of title.

_____7. A bailee who receives compensation for storing goods.

_____8. A transporter of goods offering services and facilities to the public indifferently and not in a casual or individual manner.

_____9. One carrying another's goods only on isolated occasions, serving a limited number of customers under single, long-term contract.

_____10. Method of transferring rights to title documents under which the transferee can acquire rights greater than the assignor.

_____11. A document of title made out to "bearer" or "order" of a named person.

_____12. A document of title under which delivery of goods, without surrender of the document, completely discharges the carrier or warehouser from further contractual liability.

_____13. Bills of lading that specify connecting carriers.

_____14. One taking an interest in goods sold to enforce a lien free of any rights of the persons against whom the lien was valid.

_____15. Written document representing ownership in goods.

MULTIPLE CHOICE: Select the alternative that best completes each statement below.

_____1. Transferors for value of documents of title warrant (a) the genuineness of the document (b) the rightfulness of the transfer (c) no knowledge of any fact impairing the validity of worth of the document (d) all of the above.

_____2. A bailment in which the bailee must exercise greater care than a reasonably prudent person is a bailment for the benefit of the (a) bailee (b) bailor (c) bailor and bailee (d) third person.

_____3. A nonnegotiable document of title is transferable only by (a) negotiation (b) the process of laches (c) assignment (d) ratification.

_____4. Property subject to bailment includes (a) promissory notes (b) corporate bonds (c) treasury bonds (d) all of the above.

_____5. Unauthorized use of the bailed goods by the bailee is considered (a) misappropriation (b) trespass (c) assumption of risk (d) immaterial if the possession is lawful.

_____6. A document of title issued by a carrier who promises to deliver goods to the named consignee is a (a) straight bill of lading (b) destination receipt (c) delivery order (d) sub-bill.

_____7. A bailment is not automatically terminated by (a) mutual consent (b) breach of the agreement by the bailor (c) destruction of the goods (d) accomplishment of the purpose of the bailment.

_____8. The liability a private carrier owes to the goods transported is that of (a) an insurer (b) a bailee (c) a reasonable person (d) slight care.

_____9. Essential elements to a bailment include (a) transfers of real property (b) parties known as buyer and seller (c) conveyance of title but not of possession (d) none of the above.

_____10. When a document of title is lost, the claimant of the goods (a) may seek an issuance of a substitute document from the courts (b) must find the document or surrender right to delivery (c) has lost all delivery rights (d) can use the doctrine of detrimental reliance to gain possession of the goods.

_____11. Code requirements for "due negotiation" of title documents include all of the following except (a) purchase for value (b) in good faith (c) as settlement or payment of debt (d) none of the above.

_____12. Duly negotiating documents of title (a) cuts off defenses and claims valid against the transferor (b) creates new rights in the holder (c) facilitates credit extensions based on such documents (d) all of the above.

_____13. Persons who cut off transferee rights under transfer of a non-negotiable title document include (a) bailee creditors (b) transferor creditors (c) any good faith purchaser for value (d) all of the above.

CASE PROBLEMS — SHORT ESSAY ANSWERS: Read each case problem carefully. When appropriate, answer by stating a Decision for the case and by explaining the rationale — Rule of Law — relied upon to support your decision.

1. T, a thief, bails goods stolen from owner O with carrier C and, in return, receives a negotiable bill of lading. The bill, transferred several times, is eventually duly negotiated to H. H and original owner O both claim the goods. Who wins and why?

Decision: _____

_____

Rule of Law: _____

2. Cheesemaker C sues warehouseman W for damage done to C's stored cheese, asserting W's negligence as the cause. The warehouse receipt C received from W provided: "All stored property is at the owner's risk of loss or damage from riot, fire, water, deterioration, leakage, frost, the goods being perishable or otherwise inherently defective." W failed to keep an even temperature in the storage rooms and the cheese became moldy. W argues that the warehouse receipt exempts any liability for the damage to the cheese. Who prevails? Discuss.

Decision: _____

_____

Rule of Law: _____

3. A hires B to deliver a stove to a certain address. B accidentally delivers it to the wrong house, which B cannot later locate. Is B liable for this loss? Discuss.

Decision: _____

_____

Rule of Law: _____

4. Harriet's Honey of Helena, Montana sells forty cases of honey to Sam's Sweetshop of Sioux City. Iowa. Harriet contracts with Tracy Transportation, a local trucking firm, to ship the order. Not having direct service to Sioux City, Tracy issues and forwards a bill of lading to Sam's order providing for final delivery of the honey at Sam's shop from Terry's Trucking of Tremont, Iowa. The cases of honey arrive at Terry's terminal without incident and are loaded onto one of Terry's trucks. On route to Sam's shop, the truck blows a tire, hitting a guard rail with total loss to all goods on board. Terry notifies Sam of the accident, and Sam who contacts Tracy requesting coverage for the loss. Tracy seeks your advice, which is . . .

Decision: _____

_____

Rule of Law: _____

5. Ms. Guest spends a night at Innkeeper Hotel. Guest has with her a $2,500 Swiss watch. Innkeeper has a hotel safe for protecting customer valuables. No notice of its availability is posted at the registration desk or in any of the individual guest rooms. When Guest registers, Innkeeper fails to mention the safe. Sometime during the night, following Guest's check-in, a thief enters her room and steals the watch. Who bears the loss of the watch and why?

Decision: _____

_____

Rule of Law: _____

Chapter 51

INTERESTS IN REAL PROPERTY

SCOPE NOTE

The legal doctrines relating to the ownership, use and transfer of interests in land are discussed in Chapters 51 and 52. This is an extremely technical and complicated area of law due partly to the fact that the basis for our system of real property law is in the highly formalized, intricate structure of feudal land-tenure that dominated English law during the 13th and 14th centuries. Chapter 51 introduces the study of real property law by discussing the types of ownership interests in real property. The terms and doctrines associated with freehold interests in land are examined. The chapter continues by contrasting ownership of land held by one person (ownership "in severalty") to ownership shared by several people (ownership in co-tenancy). Possessory interests in real property (reducible to control and occupancy) are distinguished from non-possessory interests (incapable of control and occupancy). The essential doctrines associated with forms of concurrent (multiple) ownership are developed. Also examined are the legal principles that control the legal relationship of co-owners (co-tenants) of real property. The chapter closes with a discussion of the types of interests one may hold in another's land and the nature of the reciprocal rights/duties among the parties to such a legal relationship.

EDUCATIONAL OBJECTIVE

1. Define real property and differentiate freehold from non-freehold interests in land.

2. Identify, outline the essential characteristics of recognized simple estates and explain the means of creating them.

3. Describe the unique characteristics of, the methods for creating, and the purposes served by a life estate.

4. Explain the types of future interests associated with qualified or conditional estates.

5. Contrast vested with contingent future interests and how they are affected by the rule against perpetuities.

6. Distinguish the various classes of leasehold estates and how they are created.

7. Discuss the methods used and the consequences of parties to a leasehold transferring their respective interests to other individuals.

311

8. Outline the rights/duties of the parties to a rental agreement and how they are influenced by such factors as condition of the premises, presence of government regulation and acts of the parties.

9. Contrast common forms of concurrent ownership in terms of their definitional characteristics, method of creation and purposes served.

10. Compare the types of easements and discuss how they are created.

11. Differentiate between profits á prendre and licenses.

CHAPTER OUTLINE

I. **Freehold Estates** — immediate possession and ownership at least for life
    A. **Fee Estates** — immediate possession
        1. Fee simple — absolute ownership of indefinite duration; transferable and inheritable
        2. Base or qualified fee — certain conditions restrict title
    B. **Life Estates** — terminable at death of life tenant or another
        1. Conventional life estates — created by agreement; parties include life tenant, remainderman, holder of reversionary interest
        2. Life estates established by law — following death of a spouse; existing under common law; changed by statutes granting forced share interest to surviving spouse
            a. Dower — held by surviving wife; in one-third of husband's real property owned during marriage
            b. Courtesy — held by surviving husband; in all of wife's real property if child from the marriage
        3. Life tenant rights — transfer land; use, make profit from the land
        4. Life tenant duties — not commit "waste"; reasonable maintenance and repair; pay taxes
    C. **Future Interests** — not immediately possessory; takes effect in future upon termination of preceding estate
        1. Reversions — held by grantor/grantor's heirs; tied to life estate
        2. Reverters — held by grantor/heirs of; tied to conditional fee
        3. Remainders — held by person other than grantor/grantor's heirs
            a. Vested remainders — no condition other than termination of intermediate estate
            b. Contingent remainders — possession subject to specified condition in addition to termination of preceding estate

II. **Leasehold Estates** — landowner (landlord) grants possession rights to another (tenant) for definite time
    A. **Creation and Duration** — usually by agreement; Statute of Frauds requires writing for periods longer than one year
        1. Definite terms — specified determinable time; automatic termination at end of specified term; certain termination date
        2. Periodic tenancy — indefinite succession of specific term; termination date uncertain; termination by proper notice
        3. Tenancy at will — terminates by act of either party at any time; uncertain termination date
        4. Tenancy at sufferance — possession without a valid lease
    B. **Transfer of Interests** — original parties to lease (landlord and tenant) seek replacement by a third party
        1. Transfers by landlord — tenant's lease valid under time of original agreement

    2. Transfers by tenant
        a. Assignment — tenant transfers all interest; has no reversion; tenant still has rent payment obligation
        b. Sublease — tenant transfers less than full interest; sublease liable to tenant, not landlord
  C. **Tenant's Rights** — determines landlord misbehavior
    1. Exclusive possession — no landlord entry without express reservation, consent, emergency
    2. Fitness for occupancy and proper maintenance — no tenant improvement duty
    3. Trade fixtures doctrine — fixture removal upon term expiration and repair liability
    4. Constructive eviction — lease terminates, rent liability ends on quiet enjoyment breach, untenable premises
    5. Implied warranty of habitability for residential leases
  D. **Tenant's Obligations** — rent payment; no damage, loss to unit
    1. Destruction of the premises — lease usually calls for landlord to repair; suspension of rent until unit usable; tenant liable for damages caused by own misbehavior
    2. Eviction or abandonment — landlord orders tenant to leave or tenant leaves prior to expiration of rental term
        a. Dispossession by landlord for breach of covenant — lease terminates upon landlord's rightful eviction
        b. Wrongful abandonment by tenant — rent payment duty ends upon re-entry, re-letting (landlord's mitigation duty)
        c. Wrongful eviction by landlord — landlord breaches quiet enjoyment right; tenant's duties are terminated; landlord liability
  E. **Landlord's Obligations/Rights**
    1. Right to rent, possession on termination; lien against personal goods for tenant wrongful abandonment and rent nonpayment
    2. Quiet enjoyment duty — not disrupt tenability
    3. Fitness for use, ordinary purpose — residential habitability warranty
    4. Repair — duty arises from statute or contract; applies to areas remaining under landlord's control; notification of known defects
    5. Return security deposit — does not apply to repair costs

III. Concurrent Ownership — ownership held by two or more persons (co-tenants)
  A. **Joint Tenancy** — survivorship characteristic; four unities requirement (time, title, interest, possession)
    1. Clear intent, proper language requirement
    2. Termination by transfer, partition action
  B. **Tenancy in Common** — estate of inheritance; unity of possession
    1. Transferable during life
    2. Termination — by transfer or partition
  C. **Tenancy by the Entireties** — joint tenancy held by husband and wife
    1. Terminated by death, divorce, mutual agreement
    2. Separate transfer prohibition
  D. **Community Property** — by statute in some states; applies to marital property; joint management rights
  E. **Condominiums** — ownership of single unit; tenant in common for rest of facility; separate mortgages
  F. **Cooperatives** — group owns whole and leases back separate units to shareholding tenants; no separate unit ownership; single mortgage; proportionate expense sharing

I V. Nonpossessory Interests — limited rights in another's land
    A.   **Easements** — use of another's land for specific purpose
        1. Types of easements — in gross (personal to parties), subsequent takers not bound, or appurtenant (runs with land), subsequent takers bound
        2. Creation of easements — act of parties; by operation of law
            a. Express grant or reservation — written agreement between parties
            b. Implied grant or reservation — arises from established use and division of land
            c. Necessity — arises through operation of law to preserve use; rights of crossage to protect accessibility
            d. Dedication — public use from owner's lot, subdivision and plat recording
            e. Prescription — arises through adverse use (nonrightful, open, notorious, continuous) for certain period of time
    B.   **Profits á Prendre** — right to remove "valuables" (trees, minerals, etc.)
    C.   **Licenses** — slightest permission to use land; protection against trespass; revocable at any time

TRUE—FALSE: Circle true or false.

T   F   1. A fee simple estate is of indefinite duration and could therefore last forever.

T   F   2. By statute in most states today, joint tenancy can be created by a conveyance "to A and B and their heirs."

T   F   3. "To A and his heirs" is the only language that can effectively create a fee simple estate today.

T   F   4. At common law, landlords had no obligation to keep rented residential premises in habitable/ tenantable condition.

T   F   5. Survivorship refers to the interest of a joint tenant passing to his heirs at his death.

T   F   6. Landlords are not held strictly/absolutely liable for harm caused by the criminal conduct of other persons.

T   F   7. A license, like an easement, creates an interest in real property.

T   F   8. Where a tenant has expressly agreed to pay rent in the rental agreement, an assignment of the lease to another person does not free the first tenant from further rent payment obligation.

T   F   9. Most courts hold that when a tenant wrongfully abandons rented premises and the landlord re-rents the premises to another, the abandoning tenant's obligation to pay rent ceases.

T   F   10. Divorce automatically terminates a tenancy by the entireties.

T   F   11. When a lease does not mention time for rent payment, rent is due and payable at the end of the rental term.

T   F   12. Under a contingent remainder, the remainderman has rights to immediate possession upon termination of the preceding estate.

KEY TERMS - MATCHING EXERCISE: Select the term that best completes each statement below.

1. Periodic tenancy	8. Constructive eviction	15. Community property
2. Life estate	9. Reversion	16. Tenant
3. Appurtenant	10. Assignment	17. Tenancy at sufferance
4. Waste	11. Profit á prendre	18. Dower
5. Remainder	12. Dominant estate	19. Tenancy at will
6. Partition	13. Contingent	20. Courtesy
7. Vested	14. Possibility of reverter	

_____1. A future interest held by one not the grantor or the grantor's heirs.

_____2. Failure to care properly for property that is held for only a limited time.

_____3. Easements that create rights and duties pertaining to the land itself and not personal to the parties that created them.

_____4. The interest retained by a grantor or his heirs when no disposition is made of the balance of a life estate.

_____5. A type of co-ownership recognized in some states creating a one-half undivided interest between spouses in property acquired during marriage.

_____6. The parcel of land that is benefited by an easement.

_____7. The doctrine that allows a tenant to abandon rented premises and terminate a lease when a landlord has failed to meet the terms of the lease.

_____8. The right to harvest the crops from the land of another.

_____9. The act of changing undivided interests in land into separate and divided interests.

_____10. A future interest that has as its only condition to possession the termination of the preceding estate.

_____11. Common law life estate that surviving husband had in deceased wife's real property.

_____12. Tenant's holding land after expiration of a lease.

_____13. Someone who has temporary use and possession of another's land.

_____14. Holding land for an indefinite period subject to termination by either party to the agreement.

_____15. Life estate held by a wife in deceased husband's real property.

MULTIPLE CHOICE: Select the alternative that best completes each statement below.

_____1. When a tenant under an eight-year lease transfers the premises to another person for a five-year period, the transfer is called a/n (a) conditional apportionment (b) assignment (c) sublease (d) equitable allocation.

_____2. A tenancy in common may be created by (a) operation of law (b) an ineffective attempt to create a joint tenancy (c) more than one instrument (d) all of the above.

_____3. A wife's dower right in her husband's property (a) is an example of a conventional life estate (b) passes to her all of his real property when he dies (c) is an example of a life estate created by operation of law (d) stems from statutory law.

_____4. A gross easement is (a) personal to the parties that created it (b) similar in purpose to a zoning restriction (c) nothing more than a negative covenant (d) much like a constructive trust.

_____5. When a landlord breaches a warranty of habitability, a tenant (a) is still bound to the lease (b) may not avoid liability for further rent (c) can sue for damages (d) is precluded from withholding rent.

_____6. The type of co-ownership by which a buyer acquires separate title to a purchased unit while also becoming a tenant in common vis-a-vis the common facilities of which the unit is a part is called a (a) condominium (b) cooperative (c) tenancy by estoppel (d) unified severalty.

_____7. Creation of concurrent ownership by the same instrument is an absolute requirement of (a) community property (b) tenancy at will (c) tenancy in common (d) joint tenancy.

_____8. Among the four "unities" that exist, the only one required of a tenancy in common is the unity of (a) possession (b) time (c) title (d) interest.

_____9. A rental agreement covering a definite period of time (a) expires automatically at the end of the stated rental term (b) terminates only upon one of the parties giving notice (c) is automatically renewed if no termination notice is given (d) none of the above.

_____10. Under common law, a tenant must repair (a) damage caused by ordinary wear and tear (b) extraordinary damage even though caused without fault (c) damages that are caused by fault (d) all of the above.

_____11. _____ is an indirect form of co-ownership that gives shareholders leasehold rights to individual units (a) tenancy by entireties (b) cooperative (c) tenant by estoppel (d) condominium.

_____12. _____ prohibits landlords from discriminating against renters on the grounds of race, sex, religion, nationality, family status, or handicap (a) no laws (b) the Uniform Housing code (c) the Fair Housing law (d) none of the above.

_____13. Landlord's obligation not to disrupt the tenant's possession and use of the premises is known as the covenant of (a) repair (b) habitability (c) no disposition (d) quiet enjoyment.

CASE PROBLEMS — SHORT ESSAY ANSWERS: Read each case problem carefully. When appropriate, answer by stating a Decision for the case and by explaining the rationale — Rule of Law — relied upon to support your decision.

1. A, B and C are joint-tenant owners of Greenacre. C conveys an interest in the land to D. Following this action, A dies. What form or forms and percentage of concurrent ownership exist between the surviving parties? Explain.

    Decision: _____

    _____

    Rule of Law: _____

2. A conveys land "to B so long as the property is used for church purposes." B sells the property to C, who builds a liquor store on the property. A and B are dead. A's heirs, B's heirs and C claim the property. Who prevails? Discuss.

    Decision: _____

    _____

    Rule of Law: _____

3. H is a tenant-in-common owner of a dairy farm with A, a joint tenant owner of a ranch with B, and a life tenant of a poultry farm. When H dies, what dower rights would his surviving wife have in these three property interests? Explain.

    Decision: _____

    _____

    Rule of Law: _____

4. A has a right to cross neighbor B's land. When B sells the land to C, may C stop A from crossing the land? Explain.

    Decision: _____

    _____

    Rule of Law: _____

5. A conveys, by deed, an undivided one-half interest in Blackacre to B and wills the other one-half interest in the same land to C, stating in both documents that C and B are to hold as "joint tenants." A dies. Are B and C joint-tenant owners of Blackacre? Explain.

    Decision: _____

    _____

    Rule of Law: _____

Chapter 52

TRANSFER AND CONTROL OF REAL PROPERTY

SCOPE NOTES

Title to real property may be transferred in many ways. Ownership may pass to government (through tax default, escheat, dedication or eminent domain) or out from government (through grants and tax sales). Events (marriage, natural forces) may trigger the passage of title. Acts by the present owner (sale, gift) or inaction by the present owner (adverse possession, mortgage foreclosure proceedings) may pass title. In Chapter 52, the legal principles controlling methods of acquiring title to real property are discussed in the context of purchase agreements, security interest in land and adverse possession.

As a general rule, owners of real property enjoy the benefits of title according to their own wishes with little outside interference. Under various circumstances, however, public (government regulation) and private (contractual controls) limitations are placed on the manner and degree to which one may enjoy the incidents of real property ownership. To protect and promote the general welfare of society, as well as to effectuate the intent of contractual provisions, restrictions determine how one may exercise title interests in land. Chapter 52 also focuses on the conflicting interests between enjoyment of the incidents of title and the general welfare of society through public and private controls on ownership.

EDUCATIONAL OBJECTIVES

1. Outline the major steps involved in purchasing real property.

2. Explain formation requirements for valid land sales contracts.

3. Define and discuss the significance of marketable title.

4. Discuss the importance of deeds and distinguish among the various types of deeds.

5. List execution requirements for a valid deed.

6. Develop the importance of delivery and recording deeds in terms of their effectiveness.

7. Define and explain the significance of adverse possession.

318

8.   Discuss the purpose and execution requirements of mortgages.

9.   Identify the rights/duties of parties to a mortgage and how their legal relationship is affected by transfers of the mortgage interest.

10. Outline various issues and problems related to discharge, foreclosure and redemption of mortgages.

11. Define and discuss the importance of eminent domain.

12. Specify how the public use, just compensation and due process doctrines relate to eminent domain.

13. Describe the purposes served by zoning ordinances.

14. Distinguish among the various ways of avoiding zoning limitations.

15. List the types and ways of creating private controls over land.

16. Discuss how restrictive covenants are interpreted and how they are terminated.

CHAPTER OUTLINE

I. Transfer of Real Property — documents, procedure, relationship of parties to land title transfers
   A.   **Contract for Sale** — Statute of Frauds application
      1.   Formation — written agreement: names; description; time; deed; price
      2.   Marketable title — implied duty of seller; free from certain defects (encumbrances, chain of title, etc.)
      3.   Implied warranty of habitability — suitable for human use, intended purpose; structural defects issue; disappearance of caveat emptor
   B.   **Deeds** — written document conveying title; party, land identification
      1.   Types of deeds — extent of liability of grantor for title defects
         a.   Warranty — grantor assures no defects: covenants of title, conveyance rights, habitability, quiet enjoyment, no encumbrances
         b.   Special warranty — grantor assures no self conduct that impairs title, but no assurances regarding acts of others
         c.   Quitclaim — grantor makes no title assurances; conveys whatever interest grantor holds
      2.   Formal requirements — valid, enforceable deed
         a.   Consideration — usually not required (gift)
         b.   Description of land — clear, certain identification; methods of description; natural boundaries, survey, metes and bounds, plat
         c.   Quantity of the estate — title interest transferred
         d.   Covenant of title — undisturbed (quiet enjoyment) ownership in buyer
         e.   Execution — proper drafting; signatures, notary acknowledgment
      3.   Delivery — triggers title transfer; intent of grantor
         a.   Physical transfer not required
         b.   Escrow — third party holds deed until specified conditions are met; grantor retains title
      4.   Recording — properly executed deed; notice of interest; protection against subsequent takers, creditors
   C.   **Secured Transactions** — land used as security in credit extension; involves debt, creditor interest in specified land; borrower (mortgagor) issues promissory note to lender (mortgagee); mortgagee provides debt satisfaction from land upon nonpayment
      1.   Form of mortgages — writing; parties named; land described; Statute of Frauds applies

        a. Recording — protect mortgage against subsequent takers and creditors

        b. Trust deed — debtor (trustor) conveys property to third party (trustee) for benefit of creditor (beneficiary): release and reconveyance on payment

    2. Rights and duties

        a. Legal theories — lien (majority view; mortgagor retains title, has possession; mortgagee has lien; default triggers mortgagee possession rights) contrasted to title (minority view; mortgagee has title, mortgagor possession; default triggers loss of possession)

        b. Release, surrender of mortgagee interest on debt payment — equity enforcement

        c. No prepayment unless contract authorization

        d. Mortgagee self-protection — mortgage, tax, expense payments vis-a-vis competing interests; redemption rights

    3. Transfer of mortgage interests — mortgagor conveys land by sale, will gift; taker of mortgaged land not liable for transferor's debt unless express, implied assumption; taking "subject to" relieves taker of debt liability; original mortgagor relieved of debt through novation

    4. Foreclosure — regaining property following default; by public, private, judicial sale; statutory limitations

        a. Strict — debt discharge

        b. Power of sale — mortgagee rights in contract; mortgagee agent of mortgagor

        c. Mortgagor redemption — retain land by debt, sale price, incidental expenses payment

        d. Deficiency judgment — mortgagor liability for sale proceeds/debt balance difference; statutory restrictions

  D. **Adverse Possession** — involuntary title passage without deed or regular formality; hostile use to owner; statute of limitation restrictions; open, continuous, notorious occupancy of another's land

II. Public and Private Controls — restrictions on property use and ownership

  A. Zoning — public control over land use

    1. Enabling acts and zoning ordinances — regulate land use in local areas: building size; population density; traffic ways; division of commerce, residential, service activity; building codes

    2. Variance — avoid regulations based on hardship

    3. Non-conforming uses — reasonable time to adjust to new restrictions; lawful use not ended immediately

    4. Judicial review of zoning — grounds for court invalidating zoning restrictions

        a. Invalidity of zoning ordinance — unreasonable application of authority; no reasonable relation to protecting health, safety

        b. Zoning amounts to a taking — restriction prevents any beneficial use

    5. Approval of subdivision master plans

  B. **Eminent Domain** — power to convert private property to public use (serves the public)

    1. Public use — condemnation power is delegatable; application to urban renewal plans

    2. Just compensation — fair market value at time of taking

  C. **Private Restrictions Upon Land Use** — contractual, deed clauses restrict land use

    1. Nature of restrictive covenants — intended for purchaser benefit; must appear in title chain

    2. Type and construction of restrictive covenants — residential lot size, building type, density limits

    3. Termination of restrictive covenants — established acceptance of past violations; changed circumstances

    4. Validity of restrictive covenants — enforcement through injunction; discriminatory restrictions not enforceable; general benefit to all owners of land affected

TRUE - FALSE: Circle true or false

T	F	1.	Most States follow the common law rule that after the land sales contract is made, risk of loss to the real property passes to the seller.
T	F	2.	A quitclaim deed could convey as much interest in land as a warranty deed.
T	F	3.	A warranty deed does not transfer an after-acquired title.
T	F	4.	The contract for the sale of land impliedly requires that the seller convey a marketable title to the buyer.
T	F	5.	Recording a deed is always necessary for title to pass from the grantor to the grantee.
T	F	6.	A mortgagor may generally assign the mortgage to a third person without having to receive the mortgagee's consent unless the mortgage agreement provides otherwise.
T	F	7.	The police power of government may be employed to regulate property use as well as to take property.
T	F	8.	The power of eminent domain may not be delegated to private enterprise.
T	F	9.	Compensation for property taken under eminent domain is determined on the basis of market value of the property condemned.
T	F	10.	The usual method for enforcing restrictive covenants is a suit for money damages.
T	F	11.	In real-estate-secured transactions, the creditor is the mortgagee and the debtor the mortgagor.
T	F	12.	The single-family, private-ownership exemption to the Fair Housing Act regulation of selling/renting residential property does not apply to racial- color-based discrimination.

KEY TERMS—MATCHING EXERCISE: Select the term that best completes each statement below.

1. After-acquired title	8. Due process	15. Allocation
2. Variance	9. Deficiency judgment	16. Foreclosure
3. Eminent domain	10. Conveyance	17. Title theory
4. Warranty deed	11. Enabling laws	18. Police power
5. Quitclaim deed	12. Trust deed	19. Confiscation
6. Adverse possession	13. Allonge	20. Redemption
7. Title insurance	14. Restrictive covenant	

_____1. A method for freeing property from zoning restrictions in cases of "particular hardship."

_____2. The statutory basis of authority for city zoning powers.

_____3. A constitutional principle protecting the interests of private property owners from unreasonable exercises of eminent domain powers.

_____4. Property ownership protection against losses stemming from title defects, liens, and encumbrances.

_____5. Private limitations placed upon how land may be used.

_____6. A method of transferring title to land involuntarily.

_____7. A deed under which grantor assumes all liability for any title defects.

_____8. Document in a secured real estate transaction conveying property to a third person to hold for the benefit of the creditor.

_____9. The power to convert private property to public use.

_____10. An action taken by the mortgagee against the mortgagor to recover any balance still owing on the debt when foreclosure proceedings are insufficient to satisfy the full debt owing.

_____11. Common law doctrine giving ownership rights and possession to the mortgagee in secured real estate transactions.

_____12. Mortgagor's right to remove a mortgage lien by paying off the debt in full.

_____13. Mortgagee's debt satisfaction rights following mortgagor's default.

_____14. Regulatory action resulting in property owner's being deprived of any and all beneficial use of their land.

_____15. Regulatory authority of government to protect public health, safety and morals.

MULTIPLE CHOICE: Select the alternative that best completes each statement below.

_____1. Private property may be taken by the government if (a) private use is to be made of the property (b) the owner is reimbursed the purchase price paid for the property (c) due process has been followed in condemnation proceedings (d) an equitable trust is established in the owner's name.

_____2. The disputed level of just compensation accompanying condemnation is determined by (a) a jury in equity (b) administrative law judges (c) state compensation boards (d) court of law.

_____3. Acknowledgment of the deed is necessary to (a) bind the grantor and grantee (b) record the deed (c) have it be effective against an escrow agent (d) all of the above.

_____4. Which of the following is not necessary for the valid transfer of land (a) delivery of the deed (b) the grantor's intention to make a transfer (c) a title search (d) grantor's issuing a deed.

_____5. Of the following, which is not an absolute requirement for adverse possession to ripen into title (a) open and continuous possession (b) constructive possession (c) possession for a required statutory time period (d) possession without owner's consent.

_____6. A marketable title is free from (a) all encumbrances except mortgages (b) all encumbrances except easements (c) zoning restrictions (d) title defects appearing in the chain of title available through land records.

_____7. Compensation for condemned property is given to (a) holders of contingent remainders (b) owners of the property taken (c) wife for her dower interest in her living husband's land (d) none of the above.

_____8. A purchaser of mortgaged real property is not personally liable for the mortgage debt unless (a) the mortgage note is pledged (b) the property is taken "subject to" the mortgage (c) the mortgage is "expressly assumed" by the purchaser (d) notice is given to the assignor.

_____ 9 The primary tool for public regulation of private land use is a (a) zoning ordinance (b) restrictive statute (c) court decision (d) condemnation proceeding.

_____10. Which of the following is not an example of restrictive covenant (a) a covenant that limits the use of property to residential purposes (b) a restriction specifying the minimum cost of each house that is built in a given area (c) a covenant against encumbrances (d) a covenant prohibiting the sale of intoxicating beverages.

_____11. In a lien theory state (a) mortgagee has title (b) mortgagor has possession and title (c) mortgagee has possession (d) none of the above.

_____12. A clause in mortgage contract allowing mortgagee to sell the property without a court order is a (a) strict redemption (b) judicial sale (c) equitable deficiency (d) power of sale clause.

_____13. Secured real estate transactions are governed by (a) state statute and common law (b) the U.C.C. (c) federal real estate laws (d) none of the above.

CASE PROBLEMS — SHORT ESSAY ANSWERS: Read each case problem carefully. When appropriate, answer by stating a Decision for the case and by explaining the rationale — Rule of Law — relied upon to support your decision.

1. A restrictive covenant banning the sale of cigarettes within the village of Bloomfield has been in existence for fifty years. For the past ten years, two tobacco shops and three pharmacies have been selling cigarettes in the village. When Frank Cooper decides to sell cigarettes from vending machines in his general store in Bloomfield, will he be prohibited by the covenant? Explain.

Decision: _____

_____

Rule of Law: _____

2. Wing and Wang Chan, husband and wife, are recent arrivees from China. Desiring to settle quickly, they hire a real estate agent and start looking for a home. They find a "priced-right" dream house and submit a purchase offer. Their bid is refused and upon further inquiry they learn that no homes in the area may be sold to persons of Asian descent according to the dictates of the original deed from the first owner of the tract development. Dismayed, the Chans seek your advice. What can you tell them?

Decision: _____

_____

Rule of Law: _____

3. A has been operating a junk yard within the city limits of Springfield for the past 35 years. The Springfield City Council passes a zoning ordinance forbidding the presence of junk yards within the city limits. The city demands that A shut down his junk yard immediately and A refuses. The city then sues A. Who wins and why?

Decision: _____

_____

Rule of Law: _____

4. L owns an undeveloped 2 acre lot in a run-down area of mixed residential and light commercial use. The city adopts an urban renewal plan for the area that provides for the location of a park on L's site. State and Federal officials have not yet approved the plan, nor has funding or a developer been located. As part of its plan, the city states that landowners who build on lots scheduled for condemnation will not be compensated for the loss of those buildings when condemnation proceedings commence. L believes the city's plan is unfair and asks for advice. What advice will you give?

Decision: _____

_____

Rule of Law: _____

5. Railroad Company R.R. wants to increase the width of its roadbeds that abut A's land. R.R. approaches A, requesting to purchase land from A. A refuses to sell the land arguing that widened roadbeds are not necessary. The railroad company fears loss of business if its tracks are not widened. Can the company force A to give up the land? Explain.

Decision: _____

_____

Rule of Law: _____

Chapter 53

TRUSTS AND
DECEDENTS' ESTATES

SCOPE NOTE

At various times during our financial lives, we might find it necessary and worthwhile to transfer control of property we own to another person to manage for our own benefit or for the benefit of a third party. Such arrangements are called trusts. Under what circumstances are trusts useful devices? What formalities are associated with the creation of a trust? What is the nature of the legal relationship between the parties to a trust? Chapter 53 focuses upon these and other matters in its discussion of the law of trusts, its vocabulary, and essential doctrines. Chapter 53 also provides a general overview of the law of testate and intestate succession and how property passes following the death of its owner. Attention is placed on the benefits /costs of dying without a will. Also discussed is the process of property distribution following death.

EDUCATIONAL OBJECTIVES

1. Explain the nature and purpose of trusts.

2. Discuss the requirements for establishing a valid, enforceable trust.

3. Identify the parties to a trust and outline their individual and mutual rights and duties.

4. Describe how the existence of a trust may come to an end.

5. Differentiate the various types and classes of trusts.

6. Differentiate testate and intestate succession.

7. Explain the nature and purpose of a will.

8. Identify the requirements for drafting a valid will.

9. List the types and respective characteristics of recognized wills.

10. Discuss the events and acts associated with altering/revoking a will.

11. Understand under what circumstances an apparently valid testamentary instrument will not be enforced

325

12. Know the rights of beneficiaries and the spouse of the decedent under a will.

13. Define and identify the problems associated with abatement and ademption.

14. Explain the purpose and role of the Uniform Probate Code.

15. Discuss how and to whom property passes when its owner dies without a valid, enforceable will.

16. Outline the probate duties of a personal representative.

17. Describe the tax consequences of death.

CHAPTER OUTLINE
I. **Trusts**
   A. **Types of Trusts**
      1. Express trusts — an oral or written trust established by voluntary action
         a. Charitable trusts — any trust that has for its purpose the benefit of the public
         b. Spendthrift trusts — a provision in a trust instrument under which the trust estate is removed from the beneficiary's control and from liability for her individual debts
         c. Totten trusts — is a bank (savings) account opened by the settlor of the trust and payable to the beneficiary on death of the settlor
      2. Implied trusts — a trust imposed upon property because of acts of the parties
         a. Constructive trusts — are imposed upon property by the equity court to rectify misconduct or to prevent unjust enrichment
         b. Resulting trusts — serve to carry out the true intent of the parties in cases where the intent was inadequately expressed
   B. **Creation of Trusts**
      1. Settlor — the person who creates the trust
      2. Subject matter — the trust property, which must consist of any definite and specific real or personal property
      3. Trustee — an individual or institution that is legally capable of holding title to and dealing with property
         a. Duties of the trustee — three primary duties are listed
         b. Powers of the trustee — determined by the settlor and state statutes
         c. Allocation of principal and income — trusts often specify how the trust property or funds shall be allocated
      4. Beneficiary — there are very few restrictions on who (or what) may be a recipient of trust property
   C. **Termination of a Trust** — as a general rule a trust is irrevocable unless the power of revocation is reserved by the settlor

II. **Decedents' Estates**
   A. **Wills** — the legal document that determines to whom the assets of a decedent will be distributed after death
      1. Mental capacity
         a. Testamentary power and capacity — the power to make a will is granted by the State; the capacity refers to limits placed upon particular persons because of mental deficiencies
         b. Conduct invalidating a will — includes duress, undue influence and fraud

      2. Formal requirements of a will
          a.   Writing — a basic requirement of a valid will
          b.   Signature — a will must be signed by the testator
          c.   Attestation — a will must be attested (certified) by witnesses, usually two or three as required by statute
      3. Revocation of a will
          a.   Destruction or alteration — tearing or burning will revoke the will and in some states erasure or obliteration may
          b.   Subsequent will — the execution of a second will does not itself revoke an earlier will
          c.   Operation of law — common law and the UPC differ on the effect marriage and divorce have on a will
      4. Effectiveness of testamentary provisions
          a.   Renunciation by the surviving spouse of the decedent spouse's will is set by statute
          b.   Abatement and ademption of a bequest — both have serious implications for beneficiaries of a will
      5. Special types of wills
          a.   Nuncupative wills — oral wills
          b.   Holographic wills — a completely handwritten will
          c.   Soldiers' and Sailors' wills — may be valid but cannot pass title to real estate
          d.   Conditional wills — a will that takes effect only on the happening of a specific condition
          e.   Joint and mutual or reciprocal wills — are types of wills involving two or more persons
          f.   Living wills — a document by which an individual states that she does not wish to receive extraordinary medical treatment in order to preserve her life
      6. Codicil — is an addition or revision of a will
  B.   **Intestate Succession** — the rules of descent that determine how intestate property passes
  C.   **Administration of Estates** — the statutory rules and procedures that control the management of the decedent's estate

TRUE—FALSE: Circle true or false.

T   F   1. Each trust has a settlor, a trustee, and a beneficiary.

T   F   2. A will takes effect only upon the death of the testator; in other words, a will is revocable at any time during life.

T   F   3. Fraud, undue influence, or duress may invalidate a will since they reflect an intent other than the testator's.

T   F   4. A beneficiary's interest in a non-spendthrift trust may be attached by creditors.

T   F   5. A second will automatically revokes the first will.

T   F   6. A resulting trust is often used to rectify fraud or to prevent unjust enrichment.

T   F   7. Stepchildren inherit from an intestate decedent to the same extent as natural children (heirs).

T   F   8. As in contract law, consideration is an essential element of an enforceable trust.

T   F   9. Even though legally created, a trust is generally revocable.

T   F   10. Legally adopted children inherit to the same extent as natural children (heirs) of the adopting parents.

T   F   11. Mutual or reciprocal wills are those in which the same instrument is made the will of two persons and is signed by them jointly.

T   F   12. An inheritance tax is imposed by the Federal government on the privilege of an heir or beneficiary to receive property from the decedent's estate.

KEY TERMS—MATCHING EXERCISE: Select the term that best completes each statement below.

1. Totten trust	8. Escheat	15. Revocation
2. Probate	9. Holographic	16. Executor
3. Attestation	10. Per capita	17. Ademption
4. Trust res	11. Spendthrift clause	18. Renunciation
5. Per stirpes	12. Charitable trust	19. Abatement
6. Express trust	13. Codicil	20. Administrator
7. Resulting trust	14. Nuncupative	

_____1. A written or oral trust in which property is transferred to a trustee for the benefit of another.

_____2. The act of witnessing a will.

_____3. The legal effect of the intentional destruction of a will by the testator.

_____4. A trust provision prohibiting the beneficiary from impairing the trust rights by an assignment of the rights.

_____5. The kind of trust that may be created when a settlor opens a bank account.

_____6. The property that is the subject matter of the trust.

_____7. Another name for an oral will.

_____8. Any trust established for the benefit of the public.

_____9. Lineal descendants of predeceased children inherit from a decedent by representation of their parent.

_____10. The procedure for managing the decedent's estate.

_____11. The person named in a will to manage the administration of the decedent's estate.

_____12. An addition to or a revision of an existing will.

_____13. The statutory right of a surviving spouse to elect to take an intestate succession statutory share of the decedent's estate rather than the share left to the spouse in the decedent's will.

_____14. Another name for a handwritten will.

_____15. A reduction in the value of the estate of the testator after the execution of his will.

MULTIPLE CHOICE: Select the alternative that best completes each statement below.

_____1. Although no particular words are necessary to create a trust, one element that must be present is the (a) formal writing (b) intent to create a trust (c) designation of a trustee (d) all of the above.

_____2. The subject matter of a trust must be (a) definite and certain (b) real property (c) intangible (d) all of the above.

_____3. A trustee who, by state law is required to invest only in those securities listed by the state, is controlled by a law that is (a) permissive (b) mandatory (c) invalid (d) tempered by reasonableness.

_____4. If a person has obtained money by duress, the person will be treated as a trustee over a (a) constructive trust (b) resulting trust (c) express trust (d) precatory trust.

_____5. The trustee must (a) carry out the trust's purposes (b) use prudence and care in the administration of the trust (c) be loyal to the beneficiary (d) all of the above.

_____6. Which of the following is not an absolute necessity for all valid wills? (a) power (b) capacity (c) intent (d) intelligence.

_____7. A codicil, like a will, must be (a) in writing (b) signed by the testator (c) witnessed (d) all of the above.

_____8. A State inheritance tax is imposed upon the (a) decedent's estate (b) executor (c) recipient of the estate (d) attorney.

_____9. A nuncupative will generally must (a) be handwritten (b) be made when no attorney is available (c) be made during the testator's last illness (d) dispose of real property only.

_____10. Since a will can be renounced, the following person cannot be disinherited by the decedent: a surviving (a) parent (b) child (c) spouse (d) none of the above can be disinherited.

_____11. A will may be revoked by (a) tearing or burning the will (b) operation of law (c) a subsequent will that is inconsistent with the original will (d) all of the above.

_____12. The formal requirements for a will do not include the need for the (a) testator's signature (b) will to be recorded (c) will to be written (d) all of the above.

_____13. The type of trust that is incorporated into a will and takes effect only on the testator's death is a (a) living trust (b) totten trust (c) testamentary trust (d) resulting trust.

CASE PROBLEMS — SHORT ESSAY ANSWERS: Read each case problem carefully. When appropriate, answer by stating a Decision for the case and by explaining the rationale — Rule of Law — relied upon to support your decision.

1. A sets up a spendthrift trust for her son, B. C is a creditor of B's to whom B owes $800 for a motorcycle. Under what circumstances can C obtain payment?

Decision: _____

_____

Rule of Law: _____

2. A appoints B trustee of a trust for the benefit of C and D. B dies. C and D petition the court to have the trust terminated. What result?

   Decision: _____

   _____

   Rule of Law: _____

3. Ted dictated a will to his nurse. It was typed, signed, and attested. In it, he divided his entire estate among his wife and children. Ted dies. Eight months later, a son is born to Ted's widow. Does the new child share in the estate? Explain.

   Decision: _____

   _____

   Rule of Law: _____

4. When Tom wrote his will, his estate was worth $35,000. Tom's will left $1,000 to A, $500 to B, and the balance to C. At the time of his death, Tom's estate was worth $1,500 after estate debts had been paid. What does C receive? Explain.

   Decision: _____

   _____

   Rule of Law: _____

5. Abby's will left her business, a pizza parlor, to her nephew, H. One year before her death, Abby sold the pizza parlor for $50,000. Is H entitled to the $50,000 in lieu of the pizza parlor? Explain.

   Decision: _____

   _____

   Rule of Law: _____

PROPERTY RESEARCH QUESTIONS: Drawing upon information contained in the text, as well as outside sources, discuss the following questions.

1. Research your State's laws on intestate succession. If you were to die without a will, how and to whom would your property pass? Is that how you would want it distributed? Draft a will distributing your property in the manner (what, how and to whom) you desire. Is it the same as the plan of distribution under intestate succession laws? Explain.

2. Assume you want to purchase a house. Trace the steps and complete drafting and processing the documents necessary for buying the home.

UNIFORM CPA EXAMINATION: INFORMATION ON BUSINESS LAW

To practice their profession, public accountants must meet various competence standards established by state accounting boards assuring minimal knowledge and skill levels. All states require candidates to demonstrate this proficiency by passing the Uniform Certified Public Accountant Examination, administered by the American Institute of Certified Public Accountants (AICPA). This two and one-half day test is given in May and November of each year and consists of four separate sections: accounting practice I and II; accounting theory; auditing; and business law.

The business law section of the CPA Examination lasts approximately three and one-half hours and consists of multiple choice and case analysis essay questions designed to test candidate knowledge over a broad range of business law rules, doctrines and concepts. These questions are similar in form to those in this Study Guide.

The breadth of business law knowledge required to pass the CPA Examination is reflected in the guidelines adopted by the AICPA Board of Examiners:

"The Business Law section tests the candidates' knowledge of the legal implications of business transactions, particularly as they relate to accounting and auditing situations, including accountant legal liability. Many of the subjects in this section are normally covered in standard textbooks on business law, auditing, taxation, and accounting. However, some subjects either are not included in such texts or are not covered in adequate depth. Important recent developments with which candidates are expected to be familiar may not yet be reflected in some texts. Candidates are expected to recognize the existence of legal implications and the applicable basic legal principles, and they are usually asked to indicate the probable result of the application of such basic principles ...."

"The Business Law section is chiefly conceptual in nature and broad in scope. It is not intended to test competence to practice law nor expertise in legal matters, but to determine that the candidates' knowledge is sufficient to enable them to recognize relevant legal issues, recognize the legal implications of business situations, apply the underlying principles of law to accounting and auditing situations, and know when to seek legal counsel, or recommend that it be sought, when appropriate."

"This section deals with federal and widely adopted uniform laws. Where there is no federal or appropriate uniform law on a subject, the questions are intended principally to test candidates' knowledge of the majority rules. Federal tax elements (income, estate or gift) are only covered where appropriate in the overall context of a question."

Business Law — Content Specification Outline

I. The CPA and the Law (10%)
- A. Common Law Liability to Clients and Third Persons
- B. Federal Statutory Liability
  1. Securities Acts
  2. Internal Revenue Code

II. Business Organizations (20%)
    A.   Agency
       1. Formation and Termination
       2. Liabilities of Principal
       3. Disclosed and Undisclosed Principals
       4. Agency, Authority, and Liability
    B.   Partnerships and Joint Ventures
       1. Formation and Existence
       2. Liabilities and Authority of Partners and Joint Owners
       3. Allocation of Profit or Loss
       4. Transfer of Interest
       5. Termination, Winding Up, and Dissolution
    C.   Corporations
       1. Formation, Purposes, and Powers
       2. Stockholders, Directors, and Officers
       3. Financial Structure, Capital, and Dividends
       4. Merger, Consolidation, and Dissolution
    D.   Estates and Trusts
       1. Formation and Purposes
       2. Allocation between Principal and Income
       3. Fiduciary Responsibilities
       4. Distributions and Termination

III. Contracts (15%)
    A.   Offer and Acceptance
    B.   Consideration
    C.   Capacity, Legality, and Public Policy
    D.   Statute of Frauds
    E.   Statute of Limitations
    F.   Fraud, Duress, and Undue Influence
    G.   Mistake and Misrepresentation
    H.   Parol Evidence Rule
    I.   Third-Party Rights
    J.   Assignments
    K.   Discharge, Breach, and Remedies

IV. Debtor-Creditor Relationships (10%)
    A.   Suretyship
       1. Liabilities and Defenses
       2. Release of Parties
       3. Remedies of Parties
    B.   Bankruptcy
       1. Voluntary and Involuntary Bankruptcy
       2. Effects of Bankruptcy on Debtors and Creditors
       3. Reorganizations

V. Government Regulation of Business (10%)
    A.   Regulation of Employment
       1. Federal Insurance Contributions Act

      2. Federal Unemployment Tax Act
      3. Worker's Compensation Acts
  B. Federal Securities Acts
      1. Securities Registration
      2. Reporting Requirements
      3. Exempt Securities and Transactions

VI. Uniform Commercial Code (25%)
  A. Commercial Paper
      1. Types of Negotiable Instruments
      2. Requisites for Negotiability
      3. Transfer and Negotiation
      4. Holders and Holders in Due Course
      5. Liabilities, Defenses, and Rights
      6. Discharge
  B. Documents of Title and Investment Securities
      1. Warehouse Receipts
      2. Bills of Lading
      3. Issuance, Transfer, and Registration of Securities
  C. Sales
      1. Contracts Covering Goods
      2. Warranties
      3. Product Liability
      4. Risk of Loss
      5. Performance and Obligations
      6. Remedies and Defenses
  D. Secured Transactions
      1. Attachment of Security Agreements
      2. Perfection of Security Interests
      3. Priorities
      4. Rights of Debtors, Creditors, and Third Parties

VII. Property (10%)
  A. Real and Personal Property
      1. Distinctions Between Realty and Personalty
      2. Types of Ownership
      3. Lessor—Lessee
      4. Deeds, Recording, Title Defects, and Title Insurance
  B. Mortgages
      1. Characteristics
      2. Recording Requirements
      3. Priorities
      4. Foreclosure
  C. Fire and Casualty Insurance
      1. Coinsurance
      2. Multiple Insurance Coverage
      3. Insurable Interest"

Students planning to take the examinations should obtain copies of *Information for CPA Candidates* issued by AICPA. Copies are available from:

>The American Institute of Certified Public Accountants
>1211 Avenue of the Americas
>New York, NY 10036

FUTURE CPA EXAMINATION DATES:

1994	May 4, 5; November 2, 3	1998	May 6, 7; November 4, 5
1995	May 3, 4; November 1, 2	1999	May 5, 6; November 3, 4
1996	May 8, 9; November 6, 7	2000	May 3, 4; November 1, 2
1997	May 7, 8; November 5, 6		

CROSS REFERENCES TABLE
Business Law Topics Appearing on CPA Examinations
Text and Study Guide Chapters

TOPIC, ESTIMATED AICPA EMPHASIS & GROUP CHAPTERS IN STUDY GUIDE:

ACCOUNTANTS AND THE LAW (10%)   7

BUSINESS ORGANIZATIONS (20%)
A.	Agency	19 and 20
B.	Partnerships and Joint Ventures	31-34
C.	Corporations	35-38
D.	Estates and Trusts	53

CONTRACTS (15%)
A.	Introduction to Contracts	9
B.	Mutual Assent	10
C.	Invalidating Assent	11
D.	Consideration	12
E.	Illegal Bargains	13
F.	Capacity	14
G.	Statute of Frauds	15
H.	Parol Evidence Rule	15
I.	Third Party Rights	16
J.	Performance, Breach and Discharge	17
K.	Remedies	18

DEBTOR—CREDITOR RELATIONSHIPS (10%)
A.	Secured Transactions	39
B.	Suretyship	40
C.	Bankruptcy	41

GOVERNMENT REGULATION OF BUSINESS (10%)
A.	Employment Law	45
B.	Federal Securities Acts	46
C.	Anti-trust	43
D.	Unfair Competition	42

UNIFORM COMMERCIAL CODE (25%)
A.	Commercial Paper	26-30
B.	Documents of Title	50
C.	Sales	21-25

PROPERTY (10%)
A.	Real and Personal Property	49-52
B.	Mortgages	52
C	Fire and Casualty Insurance	49

ANSWERS TO CHAPTER 1 — Introduction to Law
All answers are keyed to page numbers in the main text.

TRUE-FALSE

1.	T	pg 3	4.	T	pg 9	7.	F	pg 6	10.	T	pg 3
2.	T	pg 5	5.	F	pg 6	8.	T	pg 6	11.	F	pg 10
3.	F	pg 8	6.	T	pg 6	9.	F	pg 10	12.	T	pg 9

KEY TERMS — MATCHING

1.	4	pg 6	5.	14	pg 8	9.	3	pg 10	13.	2	pg 10
2.	6	pg 5	6.	7	pg 9	10.	5	pg 5	14.	18	pg 11
3.	9	pg 6	7.	13	pg 3	11.	20	pg 10	15.	19	pg 9
4.	15	pg 8	8.	10	pg 6	12.	8	pg 9			

MULTIPLE CHOICE

1.	d	pg 9	5.	d	pg 4	9.	b	pg 5	13.	d	pg 5
2.	d	pg 11, 12	6.	c	pg 11	10.	d	pg 6			
3.	a	pg 10	7.	d	pg 9	11.	a	pg 5			
4.	c	pg 10	8.	d	pg 5	12.	b	pg 9			

CASE PROBLEMS — ESSAY ANSWERS

1. This landmark U.S. Supreme Court decision would be found in the following two source books: first, in Volume 347 of the United States Supreme Court Reports at page 686, and second, in Volume 74 of the Supreme Court Reporter at page 686. This is an example of a case citation. pp. 11, 12

2. No. This is a trial in equity and equity courts do not allow jury trials. p. 9

3. No. This state has not proven beyond a reasonable doubt that Horn caused the fire and they are charged with the burden of proof. p. 6

4. If Baker owns personal property (e.g., a car), Anita may have it legally seized and sold. p. 4

5. Society may condemn John's failure to attempt a rescue as morally wrong, but the law generally imposes no legal duty on him to act. p. 4

ANSWERS TO CHAPTER 2 — Business Ethics and the Social Responsibility of Business
All answers are keyed to page numbers in the main text.

TRUE-FALSE

1.	T	pg 16	4.	F	pg 18	7.	T	pg 27	10.	F	pg 19
2.	F	pg 17	5.	F	pg 18	8.	T	pg 29	11.	F	pg 18, 19
3.	F	pg 17	6.	T	pg 23	9.	T	pg 19	12.	F	pg 21

KEY TERMS — MATCHING

1.	3	pg 16	5.	15	pg 23	9.	20	pg 20	13.	9	pg 24
2.	6	pg 18	6.	12	pg 23	10.	7	pg 20	14.	2	pg19
3.	10	pg 18	7.	13	pg 21	11.	18	pg 22	15.	16	pg 24
4.	1	pg 18	8.	11	pg 21	12.	19	pg 22			

MULTIPLE CHOICE

1.	d	pg 16	5.	b	pg 20	9.	d	pg 23	13.	d	pg 18
2.	d	pg 24	6.	c	pg 22	10.	d	pg 25			
3.	d	pg 26	7.	d	pg 22	11.	c	pg 18			
4.	a	pg 20	8.	d	pg 20	12.	b	pg 24			

CASE PROBLEMS — ESSAY ANSWERS

1. To say "whatever is legal is also moral" is too simplistic and is inaccurate. Some acts that are legal are immoral. See examples in text. p. 17

2. Ethical fundamentalists are individuals who look to a central authority to guide them in ethical decision making: Jerry Falwell, the Bible; Ayatollah Khomeini, the Koran. Criticisms: 1) The Bible and Koran do not always agree. No one yet has managed to demonstrate convincingly which authority is the "correct one." 2) The Bible cannot serve as an example of a central authority, as its proponents cannot agree on what its verses mean. p. 18

3. The theory our criminal laws apply is deontology. Deontologists judge a murderer depending on the mental processes and motives that led him to commit the crime. p. 20

4. Lawrence Kohlberg's three stages of moral development are the preconventional level, the conventional level, and the postconventional level. See his explanations and conclusions in text. p. 22

5. Corporations, like other members of society, must contribute to its betterment. They owe a moral debt to society to help make improvements, including pollution control, safe products, quality education, cures for illness, and freedom from crime. Corporations can help in each of these areas. p. 27

ANSWERS TO CHAPTER 3 — Legal Process
All answers are keyed to page numbers in the main text.

TRUE-FALSE

1.	F	pg 48	4.	F	pg 44	7.	T	pg 55	10.	T	pg 51
2.	T	pg 38	5.	T	pg 50	8.	F	pg 53	11.	T	pg 39
3.	T	pg 38	6.	T	pg 46	9.	T	pg 38	12.	F	pg 55

KEY TERMS — MATCHING

1.	6	pg 39	5.	10	pg 55	9.	2	pg 41	13.	3	pg 56
2.	5	pg 48	6.	11	pg 50	10.	13	pg 44	14.	17	pg 55
3.	14	pg 52	7.	8	pg 49	11.	12	pg 50	15.	9	pg 49
4.	15	pg 52	8.	4	pg 50	12.	20	pg 50			

MULTIPLE CHOICE

1.	d	pg 45	5.	a	pg 39	9.	d	pg 44	13.	d	pg 54
2.	a	pg 38	6.	c	pg 42	10.	d	pg 50			
3.	c	pg 52	7.	d	pg 39	11.	d	pg 44			
4.	d	pg 41	8.	b	pg 41	12.	c	pg 48			

CASE PROBLEMS — ESSAY ANSWERS

1. Remand means the original decision by the State district court is reversed by the Supreme Court. The case will now be retried in the original trial court, i.e., the district court. p. 53

2. Arbitration. Arbitration makes possible a speedy resolution to the labor/management problem and is binding. p. 55

3. No. Generally, State court decisions are not binding upon another State's courts. p. 46

4. Yes. If Malcolm is a citizen of Colorado, the Federal district court would have jurisdiction because (a) Malcolm could sue for over $50,000, and (b) "diversity of citizenship" exists, i.e., the parties are citizens of different states. p. 45

5. No. A decision of a Federal circuit court is not binding upon other circuit courts. p. 46

ANSWERS TO CHAPTER 4 — Constitutional Law
All answers are keyed to page numbers in the main text.

TRUE-FALSE

1.	T	pg 71	4.	T	pg 77	7.	F	pg 80	10.	F	pg 76
2.	F	pg 71	5.	F	pg 79	8.	F	pg 72	11.	T	pg 73
3.	F	pg 75	6.	F	pg 73	9.	T	pg 75	12.	F	pg 73

KEY TERMS — MATCHING

1.	3	pg 72	5.	7	pg 80	9.	1	pg 71	13.	17	pg 74
2.	6	pg 77	6.	9	pg 81	10.	10	pg 82	14.	19	pg 71
3.	12	pg 75	7.	11	pg 73	11.	4	pg 72	15.	14	pg 73
4.	13	pg 76	8.	15	pg 79	12.	20	pg 74			

MULTIPLE CHOICE

1.	c	pg 72	5.	d	pg 72	9.	c	pg 76	13.	d	pg 83
2.	d	pg 73	6.	b	pg 72	10.	d	pg 82			
3.	a	pg 73	7.	c	pg 82	11.	a	pg 73			
4.	b	pg 71	8.	d	pg 82	12.	b	pg 73			

CASE PROBLEMS — ESSAY ANSWERS

1. President Nixon contended that the separation of powers doctrine precluded the judicial branch of the government from reviewing the executive branch, i.e., the President's claim of executive privilege. The Supreme Court rejected this claim and ruled that the judicial, not the executive branch, interprets and decides what is the law. p. 73

2. Datsun. The commerce clause and the import-export clause of the Constitution immunize from state taxation goods that have entered the stream of commerce, whether they are interstate or foreign and whether they are imports or exports. p. 76

3. Our Constitution divides the government into three distinct and independent branches: executive, legislative and judicial. The purpose of the doctrine is to avoid excessive power in any branch of government. p. 73

4. The Tenth Amendment. This amendment states, "the powers not delegated to the United States by the Constitution, nor prohibited by it to the States, are reserved to the States respectively, or to the people." p. 75

5. The U.S. Supreme Court applies the strict scrutiny test whenever governmental action affects fundamental rights or involves suspect classifications, which include those made on the basis of race or national origin. Thus, the Court ruled in the Brown case that segregated public schools violated the equal protection guarantee. p. 83

ANSWERS TO CHAPTER 5 — Administrative Law
All answers are keyed to page numbers in the main text.

TRUE-FALSE

1.	T	pg 101	4.	T	pg 106	7.	T	pg 105	10.	F	pg 100
2.	F	pg 100	5.	F	pg 104	8.	T	pg 104	11.	T	pg 101
3.	F	pg 101	6.	F	pg 101	9.	T	pg 104	12.	F	pg 106

KEY TERMS — MATCHING

1.	3	pg 101	5.	7	pg 104	9.	1	pg 100	13.	17	pg 106
2.	6	pg 101	6.	9	pg 100	10.	10	pg 106	14.	19	pg 104
3.	12	pg 101	7.	11	pg 104	11.	4	pg 104	15.	14	pg 105
4.	13	pg 103	8.	15	pg 101	12.	20	pg 104			

MULTIPLE CHOICE

1.	c	pg 100	5.	d	pg 100	9.	c	pg 101	13.	d	pg 105
2.	d	pg 100	6.	b	pg 101	10.	d	pg 106			
3.	a	pg 101	7.	c	pg 104	11.	a	pg 106			
4.	b	pg 100	8.	d	pg 100,106	12.	b	pg 106			

CASE PROBLEMS — ESSAY ANSWERS

1. No. Juries are never used in administrative hearings. pp. 104, 105

2. Administrative Procedure Act of 1946. The Act sets basic procedures all agencies must observe, but agencies are free to fashion their own procedural rules beyond the APA minimum. p. 101

3. The three are the U.S. Constitution, the enabling Statute, and the APA. The regulation cannot violate the Constitution, the agency must not exceed the authority granted by the Statute, and it must follow the rule making procedures of the APA. p. 103

4. The substantial evidence test means if a reasonable person might reach the same conclusion as the agency, then the court will uphold the rule. p. 105

5. The arbitrary and capricious test. It requires only that the agency had a rational basis for reaching its decision. p. 105

ANSWERS TO CHAPTER 6 — Criminal Law
All answers are keyed to page numbers in the main text.

TRUE-FALSE

1.	F	pg 120	4.	F	pg 127	7.	T	pg 130	10.	F	pg 126
2.	T	pg 120	5.	F	pg 128	8.	T	pg 120	11.	T	pg 121
3.	T	pg 125	6.	T	pg 129	9.	T	pg 124	12.	F	pg 123

KEY TERMS — MATCHING

1.	6	pg 124	5.	1	pg 123	9.	8	pg 127	13.	2	pg 130
2.	5	pg 127	6.	9	pg 130	10.	4	pg 129	14.	18	pg 128
3.	12	pg 121	7.	11	pg 121	11.	20	pg 129	15.	19	pg 127
4.	13	pg 122	8.	15	pg 122	12.	17	pg 129			

MULTIPLE CHOICE

1.	d	pg 130	5.	b	pg 130	9.	c	pg 129	13.	c	pg 131
2.	d	pg 126	6.	b	pg 129	10.	d	pg 131			
3.	c	pg 130	7.	c	pg 120	11.	c	pg 129			
4.	a	pg 130	8.	d	pg 120	12.	d	pg 122			

CASE PROBLEMS — ESSAY ANSWERS

1. Entrapment. Melvin was induced to commit the crime by Allen, the F.B.I. agent. p. 128

2. Carol loses. The U.S. Supreme Court has ruled that the use of a six-member jury in a criminal case does not violate the Constitution. p. 131

3. Indictment. A grand jury, on the basis of probable cause, could vote a "true bill" and indict (charge) her with the commission of the crime. p. 129

4. No. Criminal intent without an overt act is not a crime. p. 121

5. The Supreme Court held that depriving the defendant, Gideon, of the assistance of a lawyer in a felony trial is a denial of due process. p. 130

ANSWERS TO CHAPTER 7 — Intentional Torts
All answers are keyed to page numbers in the main text.

TRUE-FALSE

1.	T	pg 142	4.	F	pg 149	7.	F	pg 148	10.	T	pg 154
2.	F	pg 144	5.	F	pg 155	8.	F	pg 142	11.	T	pg 143
3.	F	pg 145	6.	T	pg 153	9.	F	pg 146	12.	T	pg 149

KEY TERMS — MATCHING

1.	7	pg 146	5.	9	pg 148	9.	13	pg 150	13.	17	pg 147
2.	1	pg 142	6.	11	pg 146	10.	5	pg 151	14.	16	pg 147
3.	4	pg 145	7.	6	pg 149	11.	20	pg 143	15.	2	pg 146
4.	8	pg 145	8.	12	pg 149	12.	19	pg 146			

MULTIPLE CHOICE

1.	d	pg 143	5.	b	pg 145-146	9.	d	pg 154	13.	d	pg 149
2.	a	pg 146	6.	c	pg 147	10.	c	pg 153			
3.	d	pg 149	7.	d	pg 151	11.	c	pg 148			
4.	d	pg 150	8.	a	pg 153	12.	d	pg 154			

CASE PROBLEMS — ESSAY ANSWERS

1. B wins. B's consent does not extend to intentional acts of violence beyond the rules of the game. p. 154

2. Potentially, B could be guilty of battery. However, if B reasonably believed A was about to inflict death or serious bodily harm to B, then B is privileged to use even deadly force in self defense. p. 155

3. Yes. The "publication" requirement of defamation (in this case, specifically, libel) and the "publicized" requirement of invasion of privacy have both been met. pp. 147-148

4. The tort is slander. Slander is the oral publication of a defamatory statement which is not true and which injures a person's reputation. p. 146

5. B wins. A is liable for the tort of emotional distress. p. 145

ANSWERS TO CHAPTER 8 — Negligence and Strict Liability
All answers are keyed to page numbers in the main text.

TRUE-FALSE

1.	T	pg 174	4.	T	pg 187	7.	T	pg 185	10.	F	pg 183
2.	T	pg 183	5.	F	pg 186	8.	F	pg 178	11.	F	pg 178
3.	F	pg 175 -176	6.	F	pg 186	9.	T	pg 174	12.	T	pg 175

KEY TERMS — MATCHING

1.	6	pg 174	5.	1	pg 180	9.	8	pg 184	13.	3	pg 185
2.	13	pg 186	6.	14	pg 181	10.	5	pg 178	14.	10	pg 184
3.	11	pg 184	7.	2	pg 174	11.	7	pg 179	15.	9	pg 187
4.	4	pg 179	8.	20	pg 179	12.	19	pg 182			

MULTIPLE CHOICE

1.	a	pg 187	5.	c	pg 180	9.	d	pg 186-187	13.	a	pg 183
2.	d	pg 178	6.	a	pg 175	10.	c	pg 184			
3.	d	pg 186	7.	b	pg 176	11.	d	pg 178			
4.	b	pg 186	8.	c	pg 178	12.	d	pg 178-179			

CASE PROBLEMS — ESSAY ANSWERS

1. Sarah wins. Joelene was flying the plane negligently and is liable to Sarah for this tort, i.e., negligence. p. 174

2. Yes. As the person responsible for Kathy's care, Mark would have a duty to act and would be liable for not taking action. p. 178

3. No. Abner's act of leaving Baker unconscious in the middle of the street could "normally result" in additional injury to Baker. It is also foreseeable that Baker would be struck by a car, and Abner has a duty of affirmative action when there is a danger of further harm to the unconscious person. At the very least, Abner should have carried or dragged Baker out of the street. pp. 178, 183

4. $45,000. The amount of the judgment award is determined by multiplying the percentage of the defendant's negligence times the amount of damage, e.g., 90% times $50,000, which is $45,000. p. 184

5. This is an example of strict liability because this activity is so inherently dangerous to the public that absolute liability is imposed regardless of fault. p. 187

ANSWERS TO CHAPTER 9 — Introduction to Contracts
All answers are keyed to page numbers in the main text.

TRUE-FALSE

1.	T	pg 207	4.	F	pg 208	7.	F	pg 211	10.	T	pg 212-213
2.	T	pg 207	5.	T	pg 210	8.	F	pg 211	11.	T	pg 210
3.	F	pg 207	6.	F	pg 211	9.	T	pg 211	12.	F	pg 209

KEY TERMS — MATCHING

1.	15	pg 207	5.	3	pg 211	9.	9	pg 212	13.	20	pg 210
2.	5	pg 209	6.	7	pg 212	10.	2	pg 207	14.	4	pg 210
3.	12	pg 211	7.	8	pg 211	11.	18	pg 208	15.	19	pg 212
4.	1	pg 207	8.	6	pg 211	12.	16	pg 210			

MULTIPLE CHOICE

1.	a	pg 207	5.	c	pg 211	9.	c	pg 207	13.	c	pg 209
2.	d	pg 209	6.	d	pg 209	10.	c	pg 207			
3.	d	pg 212	7.	b	pg 211	11.	a	pg 207			
4.	b	pg 210	8.	d	pg 206	12.	b	pg 211			

CASE PROBLEMS — ESSAY ANSWERS

1. An implied contract is created. Sara requested and accepted Mary's services, and Sara's estate must pay Mary a reasonable amount for the services. p. 209

2. Yes. The moment Julie purchased the microscope an implied, unilateral contract existed. pp. 209-210

3. Yes. It is clearly understood from the statements of both parties that they were making and exchanging mutual promises. The parties need not use the actual word "promise" to create a bilateral contract. p. 211

4. A false statement that is material to the contract agreed upon by the parties is fraud. Fraud makes the contract voidable to the defrauded party, Joyce. p. 211

5. Yes. This is an example of a quasi-contract, or an implied-in-law contract. p. 212

ANSWERS TO CHAPTER 10 — Mutual Assent
All answers are keyed to page numbers in the main text.

TRUE-FALSE

1.	T	pg 224	4.	T	pg 225	7.	F	pg 225	10.	T	pg 233
2.	T	pg 224	5.	T	pg 230	8.	F	pg 232	11.	T	pg 227
3.	F	pg 227	6.	T	pg 231	9.	T	pg 229	12.	T	pg 231

KEY TERMS — MATCHING

1.	15	pg 232	5.	10	pg 226	9.	9	pg 232	13.	20	pg 224
2.	11	pg 231	6.	1	pg 225	10.	4	pg 233	14.	6	pg 229
3.	14	pg 232	7.	12	pg 228	11.	16	pg 228	15.	18	pg 224
4.	2	pg 225	8.	3	pg 229	12.	19	pg 229			

MULTIPLE CHOICE

1.	d	pg 232	5.	d	pg 227	9.	b	pg 232	13.	c	pg 231
2.	d	pg 228	6.	d	pg 229	10.	a	pg 224			
3.	a	pg 224-225	7.	b	pg 230	11.	d	pg 225			
4.	d	pg 225	8.	d	pg 226	12.	d	pg 228-229			

CASE PROBLEMS — ESSAY ANSWERS

1. Sam wins. The U.C.C. and the Restatement would require that Jerome accept by telegram, as requested by Sam, in order for Sam to be bound. p. 233

2. B wins. Today such unsolicited items, e.g., the candy, would be considered a gift. p. 232

3. A wins. The option is a binding promise not to revoke for one year and is enforceable against B's executor. p. 231

4. No. Statements made under circumstances of emotional stress are not offers since they lack contractual intent. p. 226

5. No. This is an example of the parties engaging in preliminary negotiations. B's letter is the actual offer, not the acceptance of the offer. p. 226

ANSWERS TO CHAPTER 11 — Conduct Invalidating Assent
All answers are keyed to page numbers in the main text.

TRUE-FALSE

1.	T	pg 248	4.	F	pg 249	7.	F	pg 248	10.	F	pg 253
2.	T	pg 251	5.	T	pg 253	8.	T	pg 252	11.	T	pg 251
3.	F	pg 247	6.	F	pg 248	9.	T	pg 253	12.	T	pg 250

KEY TERMS — MATCHING

1.	5	pg 248	5.	12	pg 252	9.	9	pg 250	13.	6	pg 249
2.	7	pg 250	6.	8	pg 252	10.	13	pg 247	14.	10	pg 247
3.	1	pg 251	7.	2	pg 253	11.	14	pg 247	15.	19	pg 251
4.	3	pg 252	8.	15	pg 248	12.	11	pg 251			

MULTIPLE CHOICE

1.	c	pg 247	5.	a	pg 250	9.	d	pg 249	13.	d	pg 248
2.	a	pg 248	6.	d	pg 250	10.	d	pg 252			
3.	b	pg 249	7.	b	pg 250	11.	d	pg 247			
4.	a	pg 249	8.	b	pg 249-250	12.	d	pg 248			

CASE PROBLEMS — ESSAY ANSWERS

1. Yes. One may have a duty of disclosure because of prior representations innocently made but which are later discovered to be untrue before making a contract. Abner's lack of disclosure is fraud. p. 250

2. No. This is an example of duress. p. 247

3. Yes. One who assents to a writing is presumed to know its contents and cannot escape being bound to its terms by contending he did not read them. Generally, a party is held to what he signs. p. 253

4. No to both questions. A prediction is normally not a factual statement and does not form the fraud. p. 251

5. No. If the subject matter of the contract (potatoes) is destroyed without fault of either loss is total, the contract is voidable by the adversely effected party (buyer) unless mistake. p. 252

ANSWERS TO CHAPTER 12 — Consideration
All answers are keyed to page numbers in the main text.

TRUE-FALSE

1.	T	pg 269	4.	F	pg 270	7.	T	pg 270	10.	T	pg 274
2.	T	pg 269	5.	T	pg 269	8.	F	pg 273	11.	T	pg 273
3.	F	pg 269	6.	T	pg 275	9.	F	pg 271-272	12.	F	pg 276

KEY TERMS — MATCHING

1.	13	pg 274	5.	7	pg 269	9.	6	pg 272	13.	16	pg 276
2.	2	pg 276	6.	4	pg 270	10.	10	pg 276	14.	14	pg 277
3.	3	pg 277	7.	5	pg 271	11.	1	pg 274	15.	18	pg 278
4.	12	pg 277	8.	11	pg 272	12.	20	pg 275			

MULTIPLE CHOICE

1.	d	pg 269	5.	c	pg 271	9.	c	pg 277	13.	c	pg 269
2.	a	pg 269	6.	c	pg 274	10.	d	pg 277			
3.	b	pg 272	7.	c	pg 273	11.	d	pg 276			
4.	d	pg 270	8.	d	pg 278	12.	d	pg 277			

CASE PROBLEMS

1. Th...

, and normally courts will uphold these charitable ...ideration. p. 277

...dered as full payment of a disputed debt, and ...ollect the remainder. p. 274

...fying a contract for the sale of goods needs no

... pay is for a past transaction. p. 275

...ght; hence, legally, his forbearance is a legal

ANSWERS TO CHAPTER 13 — Illegal Bargains
All answers are keyed to page numbers in the main text.

TRUE-FALSE

1.	F	pg 291	4.	F	pg 292	7.	F	pg 293	10.	F	pg 297
2.	T	pg 291	5.	T	pg 292	8.	T	pg 293	11.	F	pg 296
3.	F	pg 292	6.	T	pg 292	9.	F	pg 294	12.	T	pg 292

KEY TERMS — MATCHING

1.	9	pg 295	5.	8	pg 297	9.	5	pg 293	13.	3	pg 295
2.	10	pg 293-294	6.	12	pg 292	10.	15	pg 295-296	14.	19	pg 294
3.	7	pg 296	7.	2	pg 292	11.	11	pg 292	15.	1	pg 292
4.	6	pg 293	8.	14	pg 292	12.	16	pg 294			

MULTIPLE CHOICE

1.	b	pg 292	5.	c	pg 293	9.	d	pg 296	13.	c	pg 294
2.	c	pg 291-292	6.	d	pg 293	10.	a	pg 294			
3.	a	pg 292	7.	d	pg 292	11.	c	pg 296			
4.	c	pg 292	8.	c	pg 295	12.	d	pg 297			

CASE PROBLEMS — ESSAY ANSWERS

1. No. The maximum rate of interest in state Z is 8% or $80 per year on a $1,000 loan. A and B agreed to $72 interest and thus no usury. p. 293

2. Barbara wins. The statute was for revenue purposes only and not for protection of the public. p. 292

3. No. Where one person has a superior bargaining position which enables that person to impose an exculpatory clause upon another person as part of their contract, the courts tend to nullify the clause. p. 295

4. C loses. The issue is whether or not the restraint is reasonable. Since a barber shop is localized business, a restraint that prohibits a barber business anywhere in the county for a period of five years is unreasonable. p. 294

5. B loses. Since the contract is a violation of a criminal statute, it will be held unenforceable. p. 291

ANSWERS TO CHAPTER 14 — Contractual Capacity
All answers are keyed to page numbers in the main text.

TRUE-FALSE

1.	F	pg 310	4.	T	pg 312	7.	F	pg 313	10.	F	pg 314
2.	F	pg 310	5.	F	pg 310	8.	T	pg 314	11.	F	pg 312
3.	T	pg 312	6.	F	pg 311	9.	F	pg 314	12.	F	pg 313

KEY TERMS — MATCHING

1.	10	pg 313	5.	1	pg 313	9.	9	pg 312	13.	11	pg 310
2.	8	pg 314	6.	2	pg 311	10.	7	pg 312	14.	20	pg 313
3.	15	pg 311	7.	3	pg 310	11.	5	pg 312	15.	16	pg 313
4.	12	pg 314	8.	4	pg 310	12.	19	pg 310			

MULTIPLE CHOICE

1.	d	pg 312	5.	b	pg 310	9.	d	pg 313	13.	d	pg 312
2.	a	pg 312	6.	d	pg 311	10.	b	pg 314			
3.	b	pg 311	7.	b	pg 311	11.	d	pg 313-314			
4.	d	pg 312	8.	d	pg 314	12.	c	pg 314			

CASE PROBLEMS — ESSAY ANSWERS

1. The majority view is that even though a minor (Mary) misrepresents her age, she may nevertheless disaffirm the contract. p. 313

2. Contracts entered into by persons judged incompetent and who are under a guardianship appointed by a court order are void and have no legal effect. p. 313

3. No. A minor may disaffirm a contract for the sale of a chattel within a reasonable time after reaching majority age. Continued use after reaching majority age is an implied ratification. p. 312

4. A wins. An intoxicated person who is unable to comprehend the nature and effect of a contract can avoid the contract. p. 314

5. A minor is not liable for anything, including necessaries, unless they are actually furnished to the minor or used by the minor. Also, the minor is not liable if the minor is already supplied or is being supplied with the items (necessaries) by someone else, such as the minor's parents. p. 312

ANSWERS TO CHAPTER 15 — Contracts in Writing
All answers are keyed to page numbers in the main text.

TRUE-FALSE

1.	T	pg 326	4.	T	pg 329	7.	T	pg 328	10.	F	pg 335
2.	T	pg 327	5.	T	pg 332	8.	T	pg 329	11.	T	pg 334
3.	T	pg 328	6.	F	pg 326	9.	T	pg 330	12.	T	pg 335

KEY TERMS — MATCHING

1.	9	pg 328	5.	2	pg 335	9.	4	pg 330	13.	19	pg 327
2.	11	pg 332	6.	15	pg 330	10.	1	pg 333	14.	5	pg 328
3.	12	pg 327	7.	3	pg 328	11.	20	pg 327	15.	17	pg 328
4.	7	pg 335	8.	13	pg 335	12.	10	pg 326			

MULTIPLE CHOICE

1.	b	pg 330	5.	d	pg 329	9.	a	pg 328	13.	d	pg 335-336
2.	c	pg 333	6.	a	pg 330	10.	d	pg 335			
3.	d	pg 330-331	7.	d	pg 335	11.	b	pg 327			
4.	c	pg 328	8.	b	pg 330	12.	b	pg 329			

CASE PROBLEMS — ESSAY ANSWERS

1. No. The parol evidence rule does not apply whenever parties to an existing contract subsequently agree to cancel it. p. 336

2. No. Neither the Statute of Frauds nor the U.C.C. would allow this memo to bind the parties since the subject matter and quantity are not clear. p. 332

3. No. This is a contract for the sale of an interest in land and thus it is unenforceable. However, A may recover damages for the work done and damages would be the appropriate remedy. p. 334

4. A loses. The Code states that oral contracts for goods specifically manufactured for the buyer and which are not suitable for resale in the ordinary course of business are enforceable. This contract is not within the Statute of Frauds. p. 331

5. Allen loses. The party to be charged, i.e., Bernard, has not signed the letter. p. 332

ANSWERS TO CHAPTER 16 — Third Parties to Contracts
All answers are keyed to page numbers in the main text.

TRUE-FALSE

1.	T	pg 353	4.	F	pg 352	7.	T	pg 355	10.	T	pg 357
2.	F	pg 352	5.	T	pg 354 -357	8.	F	pg 355	11.	T	pg 359
3.	F	pg 353	6.	F	pg 355	9.	T	pg 355	12.	T	pg 359

KEY TERMS — MATCHING

1.	11	pg 357	5.	12	pg 356	9.	2	pg 359	13.	17	pg 354
2.	6	pg 354	6.	9	pg 358	10.	4	pg 356	14.	3	pg 354
3.	13	pg 358	7.	14	pg 356	11.	8	pg 352	15.	18	pg 353
4.	15	pg 356	8.	10	pg 358	12.	19	pg 353			

MULTIPLE CHOICE

1.	d	pg 354	5.	d	pg 355	9.	b	pg 356	13.	d	pg 357
2.	d	pg 354	6.	c	pg 359	10.	d	pg 356			
3.	d	pg 354-357	7.	a	pg 358	11.	b	pg 352			
4.	b	pg 357	8.	a	pg 359	12.	c	pg 357			

CASE PROBLEMS — ESSAY ANSWERS

1. Y wins. Y is a donee beneficiary and may recover; it does not matter that Y was unaware of the policy. p. 358

2. B wins. Because C is only an incidental beneficiary, C has no rights under the contract and cannot sue. p. 359

3. Company X wins. Since the risk assumed by the appliance company was with A, the assignment to B would be an entirely different risk to the company, and they need not take it. p. 354

4. X wins. Because E made a contract with X for a personal service, E does not have the right to delegate the duty to another. p 357

5. The majority view says Y wins because Y was prior in time. A minority view would give the wages to T because T gave first notice. p. 356

ANSWERS TO CHAPTER 17 — Performance, Breach and Discharge
All answers are keyed to page numbers in the main text.

TRUE-FALSE

1.	T	pg 370	4.	F	pg 371	7.	F	pg 375	10.	F	pg 377
2.	T	pg 370	5.	F	pg 371	8.	F	pg 375	11.	T	pg 373
3.	F	pg 370	6.	T	pg 372	9.	T	pg 374	12.	T	pg 373

KEY TERMS — MATCHING

1.	7	pg 374	5.	15	pg 375	9.	4	pg 372	13.	5	pg 373
2.	9	pg 374	6.	1	pg 375	10.	8	pg 374	14.	14	pg 375
3.	11	pg 377	7.	2	pg 375	11.	16	pg 373	15.	20	pg 372
4.	13	pg 375	8.	3	pg 377	12.	18	pg 376-377			

MULTIPLE CHOICE

1.	a	pg 375	5.	d	pg 370	9.	b	pg 373	13.	c	pg 375
2.	b	pg 376	6.	d	pg 371	10.	a	pg 375			
3.	d	pg 373	7.	c	pg 371	11.	b	pg 372			
4.	c	pg 377	8.	a	pg 372	12.	c	pg 375			

CASE PROBLEMS — ESSAY ANSWERS

1. Decision for A because this situation presents an impossibility for which neither party was responsible. This is the frustration of purpose doctrine. p. 377

2. Yes. The contract is discharged by an accord and satisfaction. p. 375

3. Yes. By novation, Z has become the new debtor and is liable for the debt. p. 375

4. Y wins. This is an example of mutual rescission. p. 375

5. B wins. The law will imply a condition concurrent whereby A and B have a duty to perform the acts of delivery and payment at the same time. The remedy of specific performance would only be granted for non-performance or failure to tender performance and, in the case of the sale of personal property, only when the property is unique. p. 372

ANSWERS TO CHAPTER 18 — Remedies
All answers are keyed to page numbers in the main text.

TRUE-FALSE

1.	T	pg 391	4.	F	pg 399	7.	F	pg 397	10.	T	pg 394
2.	F	pg 392	5.	F	pg 395-396	8.	F	pg 394	11.	T	pg 398
3.	F	pg 392	6.	F	pg 393	9.	T	pg 392	12.	F	pg 398

KEY TERMS — MATCHING

1.	4	pg 391	5.	13	pg 396	9.	6	pg 397	13.	16	pg 393
2.	9	pg 393	6.	14	pg 398	10.	10	pg 398	14.	2	pg 394
3.	11	pg 394	7.	3	pg 391-399	11.	20	pg 392	15.	18	pg 397
4.	15	pg 394	8.	12	pg 397	12.	17	pg 393			

MULTIPLE CHOICE

1.	b	pg 392	5.	a	pg 394	9.	c	pg 397	13.	a	pg 397
2.	c	pg 397	6.	b	pg 394	10.	d	pg 399			
3.	a	pg 398	7.	c	pg 392	11.	d	pg 399			
4.	b	pg 395	8.	b	pg 394	12.	d	pg 399			

CASE PROBLEMS — ESSAY ANSWERS

1. You might sue for lost profits, but under the reasoning of <u>Hadley v. Baxendale</u>, you would have to have told Ace of your need specifically to render them liable. p. 396

2. Possibly. Although punitive damages are not generally recoverable for breach of contract, if the conduct constituting the breach is also a tort (fraud), punitive damages may be obtained. p. 394

3. Probably not, because the courts would look at this as a penalty rather than a valid liquidated damage clause since the $2,000 would not bear a reasonable relationship to the amount of probable loss. p. 394

4. For all the lawnmowers A built after the repudiation, B would probably not be liable, because A could have mitigated the damages by not continuing to build. p. 396

5. Yes. B can ask for the remedy of specific performance from A because the car is unique. p. 397

ANSWERS TO CHAPTER 19 — Relationship of Principal and Agent
All answers are keyed to page numbers in the main text.

TRUE-FALSE

1.	T	pg 412	4.	T	pg 414	7.	T	pg 417	10.	F	pg 422
2.	F	pg 415	5.	F	pg 412	8.	T	pg 420	11.	F	pg 413
3.	T	pg 416	6.	T	pg 416	9.	F	pg 419	12.	T	pg 421

KEY TERMS — MATCHING

1.	7	pg 412	5.	15	pg 416	9.	12	pg 420	13.	19	pg 414
2.	6	pg 412-413	6.	10	pg 413	10.	5	pg 420	14.	17	pg 417
3.	9	pg 414	7.	13	pg 417	11.	20	pg 419	15.	18	pg 421
4.	1	pg 416	8.	3	pg 421	12.	16	pg 419			

MULTIPLE CHOICE

1.	c	pg 414	5.	b	pg 413	9.	b	pg 414	13.	a	pg 421
2.	a	pg 416	6.	d	pg 420	10.	c	pg 420			
3.	b	pg 414	7.	d	pg 415-416	11.	d	pg 419			
4.	a	pg 415	8.	a	pg 415	12.	c	pg 418			

CASE PROBLEMS — ESSAY ANSWERS

1. No. This would be considered a contract for personal services, and A cannot delegate them. This case is beyond the scope of agency purposes. p. 413

2. Yes, because A has breached the fiduciary duty to P. Agents who are employed to buy may not buy from themselves. p. 417

3. No. An agent has a duty not to make any secret profit while dealing for the principal. p. 417

4. No. The authority of the agent to perform a specific act is terminated when the act is performed. A could not sell the second painting without new authority from P. p. 420

5. When war occurs, which puts a principal and an agent in the position of hostile enemies from countries at war, the agency relationship is terminated due to supervening illegality. Thus, D no longer has authority to represent T since their agency contract has been terminated through operation of law. p. 422.

ANSWERS TO CHAPTER 20 — Relationship with Third Parties
All answers are keyed to page numbers in the main text.

TRUE-FALSE

1.	T	pg 440	4.	T	pg 439	7.	T	pg 448	10.	T	pg 443
2.	F	pg 440	5.	T	pg 442	8.	F	pg 446	11.	F	pg 440
3.	F	pg 449	6.	F	pg 450	9.	F	pg 445	12.	T	pg 444

KEY TERMS — MATCHING

1.	14	pg 449	5.	2	pg 448	9.	4	pg 439	13.	16	pg 439
2.	7	pg 439	6.	11	pg 448	10.	5	pg 438	14.	20	pg 442
3.	9	pg 442	7.	8	pg 444	11.	1	pg 439	15.	17	pg 442
4.	15	pg 439	8.	13	pg 439	12.	19	pg 439			

MULTIPLE CHOICE

1.	b	pg 444-445	5.	a	pg 452	9.	a	pg 451	13.	b	pg 443
2.	a	pg 450	6.	d	pg 444	10.	c	pg 451			
3.	c	pg 448	7.	b	pg 451	11.	b	pg 452			
4.	d	pg 450	8.	d	pg 448	12.	a	pg 442			

CASE PROBLEMS — ESSAY ANSWERS

1. Probably not. A pattern of conduct has been established, based on A's five year purchases, where C has continuously done business with P. C may assume, having no knowledge otherwise, that the established purchase pattern will continue. The apparent authority of A to act, coupled with C's lack of knowledge that A is not so authorized, gives C a right of recourse against P. p. 440

2. Yes. Agents are liable for their own wrongful and negligent acts, whether or not the principal is also liable. p. 452

3. No. An agent who makes a contract with a third person on behalf of a disclosed principal has no right of action against the third person for breach of contract. pp. 452-453

4. No. A third person can proceed to trial against both the principal and agent but if, before the entry of judgment, the third person elects to obtain a judgment against the principal alone and does obtain a judgment, the third person could not seek another judgment from the agent. An election to obtain judgment against one party irrevocably binds the third person to that choice. p. 452

5. Normally a principal is not liable for the torts of an independent contractor unless they arise from breach of non-delegable duties that are imposed by law. Usually, dangerous activity falls within non-delegatable duties. Since the duty to act safely is imposed by law, and dynamiting is a dangerous activity, P is most likely liable for X's dynamiting. T can sue P. p. 449

ANSWERS TO CHAPTER 21 — Introduction to Sales
All answers are keyed to page numbers in the main text.

TRUE-FALSE

1.	T	pg 471	4.	T	pg 474	7.	F	pg 471	10.	F	pg 481
2.	F	pg 479	5.	T	pg 480	8.	T	pg 471-472	11.	T	pg 470-471
3.	F	pg 475	6.	F	pg 479	9.	T	pg 476	12.	F	pg 474

KEY TERMS — MATCHING

1.	4	pg 470	5.	15	pg 471-472	9.	13	pg 473	13.	19	pg 472
2.	7	pg 471	6.	10	pg 474	10.	6	pg 472	14.	17	pg 476
3.	11	pg 473	7.	8	pg 479	11.	1	pg 476	15.	18	pg 479
4.	9	pg 472	8.	2	pg 477	12.	16	pg 479			

MULTIPLE CHOICE

1.	c	pg 471	5.	d	pg 474	9.	d	pg 473	13.	b	pg 481
2.	d	pg 483	6.	b	pg 474	10.	a	pg 476			
3.	b	pg 479	7.	a	pg 481	11.	c	pg 474			
4.	d	pg 477	8.	b	pg 470	12.	d	pg 475			

CASE PROBLEMS — ESSAY ANSWERS

1. Yes. Under U.C.C. 2-205, a merchant's written offer containing a statement that it will remain open for a specified period is irrevocable during the stated time. p. 476

2. No. The U.C.C. holds output and quantity contracts valid. An objective standard, based on the good faith of the parties, drawing upon prior agreements, course dealings and usages of trade is used to supply the missing term. p. 476

3. Yes. The unequal bargaining positions of the parties to the contract and the $800 purchase price for an item with a $180 fair market retail value render the agreement "unconscionable." Under section 2-302 of the U.C.C., courts have the authority to deny or limit enforcement of such unfair, harsh and indecent contracts. p. 473

4. A contract exists and Penny's additional terms are not a rejection or counteroffer. Under U.C.C. 2-207, Penny's acceptance, definitely and seasonably made, is effective. Since both parties are merchants, her additional terms will become part of the contract because the offer was not expressly limited to its terms and the additional terms probably do not materially alter the terms of the offer unless Yummy objects to them in writing within a reasonable time. p. 477

5. Wally loses. The Code states that oral contracts for goods specifically manufactured for the buyer, which are not suitable for resale in the ordinary course of business, are enforceable. This contract is not within the Statute of Frauds. p. 481

ANSWERS TO CHAPTER 22 — Performance
All answers are keyed to page numbers in the main text.

TRUE-FALSE

1.	T	pg 500	4.	T	pg 506	7.	T	pg 506	10.	T	pg 507
2.	F	pg 501	5.	F	pg 504	8.	F	pg 506	11.	F	pg 509
3.	F	pg 510	6.	T	pg 507	9.	F	pg 501	12.	T	pg 507

KEY TERMS — MATCHING

1.	7	pg 500	5.	12	pg 507	9.	10	pg 502	13.	19	pg 500
2.	3	pg 505	6.	5	pg 504	10.	11	pg 506	14.	17	pg 509
3.	6	pg 502	7.	9	pg 510	11.	20	pg 507	15.	18	pg 505
4.	15	pg 506	8.	1	pg 501	12.	16	pg 506			

MULTIPLE CHOICE

1.	a	pg 501	5.	c	pg 506	9.	d	pg 506	13.	c	pg 505
2.	d	pg 504	6.	b	pg 505	10.	b	pg 502			
3.	d	pg 502	7.	a	pg 507	11.	d	pg 505			
4.	b	pg 507	8.	c	pg 506	12.	a	pg 505			

CASE PROBLEMS — ESSAY ANSWERS

1. Probably not. Assuming that the masks were specified and identified to the contract when it was made, their total loss during the flood, before risk of loss passed to B, avoided the contract. p. 509

2. For B. Although this is a breach of an installment contract with commercial units and therefore gives rise to cause of action, S may not treat the one-day delayed payment as a material breach striking at the heart of the contract. The one-day delay is not justification to cancel the entire contract. p. 505

3. B probably wins. For H.H. to effectively revoke her acceptance, the defect in the non-conforming rifle must substantially impair the value. Arguably, the scratches and nicks do not detract from the usefulness or performance capacity of the rifle and are therefore not substantial value impairments. However, since the test for value impairment is subjective — personal to the buyer—H.H. could argue that she intended to use the gun as a showcase collector's piece, as well as for hunting, and the blemishes, foreclosing the showcase capacity, are substantial value impairments. p. 507

4. Decision for S. A merchant buyer, who has possession of rightfully rejected goods, must make reasonable efforts to resell the goods, if they are perishable, even if the seller gives the buyer no instructions. Failure to comply with the Code makes merchant buyer B liable for losses stemming from holding the perishable bananas and not selling them on seller's account. p. 506

5. S probably wins. Ordinarily, impossibility of performance (in this case, the trade embargo) does not excuse performance on the contract. But where the parties understood when they entered their contract that performance would depend upon a certain event or condition (availability of Australian widgees), the non-occurrence or termination of that presupposed basic condition (trade embargo on Australian goods) will excuse duties of performance. p. 509

ANSWERS TO CHAPTER 23 — Transfer of Title and Risk of Loss
All answers are keyed to page numbers in the main text.

TRUE-FALSE

1.	T	pg 531	4.	F	pg 528	7.	F	pg 536	10.	T	pg 533-534
2.	F	pg 526	5.	T	pg 528	8.	T	pg 535	11.	T	pg 533-534
3.	T	pg 531	6.	T	pg 531	9.	F	pg 529	12.	F	pg 532

KEY TERMS — MATCHING

1.	8	pg 525	5.	5	pg 528	9.	14	pg 532	13.	16	pg 525
2.	9	pg 530	6.	12	pg 531	10.	1	pg 535	14.	19	pg 527
3.	7	pg 526	7.	3	pg 532	11.	20	pg 528	15.	18	pg 527
4.	11	pg 530	8.	13	pg 526	12.	17	pg 528			

MULTIPLE CHOICE

1.	c	pg 528	5.	d	pg 526	9.	b	pg 532	13.	d	pg 531
2.	c	pg 528	6.	a	pg 528	10.	b	pg 531			
3.	d	pg 535	7.	a	pg 528	11.	a	pg 531			
4.	b	pg 535	8.	c	pg 532	12.	c	pg 532			

CASE PROBLEMS — ESSAY ANSWERS

1. It depends. Under old U.C.C. Article 6, failing to comply with the Article's requirements made the purchaser's goods subject to unpaid creditors claims. Thus B's creditors could proceed against the goods in A's possession. Under revised Article 6, however, the buyer's failure to comply with Article 6 requirements does not affect title to the goods but makes the buyer liable for noncompliance damages to the seller's creditors. Thus, B's creditors would have no recourse against the goods in A's possession. pp. 535-536

2. C wins. B's leaving the goods with merchant S is an act of "entrusting" under the Code. C, a buyer in the ordinary course of business, will therefore prevail. p. 530

3. A has lost title to the coat and has no rights against C. By "entrusting" the fur coat to merchant dealer B, A has given the latter power to transfer all of her rights to a buyer in the ordinary course of business, which C was. A's only recourse is money damages against B. p. 530

4. Buyer suffers the loss. When goods held by a bailee are sold to another and the goods are covered by a negotiable title document, risk of loss passes to the buyer on the latter's receipt of the document. Since grain owner delivered the title document to buyer, buyer suffers the loss. p. 533

5. Francine may recover the $1,280 from Mary since, as a merchant seller, the risk of loss remained on her as the goods had yet to be received by Francine. p. 533

ANSWERS TO CHAPTER 24—Product Liability: Warranties and Strict Liability in Tort
All answers are keyed to page numbers in the main text.

TRUE-FALSE

1.	T	pg 558	4.	F	pg 552	7.	F	pg 559	10.	T	pg 557
2.	F	pg 550	5.	F	pg 553-554	8.	T	pg 559	11.	F	pg 552
3.	T	pg 549	6.	T	pg 557	9.	F	pg 561	12.	T	pg 558

KEY TERMS — MATCHING

1.	8	pg 550	5.	6	pg 559	9.	15	pg 555	13.	16	pg 552
2.	12	pg 555	6.	10	pg 557	10.	3	pg 562-563	14.	5	pg 554
3.	7	pg 551	7.	14	pg 556	11.	4	pg 551	15.	20	pg 564
4.	9	pg 551	8.	2	pg 562	12.	18	pg 552			

MULTIPLE CHOICE

1.	a	pg 561	5.	a	pg 558	9.	c	pg 552	13.	b	pg 557
2.	c	pg 562	6.	c	pg 563	10.	d	pg 550 -551			
3.	a	pg 551	7.	b	pg 559	11.	d	pg 554			
4.	b	pg 557	8.	d	pg 555	12.	a	pg 550			

CASE PROBLEMS — ESSAY ANSWERS

1. No. Strict liability in tort does not apply to an occasional seller not in the business of selling the defective product. p. 559

2. B may revoke acceptance and seek damages from S based upon a breach of the implied warranty of merchantability. The car is obviously not fit for ordinary driving purposes. p. 553

3. A manufacturer has a duty to warn of potential hazards or foreseeable dangers arising out of the normal or probable use of a product. Where a consumer has misused a product, the manufacturer has no duty to warn about dangers therefrom and faces no liability. For the manufacturer. p. 563

4. It depends. Assuming that the rods were warranted, the seller must be notified of any breach within a reasonable time after a defect is or should have been discovered. If B fails to notify S, no damages are recoverable. If B does seasonably notify S, damages are $300: the difference between the value of the goods as accepted and the value they would have had had they been conforming to the contract. p. 557

5. C loses. Since the inedible ingredient in question, the bone, was both natural to the food consumed and its presence could have been reasonably expected, C will have to bear her own loss, based on either the natural substance or the reasonable expectation test. p. 553

ANSWERS TO CHAPTER 25 — Remedies

All answers are keyed to page numbers in the main text.

TRUE-FALSE

1.	T	pg 584	4.	F	pg 588	7.	T	pg 593	10.	F	pg 590
2.	T	pg 585	5.	T	pg 589	8.	F	pg 593	11.	T	pg 583
3.	F	pg 586	6.	F	pg 591	9.	F	pg 587	12.	T	pg 584

KEY TERMS — MATCHING

1.	1	pg 584	5.	6	pg 589	9.	12	pg 587	13.	16	pg 583
2.	13	pg 585	6.	7	pg 591	10.	4	pg 589	14.	19	pg 584
3.	2	pg 588	7.	9	pg 587	11.	20	pg 583	15.	18	pg 583
4.	5	pg 591	8.	10	pg 587	12.	17	pg 586			

MULTIPLE CHOICE

1.	b	pg 584-585	5.	b	pg 593	9.	c	pg 586	13.	c	pg 588
2.	d	pg 586	6.	a	pg 585	10.	b	pg 584			
3.	c	pg 588	7.	a	pg 587	11.	d	pg 585			
4.	c	pg 589	8.	c	pg 587	12.	b	pg 591			

CASE PROBLEMS — ESSAY ANSWERS

1. Since the seller is usually never accountable to the buyer for any profit made on a resale of the goods, B recovers nothing. p. 585

2. Since the difference between the cost of the goods purchased by B's "cover" and the contract price resulted in a $1,000 "better deal" for B, all that B might recover are incidental or consequential damages, less expenses saved as a result of S's breach. p. 588

3. B should exercise a right of recovery against S for the identified goods in which B holds a special property interest. The Code gives a buyer the right to recover goods from an insolvent seller when the seller becomes insolvent within 10 days of the first installment payment on the sales contract. To perfect this special interest in the goods, B must tender the remaining $7,500 to S. p. 589

4. B may store the nails for the seller's account, reship them to the seller or resell them for the seller's account. By disposing of them, B is neither converting them nor accepting them. B would be liable to the seller for any excess over his security interest in the goods. p. 590

5. Because the painting in this case is unique, a court of equity will issue a decree of specific performance requiring delivery of the painting from C to A rather than a money damages judgment. p. 589

ANSWERS TO CHAPTER 26 — Form and Content
All answers are keyed to page numbers in the main text.

TRUE-FALSE

1.	T	pg 613	4.	F	pg 612	7.	T	pg 617	10.	T	pg 617
2.	F	pg 616	5.	T	pg 615	8.	T	pg 616	11.	T	pg 611
3.	T	pg 610	6.	F	pg 617	9.	F	pg 616	12.	F	pg 608

KEY TERMS — MATCHING

1.	5	pg 609	5.	4	pg 609	9.	3	pg 616	13.	19	pg 615
2.	2	pg 612-614	6.	8	pg 607	10.	1	pg 609	14.	16	pg 615
3.	14	pg 615	7.	11	pg 614	11.	9	pg 609	15.	18	pg 610
4.	12	pg 612	8.	15	pg 607-608	12.	17	pg 610			

MULTIPLE CHOICE

1.	b	pg 613	5.	b	pg 615	9.	c	pg 616	13.	a	pg 617
2.	d	pg 616	6.	d	pg 611	10.	a	pg 615			
3.	d	pg 610	7.	d	pg 607	11.	b	pg 606-608			
4.	b	pg 608	8.	a	pg 606-607	12.	b	pg 610			

CASE PROBLEMS — ESSAY ANSWERS

1. S wins. Where words and figures on an instrument are in conflict, the words, unless unclear themselves, are controlling. B must come up with the $810 difference. p. 618

2. None. Provisions in commercial paper granting the obligor the option to extend the maturity date for a definite time period do not affect negotiability. p. 616

3. Yes. Auxiliary clauses of this nature do not affect the sum certain due on the instrument. The note is therefore negotiable. p. 614

4. Yes. Any symbol is sufficient as a signature so long as the person signing has adopted it and intends it to be their authentic signature. p. 612

5. No. A bare indebtedness acknowledgement, such as an "I.O.U.," is not a negotiable instrument carrying with it an obligation of payment to its holder. M has made no promise of payment at all. p. 612

ANSWERS TO CHAPTER 27 — Transfer
All answers are keyed to page numbers in the main text.

TRUE-FALSE

1.	T	pg 630	4.	F	pg 630	7.	T	pg 635	10.	F	pg 636
2.	F	pg 635	5.	T	pg 635-636	8.	F	pg 635	11.	T	pg 631
3.	T	pg 636	6.	F	pg 635	9.	T	pg 635	12.	F	pg 630

KEY TERMS — MATCHING

1.	4	pg 634	5.	15	pg 630	9.	12	pg 635-636	13.	16	pg 630
2.	14	pg 636	6.	13	pg 634	10.	7	pg 630	14.	6	pg 630
3.	5	pg 634	7.	10	pg 635	11.	18	pg 630	15.	19	pg 636
4.	1	pg 630	8.	2	pg 630	12.	20	pg 635			

MULTIPLE CHOICE

1.	d	pg 630	5.	c	pg 636	9.	b	pg 636	13.	d	pg 634
2.	c	pg 635	6.	b	pg 634	10.	a	pg 636			
3.	d	pg 634	7.	d	pg 638	11.	a	pg 630			
4.	a	pg 633	8.	b	pg 634	12.	b	pg 634			

CASE PROBLEMS — ESSAY ANSWERS

1. For X. Indorsees, under a conditional indorsement, have no rights to payment until the stated condition is met. The maker of a note conditionally indorsed is not discharged from the instrument if payment is made inconsistent with the stated restriction. Since the note in question was presented for payment three days prior to the occurrence of the event that would trigger X's obligation to pay, X may properly dishonor Z's presentment for payment. p. 635

2. An indorsement which conveys less than the entire amount of a note is not an effective negotiation. This type of indorsement is effective only as an assignment. p. 633

3. Only if X's signature appeared on the note. Since the bearer paper became order paper through P's special indorsement, any further negotiation of the note would require X's indorsement. M may rightfully refuse payment to F if the note does not contain X's signature. p. 632

4. Yes. Anyone who possesses bearer paper is a holder entitled to payment. p. 631

5. To protect the interest in the instrument, B can convert the blank indorsement to a special indorsement by writing over A's signature any restriction not contrary to the type of indorsement. Thus, B may write "Pay to the order of B" to protect the interest. p. 635

ANSWERS TO CHAPTER 28 — Holder in Due Course
All answers are keyed to page numbers in the main text.

TRUE-FALSE

1.	T	pg 654	4.	F	pg 656	7.	T	pg 654	10.	T	pg 663
2.	T	pg 652	5.	T	pg 655	8.	F	pg 659	11.	F	pg 659
3.	F	pg 652	6.	F	pg 658	9.	T	pg 655	12.	F	pg 652

KEY TERMS — MATCHING

1.	4	pg 650	5.	6	pg 658	9.	1	pg 657	13.	18	pg 657
2.	2	pg 654	6.	13	pg 658	10.	12	pg 658-659	14.	17	pg 655
3.	7	pg 659	7.	10	pg 659	11.	19	pg 650	15.	9	pg 658
4.	3	pg 659	8.	11	pg 658	12.	16	pg 659			

MULTIPLE CHOICE

1.	d	pg 657	5.	d	pg 658	9.	d	pg 664	13.	c	pg 659
2.	a	pg 663	6.	b	pg 660	10.	c	pg 655			
3.	d	pg 654	7.	c	pg 650	11.	a	pg 652-653			
4.	a	pg 657	8.	b	pg 658	12.	b	pg 655			

CASE PROBLEMS — ESSAY ANSWERS

1. H is holder of the full $1,000 face value of the note. A holder is not required to pay the full face amount to give value, but only the amount agreed upon with the transferor. p. 653

2. No. One not a holder in due course cannot cleanse paper by transferring the paper to and re-acquiring it from a holder in due course. P cannot use the shelter rule to profit from wrongdoing. p. 657

3. S's alteration is not a material one that would operate to discharge M on the instrument. Changing figures to comply with the controlling written number is not a material change. p. 660

4. Probably not. Under the Code, notice must be received in a timely manner sufficient to provide a reasonable opportunity to act on it. Such is not the case here. p. 654

5. No. Based on a FTC regulation, effective May 1976, holders of commercial paper issued in connection with consumer credit transactions acquire the paper subject to all claims, defenses and demands, including fraud and defective goods, which the consumer debtor could have asserted against the payee on the instrument. p. 663

ANSWERS TO CHAPTER 29 — Liabilities of Parties
All answers are keyed to page numbers in the main text.

TRUE-FALSE

1.	T	pg 678	4.	F	pg 680	7.	F	pg 685	10.	T	pg 689
2.	T	pg 678	5.	T	pg 683	8.	T	pg 680	11.	T	pg 686
3.	F	pg 682	6.	T	pg 683	9.	F	pg 687	12.	F	pg 689-690

KEY TERMS — MATCHING

1.	4	pg 681	5.	9	pg 685	9.	13	pg 691	13.	1	pg 678
2.	11	pg 681	6.	7	pg 678	10.	12	pg 686	14.	20	pg 686
3.	14	pg 686	7.	2	pg 686	11.	18	pg 678	15.	17	pg 692
4.	8	pg 681	8.	6	pg 682	12.	16	pg 678			

MULTIPLE CHOICE

1.	c	pg 678	5.	c	pg 685	9.	b	pg 679	13.	a	pg 687
2.	d	pg 681	6.	a	pg 684	10.	d	pg 693-694			
3.	b	pg 682	7.	c	pg 686	11.	c	pg 680			
4.	b	pg 685	8.	a	pg 682	12.	b	pg 687			

CASE PROBLEMS — ESSAY ANSWERS

1. M can collect on the instrument from the drawer, A, to the original tenor of $500. When certification is at the request of the drawer, the drawer is not relieved of secondary liability on the instrument. p. 682

2. A's willingness and ability to pay at the specified place, i.e., the bank, is the equivalent of tender of payment. A is liable for the face amount and interest accrued at the time payment was due, but not for additional interest thereafter or for subsequent costs and attorney's fees. p. 691

3. No. H's actions constitute improper presentment. The drawee can require the holder to adhere to the terms of the instrument (presentment only at the main office of the drawee) without causing a dishonor. p. 684

4. M is liable. By having failed to identify P, P is not obligated on the instrument to H, and M is solely bound to make payment. p. 679

5. H wins. Since the maker, M, is in the best position to know the original amount of the instrument, when M pays the altered amount to the innocent party, H, M absorbs the loss. p. 690

ANSWERS TO CHAPTER 30 — Bank Deposits, Collections, and Fund Transfers
All answers are keyed to page numbers in the main text.

TRUE-FALSE

1.	T	pg 712	4.	F	pg 707	7.	T	pg 712	10.	T	pg 713
2.	F	pg 706	5.	F	pg 711	8.	F	pg 708	11.	F	pg 707
3.	T	pg 710	6.	T	pg 712	9.	F	pg 708	12.	T	pg 707

KEY TERMS — MATCHING

1.	1	pg 706	5.	14	pg 709	9.	2	pg 713	13.	18	pg 705
2.	3	pg 706	6.	15	pg 711	10.	6	pg 709	14.	16	pg706-707
3.	13	pg 706	7.	8	pg 714	11.	17	pg 708	15.	19	pg 712
4.	7	pg 707	8.	11	pg 708	12.	20	pg 713			

MULTIPLE CHOICE

1.	a	pg 708	5.	b	pg 711	9.	d	pg 707	13.	b	pg 707
2.	d	pg 710	6.	c	pg 709	10.	a	pg 711			
3.	c	pg 713	7.	b	pg 710	11.	d	pg 714			
4.	c	pg 708	8.	a	pg 715	12.	c	pg 716			

CASE PROBLEMS — ESSAY ANSWERS

1. C wins. A payor bank receiving an item properly payable from a customer's account that lacks sufficient funds to cover the designated amount, may pay the item, charge the account, and seek reimbursement from the customer for both the overdraft created by the item and any service charges connected with its handling. p. 711

2. Cathy will be liable for only $50 of the withdrawals if she notifies her bank of the card's disappearance within two days after she knows of its absence. After two days, she will be liable for the full amount of Frank's withdrawals up to a maximum of $500 if she notifies the bank within 60 days of the card's absence. p. 715

3. H may bring an action for payment against B because a stop payment order does not automatically relieve the drawer of liability to the holder. Since H is a holder in due course of a negotiable instrument arising from a non-consumer transaction, the personal defense of failure of consideration may not be used by B to avoid payment to H. p. 711

4. Under the U.C.C., a bank may fix a time at or after 2:00 p.m. as a cut-off hour for handling items and making appropriate entries on its books. This rule permits the bank to extend the banking day until a later hour without starting the running time for the midnight deadline. An item, having been received after the cut-off time, is deemed to be received at the opening of business on the next banking day. In this case, the next banking day is Monday and the midnight deadline is thus on Tuesday. Here, the bank did not act until Wednesday. Therefore it did not act seasonably. p. 708

5. P wins. The payor bank's authority to honor checks drawn by its customers is not affected by the incompetence of a customer at the time collection is undertaken and payment made when the bank is, in fact, not aware of the adjudication of incompetence. The bank may make payment without incurring any liability. p. 712

ANSWERS TO CHAPTER 31 — Nature and Formation
All answers are keyed to page numbers in the main text.

TRUE-FALSE

1.	F	pg 736	4.	F	pg 735	7.	F	pg 741	10.	T	pg 735
2.	T	pg 735	5.	T	pg 740	8.	T	pg 737	11.	F	pg 743
3.	T	pg 735	6.	F	pg 741	9.	F	pg 735	12.	T	pg 743

KEY TERMS — MATCHING

1.	13	pg 742	5.	7	pg 736	9.	3	pg 734	13.	18	pg 743
2.	12	pg 736	6.	10	pg 735	10.	2	pg 741	14.	5	pg 736
3.	1	pg 735	7.	14	pg 736	11.	20	pg 740	15.	9	pg 736
4.	4	pg 736	8.	8	pg 740	12.	16	pg 737			

MULTIPLE CHOICE

1.	a	pg 742	5.	b	pg 741	9.	d	pg 741	13.	c	pg 737
2.	d	pg 741	6.	c	pg 735	10.	c	pg 736			
3.	a	pg 740	7.	b	pg 737	11.	d	pg 735			
4.	a	pg 736	8.	d	pg 741	12.	d	pg 736			

CASE PROBLEMS — ESSAY ANSWERS

1. Yes. They have an agreement to share the profits and continue to manage the business. This constitutes a partnership. p. 737

2. Yes. C is an ostensible partner and is liable to persons who have extended credit in good faith relying on the belief that C is a partner. p. 736

3. No. An adjudicated incompetent person's contracts, including a partnership agreement, are void. p. 740

4. C is a dormant partner since C is both a secret and a silent partner. p. 736

5. No. The Statute of Frauds requires that a contract to form a partnership to continue for a period longer than one year requires a writing to be enforceable. p. 737

ANSWERS TO CHAPTER 32 — Duties, Rights, and Liabilities
All answers are keyed to page numbers in the main text.

TRUE-FALSE

1.	T	pg 754	4.	F	pg 756	7.	F	pg 757	10.	T	pg 754
2.	T	pg 756	5.	T	pg 762	8.	F	pg 761	11.	T	pg 758
3.	F	pg 756	6.	T	pg 757	9.	F	pg 762	12.	T	pg 758

KEY TERMS — MATCHING

1.	8	pg 757	5.	4	pg 758	9.	11	pg 754	13.	7	pg 758
2.	1	pg 757	6.	9	pg 758	10.	6	pg 756	14.	10	pg 757
3.	2	pg 758	7.	15	pg 760	11.	20	pg 756	15.	19	pg 755
4.	3	pg 754	8.	14	pg 760	12.	17	pg 756			

MULTIPLE CHOICE

1.	a	pg 756	5.	d	pg 760	9.	c	pg 761	13.	c	pg 756
2.	d	pg 759	6.	a	pg 760	10.	d	pg 756			
3.	d	pg 754	7.	d	pg 757	11.	d	pg 755			
4.	c	pg 758	8.	b	pg 758	12.	b	pg 756			

CASE PROBLEMS — ESSAY ANSWERS

1. B and C win. P does not become a partner and is not entitled to participate in the management of the partnership. P is only entitled to receive her share of the profits and to participate in the event of liquidation. p 757

2. Q wins. Unanimous agreement among all the partners is required when a matter involves changing the terms of the partnership agreement. p. 757

3. A loses. The Uniform Partnership Act provides that, unless otherwise agreed, no partner is entitled to compensation for acting in the partnership business. p. 757

4. The partners prevail. The transfer is outside the scope of the partnership. A lacked authority to act alone. The Uniform Partnership Act provides that the assignment of partnership property for the benefit of creditors must be authorized by all partners to bind the partnership. p. 759

5. No. A partner may not sue the partnership for damages, but if the partner is denied a formal accounting, then the partner may sue in equity for an accounting. p. 758

ANSWERS TO CHAPTER 33 — Dissolution, Winding Up, and Termination
All answers are keyed to page numbers in the main text.

TRUE-FALSE

1.	T	pg 775	4.	F	pg 775	7.	T	pg 778	10.	T	pg 778
2.	T	pg 775	5.	T	pg 773	8.	F	pg 774	11.	T	pg 773
3.	F	pg 773	6.	T	pg 775	9.	F	pg 777	12.	F	pg 773

KEY TERMS — MATCHING

1.	8	pg 775	5.	4	pg 777	9.	11	pg 775	13.	12	pg 774
2.	1	pg 776	6.	9	pg 777	10.	6	pg 773	14.	13	pg 774
3.	7	pg 773	7.	5	pg 774	11.	20	pg 778	15.	17	pg 776
4.	3	pg 778	8.	14	pg 774	12.	16	pg 778			

MULTIPLE CHOICE

1.	a	pg 775	5.	a	pg 775	9.	d	pg 774	13.	b	pg 773
2.	d	pg 773	6.	a	pg 773	10.	d	pg 774			
3.	b	pg 774	7.	d	pg 777	11.	d	pg 778			
4.	a	pg 774	8.	b	pg 778	12.	c	pg 777			

CASE PROBLEMS — ESSAY ANSWERS

1. Yes on both counts. If the partnership agreement allows X and Y to continue the business, they may, and Z may be discharged from her liabilities to existing creditors by a novation. p. 778

2. Z must give actual notice of her retirement to persons with whom the partnership regularly does business and to persons who had extended credit to the partnership prior to dissolution, and give constructive notice by newspaper publication to the general business community. p. 778

3. C will receive $15,000. The total value of the firm's assets ($100,000) is reduced by the amount of outstanding debts, leaving $60,000 available for distribution to the partners. Capital contributions ($5,000 per partner) must be subtracted from this amount. This leaves $45,000 to be divided equally among three partners. p. 776

4. Yes. A partner can apply for dissolution by court order since partner A is guilty of conduct prejudicial to the business and has willfully breached the partnership agreement. p. 774

5. X wins. Even though C retired with the consent of the other partners, who agreed to assume full liability for all old partnership debts, C is still liable to creditors whose claims arose prior to dissolution. C's recourse would be to seek indemnification from A and B for their failure to live up to the agreement. p. 778

ANSWERS TO CHAPTER 34 — Limited Partnerships
All answers are keyed to page numbers in the main text.

TRUE-FALSE

1.	F	pg 792	4.	T	pg 801	7.	F	pg 793	10.	F	pg 796
2.	F	pg 793	5.	F	pg 798	8.	T	pg 793	11.	T	pg 794
3.	T	pg 801	6.	T	pg 797	9.	T	pg 794	12.	T	pg 801

KEY TERMS — MATCHING

1.	5	pg 793	5.	10	pg 793	9.	7	pg 797	13.	12	pg 796
2.	8	pg 794	6.	13	pg 800	10.	15	pg 801	14.	17	pg 794
3.	6	pg 798	7.	1	pg 799	11.	20	pg 796	15.	19	pg 794
4.	9	pg 801	8.	2	pg 800	12.	4	pg 797			

MULTIPLE CHOICE

1.	d	pg 798	5.	d	pg 797	9.	b	pg 799	13.	d	pg 800
2.	d	pg 793	6.	b	pg 794	10.	c	pg 793			
3.	c	pg 795	7.	c	pg 801	11.	c	pg 793			
4.	d	pg 793	8.	a	pg 801	12.	c	pg 793			

CASE PROBLEMS — ESSAY ANSWERS

1. No. Absent a provision in the partnership agreement, a limited partner has limited personal liability and does not share in the losses of the partnership beyond her capital contribution. p. 796

2. C can sue both A and B. A limited partner whose name is used as part of the partnership name renders the limited partner liable as a general partner to any creditor who did not know of the limited partnership. In addition, since the words "limited partnership" must be in the partnership name, B is also liable for this reason. p. 793

3. No. The death of a limited partner does not dissolve the limited partnership. p. 798

4. Yes. If all partners, general and limited, agree in writing, the new general partner may be added. p.795

5. The certificate shall contain the name of the limited partnership, the location of the business office, the names and addresses of each general and limited partner, the latest date upon which the limited partnership is to dissolve, and any other matters the general partners decide to include in the certificate. p 793

ANSWERS TO CHAPTER 35 — Nature, Formation, and Power
All answers are keyed to page numbers in the main text.

TRUE-FALSE

1.	T	pg 818	4.	F	pg 824	7.	T	pg 815	10.	F	pg 815
2.	T	pg 827	5.	F	pg 828	8.	T	pg 816	11.	F	pg 815
3.	T	pg 822	6.	T	pg 830	9.	F	pg 816	12.	T	pg 822

KEY TERMS — MATCHING

1.	3	pg 816	5.	8	pg 822	9.	9	pg 830	13.	1	pg 817
2.	2	pg 825	6.	7	pg 820	10.	11	pg 817	14.	19	pg 817
3.	5	pg 822	7.	14	pg 829	11.	17	pg 817	15.	16	pg 817
4.	6	pg 827	8.	12	pg 824	12.	18	pg 819			

MULTIPLE CHOICE

1.	c	pg 821	5.	a	pg 820	9.	d	pg 830	13.	d	pg 817
2.	a	pg 816	6.	c	pg 825	10.	c	pg 822			
3.	d	pg 816	7.	b	pg 828	11.	d	pg 817			
4.	c	pg 822	8.	d	pg 830	12.	d	pg 817			

CASE PROBLEMS — ESSAY ANSWERS

1. Yes. If the business is operated as a corporation, the business' debts can be satisfied only from assets of the corporation. C's personal assets would be protected. p. 816

2. Possibly. A corporation may be liable for crimes committed by its agents or employees and punished for the violation by a fine. p. 830

3. Contracts made by a promoter for a corporation not yet formed are binding only on the promoter. The corporation becomes liable if it ratifies the contract after the corporation is formed, but the promoter usually also remains liable. p. 820

4. No. A promoter has a fiduciary duty to the initial shareholders and the corporation and cannot retain secret profits resulting from this relationship. p. 820

5. No. The case illustrates the formation of a de facto corporation. The corporation would be liable to the customer. A, B, and C would not be personally liable. Only the State can challenge the existence of a de facto corporation. Under the Revised Act, liability is imposed on persons who purport to act as a corporation only if they know there is no proper incorporation. A, B, and C did not know and are not personally liable. p. 826

ANSWERS TO CHAPTER 36 — Financial Structure
All answers are keyed to page numbers in the main text.

TRUE-FALSE

1.	F	pg 844	4.	F	pg 852	7.	F	pg 850	10.	T	pg 858
2.	T	pg 849	5.	F	pg 852	8.	F	pg 857	11.	T	pg 846
3.	F	pg 851	6.	F	pg 843	9.	T	pg 860	12.	F	pg 853

KEY TERMS — MATCHING

1.	7	pg 845	5.	8	pg 843	9.	10	pg 843	13.	17	pg 843
2.	6	pg 857	6.	5	pg 859	10.	14	pg 850	14.	18	pg 851
3.	2	pg 859	7.	12	pg 846	11.	20	pg 847	15.	19	pg 853
4.	4	pg 859	8.	9	pg 845	12.	16	pg 844			

MULTIPLE CHOICE

1.	d	pg 858	5.	d	pg 856	9.	c	pg 860	13.	d	pg 859
2.	d	pg 847	6.	a	pg 857	10.	d	pg 858			
3.	b	pg 854	7.	d	pg 859	11.	c	pg 854			
4.	b	pg 850	8.	d	pg 858	12.	a	pg 853			

CASE PROBLEMS — ESSAY ANSWERS

1. No. The majority position states that in the absence of fraud, the judgment of the board of directors as to the value of the consideration received for shares shall be conclusive. p. 847

2. Yes. If provided for in the articles of incorporation, a corporation does have the power of redemption. To protect creditors, however, most states have statutory restrictions upon redemption that may overrule the articles of incorporation (charter) and the Revised Act does not permit redemption if the corporation would be unable to pay its debts as they become due in the usual course of its business. p. 855

3. Yes. A corporation becomes the debtor of its shareholders when a cash dividend is properly declared. The shareholders may enforce their claims as unsecured creditors in a court of law. p. 856

4. B wins. A has breached A's warranty that the transfer is effective and rightful. Neither party is owner of the stock. p. 860

5. A wins. An issuer who registers the transfer of a certificated security upon an unauthorized indorsement is subject to liability for improper registration. p. 860

ANSWERS TO CHAPTER 37 — Management Structure
All answers are keyed to page numbers in the main text.

TRUE-FALSE

1.	T	pg 889	4.	T	pg 890	7.	T	pg 895	10.	F	pg 881
2.	T	pg 876	5.	T	pg 890	8.	T	pg 888	11.	T	pg 876
3.	F	pg 886	6.	F	pg 887	9.	F	pg 889	12.	F	pg 895

KEY TERMS — MATCHING

1.	15	pg 884	5.	11	pg 893	9.	2	pg 882	13.	7	pg 888
2.	4	pg 888	6.	12	pg 893	10.	14	pg 881	14.	18	pg 877
3.	8	pg 893	7.	9	pg 888	11.	16	pg 892	15.	5	pg 890
4.	10	pg 893	8.	6	pg 895	12.	20	pg 890			

MULTIPLE CHOICE

1.	a	pg 893	5.	b	pg 888	9.	d	pg 881	13.	d	pg 891
2.	d	pg 890	6.	c	pg 890	10.	a	pg 893			
3.	d	pg 888	7.	a	pg 888	11.	d	pg 876			
4.	d	pg 887	8.	d	pg 887	12.	d	pg 879			

CASE PROBLEMS — ESSAY ANSWERS

1. Because the vote is cumulative, X has 30 votes. X may give all 30 votes to one director or apportion the 30 votes between two or among all three of the candidates. p. 881

2. No. Because of an officer's fiduciary duty and the "corporate opportunity" doctrine, A must make full disclosure of the opportunity to the corporation before A purchases the land. pp. 893, 894

3. No. Unless all the directors signed a consent in writing to vote without a meeting, they do not have the power to bind the corporation when acting individually. p. 888

4. X wins. Absent fraud, a court will not hold X liable for damages if X is using good judgment which later proves to be financially unsound. p. 891

5. X is liable. Either directors or officers may be held liable for not fulfilling their duty of diligence to the corporation. p. 892

ANSWERS TO CHAPTER 38 — Fundamental Changes
All answers are keyed to page numbers in the main text.

TRUE-FALSE

1.	F	pg 915	4.	T	pg 917	7.	F	pg 917	10.	F	pg 922
2.	F	pg 915	5.	F	pg 917	8.	T	pg 914	11.	F	pg 915
3.	T	pg 917	6.	F	pg 921	9.	T	pg 919	12.	T	pg 921

KEY TERMS — MATCHING

1.	3	pg 917	5.	9	pg 913	9.	12	pg 917	13.	1	pg 917
2.	2	pg 917	6.	6	pg 920	10.	13	pg 921	14.	11	pg 920
3.	15	pg 913	7.	7	pg 922	11.	20	pg 916	15.	17	pg 921
4.	4	pg 916	8.	8	pg 919	12.	16	pg 918			

MULTIPLE CHOICE

1.	d	pg 921	5.	d	pg 921	9.	d	pg 920	13.	b	pg 921
2.	d	pg 914	6.	d	pg 920	10.	d	pg 921			
3.	d	pg 920	7.	d	pg 920	11.	d	pg 914			
4.	d	pg 920	8.	b	pg 922	12.	b	pg 915			

CASE PROBLEMS — ESSAY ANSWERS

1. Upon dissolution, the assets of the corporation are liquidated and used first to pay creditors and the expenses of liquidation. A will be paid ahead of all the shareholders. p. 921

2. No. The Revised Act requires a written demand for the money on a form provided by the corporation within a time period set by the corporation. Unless Abby makes the demand within that time period, she is not entitled to payment for her shares. p. 919

3. No. Only the dissenting shareholders of the subsidiary corporation have the right to obtain payment for their shares from the parent corporation. p. 917

4. Merger, consolidation, the purchase of the assets of one corporation by the other, or dissolution of one corporation are all possible remedies. pp. 915, 921

5. Yes. When one corporation becomes the parent over another, no change is made in the legal existence of either, i.e., the separate existence of both corporations is not affected by the exchange. p. 916

ANSWERS TO CHAPTER 39 — Secured Transactions in Personal Property
All answers are keyed to page numbers in the main text.

TRUE-FALSE

1.	F	pg 938	4.	T	pg 946	7.	T	pg 941	10.	T	pg 938 -939
2.	T	pg 939	5.	F	pg 946	8.	F	pg 956	11.	F	pg 941 -942
3.	F	pg 945	6.	T	pg 949	9.	T	pg 939 -940	12.	F	pg 948

KEY TERMS — MATCHING

1.	5	pg 940	5.	1	pg 946	9.	12	pg 941	13.	15	pg 940
2.	7	pg 939	6.	13	pg 942	10.	3	pg 940	14.	20	pg 942
3.	9	pg 945	7.	8	pg 941	11.	19	pg 938	15.	18	pg 956
4.	10	pg 949	8.	2	pg 940	12.	16	pg 939			

MULTIPLE CHOICE

1.	c	pg 951	5.	c	pg 952	9.	d	pg 951	13.	c	pg 954
2.	b	pg 939	6.	c	pg 939	10.	b	pg 946			
3.	d	pg 939	7.	a	pg 952	11.	d	pg 941			
4.	b	pg 941	8.	c	pg 946	12.	a	pg 946			

CASE PROBLEMS — ESSAY ANSWERS

1. S wins. Under a conditional sales contract, the seller retains "title" in the goods as a security until they are fully paid for. When the buyer defaults on the contract, the seller may usually recover the goods. p. 939

2. L has incorrectly identified the collateral. The books are likely equipment under the U.C.C.'s broad definition of this term. p. 940

3. Unless the agreement between debtor and creditor provides otherwise, the secured creditor has rights to sale proceeds upon transfer of the collateral. Assuming the agreement between L and B did not speak to this issue, B may assert a claim against the $1,000. p. 945

4. L has priority since that security interest was perfected first and C could have found out about it by checking the recorded financing statement. p. 951

5. Assuming that following default B did not sign a written waiver of any rights, S's actions are improper since B has paid at least 60% of the original $2,500 debt. S must therefore sell the repossessed unit within 90 days after repossession and reimburse B for any amount of the sale proceeds that exceed the debt balance, plus expenses associated with repossession and resale. p. 957

ANSWERS TO CHAPTER 40 — Suretyship
All answers are keyed to page numbers in the main text.

TRUE-FALSE

1.	F	pg 975	4.	F	pg 977	7.	T	pg 979	10.	T	pg 977
2.	T	pg 975	5.	T	pg 977	8.	F	pg 976	11.	T	pg 977
3.	F	pg 975	6.	F	pg 979	9.	T	pg 977	12.	F	pg 978

KEY TERMS — MATCHING

1.	6	pg 973	5.	2	pg 976	9.	13	pg 977	13.	8	pg 976
2.	15	pg 974	6.	4	pg 977	10.	14	pg 975	14.	17	pg 979
3.	1	pg 975	7.	10	pg 976	11.	20	pg 974	15.	18	pg 975
4.	11	pg 975	8.	12	pg 975	12.	16	pg 975			

MULTIPLE CHOICE

1.	a	pg 973	5.	d	pg 978	9.	a	pg 975	13.	d	pg 977
2.	b	pg 973	6.	d	pg 979	10.	d	pg 979			
3.	c	pg 976	7.	b	pg 979	11.	a	pg 979			
4.	a	pg 975	8.	c	pg 975	12.	c	pg 974			

CASE PROBLEMS — ESSAY ANSWERS

1. Unless Samantha has knowledge of this extension, consents to it, or Casper has expressly reserved his remedies against her, she is discharged from the agreement and has no further payment liability. p. 979

2. Probably not. Absent the application of the main purpose doctrine to this case, the general rule under the Statute of Frauds controls. Since Bea's promise was not in writing, it is not enforceable. p. 975

3. Cindy wins. When the debtor, owing several loans to one creditor, makes an undesignated payment, the creditor may apply the money to any of the debts in any manner. Thus, the full $5,400 is still owing and Cindy may seek that from Cecil. p. 979

4. Sal is released from the contract since sureties are discharged from their payment obligations to the extent of the value of security interests released or impaired by the creditor. p. 979

5. Cityville may enforce Sally's payment obligation since bankruptcy discharge of the principal debtor does not release the surety. p. 977

ANSWERS TO CHAPTER 41 — Bankruptcy
All answers are keyed to page numbers in the main text.

TRUE-FALSE

1.	F	pg 989	4.	T	pg 994	7.	F	pg 991	10.	T	pg 991
2.	T	pg 990	5.	F	pg 994-995	8.	T	pg 1001	11.	T	pg 994
3.	F	pg 992	6.	F	pg 992-993	9.	T	pg 1004	12.	F	pg 1004

KEY TERMS — MATCHING

1.	12	pg 988	5.	5	pg 992	9.	15	pg 1000	13.	19	pg 995
2.	3	pg 1006	6.	1	pg 995	10.	8	pg 1005	14.	17	pg 1001
3.	4	pg 1007	7.	2	pg 993	11.	20	pg 991	15.	18	pg 1006
4.	11	pg 989	8.	7	pg 1005	12.	16	pg 994			

MULTIPLE CHOICE

1.	c	pg 990	5.	d	pg 989	9.	b	pg 1002	13.	d	pg 991
2.	b	pg 992	6.	c	pg 997	10.	c	pg 1002			
3.	b	pg 996	7.	a	pg 995	11.	b	pg 1007			
4.	a	pg 991	8.	d	pg 993	12.	a	pg 1001			

CASE PROBLEMS — ESSAY ANSWERS

1. No. Student loans are non-dischargeable debts for five years after they become due. p. 995

2. No. Since the agreement was made after D's discharge, it is unenforceable under the 1978 Bankruptcy Reform Act. p. 994

3. Creditors 1, 2, and 3 hold some degree of priority claims. The portion of their debts given priority status must be fully satisfied before any general unsecured creditors receive payment. Accordingly, Creditor 1 receives $10,000, Creditor 2 $2,000, and Creditor 3 $6,000, totalling $18,000 of priority claims satisfied. This leaves $27,000 to apply to the remaining $36,000 in unsecured debt: $7,000 to Creditor 1; $6,000 to Creditor 2; $12,000 to Creditor 4; and $11,000 to Creditor 5. Creditor 6 will not share in debtor's estate since they failed to list their claim with the court. The $27,000 will be divided pro rata among Creditors 1, 2, 4, and 5. Each will receive 75% (27,000/36,000 or 3/4) return on the debt owed them: Creditor 1 receives $5,200; Creditor 2 receives $4,500; Creditor 4 receives $8,250; and Creditor 5 receives $9,000. p. 998

4. Dingle's transfers constitute a fraudulent conveyance. It can result in Doodles being denied discharge as well as the trustee avoiding the transfers and bringing the boat and car back into Doodle's estate. p. 997

5. The transfer is legal since before it can be a voidable preference, Paddywack must be insolvent or the transfers must make him insolvent. Here, Paddywack is solvent (assets exceeding liabilities). p.996

ANSWERS TO CHAPTER 42 — Protection of Intellectual Property

All answers are keyed to page numbers in the main text.

TRUE-FALSE

1.	T	pg 1018	4.	F	pg 1024	7.	T	pg 1023	10.	F	pg 1021
2.	T	pg 1018	5.	T	pg 1021	8.	F	pg 1021	11.	T	pg 1020
3.	F	pg 1022	6.	F	pg 1023	9.	T	pg 1024	12.	F	pg 1020

KEY TERMS — MATCHING

1.	14	pg 1018	5.	2	pg 1019	9.	6	pg 1019	13.	18	pg 1022
2.	1	pg 1018	6.	7	pg 1021	10.	3	pg 1018	14.	19	pg 1019
3.	15	pg 1021	7.	4	pg 1019	11.	17	pg 1020	15.	16	pg 1022
4.	9	pg 1019	8.	10	pg 1020	12.	20	pg 1025			

MULTIPLE CHOICE

1.	b	pg 1024	5.	a	pg 1025	9.	b	pg 1023	13.	b	pg 1025
2.	d	pg 1018	6.	c	pg 1019	10.	a	pg 1022			
3.	c	pg 1021	7.	c	pg 1024	11.	d	pg 1020			
4.	b	pg 1020	8.	a	pg 1021	12.	c	pg 1024			

CASE PROBLEMS — ESSAY ANSWERS

1. Probably not. Since "Lantern" is related to the function and purpose of Larry's lamps, he cannot tie up the word for exclusive application to his lamps. p. 1020

2. Toys Mfg., Inc. may restrain A and B, through an injunction, from using the special knowledge and skills they developed while employed at Toys for the benefit of Playthings. If Toys were not allowed to so protect its trade secrets, Playthings would gain an unfair competitive advantage at Toys' expense. p. 1019

3. Probably not. Natural substances are not patentable. Discovering the usefulness of an already existing and known bacteria does not meet the requirements of a human-made or modified invention. Only if Doctor Science's efforts amount to genetically engineering the bacteria could it be patentable. pp. 1023-1024

4. The Puffers. By failing to register their copyright, the Eskimos are foreclosed from bringing an infringement action against the Puffers. p. 1022

5. Home Products has violated the Lanham Act by intentionally and knowingly using a counterfeit mark. Accordingly, H. P. faces fines upwards of $1 million and all "Clean and Smooth" cans marked with a "P" may be confiscated and destroyed. p. 1021

ANSWERS TO CHAPTER 43 — Antitrust
All answers are keyed to page numbers in the main text.

TRUE-FALSE

1.	T	pg 1040	4.	T	pg 1040	7.	T	pg 1050	10.	F	pg 1046
2.	T	pg 1045	5.	F	pg 1049	8.	F	pg 1040	11.	T	pg 1039
3.	F	pg 1046	6.	F	pg 1044	9.	T	pg 1041	12.	F	pg 1041

KEY TERMS — MATCHING

1.	3	pg 1046	5.	14	pg 1043	9.	6	pg 1045	13.	16	pg 1050
2.	7	pg 1044	6.	13	pg 1050	10.	12	pg 1043	14.	11	pg 1047
3.	15	pg 1041	7.	4	pg 1043	11.	17	pg 1042	15.	5	pg 1049
4.	9	pg 1040	8.	10	pg 1041	12.	20	pg 1042			

MULTIPLE CHOICE

1.	d	pg 1049	5.	a	pg 1045	9.	b	pg 1041	13.	b	pg 1048
2.	b	pg 1051	6.	c	pg 1047	10.	d	pg 1049			
3.	d	pg 1042-1043	7.	a	pg 1051	11.	a	pg 1045			
4.	c	pg 1051	8.	c	pg 1049	12.	c	pg 1045			

CASE PROBLEMS — ESSAY ANSWERS

1. This is an example of an exclusive supply contract that might be a violation of antitrust statutes (Section 3 of the Clayton Act) if it results in a considerable reduction of competition or has the effect of establishing a monopoly. p. 1045

2. This is an example of resale price maintenance (vertical price fixing). This practice was once legal under state Fair Trade Acts but is now a per se violation of the Sherman Antitrust Act when interstate commerce is affected. p. 1042

3. Probably. Since the contract between Home Furnishings and the distributor calls for lower prices than competitors of Home Furnishings pay, this could amount to the type of price discrimination prohibited by Section 2 of the Robinson-Patman Act. For the price differentials not to be violations, they would have to be justified on the basis of legitimate business reasons. p. 1049

4. Yes. Since Pewtrid raised the price on the paint to be purchased, and the sales price for the three gallons of paint was more than the usual retail price for two gallons, the ad campaign was deceptive by referring to the third gallon as "free." p. 1051

5. Yes. Since the practice of law is professional commerce, and lawyers are sellers of professional services, agreements between these sellers to establish minimum prices at which their services are sold is prohibited under the Act. p. 1042

ANSWERS TO CHAPTER 44 — Consumer Protection
All answers are keyed to page numbers in the main text.

TRUE-FALSE

1.	F	pg 1067	4.	F	pg 1079	7.	F	pg 1076	10.	T	pg 1068
2.	T	pg 1072	5.	F	pg 1066	8.	F	pg 1080	11.	F	pg 1067
3.	T	pg 1076	6.	T	pg 1069	9.	F	pg 1072	12.	T	pg 1077

KEY TERMS — MATCHING

1.	5	pg 1076	5.	9	pg 1081	9.	4	pg 1068	13.	17	pg 1076
2.	7	pg 1067	6.	12	pg 1066	10.	1	pg 1075	14.	13	pg 1077
3.	8	pg 1071	7.	10	pg 1067	11.	19	pg 1075	15.	18	pg 1079
4.	15	pg 1074	8.	14	pg 1070	12.	16	pg 1072			

MULTIPLE CHOICE

1.	c	pg 1076	5.	c	pg 1067	9.	b	pg 1075	13.	a	pg 1078
2.	b	pg 1074	6.	b	pg 1074	10.	c	pg 1080			
3.	d	pg 1076	7.	d	pg 1072	11.	b	pg 1068			
4.	a	pg 1075	8.	a	pg 1073	12.	d	pg 1071			

CASE PROBLEMS — ESSAY ANSWERS

1. Jackson is not liable for any of the $250. Since the card was neither requested nor accepted, the entire loss for its unauthorized use falls on Plakton Petroleum as provided for under the FCCPA. p.1079

2. According to provisions in the FCCPA, an employer may not fire employees simply because creditors of employees have exercised a right of wage assignment or garnishment against them. In this case, E's threat of discharge is improper and illegal. p. 1080

3. The final $1,600 payment is called a balloon payment. In such cases, a debtor unable to meet the amount is not automatically in default with the possibility of losing the goods. In some states, balloon payment clauses are void and prohibited. In others, B may refinance the $1,600 on the same terms as the prior payment of $5,600 without any penalty. p. 1078

4. The Magnuson-Moss Act applies only where written warranties accompany the sale of goods or services. The Act does not require that such warranties be given. Since, in this case, no warranty was given by S, B has no rights under Magnuson-Moss. p. 1073

5. Under the Federal Interstate Land Sales Full Disclosure Act, purchasers of land through an interstate promotional campaign must be provided a "statement of record" or property report prior to entering a contract of sale with the real property seller. When sellers fail to provide such a statement, buyers may cancel their contracts with the seller any time within two years after the contract was signed. Since in this case H and W were never given a report from S, you should advise them to exercise their revocation rights as allowed under the ILSFDA. p. 1074

ANSWERS TO CHAPTER 45 — Employment Law
All answers are keyed to page numbers in the main text.

TRUE-FALSE

1.	T	pg 1107	4.	T	pg 1096	7.	T	pg 1100	10.	F	pg 1104
2.	F	pg 1096	5.	F	pg 1098	8.	T	pg 1106	11.	T	pg 1099
3.	F	pg 1093	6.	F	pg 1097	9.	T	pg 1106	12.	F	pg 1104

KEY TERMS — MATCHING

1.	4	pg 1094	5.	15	pg 1097	9.	13	pg 1106	13.	17	pg 1098
2.	7	pg 1094	6.	10	pg 1104	10.	6	pg 1105	14.	19	pg 1100
3.	11	pg 1095	7.	8	pg 1107	11.	16	pg 1094	15.	18	pg 1101
4.	9	pg 1095	8.	2	pg 1107	12.	20	pg 1095			

MULTIPLE CHOICE

1.	d	pg 1093	5.	d	pg 1097	9.	b	pg 1107	13.	c	pg 1095
2.	c	pg 1094	6.	b	pg 1097	10.	a	pg 1106			
3.	a	pg 1096	7.	a	pg 1101	11.	d	pg 1095			
4.	c	pg 1096	8.	c	pg 1105	12.	d	pg 1102			

CASE PROBLEMS — ESSAY ANSWERS

1. Probably not. Since stock clerks and yard attendants are most likely different with different responsibilities, they may have different salary scales without violating the Equal Pay Act. p. 1096

2. Aerospace wins. Federal age discrimination laws apply only to persons at least 40 years old. p. 1100

3. Fortisque wins if his opinions carry no direct reprisal or threat of coercion against his workers. This falls under the employer free speech section of the Taft-Hartley Act. p. 1095

4. Charlene wins. OSHA forbids discharge of employment based on employees exercising their rights under the Act. p. 1104

5. Folsum wins. The union's action is a prohibited secondary boycott under the terms of Taft-Hartley and amounts to a union unfair labor practice. p. 1095

ANSWERS TO CHAPTER 46 — Securities Regulation
All answers are keyed to page numbers in the main text.

TRUE-FALSE

1.	F	pg 1126	4.	T	pg 1134	7.	F	pg 1138	10.	F	pg 1127
2.	F	pg 1127	5.	F	pg 1135	8.	T	pg 1126	11.	T	pg 1126
3.	T	pg 1129	6.	T	pg 1132	9.	T	pg 1141	12.	T	pg 1132

KEY TERMS — MATCHING

1.	15	pg 1126	5.	3	pg 1142	9.	9	pg 1131	13.	16	pg 1131
2.	5	pg 1127	6.	7	pg 1138	10.	10	pg 1131	14.	18	pg 1133
3.	12	pg 1127	7.	8	pg 1138	11.	20	pg 1126	15.	19	pg 1139
4.	1	pg 1129	8.	6	pg 1140	12.	17	pg 1128			

MULTIPLE CHOICE

1.	a	pg 1127	5.	d	pg 1129	9.	c	pg 1143	13.	a	pg 1140
2.	c	pg 1129	6.	c	pg 1127	10.	b	pg 1135			
3.	d	pg 1128	7.	d	pg 1134	11.	d	pg 1139			
4.	a	pg 1129	8.	a	pg 1135	12.	d	pg 1139			

CASE PROBLEMS — ESSAY ANSWERS

1. No. Under Regulation A, although Ajax is exempt for registration purposes, it still must file a notification and an offering circular with the SEC. p 1132

2. Since this transaction meets the definition of "short-swing" trading by "insiders," Brown is liable for the profits to the corporation and its shareholders. p. 1141

3. No. Under Section 3 of the 1933 Securities Act, securities marketing by non-profit organizations are exempt from registration requirements. p. 1129

4. Yes. Since an untrue statement was made by Explorations in its registration statements, I is entitled to a return of his investment plus interest. Because Sammy and Edith were named as directors in the registation, they are liable to I unless they can apply the defense of due diligence to their case. p. 1134

5. No. Since XYZ's assets are less than $5 million and the class of equity securities shareholders is less than 500, it does not have to register these securities. p. 1136

ANSWERS TO CHAPTER 47 — Accountant's Legal Liability
All answers are keyed to page numbers in the main text.

TRUE-FALSE

1.	T	pg 1162	4.	F	pg 1164	7.	F	pg 1166	10.	F	pg 1166
2.	F	pg 1163	5.	T	pg 1166	8.	F	pg 1167	11.	T	pg 1166
3.	T	pg 1163	6.	F	pg 1166	9.	T	pg 1167	12.	F	pg 1163

KEY TERMS — MATCHING

1.	9	pg 1163	5.	2	pg 1167	9.	4	pg 1166	13.	18	pg 1162
2.	11	pg 1163	6.	15	pg 1167	10.	1	pg 1166	14.	14	pg 1163
3.	12	pg 1163	7.	3	pg 1163	11.	16	pg 1167	15.	20	pg 1163
4.	7	pg 1163	8.	13	pg 1166	12.	17	pg 1162			

MULTIPLE CHOICE

1.	c	pg 1162	5.	c	pg 1166	9.	c	pg 1167	13.	b	pg 1167
2.	a	pg 1166	6.	d	pg 1166	10.	a	pg 1162			
3.	d	pg 1165	7.	a	pg 1167	11.	d	pg 1165			
4.	b	pg 1166	8.	b	pg 1166	12.	c	pg 1165			

CASE PROBLEMS — ESSAY ANSWERS

1. Since accountant explicitly agreed to furnish a final report by May 15th and time was of the essence, failure to meet this deadline constitutes a material breach, which discharges client's payment obligation. p. 1163

2. Accountant's failure to follow up on the discrepancies may constitute negligence, opening liability to the parties as "foreseeable plaintiffs" for compensatory damages. But since no fraud was involved on accountant's part, no basis for punitive damages exists. p. 1163

3. Accountant wins. As owner of the working papers, accountant is not obligated to give them over to client. p. 1166

4. Accountant has substantially performed on the contract. As such, contractually agreed upon compensation is due from client, reduced by damages caused by accountant's delay. p. 1163

5. Prosecutor wins. Accountant must testify since federal law does not recognize an accountant/client privilege. p. 1166

ANSWERS TO CHAPTER 48 — International Business Law
All answers are keyed to page numbers in the main text.

TRUE-FALSE

1.	F	pg 1187	4.	T	pg 1185	7.	T	pg 1190	10.	T	pg 1184
2.	T	pg 1186	5.	F	pg 1185	8.	F	pg 1190	11.	T	pg 1186
3.	F	pg 1186	6.	T	pg 1185	9.	F	pg 1188	12.	F	pg 1190

KEY TERMS — MATCHING

1.	6	pg 1186	5.	18	pg 1184	9.	15	pg 1187	13.	12	pg 1189
2.	11	pg 1185	6.	13	pg 1186	10.	2	pg 1190	14.	1	pg 1189
3.	9	pg 1185	7.	14	pg 1187	11.	19	pg 1190	15.	4	pg 1188
4.	16	pg 1185	8.	10	pg 1187	12.	20	pg 1189			

MULTIPLE CHOICE

1.	b	pg 1187	5.	c	pg 1185	9.	c	pg 1188	13.	c	pg 1184
2.	c	pg 1187	6.	b	pg 1190	10.	d	pg 1190			
3.	d	pg 1187	7.	a	pg 1190	11.	b	pg 1188			
4.	a	pg 1186	8.	d	pg 1188	12.	a	pg 1190			

CASE PROBLEMS — ESSAY ANSWERS

1. Tell Glewbenstein officials to enact laws preventing foreign investors and businesses from owning more than 49% of the glue company formed. Also, the laws should state that Glewbensteinians comprise a majority of the workers and management in the company. p. 1190

2. Since Section 1 of the Sherman Act allows application of U.S. antitrust laws to foreign businesses, the agreement in question is probably illegal trade restraint in violation of this Act and therefore void. p. 1189

3. Probably not. Today, only public, not commercial, acts of a foreign government are immune from a host country's laws and courts. Marketing the gambling seminar submits the Monaco government to U.S. jurisdiction over disputes arising out of conducting the business. p. 1186

4. Since international commercial activity carries complications arising from language, customs, legal system and currency differences, advise the parties to include in their contract the following clauses: controlling language; choice of legal system; definition of important terms; acceptable medium and method of payment; unforeseeable event risk-of-loss apportionment. p. 1188

5. Only an official United Nations agency may seek advisory jurisdiction from I.C.J. Advisory opinions cannot be sought by individuals or governments. p. 1185

ANSWERS TO CHAPTER 49 — Introduction to Property and Property Insurance
All answers are keyed to page numbers in the main text.

TRUE-FALSE

1.	T	pg 1206	4.	T	pg 1211	7.	T	pg 1211	10.	T	pg 1209
2.	T	pg 1214	5.	F	pg 1211	8.	T	pg 1209	11.	F	pg 1215
3.	F	pg 1209	6.	F	pg 1215	9.	F	pg 1208	12.	T	pg 1208

KEY TERMS — MATCHING

1.	3	pg 1208	5.	4	pg 1208	9.	1	pg 1210	13.	20	pg 1216
2.	7	pg 1209	6.	5	pg 1214	10.	15	pg 1213	14.	17	pg 1206
3.	9	pg 1207	7.	8	pg 1212	11.	18	pg 1210	15.	19	pg 1215
4.	12	pg 1207	8.	11	pg 1207	12.	16	pg 1210			

MULTIPLE CHOICE

1.	b	pg 1213	5.	b	pg 1213	9.	a	pg 1209	13.	a	pg 1212
2.	d	pg 1210	6.	a	pg 1215	10.	c	pg 1208			
3.	a	pg 1210	7.	d	pg 1215	11.	b	pg 1206			
4.	c	pg 1210	8.	d	pg 1208	12.	d	pg 1207			

CASE PROBLEMS — ESSAY ANSWERS

1. This is an example of title transfer through accession. Since Ragmuffin's taking of the fabric pieces was based on the innocent mistaken belief that they were abandoned, and through Ragmuffin's work the value of the pieces has increased and their identity substantially changed, Ragmuffin will own the coat. Josephine's only remedy is reimbursement for the value of the pieces of cloth in their original, not improved, state. p. 1211

2. Sam probably must keep the money. The law generally presumes that donees accept gifts when the property does not impose a burden on them and they are benefited from it. Since Sam remained silent for six months after receiving the money order, he is presumed to have accepted it. p. 1210

3. Since the ring was on the floor when it was discovered, it would probably be considered lost and not misplaced. Therefore, Brown, the finder, would have superior rights to the ring vis-a-vis Smith. Brown wins. p. 1212

4. Audrey recovers $30,000. She is under-insured under her "valued" policy, which calls for the insurer to pay the value specified in the policy and not the actual value at the time of loss. p. 1214

5. M and F probably have superior rights to the items in question. The goods are most likely fixtures since they have been so firmly attached to the home as to lose their identity as personal property and have become part of the home. In addition, they most likely cannot be removed without material damage. Therefore, they were sold with the house to M and F. p. 1208

ANSWERS TO CHAPTER 50 — Bailments and Documents of Title
All answers are keyed to page numbers in the main text.

TRUE-FALSE

1.	T	pg 1234	4.	F	pg 1228	7.	F	pg 1233	10.	T	pg 1231
2.	T	pg 1234	5.	T	pg 1226	8.	T	pg 1232	11.	F	pg 1235
3.	F	pg 1233	6.	F	pg 1229	9.	F	pg 1233	12.	T	pg 1235

KEY TERMS — MATCHING

1.	4	pg 1232	5.	12	pg 1231	9.	13	pg 1232	13.	20	pg 1234
2.	5	pg 1227	6.	11	pg 1226	10.	15	pg 1235	14.	17	pg 1234
3.	3	pg 1226	7.	2	pg 1231	11.	19	pg 1235	15.	18	pg 1232
4.	6	pg 1233	8.	14	pg 1231	12.	16	pg 1235			

MULTIPLE CHOICE

1.	d	pg 1236	5.	b	pg 1229	9.	d	pg 1227	13.	b	pg 1236
2.	a	pg 1229	6.	a	pg 1234	10.	a	pg 1237			
3.	c	pg 1235	7.	b	pg 1228	11.	c	pg 1235			
4.	d	pg 1227	8.	b	pg 1232	12.	d	pg 1236			

CASE PROBLEMS — ESSAY ANSWERS

1. The owner. The holder of a negotiable bill issued to a thief following bailment of stolen goods acquires no right to the goods as against the true owner, regardless of intervening due negotiation. A thief who delivers goods to a carrier and receives a negotiable document cannot extinguish the true owner's title. p. 1236

2. C wins. U.C.C. 7-204(1) holds W's obligation to C as that of a reasonably careful warehouseman. In this case, reasonable care would have avoided the damage to the cheese. Although W may limit by contract the extent of liability by fixing a damages maximum, the duty of reasonable care cannot be completely waived. p. 1233

3. Yes. B, as the bailee for hire, has an absolute duty to deliver the goods to the right person. The innocent misdelivery is a conversion of the goods and B is not excused from liability. p. 1230

4. Tracy, as the originating carrier receiving the cases of honey from Shipper Helen, issuing a through bill of lading naming same as taker, is liable to Sam for the loss. Tracy, however, has reimbursement rights against Terry. p. 1234.

5. Innkeeper suffers the loss. By Statute, innkeepers may avoid their common law strict liability for the belongings of their guests by providing a safe for guest use and posting notice of its existence. Here, however, no notice was given Guest of Innkeeper's safe. Innkeeper is therefore the insurer of Guest's watch under common law. p. 1232

ANSWERS TO CHAPTER 51 — Interests in Real Property
All answers are keyed to page numbers in the main text.

TRUE-FALSE

1.	T	pg 1250	4.	T	pg 1258	7.	F	pg 1262	10.	F	pg 1259
2.	F	pg 1259	5.	F	pg 1259	8.	T	pg 1255	11.	T	pg 1255
3.	F	pg 1251	6.	T	pg 1258	9.	T	pg 1257	12.	F	pg 1252

KEY TERMS — MATCHING

1.	5	pg 1252	5.	15	pg 1260	9.	6	pg 1259	13.	16	pg 1253
2.	4	pg 1251	6.	12	pg 1261	10.	7	pg 1252	14.	19	pg 1254
3.	3	pg 1261	7.	8	pg 1257	11.	20	pg 1252	15.	18	pg 1251
4.	9	pg 1252	8.	11	pg 1262	12.	17	pg 1254			

MULTIPLE CHOICE

1.	c	pg 1255	5.	c	pg 1258	9.	a	pg 1254	13.	d	pg 1257
2.	d	pg 1259	6.	a	pg 1260	10.	c	pg 1256			
3.	c	pg 1251	7.	d	pg 1259	11.	b	pg 1260			
4.	a	pg 1261	8.	a	pg 1259	12.	c	pg 1257			

CASE PROBLEMS — ESSAY ANSWERS

1. Initially, A, B and C each have a one-third undivided interest in the land. Upon C conveying a one-third interest to D, D becomes a tenant in common with A and B, who remain joint-tenant owners of Greenacre for their two-thirds interest. When A dies, B acquires A's undivided one-third interest by right of survivorship and, as a result, holds a two-thirds interest as a tenant in common with D, who has an undivided one-third interest. p. 1259

2. A's heirs. The qualification, which limited the fee estate in the land, runs against all subsequent owners. When the property no longer is used for the specific purpose mentioned, it automatically reverts to the grantor or the grantor's heirs through "possibility of reverter." p. 1252

3. H's wife has dower or inheritance rights only in real property held in fee simple or its equivalent by H. Since H's interest in the dairy farm is the only estate of inheritance (held in fee simple), his wife will have no rights or interests in the joint tenancy property (ranch) or the life tenancy property (poultry farm). W will only receive H's interest in the dairy farm. p. 1259

4. It depends. If A's land is the dominant parcel of an appurtenant easement, then it is not necessary to refer specifically to that easement in the deed from B to C in order to give A the ongoing use of the easement over C's land. But if A's easement is in gross, then it must be mentioned in the deed from B to C, otherwise it is extinguished. p. 1261

5. No. Since B and C acquire their interests by different instruments, which take effect at different times, the unities of time and title are lacking from the "four unities" required for joint tenancy. B and C are therefore tenants in common. p. 1259

ANSWERS TO CHAPTER 52 — Transfer and Control of Real Property
All answers are keyed to page numbers in the main text.

TRUE-FALSE

1.	F	pg 1277	4.	T	pg 1277	7.	F	pg 1282	10.	F	pg 1286
2.	T	pg 1278	5.	F	pg 1279	8.	F	pg 1284	11.	T	pg 1280
3.	F	pg 1278	6.	T	pg 1281	9.	T	pg 1284	12.	T	pg 1277

KEY TERMS — MATCHING

1.	2	pg 1283	5.	14	pg 1285	9.	3	pg 1284	13.	16	pg 1281
2.	11	pg 1283	6.	6	pg 1282	10.	9	pg 1282	14.	19	pg 1284
3.	8	pg 1284	7.	4	pg 1278	11.	17	pg 1280	15.	18	pg 1283
4.	7	pg 1277	8.	12	pg 1280	12.	20	pg 1281			

MULTIPLE CHOICE

1.	c	pg 1284	5.	b	pg 1282	9.	a	pg 1283	13.	a	pg 1280
2.	d	pg 1284	6.	d	pg 1277	10.	c	pg 1286			
3.	b	pg 1279	7.	b	pg 1284	11.	b	pg 1280			
4.	c	pg 1279	8.	c	pg 1281	12.	d	pg 1282			

CASE PROBLEMS — ESSAY ANSWERS

1. Due to the two tobacco shops and three pharmacists selling cigarettes in violation of the dictates of the restrictive covenant, Frank can persuasively argue that the character of the area has changed and that the covenant has been abandoned. There would thus be no justification for enforcing the covenant against him. p. 1286

2. Racially based restrictive covenants are invalid and therefore unenforceable stemming from the 1947 U.S. Supreme Court decision. Advise the Chans to resubmit the bid and if they are turned down again for the same reason, bring action against the sellers to invalidate the restriction. p. 1286

3. A prevails. Zoning ordinances may not be used to immediately end a lawful use of property existing prior to the passage of the ordinance. A will be permitted to operate the junkyard for a reasonable time. p. 1283

4. Zoning ordinances that result in a "taking" of property without compensation are invalid. If the effect of a zoning restriction is to render nearly any beneficial use of property impossible, then the ordinance is an invalid confiscation. The city is not certain whether its urban renewal plan will ever go into effect. During the interim, L is essentially barred from pursuing beneficial development of the site, given the plan's building compensation restriction. L should therefore argue that this part of the plan amounts to a confiscation and seek to invalidate it. p. 1284

5. Possibly. The power of eminent domain can be delegated to R.R. if the increased width of the tracks would result in improved service to the public and therefore constitute promoting a "public purpose." p. 1284

ANSWERS TO CHAPTER 53 — Trusts and Decedents' Estates
All answers are keyed to page numbers in the main text.

TRUE-FALSE

1.	T	pg 1302	4.	T	pg 1304	7.	F	pg 1311	10.	T	pg 1311
2.	T	pg 1305	5.	F	pg 1308	8.	F	pg 1302	11.	F	pg 1309
3.	T	pg 1306	6.	F	pg 1302	9.	F	pg 1305	12.	F	pg 1311

KEY TERMS — MATCHING

1.	6	pg 1300	5.	1	pg 1301	9.	5	pg 1310	13.	18	pg 1308
2.	3	pg 1307	6.	4	pg 1303	10.	2	pg 1311	14.	9	pg 1309
3.	15	pg 1307	7.	14	pg 1309	11.	16	pg 1311	15.	19	pg 1308
4.	11	pg 1301	8.	12	pg 1301	12.	13	pg 1309			

MULTIPLE CHOICE

1.	b	pg 1302	5.	d	pg 1303	9.	c	pg 1309	13.	c	pg 1302
2.	a	pg 1303	6.	d	pg 1306	10.	c	pg 1308			
3.	b	pg 1304	7.	d	pg 1309	11.	d	pg 1307			
4.	a	pg 1302	8.	c	pg 1311	12.	b	pg 1307			

CASE PROBLEMS — ESSAY ANSWERS

1. If properly created, creditors of a beneficiary of a spendthrift trust cannot attach the trust fund or its income but must wait until the income is received by the beneficiary to obtain payment. p. 1301

2. The death of the trustee does not terminate the trust. Nor will the court terminate the trust simply because all beneficiaries ask for it. The court will decide according to the trust purposes of the settlor. p. 1305

3. Yes. The birth of a child after execution of a will may revoke the will at least as far as that child is concerned. p. 1308

4. Nothing. This is an example of abatement. Specific gifts must be satisfied first. p. 1308

5. No. This is an example of ademption; the will provision is impossible to perform. p. 1308